Opportunity Structures in Diaspora Relations: Comparisons in Contemporary Multilevel Politics of Diaspora and Transnational Identity

EDITED BY

Gloria Totoricagüena

Center for Basque Studies
University of Nevada, Reno
Reno, Nevada

This book was published with generous financial support from the Basque Government.

Center for Basque Studies
Conference Papers Series, No. 4

Center for Basque Studies
University of Nevada, Reno
Reno, Nevada 89557
http://basque.unr.edu

Library of Congress Cataloging-in-Publication Data

Opportunity structures in diaspora relations : comparisons in contemporary multi-level politics of diaspora and transnational identity / edited by Gloria Totoricaguena.
    p. cm. -- (Conference papers series / Center for Basque Studies ; No. 4)
    Includes bibliographical references and index.
    ISBN 978-1-877802-72-0 (pbk.) -- ISBN 978-1-877802-73-7 (hardcover) 1. Emigration and immigration--Congresses. 2. Transborder ethnic groups--Congresses. 3. Human geography--Congresses. I. Totoricagüena, Gloria P. (Gloria Pilar), 1961- II. University of Nevada, Reno. Center for Basque Studies. III. Title. IV. Series.

    JV6011.O77 2007
    304.8--dc22

                                                                2007050002

The Center for Basque Studies wishes to gratefully acknowledge the generous financial support of the Bizkaiko Foru Aldundia / Provincial Government of Bizkaia for the publication of this book.

Bizkaiko Foru
Aldundia
Kultura Saila

Diputación Foral
de Bizkaia
Departamento de Cultura

Opportunity Structures in Diaspora Relations: Comparisons in Contemporary Multilevel Politics of Diaspora and Transnational Identity

EDITED BY

Gloria Totoricagüena

CONTENTS

Acknowledgments

The Center for Basque Studies' international symposium on diaspora studies, "Opportunity Structures in Diaspora Relations: Comparisons in Contemporary Multilevel Politics of Diaspora and Transnational Identity," was held on April 27–29, 2006, at the University of Nevada, Reno campus with generous funding from a grant from the Basque Autonomous Community Office of the Presidency and the Basque Autonomous Community Departments of Education and of Culture. Participants were leading academic scholars in their disciplines or areas of diaspora mobilization. The debates lasted throughout breakfasts, lunches, and dinners, as well as on bus rides to and ferry boat rides on Lake Tahoe. The papers presented here are the results of presentations followed by discussions and by further reflection by each author.

I would like to thank Center for Basque Studies personnel for the assistance with conference organization, especially Jill Berner and Kate Camino, as well as CBS professors Linda White, Sandra Ott, and Xabier Irujo for their suggestions, assistance, and attendance at the conference.

Editing for these articles was meticulously performed by Bud Bynack with production assistance from Jill Berner, and I thank them for their expertise. Ms. Berner manages several publications per year from the CBS, and her attention to detail is always exceptional. It has truly been a pleasure to work with both of these individuals.

Gloria Totoricagüena
Reno, Nevada, 2007

Introduction

In the social sciences, the narrative implied by the use of the term "diaspora" has often tended to focus on a negative interpretation of displacement, discrimination, and oppression. However, simultaneously, academics and intellectuals now are using the term to discuss the benefits of multiple and multilayered identities, creolization, creating a home away from home, and of the many opportunities resulting from the effects of globalization that enable and enhance the mobilization of diaspora identities around the globe. The various categorizations and definitions of "diaspora" are expertly delineated herein by preeminent scholars in diaspora studies William Safran, Robin Cohen, and Gabriel Sheffer.

The aim of the Center for Basque Studies 2006 international symposium, "Opportunity Structures in Diaspora Relations: Comparisons in Contemporary Multilevel Politics of Diaspora and Transnational Identity," was to gather several of the world's leading scholars in diaspora studies to compare definitions, realities, case studies, and approaches from different disciplines and to discuss and debate the possibilities for future interdisciplinary investigation. World-renowned experts in political science, history, anthropology, sociology, and economics presented their research on such topics as the main characteristics and organizational structures of contemporary ethnonational diasporas and how the relationships with their homelands and host-society governments might develop. Common questions raised throughout the various discussions addressed the communal strategies and tactics used by diasporas to articulate their own identities and to act effectively with respect to both their hostlands and their homelands, the circumstances in which they employ such approaches, and which of them are most effective at influencing local or global affairs, particularly the foreign policy of the central governments. The essays by Kim D. Butler, Michele Laguerre, William Safran, Gabriel Sheffer, and Gloria Totoricagüena address these questions from a variety of angles, using diverse examples to do so.

The effects of these strategies and tactics, and of ethnonational identity maintenance in general, influence social and political security issues, both domestically and in foreign policy. Examples examined here include issues ranging from the problematics of the decision to record Basque identity in the U.S. Census, analyzed by William A. Douglass, to Robin Cohen's questioning definitions of hybridity and "creole" in the America South and the United Kingdom, to Nergis Canefe's investigation of the Canadian liberal democratic ethics of citizenship and belonging and Muslim individual and communal identity. Michel Laguerre uses the Jewish quarter in Paris to analyze the social integration of European neighborhoods and the relations of the neighborhood with city hall, which he argues are necessary to understanding manifold globalization.

Modern diasporas are composites of diasporas formed in different eras that necessarily interact and cross-pollinate each other. Using the case of the multilayered African diaspora as an example, Kim Butler explores the use of diaspora as a political strategy in multiple contexts, illuminating the vast difference in political options of recent emigrants from nation-states versus those held by descendants of slave-era dispersals from a generic continental homeland. She asks to what extent it is possible to coordinate strategies toward a collective transnational political agenda. Do these disparities in political realities mitigate against a shared diaspora consciousness, especially when the type of diasporization is markedly different? The African diaspora is a metadiaspora that consists of many constituent diasporas (i.e., Ghanaian, Garifuna, Indian Ocean, Caribbean), and just as individuals hold multiple layers of identity, so also do diasporas exist at the meta and micro levels simultaneously. This suggests that the overall landscape of diaspora politics is an interaction between differently bounded diaspora communities. Butler examines instances of diaspora mobilization in a variety of contexts within the African diaspora and suggests that today's political and technological climate favors types of diaspora politics (and forms of identity consciousness) that differ from those prevalent in the past. She closes by considering how the salience of discrete diasporas' politics might affect the possibilities for pandiaspora politics in the future.

Among other things, liberal democratic citizenship is meant to symbolize respect for difference, institutionalized tolerance for disagreement, and legal protection of freedoms of expression and choice. Nergis Canefe argues that Canada constitutes no exception in terms of the formal embrace of this rendition of citizenship and that compared with its southern neighbor, Canada is apt to be seen as the paradigmatic example of such a conception put into practice. However, from within Canada, the picture looks somewhat different, and Muslims who either recently acquired citizenship or assumed landed immigrant status are finding themselves without full and accepted participation in Canadian social, political, and economic life, compared with others who belong to the Northern European or Francophone traditional Canadian society.

Canefe's article presents the case that what is grossly overlooked in the grand scheme of institutional reform and political optimism is that the changes to the "citizenship contract" in any given society have always been made within the context of existing norms of sociopolitical membership. In other words, they take place with direct reference to already-determined criteria for qualifications regarding full membership, the legal process of naturalization being the tip of the iceberg. She writes that there is a "starting line" in each society cum political community regarding the minimums of acceptance for full participation with protected rights, and also, by default, regarding the agreed-upon principles of exclusion. Integration or assimilation forces immigrants into conforming to national stereotypes. At the current stage of the history of Canadian society, religion—especially when combined with ethnicity, race, and class—constitutes a key component of the silent barrier that separates those who categorically qualify for becoming a "true Canadian" and those who, at best, can only approximate "Canadianness."

At first sight, writes Robin Cohen, "creolization" and "diaspora" are separate forms of cultural politics with different sensibilities and trajectories. However as he concentrates on comparative and historical examples of Creoles and creolization, we find that the core of the concept centers on the cross-fertilization that takes place between different cultures when they interact. He describes creolization as a form of "fugitive power," highlighting the hidden power resulting from collective shifts in attitudes and social behavior. When creolizing, participants select particular elements from incoming or inherited cultures, endow these with meanings different from those they possessed in the original culture, and then merge these to create totally new varieties that supersede the prior forms. Creolization is a "here and now" sensibility that erodes the old roots and stresses the new growth in a new place of identification. A diasporic consciousness, by contrast, reflects a degree of unease with the here and now and the current location. Cohen illustrates how "home" or "homeland" is reconstructed and revalorized through fabulation, historical memory, and social organization. It provides a continuing pole of attraction and identification. By contrasting these two forms of cultural politics, he illuminates both, and he also finds possibilities and examples of convergence between them. Cohen affirms mixed identities, hybridity, and "everyday cosmopolitanism."

William A. Douglass's contribution describes how the Basque American census count developed, replacing an approach in which Basques were asked to identify themselves as "Spanish," "French" or other nationals by the U.S. census. When this occurred, Basques became one of the best-documented small ethnic groups in the United States. He discusses the state's preeminent role in counting its citizens for purposes of taxation, military conscription, and making public policy, as well as the importance of census numbers for the sociopolitical status of ethnic groups. Douglass gives a historical overview of informal counts of Basques in the western United States before leading us into an analysis of how Basques came to be depicted in the current U.S. census. He questions the Basque government's use of the figure "nine million" Basques worldwide because of the difficulty in defining who counts as a Basque, in addition to a lack of detailed ethnic census taking in the twenty countries where there exist known Basque diaspora communities. Additionally, Douglass points out possible misrepresentations and overcounting in the Basque case because of a combination of policies used for rural-area counting, as well as because of the use of statistical formulas.

The Basque American case study underscores dilemmas within diaspora studies, including who defines who will be categorized and how that category of "ethnics" itself will be defined. Douglass queries the underlying assumptions and presumptions of efforts at identifying ethnic populations. How comprehensive and reliable are the results? How relevant and useful are they for our purposes?

Michel S. Laguerre's study considers the social integration of European neighbor-hoods prevalent in countries that are being integrated into the European Union, specifi-cally looking at how national plans for the renovation of cities connect the various levels of identity and government: local, state, and global. This manifests itself in the double adaptation of these neighborhoods—at the country level, in terms of the urban policies of city hall, and also at the level of the European Union, in terms of immigration policy, since the European Parliament can overrule some local practices. The reengineering of local practices is being carried out at the same time that diasporic residents of these neighborhoods are entertaining transnational relations with their homelands and other geographically dispersed diasporic sites. This adds another layer of complexity to the globalization process. Laguerre chooses the Jewish quarter in Paris for this study because of the light it sheds on neighborhood globalization and diasporic politics in the European Union.

The controversy over the mayor's proposal to modernize the Jewish Quarter of Paris hinged on two main arguments, according to Laguerre. The proponents of the plan (the city hall officials) claimed that the quarter should match the reality of the rest of Paris. The opponents of the plan (residents of the Jewish quarter and its merchants) believed that it was important to preserve the villagelike life that had provided a protective niche for the maintenance of their culture and identity. From the viewpoint of city hall, the plan called for minimal change, while local Jewish merchants saw it as a major intervention that would destroy the last bastion of Jewish life in Paris. Laguerre's article examines how, in this case, the renovation of an ethnic neighborhood was negotiated at the interface of the local with the global by giving examples of the global conversation being played out via the Internet. Furthermore, it shows how the dynamic of globalization from below and globalization from above affect the decision-making process in urban planning.

The relationship between the democratic or nondemocratic systems of host coun-tries and the persistence of diaspora identity is the theme of William Safran's research published here. He explores which political systems and opportunity structures are more conducive to enabling or facilitating the maintenance of an ethnic identity away from a homeland. He notes that authoritarian centralized states are thought to obstruct and hin-der the maintenance of ethnic identity, while democratic systems, often publicly devoted to multiculturalism, are expected to nurture diasporic identities. However, he also ques-tions whether some democratic states' public policy of the redistribution of wealth may actually initiate a breakdown of ethnic community self-help, because individuals become economically or socially dependent on the state, instead of on their own ethnic commu-nity. An authoritarian regime may be so oppressive as to actually heighten the group sense of identity in opposition to and in defense against a dominating cultural force. Citing many examples, Safran distinguishes between democratic, centralized, "mono-chromatic" political systems and those that are also democratic, but pluralistic.

The depth and continuity of diasporic identity are strongly affected by the policies of the hostland, such as naturalization, integration, and the legitimation of immigrant particularisms. In this regard, globalization has produced an important change in context. In particular, the tools of telecommunications are greatly enhancing the individual's and the group's realities of being both "here" and "there." Globalization has made national boundaries more permeable, facilitated transpolitical relations, and engendered a rethinking of the concept of citizenship, thereby clouding the distinction between indigenous and diaspora status. Because many of Safran's points are subject to debate, he also raises questions about the way in which arguments concerning the relationship between political context and diaspora identity might be substantiated or falsified by systematic comparative analysis.

Gabriel Sheffer commences his work with a concise overview of his categorization and definition of the various types of diasporas—including those migrants who are *not* in diaspora—and clearly states that he believes the economic, political, and social influences of diasporas and diasporans will continue to increase. He defines and then outlines the most critical challenges facing both transstate and transnational diasporas. He advises "core and peripheral members to clarify their individual and collective identity and identification" and reminds us that maintaining the nonessentialist primordial elements of their ethnic identity is also difficult.

The second major challenge is connected to the need to define and delineate the actual and virtual boundaries of these communities, which are quite fluid and permeable. The effects of globalization make this additionally difficult. Another issue facing these entities concerns the question of "homeland" or "center" and the effort to define and to recognize the actual or virtual location of the particular diaspora's origin or center point. Relations between diaspora individuals as well as between their diaspora institutions are also significant. A fourth area of concern raises the common question of dual loyalty and the diaspora's preference for the homeland or for the new host country. Finally, Sheffer raises the issue of the strategic and tactical policies and activities (including violence and terrorism) that are used in attempts to achieve the interests of the various types of diasporas.

Differentiating between "diaspora" and "dispersion," Khachig Tölölyan begins his work by defining and categorizing various groups and experiences. He then moves into a discussion of "soft power" and "stateless power," referring to diaspora elites and their abilities to influence social and cultural services that states no longer, or never did, perform. The "stateless power" of diaspora includes their capacities to design and establish organizations and institutions within the community; as well as to "extend the diasporan community's reach, through financial contributions, political lobbying, and media representations, to influence policies and legislation, indeed, to participate energetically in the public sphere" and to create and maintain relations among various actors that influence outcomes. He gives a detailed case study of the Armenian diaspora and analyzes how diasporas both act and react in relationship to homeland issues, and how the Armenian diaspora has mobilized, including militarily, in regards to particular political and social changes. The timing of such mobilizations and homeland specific political and economic development can affect and effect the efficacy and level of influence diaspora groups will have.

The efforts of the U.S. Armenian diaspora have kept Azerbaijan and Turkey on notice that they do have political power to influence the debate about what U.S. actions in the Transcaucasus would best serve America's interest, and increasingly Armenians in Paris and London are showing influence in the European Union policy discussions. Tölö-lyan also illustrates the difficulties of diaspora involvement in internal homeland politics as the homeland's foreign affairs, strings that are attached to financial remittances, and how dominant diasporic partisan factions have formed alliances with their counterparts in Armenia. The diaspora communities are often impediments to conflict resolution.

Gloria Totoricagüena argues that the presence of nonstate actors in foreign policy is not a new phenomenon; however, their pursuits are now greatly facilitated by trans-formations in the power of the state, telecommunications, the global economy, and the emergence of global culture. In contemporary world affairs, diplomacy is unambiguously multilayered, and paradiplomacy—as a postmodern deconstruction of state diplomacy—has increasing influence in international relations. Though the relations of regional governments and diaspora communities remain clearly inferior in the statecraft of "high" and "low" politics, she indicates that culture and identity politics are no longer singularly dominated by statecentric networks and are moving into the realm of ethnic alliances such as homeland-diaspora transnational relations.

Although the primary unit of analysis in foreign affairs has been the state, Totori-cagüena offers that for centuries, noncentral government actors have always engaged in transborder activities. Using quantitative and qualitative examples from the case of the government of the Basque Autonomous Community and the nearly two hundred Basque diaspora organizations in twenty-two different countries, her article aims to discuss the localization of international relations and the significance of noncentral governments in homeland-diaspora relations. She analyzes global activities of noncentral governments that promote a separatist or independentist message in programs and projects with entities in other countries. She asks whether Basque homeland institutions are using their trade and cultural missions abroad as protoembassies or protoconsulates of a potentially sovereign state. What is the opportunity structure presently in place for diasporas to act in foreign policy, and do diasporas have the capacity for independent political action?

As the contributions in this volume amply demonstrate, opportunity structures for diasporas in postmodern and transstate social, economic, and political systems are many. What follows is a diverse set of research articles with perspectives from various case studies, using divergent theories to describe and to analyze the definitions of transnationalism and diaspora existences, the mobilizing practices and the political implications of such entities, and the possibilities for future applications of these practices in the globalized context.

Gloria Totoricagüena

Multilayered Politics in the African Diaspora:
The Metadiaspora Concept and Minidiaspora Realities

By Kim D. Butler

Narratives of diaspora once focused on oppression and displacement. Today, they focus on diaspora as a potential strategy of empowerment. The ability to harness that potential varies greatly from one diaspora to the next; these differences are evident between different branches of single diasporas as well. In seeking to understand better the nature of diaspora politics, it is useful to consider how such diversity interacts within complex diasporas and how it affects the collective political possibilities of the diaspora as a whole.

We tend to think of diasporas as a hub-and-spoke model: Imagine a wheel with a single homeland at the center from which spokes extend to discrete diaspora communities. Not all diasporas are such simple constructions. Many modern diasporas are composites of diasporas formed in different eras that necessarily interact and cross-pollinate each other, as is the case with the African diaspora. To reflect its complexities, I use the term "metadiaspora" to refer to the umbrella category of all peoples dispersed from the African continent. Such a construction allows for the consideration of not only the whole, but also its constituent diasporas in their own right, each of which has conditions fostering a particular set of political ideologies, strategies, and possibilities. The African metadiaspora consists of many constituent diasporas (i.e., Ghanaian, Garifuna, Indian Ocean, Caribbean). Just as individuals hold multiple layers of identity, so also do diasporas exist at the meta and micro levels simultaneously. The overall landscape of diaspora politics is thus an interaction between differently bounded diaspora communities.

As a multilayered diaspora, the African example illuminates the vast difference in political options for recent emigrants from nation-states versus the slave-era dispersals from a generic continental homeland. To what extent is it possible to coordinate multiple types of strategies toward a collective transnational political agenda? Are diasporas deployed differently by groups and individuals who have experienced mobility as compared with those whose lives are rooted in new homelands or who perhaps are the descendants of subsequent waves of diasporization? Do these disparities in political realities mitigate against a shared diaspora consciousness and the potential for collective metadiaspora mobilization?

The first example of diasporas' deployment considered here looks at newer African diasporas, those coming from modern African states, and the types of diaspora politics reflected in their organizations. The second considers how different sectors of the African diaspora interact in New York City's racialized environment. The third looks at instances of larger-level diaspora mobilization at the continental and diaspora-only level. A central premise in what follows is that today's political and technological climate favors types of diaspora politics (and forms of identity consciousness) that are different from those prevalent in the past. This results in a conglomeration within the African diaspora of very different types of constituent diasporas. It concludes with a brief consideration of how these discrete diaspora politics might become part of the ideological and political discourse of the pandiaspora community.

The Diversity of the African Diaspora

All diasporas, by definition, are multifaceted. Each site or remigration constitutes its own community within the larger whole. Just as important, many diasporas are also multilayered. The descendants of the initial migrants are eventually joined by new waves of people departing from the same homeland. Both principles are essential for understanding the diversity and dynamism of diasporas.

The African diaspora is, by some measures, the most diverse of all diasporas, as well as the oldest. Africa is the point of origin from which humankind scattered throughout the globe. It is the site of major migratory movements in antiquity. Some of these, such as the great Bantu migration, were contained within the continent; others involved travels across the seas to Oceania and, as argued by Ivan Van Sertima, to the Americas.[1] Every era of human history has seen migrations from Africa. Because of this diversity, at least two theoretical issues immediately have faced scholars of the African diaspora. The first is the question of whether all these migrations should be considered part of the diaspora. In the first widely cited paper on the subject, George Shepperson was unequivocal. His definition limited the concept of an African diaspora to "the study of a series of reactions

The author thanks research assistant Kimberly Jacobs, Khachig Tölölyan, and the participants and organizers of the 2006 diaspora politics conference at the Basque Center of the University of Nevada, Reno, for their invaluable contributions to this paper, along with special thanks to Gloria Totoricagüena for her development of this project on comparative diaspora politics.

1. Ivan Van Sertima, *They Came Before Columbus* (New York: Random House, 1976); Joseph E. Harris, "The African Diaspora in World History and Politics," in *African Roots/American Cultures: Africa in the Creation of the Americas*, ed. Sheila Walker (Lanham, MD: Rowman and Littlefield, 2001), 104–7.

to coercion, to the imposition of the economic and political rule of alien peoples in Africa, to slavery and imperialism."[2] The second is whether the major circuits of dispersion should be thought of as unique diasporas or as part of one great African diaspora. The Africanists who first employed the construct conceived of a single African diaspora composed of discrete streams.[3]

The boundaries of the African diaspora are still contested terrain. However, the past half century of scholarship has provided some useful guideposts. As Colin Palmer has suggested, there is a fundamental difference between the migrations of antiquity and those constituting the modern African diaspora. He distinguishes five historical phases within the development of the African diaspora.[4] Modifying Palmer's periodization slightly, I employ the notion of a modern African diaspora composed of four principal streams.

The most visible of these resulted from the traumatic transatlantic slave trade. The experiences of this community first suggested to scholars of Africa that the concept of a diaspora could be a useful construct for understanding the complicated identities, relationships, and politics of peoples of African descent on a global level. The approximately eleven million souls who survived the brutality of the Middle Passage came to constitute what is often considered the archetypical African diaspora, along with their descendants concentrated in the Americas and the Caribbean. I refer to this community as the Afro-Atlantic diaspora.[5]

Africans were also moving in other directions, even as the Afro-Atlantic diaspora was taking shape. A much older commercial network trading in slaves across the Indian Ocean dates back to the first or second century A.D. and was responsible for African

---

2. George Shepperson, "The African Abroad or the African Diaspora," in *Emerging Themes in African History: Proceedings of the International Congress of African Historians held at University College, Dar es Salaam, October 1965*, ed. T. O. Ranger (London: Heinemann Educational, 1968), 153.

3. See the proceedings of the First African Diaspora Studies Institute in Joseph E. Harris, ed., *Global Dimensions of the African Diaspora*, 1st ed. (Washington: Howard University Press, 1982); and Harris, "The African Diaspora in World History and Politics."

4. Colin Palmer, "Defining and Studying the Modern African Diaspora," *Perspectives* (newsletter of the American Historical Association), September 1998: 22–25.

5. Recent scholarship has begun to identify discrete diasporas within this larger aggregate, a project greatly assisted by the compilation of the records of thousands of individual slaving voyages. See David Eltis, Stephen Behrendt, David Richardson, and Herbert S. Klein, *The Trans-Atlantic Slave Trade: A Database on CD-ROM* (Cambridge: Cambridge University Press, 1999), and Gwendolyn Midlo Hall, *Afro-Louisiana History and Genealogy Database* (Baton Rouge: Louisiana State University Press, 2000). For works tracing specific African diasporas into the Americas using a variety of approaches, see, for example, Linda Heywood, ed., *Central Africans and Cultural Transformations in the African Diaspora* (Cambridge: Cambridge University Press, 2002); Maureen Warner-Lewis, *Central Africa in the Caribbean: Transcending Time, Transforming Cultures* (Barbados: University of the West Indies Press, 2003); M. Thomas J. Desch-Obi, "Engolo: Combat Traditions in African and African Diaspora History," Ph.D. diss., UCLA, 2000; and Toyin Falola and Matt D. Childs, eds., *The Yoruba Diaspora in the Atlantic World* (Bloomington: Indiana University Press, 2004). It should also be noted that as research expands on other branches of the African diaspora, it is challenging the notion of a quintessential or archetypical diaspora modeled on any single branch. See Ruth Simms Hamilton, ed., *Routes of Passage: Rethinking the African Diaspora*, vol. 1, part 1 (East Lansing: Michigan State University Press, 2007).

relocations to India, Pakistan, Iraq, Iran, Turkey, Yemen, Pakistan, and probably as far as China.[6]

European military and commercial involvement in Africa culminated in colonization in the nineteenth and twentieth centuries. Subsequent migrations of Africans between the continent and colonial capitals led to the creation of many diasporan communities in Europe. In contrast to the mass arrivals of the slave era, the greater percentage of individual migrations in this stream did not always result in de facto "community." Children born to African-European couples were frequently raised as part of a nationally defined, rather than African or black community.[7]

The possibilities for economic opportunities and safe haven from untenable situations at home have continued to draw continental Africans and African descendants in the diaspora to an ever growing list of places that have become diaspora capitals.[8] This fourth and most recent stream of the African diaspora is developing within the context of vastly improved transportation and telecommunications technology that, I contend, significantly distinguishes it from earlier branches. While these are the principal dispersals from the continent considered as a whole, there are also many dispersals from single locations within Africa to destinations elsewhere in the continent and abroad.

I have argued elsewhere that the particular reasons for and conditions of any diasporization leave a fundamental imprint on that diaspora that will, in turn, inform its subsequent politics, culture, and identity.[9] Each of these four branches of the African diaspora differed in the forces leading to their respective dispersals, as well as in the context of their evolving experiences abroad. For example, the primacy of race in the Afro-Atlantic diaspora does not have the same resonance for other sectors of the African diaspora. What has changed in recent times is that those dynamics no longer exist in geographic isolation. Today, multiple sectors of the diaspora coexist in the same space and time.

Diversity within diasporas is often posited geohistorically, because dispersed communities have resettled and followed distinct, yet interlinked trajectories. In other words, we think of the constituent segments of a diaspora as location A, B, C, and so on. While this is an appropriate mapping approach for certain research questions, it does not capture the complexity of overlapping waves of diaspora arrivals or remigrations that bring branches of the diaspora together in one location.

---

6. Shihan de S. Jayasuriya and Richard Pankhurst, eds., *The African Diaspora in the Indian Ocean* (Trenton, NJ: Africa World Press, 2003); Joseph E. Harris, *The African Presence in Asia: Consequences of the East African Slave Trade* (Evanston, IL: Northwestern University Press, 1971).

7. Tina Campt, *Other Germans: Black Germans and the Politics of Race, Gender, and Memory in the Third Reich* (Ann Arbor: University of Michigan Press, 2004).

8. Khalid Koser, ed., *New African Diasporas* (London: Routledge, 2003); Nicolas van Haer, *New Diasporas* (Seattle: University of Washington Press, 1998).

9. Kim D. Butler, "Defining Diaspora, Refining a Discourse," *Diaspora* 10, no. 2 (2001): 189–219.

Yet another level of complexity occurs when a single location generates distinct diasporas. If, for example, one considers the global coordinates of approximately 8 degrees north latitude and 4 degrees east longitude, a person departing in 1800 would have left Oyo; a person departing in 1900 would have left a British colony; a person departing in 2000 would have left Nigeria. While they are all the same bit of land, each departure was from a differently imagined homeland. Today, individuals connected to each of these migrations could easily live together in the same city. It is readily apparent that the choices made by an enslaved African are circumscribed by conditions not faced by a Nigerian today, with access to international calling cards, DVDs of Nigerian movies, the Internet, airlines, and so on. What I wish to emphasize here is that some of those conditions of being in diaspora for a modern-day Nigerian are shaped by the prior history of the African diaspora, as well as by the contemporary realities of new migrations from multiple diasporas. While the histories of each branch of the African diaspora may be in dialogue, the question remains as to whether the conditions for diasporas formed in the digital age will support metadiaspora consciousness and political viability. This essay seeks to interrogate how, as these various diaspora sectors coexist in the same place and time, their disparate political sensibilities interact to produce "diaspora politics."

The diversity of the African diaspora has caused its scholars to be very cognizant of the juxtaposition of particularity and commonality that characterizes diasporas. As noted in 1999 by historian Thomas Holt and elaborated further by Brent Edwards, it is precisely this interplay of sameness and difference, which Edwards terms *décalage*, that provides a framework for understanding the nature of the African diaspora.[10] The concept can be pushed even further to yield a more nuanced analysis of diaspora politics. Each constituent diaspora community has its own politics based on its unique places and times. In addition to constituent communities dispersed from a common homeland to different locations, the African metadiaspora also has constituent diasporas of different homelands and conditions of dispersal.[11] These necessarily interact at moments of the mobilization of metadiaspora politics. Metalevel diaspora politics can therefore operate in multiple ways, such as through collaboration to work on common local goals or under the umbrella auspices and direction of a metalevel homeland. In this regard, the African diaspora is affected by the fact that the homeland—Africa—did not exist as a cohesive political entity at the time of dispersal and only relatively recently has begun continental-

---

10. Thomas C. Holt, "Slavery and Freedom in the Atlantic World: Reflections on the Diasporan Framework," in *Crossing Boundaries: Comparative Histories of Black People in Diaspora*, ed. Darlene Clark Hine and Jacqueline McLeod (Bloomington: Indiana University Press, 1999), 36. This argument was elaborated as the concept of *décalage* by literary scholar Brent Edwards in *The Practice of Diaspora: Literature, Translation, and the Rise of Black Internationalism* (Cambridge. MA: Harvard University Press, 2003).

11. For example, the African metadiaspora includes the national diaspora of Somalia and the diaspora of the Caribbean region. In noting this, I differ with Robin Cohen's characterization of the Caribbean as a "cultural diaspora." While the spread of culture may be studied using a diaspora framework, this does not preclude the Caribbean being studied as a formal diaspora in its own right. See Robin Cohen, "The Diaspora of a Diaspora: The Case of the Caribbean," *Social Science Information* 31 (1992): 159–69.

level coordination through the Organization for African Unity and its successor, the African Union. However, the African Union is limited in its authority to legislate policies vis-à-vis the African diaspora (such as citizenship or voting rights) that are currently implemented individually by its member states.

Because different options are available to individuals and groups who may otherwise appear to be members of the same metadiaspora, political theories of diaspora must necessarily consider how these more circumscribed politics operate in relation to the larger whole. This is not a minor issue. All diasporas have an internal politics—the personal politics of belonging—that operates on different axes for each diaspora. On the one hand, individuals negotiate their own belonging to the diaspora (as well as their understanding of how others belong). On the other, hostlands and homelands also mediate belonging, which, in turn, affects the degree to which individuals feel the need to affirm a diaspora community. Within the African diaspora, race continues to be a powerful factor shaping diaspora affinities, a factor that varies widely, even between individuals.

A mobilization of diaspora at the metalevel would require bridging its natural disaggregations of spatial locations and, at the same time, the disparate layers of communities within any single location. What types of issues inspire such mobilizations? Do people shift the tactics appropriate for constituent diasporas when working for the whole, or do they combine to maximize their varying locations to create multifaceted strategies for metalevel goals? Also, is it possible to have a decentered diaspora politics in which the homeland is not a principle actor, but merely the "glue" that defines the community? To move diaspora political theory forward, it is necessary to begin exploring such questions. This essay represents an opening salvo aimed toward that end.

The Metadiaspora in African Experience

As previously noted, what is commonly understood today as "the" African diaspora is more properly labeled "the modern African diaspora." The reference to the modern age is not merely a temporal distinction. One cannot understand modernity without understanding the African diaspora. Embedded in its formation are the roots of modern transnationalism and the social philosophies of dominance, exploitation, and stratification that lubricate the engine of modern capitalism. As African raw materials and eventually people came to circulate around the globe, the concept of Africa consolidated as an overarching umbrella for the continent's diverse millions.[12] Specifically, the idea that the role of Africa was to generate wealth for non-Africans gave rise to a common cause among the targets of that exploitation. The broadly shared imposition of racialist inequality and exploitation over time may possibly be the key link between distinct African diasporas to form an African metadiaspora. As Michelle Wright noted in 2004, "Any truly accurate

---

12. Despite Africa's geological diversity, early geographers considered it a single continent, thus linking its many peoples collectively as "Africans." This was not the only option, as evidenced by the classification of the Eurasian land mass as two distinct continents.

definition of an African diasporic identity . . . must somehow simultaneously incorporate the diversity of Black identities in the diaspora yet also link all those identities to show that they indeed constitute a diaspora rather than an unconnected aggregate of different peoples linked only in name."[13] Does the construct of a unitary Africa and the social concept of blackness form the basis of the modern African diaspora identity? Neither is an inherent racial identity or necessarily congruent with many of the ways peoples of African descent construct identity.

This juxtaposition between discrete communities of the African diaspora and the undeniable realities of race politics characterizes the way that diaspora has been understood in the African case. While culture may be evoked as the basis for common ground, it is difficult to argue for any single identifiable "African culture" beyond broad, sweeping generalizations about such things as ancestor and elder veneration that can certainly apply to other world cultures. Rather, it has been the politics of race that has mobilized a sense of common cause, serving as the operative and constitutive basis of the African metadiaspora. The economic and political challenges of Africa and its diasporas are inextricably bound to the racialized practices of slavery and predatory colonialism and continue to be understood through a racially sensitive filter. That legacy is shared, albeit with some variation, by the three major geographic branches of the African diaspora in the Americas, Europe, and Asia.[14] The power relations of race are such that, regardless of how African descendants view themselves, their lives have historically been circumscribed within race constructs that forced responses and identifications with this shared political cause. When the African diaspora has been mobilized at the metalevel, it has been around such issues as slavery, racism, and anticolonialism. The sense that the fates of Africans "at home" and abroad are linked is a dominant theme in transnational African politics.

What I wish to underscore here is that the African metadiaspora in the modern era is, essentially, a political project.[15] It does not merely exist; rather, it must be mobilized toward some end. Culture serves as a binding agent insofar as it articulates the commonality of experience and shared cause. For example, blacks from the Caribbean, Africa, the southern United States, Latin America, and elsewhere encountered each other as well as descendants of older Afro-Dutch and Afro-British black communities in New York in the nineteenth and twentieth centuries. That experience, set in the context of contemporary politics and culture, gave rise to the Harlem Renaissance, which expressed artistically the concept of a "new Negro" composed of diverse elements. Similar dynamics inspired

---

13. Michelle Wright, *Becoming Black: Creating Identity in the African Diaspora* (Durham, NC: Duke University Press, 2004), 2.

14. Edward Alpers illustrates how, despite significant historical differences, the tropes of slavery mark the Indian Ocean branch of the African diaspora with patterns common throughout the Atlantic branch. Edward A. Alpers, "The African Diaspora in the Indian Ocean: A Comparative Perspective," in *The African Diaspora in the Indian Ocean*, 19–50.

15. See also Edmund T. Gordon and Mark Anderson, "The African Diaspora: Toward an Ethnography of Diasporic Identification," *Journal of American Folklore* 112/445 (Summer 1999): 285.

Negritude in the French Caribbean and Europe, Afrocubanismo in Cuba, and other manifestations whose dialogues wove a cultural foundation for the pan-African political movement.[16] In these moments, the arts and culture both expressed and reinforced a sense of community, a black cultural vernacular, that subsequently informed diaspora and pan-Africanist sensibilities and politics.[17]

The twentieth century provided no shortage of antiblack and anti-African actions toward which political action could be directed. In 1912, black residents of Oriente Province in Cuba staged an attack on government offices responsible for dispossessing their lands to give to new U.S. entrepreneurs. The protest was a popular uprising in conjunction with broader demands of citizenship in the newly created nation. However, the rebels also explicitly denounced the persistence of racial discrimination, which resulted in considerable support from other Afro-Caribbean workers. The Guantánamo Sugar Company, for example, was targeted by Haitians who maintained "they were very badly treated for being black."[18] The violent government reprisals that followed targeted *blacks*; included in the tally of dead of approximately six thousand were non-Cuban black migrant workers who had no part in the protest.

The politics of race have historically bound African diaspora peoples across diversity. However, this plays out in a variety of ways, based on the geographic, social, and economic location of individuals and communities within the diaspora. As a result, various segments of the African diaspora have experienced racism differently. It is important to note that the racialized conceptualization of the diaspora held most sway where race was utilized as a rationale for inequitable practices.[19] Race as an obstacle became a rallying point for mobilizing potential collective power. It is possible to read an explicitly black African diaspora historicized in the black popular press in locations where racial pressures were high, most notably in the *Negro World*, the publication of the Universal Negro Improvement Association.[20] Racialized practices, and slavery in particular, tied to a pancontinental conflation of Africa, sustained identities and identifications of succeeding generations as Africans in diaspora, rather than as immigrants assimilated to their respective destinations. Yet elsewhere in the African diaspora, and for those living in

---

16. Wright, *Becoming Black*; Robin Moore *Nationalizing Blackness: Afrocubanismo and Artistic Revolution in Havana, 1920–1940* (Pittsburgh, PA: University of Pittsburgh Press, 1997); Edwards, *The Practice of Diaspora.*

17. This is one of several cultural idioms available to the African diaspora. Others, such as Caribbean *creolité* or national hostland cultures, reflect and reinforce smaller units within the metadiaspora.

18. "Un independiente to Brooks" (1912), cited in Aline Helg, *Our Rightful Share: The Afro-Cuban Struggle for Equality, 1886-1912,* (Chapel Hill: University of North Carolina Press, 1995), 209; Louis A. Pérez, "Politics, Peasants and People of Color: The 1912 'Race War' in Cuba Reconsidered," *Hispanic American Historical Review* 66 (August 1986): 509–39.

19. I have proposed elsewhere that a specific type of antidiscriminatory mobilization emerges from individuals who perceive that either race or Africanity is the principal factor limiting their prerogatives. This is but one possible response to the pressures of white supremacy and exploitation and is characterized by its engagement with, rather than withdrawal from, hegemonic structures and practices. Kim D. Butler, *Freedoms Given, Freedoms Won: Afro-Brazilians in Post-Abolition São Paulo and Salvador* (New Brunswick, NJ: Rutgers University Press, 1998), ch. 2.

20. The journal circulated weekly in many areas where Caribbean workers were establishing themselves in highly racialized postabolition economies, such as the fruit plantations and railway and canal projects in the Americas.

situations where race was not a primary factor affecting life options, race has played a far less salient role.

Diaspora political theory must therefore be able to deal simultaneously with meta-constructs and the millions of microlevel interations of which they are constituted. The interactions of diasporas with one another and between segments of the same diaspora may differ for individuals situated differently within that diaspora. The example of recent migrations of African nationals illustrates significant differences in the way a recent diaspora is imagined and mobilized when compared with the pan-Africanism of the early twentieth century.

New African Diasporas

The rapid pace of African emigration beyond the continent in recent decades has alerted scholars to the necessity of distinguishing between those diasporas formed by the Atlantic and Indian Ocean slave trades and newer diasporas in the postcolonial era. The first and most obvious distinction is the nature of their status as "free" versus enslaved emigrants. While it may be argued that economic constraints and restrictions at border sites such as the Strait of Gibraltar have forced many African migrants into situations closely resembling slavery, their status as free persons has allowed them to select routes of their choice.[21] Whereas destinations in the Americas and the Caribbean figured prominently in the Atlantic slave trade, Europe is now the principal region for Africans leaving the continent. A 2004 study by the Sussex Centre for Migration Research reported that between 1995 and 2000, the mean annual flow to Europe was 84,226, compared with 35,404 traveling to the United States. This data, based on official immigration statistics, necessarily undercounts illegal migrants, but nonetheless reveals important patterns. Of the six countries with the largest numbers of emigrants, only Ethiopia had a significant majority (65 percent) moving to the United States. Nigeria and Ghana had roughly equal distributions between the two regions, with 48 percent and 56 percent, respectively, choosing Europe over the United States. A regional breakdown reveals Europe's centrality in African migration overall.

---

21. The attempts by sub-Saharan Africans to enter the European Union through Morocco, either via the sea crossing or by entering the Spanish enclave at Melilla, has reached critical proportions, yet sustainable policy accords between the European Union, Spain, and the African nations remain to be secured. The practice of marking "sub-Saharan" Africans in the press semantically reinforces perceived racial, ethnic, and cultural differences with North Africans, who also represent a considerable presence in Europe. Though not the subject of this essay, the self-identification of North Africans in diaspora, whose home media draws heavily on the concept of a Middle Eastern/Arab/Muslim diaspora, is a necessary area of consideration for African diaspora studies. Are these people leaving an "African" homeland or continuing an older dispersion that has passed through African sites?

TABLE 1:

Mean Annual Emigration Flows from Africa, 1995–2000, by Region
(percentages rounded to nearest whole number)

	To Europe	To United States
From: East Africa	14,385 (56%)	11,095 (44%)
Central Africa	8,400 (88%)	1,171 (12%)
Western Africa	32,642 (62%)	19,980 (38%)
Southern Africa	20,385 (87%)	3,158 (13%)
TOTAL AFRICA*	84,225 (70%)	35,404 (30%)

Source: Richard Black, Working Paper C6, "Migration and Pro-Poor Policy in Africa," Sussex Centre for Migration Research, Development Research Centre on Migration, Globalisation and Poverty, 2004, Appendix 1, 20–21.

* The figures are corrected here from incorrect totals provided in the original and include 8413 "other" sending sites in the total African emigration rate to Europe.

Despite the increasing rates of migration to Europe, the African immigrant population in the United States remains numerically significant, with 1.8 million African-born persons recorded in its 2000 census.[22] Continental African migration has elicited significant research into their diasporic economic and political activities, clearly underscored by questions concerning the implications of such mobilizations in places where they have settled, as well as in Africa. A first question to ask is: What levels of diaspora are being invoked, and why? Are these migrants functioning as members of "African" diaspora communities who consider the entire continent as their "homeland," or is the homeland anchor more narrowly conceived? It is, of course, possible to sustain multiple affinities simultaneously, but actual patterns in political and economic practice suggest that newer African diasporas are anchored in subcontinental units (i.e., hometown, national, or other specific networks) with corresponding administrative structures. This is a far different relationship with an African homeland than that available to most of the slave-era descendants, who lack documented ties to any specific African polity.

Chukwu-Emeka Chikezie has characterized contemporary African diaspora homeland relationships through the metaphor of the Yoruba concept of *kporapko*, the invocation of one's local society as a primary level of loyalty or patriotism.[23] Chikezie describes a speech by a Nigerian judge in London who, after acknowledging other high officials at the dais, proceeded "to do *kporapko*" by recognizing the head of his village, also in attendance.

---

22. Percy Claude Hintzen and Jean Muteba Rahier, "Introduction: From Structural Politics to the Politics of Deconstruction: Self-Ethnographies Problematizing Blackness," in Percy Claude Hintzen and Jean Muteba Rahier, eds., *Problematizing Blackness: Self-Ethnographies by Black Immigrants to the United States* (New York: Routledge, 2003), 1.

23. Chukwu-Emeka Chikezie, "Accountability, Africa and Her Diaspora," www.opendemocracy.net/globalization-accountability/africa_2869.jsp (last accessed July 28, 2007).

He argues that a combination of African traditions privileging patriotism at the local level and the challenges faced by modern African states has channeled African diaspora mobilization toward nonstate-based networks.[24] Such networking may be, in part, a function of immigrant patterns. Recent immigrants maintain involvement with the hometown, but gradually shift their focus over time to broader-based ethnic and cultural affiliations in the hostlands. Indeed, this was the pattern observed among Ghanaians in Toronto by Takyiwaa Manuh.[25] A closer look at the eras of migration (1960s–70s versus 1980s–90s) suggests that technology might be another factor at play. The ease of international communication makes it far easier for recent immigrants to keep hometown-based networks functional in the diaspora, perhaps delaying or obviating the creation of national and metadiaspora-level networks. Departing populations no longer simply disappear from their homelands. The choices of contemporary diasporas as to their relationships with "home" have serious implications for African states.

One such issue addressed by Chikezie is the way diasporas circumvent central states to send remittances and invest in development projects. As a result, development is closely tied to those regions with strong diasporas, as opposed to having a central clearinghouse decide on the distribution of expatriate funds at the national level.[26] After his election in 2001, the Ghanaian president, John Kufuor, outlined a specific role for the diaspora in his development strategy, detailed in a Poverty Reduction Strategy Paper (PRSP). Chikezie notes:

> But here Ghana's own version of *kporapko* stands in the way, somewhat, of the government's grand vision. For the PRSP rather assumes that all Ghanaians abroad are signed up to develop this construct called Ghana. Most actually focus on specific locations within Ghana. Groups from the southern Ashanti region, for instance, typically channel their efforts via the chief's stool to which they bear allegiance. This sets up a potentially tricky constitutional conundrum.[27]

Chikezie's observation highlights the important role of substate and nonstate types of relationships, such as town and fraternity networks that operate transnationally within the African diaspora. While these may be mediated by the state, their actual activities are informed by what is conceived of as "homeland."

---

24. Ibid.

25. Takyiwaa Manuh, "'*Efie*' or The Meanings of 'Home' among Female and Male Ghanaian Migrants in Toronto, Canada and Returned Migrants to Ghana," in Koser ed., *New African Diasporas*, 145.

26. A UK-based report in 2004 corroborates this conclusion, noting that remittances from Ghanaians abroad concentrated on their hometowns in the south, rather than on the more impoverished north. The Centre on Migration, Policy, and Society (COMPAS), "The Contribution of UK Based Diasporas to Development and Poverty Reduction," Oxford, April 2004, 13. This same pattern is evident elsewhere in the African diaspora, such as in Mexico's Costa Chica along the Pacific coast, where emigrants finance their families and construct homes for their eventual return. Such support does not address the underlying problems leading to emigration, making the diaspora a fundamental part of the economic infrastructure in such situations.

27. Chikezie, "Accountability, Africa and Her Diaspora."

In this regard, one of the significant factors distinguishing contemporary from older African diasporas is the relative relationship of the state. In the Americas, where enslavers strove to control all aspects of the lives of Africans, the scope and types of networks they created were greatly limited.[28] They were characterized by being trans*cultural*, in bringing together Africans (and others) of diverse backgrounds into a shared creole culture. Rarely could they function trans*nationally*, because of restrictions on black mobility. Thus, autonomous, African-based cooperative institutions in the Americas began with severe limitations on both type and scope. In contrast, throughout the continent, there is a vibrant history of nonstate social networks, both precolonial and more recent, that complement state functions. A particularly transnational articulation of this phenomenon dates back at least to the start of the modern era in Muslim-led political states of northern and western Africa with the incursion of Arab trade associations and Muslim religious institutions. Nonstate transnational institutions assumed responsibilities supplementing the functions of the clerical and, later, the colonial and independent government. One such example is the Mouride brotherhood founded in Senegal in the 1880s by Sheik Amadou Bamba. It is one of four major Senegalese Sufi brotherhoods. The others are the Tidianyya, Quadryya, and Layenne. As Bruno Riccio notes, the brotherhoods provide a system of spiritual, economic, and political support that has helped their members negotiate the instabilities of the twentieth century, but also, significantly, has translated well as their members began looking to new opportunities overseas. Riccio argues that the Senegalese diaspora community in Italy is deeply influenced by Mouride strategies, including a fluidity that subverts reified notions of ethnic boundaries.[29]

Another phenomenon challenging the primacy of nation for African diasporas is the lack of equivalence between precolonial nations and those carved by European powers in the nineteenth century. Somalis in diaspora, for example, are not all citizens of Somalia; some are nationals of Ethiopia, Kenya, and Djibouti. Also, not all Somalians are Somali ethnics. These boundaries of ethnic nations and smaller, family-based communities all coexist in diaspora. This not only troubles the concept of homeland, but has practical implications for the ways in which the diaspora can be conceived and organized. For the Somalis, diversity within the diaspora has proven to be a challenge to a cohesive national diaspora.[30]

Two points are important here. First, recent African diasporas have inherited a rich history of nonstate institutions and collectivities that are often carried into diaspora. Second, the ability to maintain and successfully utilize these networks may well challenge the degree to which diaspora consciousness is anchored by common ties to either the state or the continent.

---

28. The primary forms of African-based associations in the slave-era Americas and Caribbean were religious sodalities (ostensibly for the veneration of Catholic saints), responsible for such functions as burials and mutual financial assistance; more explicitly, African and often clandestine religious practices addressed healing and spiritual concerns. Other types of association eventually emerged from these roots.

29. Bruno Riccio, "More Than a Trade Diaspora: Senegalese Transnational Experiences in Emilia-Romagna (Italy)," in Koser, ed., *New African Diasporas*, 95–110.

30. Marc-Antoine Pérouse de Montclos, "A Refugee Diaspora: When the Somali Go West," in Koser, ed., *New African Diasporas*, 37–55.

Research on African immigrants in Europe, the United States, and Canada suggests a pattern in which associations based on the original homeland or nation lead to, first, pan-African collaborations and, eventually, a broader metadiaspora sensibility. In the United Kingdom, for example, organizations of Ghanaians, Nigerians, and other African diaspora groups joined forces in 1994 to create the African Foundation for Development (AFFORD). In 2005, an African Diaspora Community Forum convened representatives of Ethiopian, South African, and other African expatriates in Ottawa, Canada, to consider ways to mobilize resources to benefit Africa generally, with specific reference to the African Union as an organizational vehicle.[31] This collaboration is not new. The history of the African diaspora is marked by its extraordinary heterogeneity as people from diverse backgrounds have come together in "African" communities abroad.[32] The degree to which recently constituted African diaspora groups expand their activities and interests to a more broadly conceived sense of community will affect the future possibilities of metadiaspora politics. The ethnic and political contexts of hostlands, as well as the modalities of global and regional politics, should be considered important factors influencing pandiaspora affinities.

New African diasporas have also changed the landscape of the ways in which diasporas relate to African homelands. Earlier iterations of African diasporas formed through the slave trade have little direct connection to specific modern African states. Some have "adopted" specific African national identities through resettlement, such as the African Brazilians who created their own communities along the Benin coast, or U.S. expatriates who relocated to Ghana.[33] Others have taken on virtual African national or ethnic identities through cultural practices such as New World expressions of Akan and Yoruba. The Jamaican-based Rastafarian religion posits Haile Selassie's homeland of Ethiopia as a place of refuge from the "Babylon" experience in diaspora. Since actual ancestry cannot be traced for millions of African descendants, such affiliations of generationally distant diasporas have a tenuous role in African politics. For this diaspora, the homeland is a generic "Africa" that did not exist in formal organizational form prior to the creation of the Organization of African Unity. The stake of the diaspora in African politics was recognized on the continental level with the creation of a section within the African Union and the formation of the Western Hemisphere African Diaspora Network. As the process moved forward, it immediately became clear that there was a significant difference

---

31. COMPAS, "The Contribution of UK-based Diasporas to Development and Poverty Reduction"; African Diaspora Community Forum, "Report of the Proceedings," Ottawa, April 25, 2005.

32. There is extensive literature on the composition of "creole" communities in the Americas. One longstanding debate centers on the degree to which specific African cultures maintained discernible integrity in diaspora. On the creolization argument, see Sidney Mintz and Richard Price, *The Birth of African-American Culture: An Anthropological Perspective* (Boston: Beacon Press, 1992). Examples of research on regional cultures include Maureen Warner, *Central Africa in the Caribbean: Transcending Time, Transforming Culture* (Kingston: University of the West Indies Press, 2003); Linda Heywood, ed., *Central Africans and Cultural Transformations in the American Diaspora* (New York: Cambridge University Press, 2002); Toyin Falola and Matt D. Childs, eds., *The Yoruba Diaspora in the Atlantic World* (Bloomington: Indiana University Press, 2004).

33. J. Michael Turner, "Les Brésiliens: The Impact of Former Brazilian Slaves upon Dahomey," Ph.D. diss., Boston University, 1975.

between the locations and political perspectives of those with identifiable ties to specific nations and the slave trade–era diasporas.

African expatriate communities formed in recent decades are well positioned to have direct involvement in their respective homelands. In the case of Eritrea, members of its diaspora helped draft its first constitution after independence in 1993, in which expatriates were granted voting rights.[34] The role of diasporas and the depth of generational distance to be included in national and continental diasporas are now matters of great debate for both diasporas and homelands.

Ghana provides a particularly interesting case study in this regard. Ghana's role as the harbinger of African liberation after its independence in 1957 attracted "returnees" from the diaspora, including, most notably, U.S. scholar and activist W. E. B. du Bois.[35] In recent decades, the Ghanaian government has become increasingly interested in its relationships with its nationals abroad. It began sponsoring a "homecoming" targeted at economic initiatives with expatriate Ghanaians. With its slave depots declared UNESCO World Heritage Sites, Ghana has also actively promoted itself as a site of "heritage tourism" for the broader diaspora. In the spring of 2007, they sponsored the Golden Homecoming, specifically targeting the global African diaspora in commemoration of the fiftieth anniversary of Ghana and the two hundredth anniversary of Britain's abolition of the slave trade.

Associated with the Golden Homecoming 2007, the Ghana Homecoming Queen beauty pageant reveals significant insight into colloquial understanding of the scope of the Ghanaian diaspora. First, the regional sites for the selection of "beautiful young Ghanaian ladies" provides some idea of the geographic locations of the national diaspora:

Region	Audition Site(s)
The Americas	New York, U.S.A.
Europe	London, UK, and Amsterdam, Holland
Asia/Pacific	Tokyo, Japan
Southern & Central Africa	Johannesburg, South Africa
East & North Africa	Nairobi, Kenya
West Africa	Lagos, Nigeria
Ghana	Accra and Kumasi

Source: Ghana Homecoming Queen Web site: http://www.ghanahomecomingqueen.com (last accessed July 29, 2007).

---

34. SAHAN Wetenschappelijk Adviesbureau, "Mobilizing African Diaspora for the Promotion of Peace in Africa," policy report for the Netherlands Ministry of Foreign Affairs, Sub-Sahara Department (Amsterdam, May 2005), 8.

35. For further discussion of the complex dialogues between African Americans and Ghana see, for example, Edward Bruner, "Tourism in Ghana: The Representation of Slavery and the Return of the Black Diaspora," *American Anthropologist* 98, no. 2 (1996): 290–304, and Jemima Pierre, "Race Across the Atlantic: Mapping Racialization in Africa and the African Diaspora," Ph.D. diss., University of Texas at Austin, 2002. On repatriates, see O. Lake, "Toward a Pan-African Identity: Diaspora African Repatriates in Ghana," *Anthropological Quarterly* 68, no. 1 (January 1995): 21–51.

Second, the eligibility requirements carry an implicit understanding of Ghanaian belonging that would effectively exclude the diaspora returnees so warmly welcomed in the official public relations documents:

Eligibility Requirements for Ghana Homecoming Queen 2007

1. Be between the ages of 18 and 25 years
2. Have an idea about the history of Ghana
3. Be of Ghanaian origin (both of one parent or grandparent [sic]) or be a Ghanaian passport holder*
4. Be able to understand at least one Ghanaian language
5. Be 5.4 ft. tall or above
6. Be able to understand and speak English
7. Be ready to travel to Ghana for two weeks between February and March 2007 (all expenses paid)

* I read this to mean that at least one parent and at least one grandparent must be Ghanaian.

Of relevance here are the ways in which the organizers identify "their" diaspora—not only is it a community of people bound ancestrally and/or as citizens to the nation, but they must also have some cultural fluency in indigenous Ghana, as well as in its colonial experience (expressed in the English-language requirement). The contest also reinforces a national (as opposed to hometown) diaspora axis that is highly gendered. The expatriate experience necessarily entails cultural change, yet these young women contestants are used to embody a standardized and reified concept of "Ghanaianness."

As African homelands reach out to "the diaspora" through the mechanism of national governments, nation-based diasporas are mobilized in a way not possible for descendants from those same countries who were forcibly removed through slavery. Indeed, transnational organizing between members of specific nation-based diasporas is an important phenomenon within more recent African diaspora communities. A 2004 report by the Centre on Migration, Policy and Society (COMPAS) at the University of Oxford noted that Ghanaians had organized across Germany, the Netherlands, and the UK, and Somalis had established links across Scandinavia, the Netherlands, and the UK.[36]

The mobilization of nation-based diasporas provides a vehicle for policy intervention in both homelands and hostlands. A Dutch study in 2005 analyzed some efforts by African diasporas to influence Dutch foreign policy vis-à-vis their homelands. In the case of conflict-torn areas, they found that in the absence of effective central governments, diasporas were lobbying for the interests of their specific factions back home. This targeted support worked to perpetuate political fragmentation in the homeland. The report concluded that "the long-distance involvement of the diaspora in the homeland power struggles is only reinforcing the divisive domestic politics. It also makes it impossible for the rival political factions to achieve reconciliation for the common good of the whole

---

36. COMPAS, "The Contribution of UK-based Diasporas to Development and Poverty Reduction," 21.

population in the homeland. In this respect the diaspora are part of the problem rather than the solution."[37] If, however, a strong central government can effectively mobilize its diaspora, such efforts could potentially provide great support.[38] The Cape Verdean president, Aristides Pereira, recognized this, shifting his government's position toward embracing its expatriates in the United States. Laura Pires-Hester characterizes this as "strategic use of the [bilateral diaspora] ethnicity resource," noting, significantly, that the benefits are also bilateral: "strategic use of the ethnicity resource may be a way of leveling the playing field for those populations which were previously absent from the field. The emergence of bilateral diaspora ethnicity among Cape Verdean-Americans suggests the possibility of utilizing this asset to improve positions where people are *actually* and where they are *ancestrally*."[39]

The ability to leverage hostland policy became an important tool in the struggle to end apartheid rule in South Africa. Black organizations around the world, in collaboration with other humanitarian supporters, successfully exerted pressure both on governments and on private businesses to boycott South Africa, resulting in the government's ultimate demise. A sense of "bilateral diaspora ethnicity"—in this case, a collective claim to the experience of blackness and/or Africanity—was arguably a factor for many participants in this movement as they called upon their nations of residence to assist anti-apartheid efforts.[40] Because closer analysis of the South African case is beyond the scope of this discussion, I will merely call attention to one point of relevance for metadiaspora politics. Despite their length of residence (part of their argument for rights to African soil), Afrikaners drew their power from the colonial dominance of the Dutch and British Empires, positioning the anti-apartheid struggle in the context of other African independence movements. As noted above, the pan-Africanist movement mobilized the metalevel diaspora toward clearly defined goals of national liberation. With the fall of the apartheid regime, formal anticolonialism is no longer relevant. It remains to be seen if other issues will motivate metadiaspora activism for African causes.

The transnational networks discussed above reflect some of the ways in which recent diasporas from Africa have contributed to a broader range of political activity and possibility within the larger diaspora. Given the improvements of modern technology, it is

---

37. SAHAN Wetenschappelijk Adviesbureau, "Mobilizing African Diaspora for the Promotion of Peace in Africa," 47.

38. O. B. C. Nwolise, "Blacks in the Diaspora: A Case of Neglected Catalysts in the Achievement of Nigeria's Foreign Policy Goals," *Journal of Black Studies* 23, no. 1 (September 1992): 117–34.

39. Laura Pires-Hester, "The Emergence of Bilateral Diaspora Ethnicity Among Cape Verdean-Americans," in *The African Diaspora: African Origins and New World Identities*, ed. Isidore Okpewho, Carole Boyce Davies, Ali A. Mazrui, (Bloomington: Indiana University Press, 1999), 497 (italics in the original).

40. I use the concept of experiencing blackness/Africanity to underscore that it is not a passive ethnic identity, but, rather, the dynamics of engaging with a world in which those two variables continue to mediate interactions at all levels. George Frederickson argues that this experience of blackness in the United States was an important factor in forging solidarity with the South African struggle. George M. Frederickson, *Black Liberation: A Comparative History of Black Ideologies in the United States and South Africa* (New York: Oxford University Press, 1995).

unclear whether today's increased efficiency of typical immigrant hometown networks mitigates against a more broadly conceived continental "African" homeland. While Africans are clearly working together in the diaspora, such collaborations may often be more appropriately categorized as coalitions of several diaspora communities. These collaborations include not only different national diasporas, but different generations of diaspora, as well. For a closer look at some of the interactions that contribute toward this process, it is instructive to turn to the case of New York City.

New York: The Many Layers of African Diaspora

New York City illustrates the vital interplay between diverse eras of the African diaspora, as well as the diverse sites of origin in a single location. Since its inception as a Dutch commercial port in the early seventeenth century, successive waves of Africans and African descendants have come to create a multifaceted African diaspora community. Even in its earliest days, that community included Africans from diverse parts of the continent, as well as those trafficked through other colonies. The names of the enslaved, such as Swan Van Loange, Domingo Angola, and Maria Portogys, underscored the city's cosmopolitanism.[41] Since then, there has been an unbroken stream of new arrivals from other U.S. states, the Caribbean, and Africa. New York state has the nation's largest black community, with 3.2 million people categorized as "black or black combination," a new census category initiated in 2000. Most (2.1 million) live in New York City. Categories in the national census do not permit an accurate count of the national origins subsumed under the "black" ethnic label. However, African descendants constituted a significant segment of the city's 35.9 percent foreign-born population at the time of the 2000 census, and approximately one in three black New Yorkers was born abroad. Of these, 92,435 were African-born; another 591,660 were from the predominantly black Caribbean countries of Guyana, Haiti, Jamaica, and Trinidad.[42] Added to this rich mix of nationalities are African descendants from a host of other countries, as well as second-generation and third-generation children of immigrants circulating in diverse cultural ambits.[43] Because of real-estate lending and leasing practices, people of African descent

41. The names suggest connections to Loango and Angola in Africa, as well as to Portugal. Joyce D. Goodfriend, "Black Families in New Netherland," *Journal of the Afro-American Historical and Genealogical Society* 5 (1984): 94–107; Allison Blakely, *Blacks in the Dutch World: The Evolution of Racial Imagery in a Modern Society* (Bloomington: Indiana University Press, 1993).

42. Department of City Planning, Population Division, City of New York, *The Newest New Yorkers: Immigrant New York in the New Millennium* (New York: Department of City Planning, 2004), 13, 44; "Immigrants Swell Numbers In and Near City," *New York Times*, August 15, 2006, B1. Such data would not include the children of immigrants. Though Guyana is located on the South American mainland, it is culturally associated with the circum-Caribbean.

43. Mary Waters includes the second generation in her analysis of ethnonational identities of black immigrants to New York City in Mary C. Waters, *Black Identities: West Indian Immigrant Dreams and American Realities* (New York: Russell Sage Foundation, 1999).

find themselves together in "black" residential concentrations, the largest of which are in Brooklyn, Queens, and Harlem.[44]

Thus, within New York's "black" community are vibrant communities of "Africans," "West Indians," "Guyanese," and so on, coming together in racially black-majority neighborhoods where their children further the interactions across disparate ethnic groups. As such, this community reflects a key principle of diasporas, which Gloria Totoricagüena calls "interconnected disconnectedness" for the Basque diaspora, or, as noted above, *décalage* for the African-diaspora.[45] While it is clear how this functions on a cultural level, its political concomitants have yet to be fully explored.

Each community has a distinct set of political traditions and options, mediated, in part, by available diaspora and homeland networks. Until relatively recently, African descendants of diverse nationalities were assimilated into "black" New York. Perhaps due to an upswing in immigration and its new technological contexts, a historically diverse black community has become newly aware of that diversity.[46] Consideration of these differences has thus far been filtered through the lens of immigration studies, particularly for analyzing the different trajectories of U.S.-ancestry versus Caribbean-ancestry blacks. Rather than perpetuate stereotypes about contrasting *values* held by industrious and entrepreneurial Caribbean-Americans in comparison to "lazy" black Americans, it may be more useful to consider contrasting *options*. Recent immigrants have the option of transnational networks and identities as an alternative to exclusive reliance on state-based citizenship networks, particularly when the latter option is biased against equal opportunity. Stated another way, the maintenance of transnational and homeland networks and identities offers greater options for success today than the exclusive focus on assimilation promoted as the American ideal. However, what makes sense economically and socially also has complex political implications.

In a 2005 article, Brett St. Louis recounted the case of Ethiopian Abdulaziz Kamus, who questioned the decision of a public project on cancer among African Americans to exclude African immigrants. He asked, "But I am African and I am an American citizen; am I not African-American?" Regardless of the technical accuracy of his assertion, the project directors concluded that he could not claim group membership.[47] For some, the African American community is defined by a shared historical experience in which

---

44. Craig S. Wilder, *A Covenant With Color: Race and Social Power in Brooklyn* (New York: Columbia University Press, 2000).

45. Gloria Totoricagüena, *Identity, Culture, and Politics in the Basque Diaspora* (Reno: University of Nevada Press, 2004); Edwards, *The Practice of Diaspora*.

46. Philip Kasinitz, *Caribbean New York: Black Immigrants and the Politics of Race* (Ithaca, NY: Cornell University Press, 1992), 7. An important study investigating the formations of intradiaspora attitudes is Jennifer V. Jackson and Mary E. Cothran, "Black Versus Black: The Relationships Among African, African-American, and African Caribbean Persons," *Journal of Black Studies* 33, no. 5 (May 2003): 576–604.

47. Brett St. Louis, "The Difference Sameness Makes: Racial Recognition and the 'Narcissism of Minor Differences,'" *Ethnicities* 5, no. 3 (2005): 344.

immigrants did not participate.[48] As Toni Morrison argues, a fundamental part of the immigrant experience is that "the move into mainstream America always means buying into the notion of American blacks as the real aliens. Whatever the ethnicity or nationality of the immigrant, his nemesis is understood to be African American."[49] The paradox for other African-descended immigrants is that antiblack discrimination both forces them to confront the African American race experience and simultaneously prompts many to distance themselves by accessing other networks and identities. Numerous studies have probed the complex issues of identity and affiliation confronted by immigrants of African descent, but rarely with an eye to the implications for diaspora politics. If, as Pedro Noguera argues, immigrants strategize against discrimination by asserting their membership in transnational communities ("anything but black"), they make possible certain types of homeland-diaspora politics.[50] At the same time, racism creates common political cause among disparate members of the African diaspora.

New York City is a site where many of Africa's diasporas live together in a racialized setting that conflates blackness with membership in the African metadiaspora. Not only are various geographic locations represented, but so also are different temporal eras of the African diaspora.

Diallo, Dourismond, and Diaspora: Negotiating Multilayered Politics in the Metadiaspora

Where various waves of diasporization overlap in any single location, the politics of that place may mobilize the pandiaspora community or pandiaspora activism. In this regard, New York City provides a rich context for exploring multilayered diaspora politics. It has continued to receive new waves of African diasporas throughout its history. Among recent immigrants was twenty-two-year-old Amadou Diallo, the son of Guinean entrepreneurs, who had moved to New York after completing a year-long computer science program in Singapore. He had settled into an apartment with four other young men from Guinea in a small neighborhood popular with Guineans and other West Africans, a community that had also helped him set up a street-vending business. Shortly before 1:00 A.M. on February 4, 1999, Diallo was gunned down by police inside the entryway of his apartment house. He was unarmed. In the darkness outside, four police officers assigned to a special task force targeting illegal guns saw what they perceived as a "suspicious"

---

48. The presidential candidacy of Illinois senator Barack Obama has engendered renewed debate on this issue. Obama, of Kenyan and white American ancestry, was raised in Indonesia and Hawaii in the otherwise white household of his mother and maternal grandparents. Leslie Fulbright, "Obama's Candidacy Sparks Debates on Race," *San Francisco Chronicle*, February 19, 2007, A1.

49. Toni Morrison, "On the Backs of Blacks," *Time*, special issue, Fall 1993, 57.

50. Pedro A. Noguera, "Anything but Black: Bringing Politics Back to the Study of Race," in Hintzen and Rahier eds., *Problematizing Blackness*.

black man and opened fire, shooting forty-one bullets at the young man's body. Many of the nineteen shots that hit him struck after he had already collapsed.[51]

The incident came in the wake of the brutalization in August 1997 of a Haitian immigrant, Abner Louima, who, while in police custody, was beaten and sodomized with a broom handle until his internal organs were ruptured. Diallo's killing came to be seen in the context of systematic racialized violence against blacks in New York. In a highly publicized case in September 1983, twenty-five-year-old Michael Stewart was arrested for painting graffiti and possession of a marijuana stub. Thirty-two minutes after being taken into custody, he arrived at Bellevue Hospital in a coma due to a severe beating that resulted in his death two weeks later. Other incidents involved police procedures that resulted in black deaths. In May 2003, police broke into the apartment of Alberta Spruill, a fifty-seven-year-old city employee whose apartment had been mistakenly identified as a site for drug dealing. The shock triggered a cardiac crisis, but treatment was delayed while police continued their search. Truill died at the scene. It was characterized by many activist groups as an example of police insensitivity. *The Internationalist*, a socialist newspaper, declared "Alberta Spruill is dead because she was black. *This was racist police murder!*"[52] A similar sentiment was expressed by a Haitian protesting the Louima assault, "It wasn't a Haitian thing, it was a black thing. Being Haitian, didn't mean anything. It was that he was black." This commentator, however, also indicated that "even as the Haitian community weaves itself into the fabric of the U.S., it will always keep part of itself separate," illustrating how the mobilization of a panblack cause did not fully supersede particular identities.[53]

The killing of Amadou Diallo underscored the reality and inevitability of race for black New Yorkers. "I think because of the color," Saikou Diallo, Amadou's father, replied when asked the reasons why New York City police unleashed such excessive firepower against his son.[54] Diallo's violent death engendered broad community reaction from black and other constituencies, who labeled it as a racialized incident. Public outcry led to an investigation by the New York Office of the Attorney General. The report documented that police were stopping blacks and Hispanics at a markedly higher rate than whites and concluded that differential treatment was a significant factor in this disparity.[55] Regardless of the ethnic identities held by individuals, perceptions of race imposed upon blacks a shared burden and common cause.

Relevant to the present discussion is the effect of the crosscutting issue of race on the various African diaspora communities present in New York, the political strategies

---

51. For a detailed account of the shooting and Diallo's family biography, see Kadiatou Diallo and Craig Wolff, *My Heart Will Cross This Ocean: My Story, My Son, Amadou* (New York: Ballantine, 2003).

52. "Alberta Spruill: Victim of NYPD Killer Elite," *The Internationalist*, May 2003. Emphasis in original.

53. "In Search for Justice, Haitians Find Political Voice," *Christian Science Monitor*, April 20, 1999, 2.

54. *Washington Post*, April 1, 2000, C1.

55. Office of the Attorney General, State of New York, Civil Rights Bureau, "Report on Stop and Frisk," December 1, 1999, ix.

mobilized by each, and the degree to which those various approaches might work together. When Kadiatou Diallo, Amadou's mother, arrived in New York to claim her son's body, she was met by several competing contingents. Given the political climate, with Mayor Rudolph Giuliani campaigning against former first lady Hillary Clinton in a senatorial election, the mayor's office sent a police escort to take her directly to the site of the killing and later to a hotel booked and paid for by the city. Also there, but not permitted to ride with Mrs. Diallo, was Mahawa Bangoura of the Guinean Embassy. Later that day, Mohammed Diallo, president of the Guinean Association in New York, met with Mrs. Diallo at her hotel to assure her of their community's support. Indeed, Amadou's West African friends and family, as well as other well-wishers, were there to meet his mother, both at the small Bronx apartment and at the hotel. The local black community was also in action; Reverend Al Sharpton met Kadiatou Diallo at the hotel, fresh from a community rally, and arranged for her to talk with Jesse Jackson by phone from Chicago. The following day, at the funeral in the Islamic Cultural Center, the mayor and police commissioner appeared without invitation, and Reverend Sharpton was there to take her directly to a rally at his headquarters.[56]

The mobilization protesting the Diallo shooting emerged not from West African governmental representatives, but from a network of civil-rights and human-rights activists well versed in U.S. race politics. Reverend Al Sharpton and his organization, the National Action Network, took the lead by staging frequent public rallies and meetings with Diallo's mother. Prominent lawyer Johnnie Cochran assumed control over the court case, supplanting the lawyer contracted by Diallo's father. As Kadiatou Diallo came to understand, black Americans viewed Amadou's death as their own tragedy:

> Joining up with the black community in New York was not second nature for me. . . . The anger expressed by people at rallies for Amadou was built on a history that I did not have and could not know. . . . Our pasts and our futures now intersected through Amadou. As parents, grandparents, brothers, and sisters of black men, we shared the same anger and fear. If my grief was more immediate, theirs had lasted lifetimes and become their companion, something that walked with them always.[57]

For black New Yorkers, Amadou Diallo was symbolic of the demonization of all black men used to justify their brutalization throughout the history of the Americas. Therefore, when Haitian immigrant Patrick Dourismond was killed by police in Brooklyn (and his juvenile arrest record illegally released by Mayor Rudolph Giuliani to justify the police action), black organizers were ready to spring to action. In this case, however, they encountered a well-established Haitian community with its own network of organizations. Though it framed the problem in the same way as a case of racial profiling, local

---

56. Kadiatou Diallo and Craig Wolff, *My Heart Will Cross This Ocean*, 221–52; *New York Times*, February 10, 1999 B6, 1.

57. Ibid., 247. The trial, moved out of the city to a predominantly white jurisdiction, resulted in acquittal for all officers.

Haitian Americans utilized tools of mobilizing particular to that immigrant community. By announcing upcoming rallies and marches in Kreyol-language media, organizers were able to mobilize a visible opposition of Haitians and other French-language speakers, but the broader black local community was less aware of those events than they had been of the rallies around the Diallo case. [58]

Situations of crisis that require political mobilization are natural sites for the activation of a diaspora insofar as the diaspora "functions" toward specific ends. However, *which* diaspora gets mobilized sometimes brings different branches of the diaspora into conflict. A Brooklyn electoral campaign in 2000 between Brooklynites of Caribbean and African American backgrounds, respectively, exposed some of the tensions between the two communities as ethnically sensitive appeals were made to constituents. That dynamic was repeated in 2007; one Brooklyn-born candidate was reported to have made disparaging remarks about the Haitian background of the eventual winner. The press emphasized the varied ethnicities of the candidates and the fact that the eventual victor was the first Haitian elected to the city council. The vacating official had herself emphasized her Caribbean background.[59]

Fortunately, points of diaspora convergence do not always involve tensions and crises. One of the city's largest public festivals is the West Indian American Day Carnival, founded in 1967 by Trinidadian immigrant Carlos Lezama. In itself, the annual Labor Day celebration helped forge community among the various Caribbean nations represented in New York, each of which has its own carnival traditions. Situated in the heart of Brooklyn's black neighborhoods, the event has attracted locals whose origins lay outside the Caribbean and has helped instill a sense of Caribbean belonging in subsequent generations.[60] The Brooklyn carnival is widely recognized in the Caribbean. Similar celebrations have developed in Toronto (Caribana), Miami, Notting Hill, and Houston

---

58. Though I am highlighting the deployment of Haitian diaspora resources here, I do not wish to understate the level of concern and involvement from other segments of New York's black community regarding the Dorismond case.

59. "Bitter Primary Contest Hits Ethnic Nerve Among Blacks," *New York Times*, August 31, 2000, A1. In 2007, press coverage of another election in Brooklyn's highly diverse Fortieth City Council District (the author's home district) focused overwhelmingly on the national backgrounds of the candidates, rather than on their policy positions. See for example, Jonathan P. Hicks, "Haitian Candidate Seeks to Add His Voice," *New York Times*, February 5, 2007, B1, and "Council Race Shows District's Diversity: Brooklyn's Special Election Candidates from Haiti, Pakistan Could Make History If They Win Seat" *Newsday* (NY), February 20, 2007, A18. The election was being monitored by foreign news outlets, as well. "New York Could Get First Pakistani as City Council Member," *The International News* (Pakistan) http://www. thenews.com.pk/daily_detail.asp?id=43662, February 20, 2007 (last accessed July 29, 2007).

60. The parade route ends in Crown Heights, a neighborhood whose largest ethnic groups are African Americans, Caribbean Americans, and Hasidic Jews. A riot erupted in 1991 after seven-year-old Gavin Cato and his cousin Angela were struck by a car driven by Israeli Yosef Lifsh, who immediately fled to Israel to avoid prosecution. Cato was killed immediately. Tensions mounted over what was perceived as a lack of concern for black life, and an angry protest escalated into the murder of a Hasidic student, Yankel Rosenbaum. The incident was framed ethnically as "Hasidics" versus "blacks." The West Indian Day Carnival, which followed shortly thereafter and falls around the start of Jewish High Holy Days, was seen by police as a potential site of further tension because it was a predominantly "black" event. It has since been heavily policed, including the placing of sharpshooters on rooftops, assignment of a police detail to every float, tight restrictions on public mobility through the use of barriers, and prohibition of alcohol sales.

(Caribfest), and Montreal (Carifiesta), as well as in other cities with significant Caribbean populations.

The negotiations between the African metadiaspora and smaller diasporic constructs are well illustrated by the case of Hispanic blacks. While groups such as Haitians and some African nationals are non-English speakers, they nonetheless live in English-speaking black neighborhoods. In contrast, Spanish-language groups are increasingly being conceived as a distinct ethnicity. Blacks from Spanish-speaking countries are typically incorporated into "Latino," rather than "black" communities, though they, too, are part of the African diaspora. The experiences of Dominicans and Puerto Ricans in New York have given rise to a reflective analysis of race, both in diaspora as well as at home. One study of Dominicans raised in the United States showed that the longer the period of residence, the higher the likelihood they would identify themselves as "black."[61]

This experience among Afro-Latinos signals a process of negotiation that is evident in other African diaspora branches, as well. Milton Vickerman has documented the evolution of ethnic identity for Jamaicans in New York, concluding that racialization causes them to "attempt to distance themselves from unflattering assumptions about blacks."[62] However, as Mary Waters shows, by the second generation, their children tend to adopt "black" identities more readily.[63]

There are two important points here. First, diaspora consciousness evolves through dialogue as distinct branches intersect and interact, and this process also involves how members of the diaspora are perceived by others. Second, each sector of the diaspora engages in multiple ways of community making simultaneously. These multiple levels of diaspora politics within a metadiaspora have the potential of working either together or separately. Thus, the civil-rights experience of the African American community helped bring visibility to the tragedy of Amadou Diallo's death. Future work on political theory may provide more insight into the convergences and divergences of diaspora activism.

Emerging Configurations of Diaspora

Some segments of the African diaspora have a long history of intraregional dialogue and cooperative efforts at both formal and informal levels. Such is the case with the Afro-Atlantic region, stemming in part from shared histories of political and cultural formation. Observers of slave societies have noted that, as heterogeneous communities

---

61. Silvio Torres-Saillant, "The Tribulations of Blackness: Stages in Dominican Racial Identity," *Latin American Perspectives* 25, no. 3 (1998): 142. In the 1990 census, 50 percent of Dominicans in New York City identified themselves as "other" (mixed race), and 25 percent as black. The Minority Rights group estimated that up to 90 percent of Dominicans have some African ancestry. Patricia R. Possar and Pamela M. Graham, "Dominicans: Transnational Identities and Local Politics," in *New Immigrants in New York*, ed. Nancy Foner, rev. ed., (New York: Columbia University Press, 2001), 256; Minority Rights Group, *No Longer Invisible: Afro-Latin Americans Today* (London: Minority Rights Group, 1995).

62. Milton Vickerman, "Jamaicans: Balancing Race and Ethnicity," in Foner, ed., *New Immigrants in New York*, 210.

63. Mary Waters, "Ethnic and Racial Ideologies of Second Generation [Jamaicans]," in *The New Second Generation*, ed. Alejandro Portes, (New York: Russell Sage Foundation, 1996).

of Africans settled in American settings, new cultures emerged that blended the various African matrices with European, indigenous, and Asian elements, all taking shape within their distinct socioeconomic and political contexts. These creole cultures arose from similar roots and served similar functions throughout the Afro-Atlantic world.[64] Because the secondary migrations concomitant with the abolition of slavery rarely relocated people to Africa, but rather to other destinations in the Americas, Caribbean, and colonial European states, these migrations further disseminated cultural elements that might have been concentrated within single regions or colonial spheres. Consequently, because creole culture, rather than any specific African culture, is the basis of the Afro-Atlantic community as a whole, "homeland" necessarily occupies a quite different space for this branch of the African diaspora. For slave-era diasporas (in both the Atlantic and Indian Oceans), while diaspora may well be invoked as a mode of interaction with Africa, it is also potent as a strategy for empowerment in the hostland.[65] Indeed, when Marcus Garvey announced the founding objectives of the Universal Negro Improvement Association and African Communities League (UNIA-ACL)—that most emblematic of diaspora organizations—in 1914, he simultaneously issued a set of corresponding local objectives for Jamaica.[66]

Diaspora is particularly important in the Afro-Atlantic world because it represents an alternative for negotiating the full benefits of citizenship in societies whose very infrastructure is predicated on anti-African exploitation and exclusion. With the abolition of slavery and with national independence, African descendants throughout the Americas began challenging barriers to equity in both the constitutional arena and informal social practice.[67] They framed their struggles in national contexts, leading to such initiatives as the black political parties formed by the Cuban Independent Party of Color in 1912 and the Brazilian Black Front in 1933. In the United States, numerous organizations emerged to combat rampant lynching and segregation. Intellectuals and activists clearly understood how issues facing the black world intersected; strategies, however, were nationally based.

The UNIA-ACL proposed a new political alternative. Leveraging the unified power and resources of the entire diaspora and strengthening the African homeland would result in increased autonomy and power locally. Indeed, many who purchased shares in the failed Black Star Line did so not to resettle in Africa, but to improve their lives locally. Another organization, the African Blood Brotherhood, saw the potential of concentrating diaspora resettlement in South America, which already had a large black population. Cyril Briggs, the head of the organization, saw African continental and diaspora

---

64. Butler, *Freedoms Given*, 61–62.

65. The terminology of "homeland" and "hostland" used by diaspora scholars is often an awkward fit when the initial dispersal may have occurred centuries before. It is used here for consistency, but we may wish to consider alternatives.

66. Judith Stein, *The World of Marcus Garvey: Race and Class in Modern Society* (Baton Rouge: Louisiana State University Press, 1986), 30–31.

67 This dynamic of the continental Americas is less applicable in the Caribbean, which remained under colonial rule until the mid-twentieth century, and had a lesser degree of white political hegemony.

empowerment as interlinked: "with African liberty effected and Africa returned to the Africans two rich continents would be dominated by the African races."[68]

Whereas other diasporas may have clearly defined homeland agendas (i.e., restoration of an ancestral territory), the nature of its historical formation has centered the Afro-Atlantic diaspora's political raison d'être on antiblack racism. In this regard, the Afro-Atlantic diaspora often functions as a *black* diaspora as well as an *African* diaspora. The common cause of race (both positive and negative) has arguably played as strong a role in consolidating a sense of community and shared experience in the Afro-Atlantic world as relationships with an African homeland.

When, therefore, a host of nongovernmental organizations convened in Santiago, Chile, to draft a plan of action for the United Nations' World Conference on Racism, African descendants articulated a seventeen-point agenda designed to rectify slavery's legacy of persistent inequities.[69] Working within a larger body that included the representatives of indigenous groups, women, migrants, poor people, children, and "other vulnerable groups," this meeting was part of a continuous history of communication between the black populations of the Americas. While much of that interaction has been informal, periodic cultural, intellectual, and political conferences have facilitated intradiaspora communication, such as the three meetings of the Congress of African Culture in the Americas held in Colombia, Panama, and Brazil between 1977 and 1980.[70]

Diaspora mobilization is generally considered as it relates to a homeland axis. These mobilizations of Afro-Atlantic diaspora, while predicated on shared African ancestry, did not center their activities on the common homeland. Ancestry alone was not being invoked; rather, it was their collective continuing experience of discrimination rooted in the history of slavery. Because of this, diaspora provided a language and framework through which to interpret and address localized concerns. This constituent diaspora mobilization would subsequently become important for new metadiaspora initiatives with the African Union.

One of the most significant developments serving to reconfigure the African diaspora is the shifting role of Africa itself as a political entity. The formal state organization of the homeland is an essential factor affecting the options available to the diaspora. Until the late twentieth century, no single political structure represented Africa, thus making it impossible to shape homeland-diaspora policy. This changed with African independence and the founding of the Organization of African Unity in 1963. Whereas sectors of

---

68. Cyril Briggs, cited in Teresa Meade and Gregory Alonso Pirio, " In Search of the Afro-American 'Eldorado': Attempts by North American Blacks to Enter Brazil in the 1920s," *Luso-Brazilian Review* 25, no. 1 (1988): 89.

69. World Conference against Racism, Racial Discrimination, Xenophobia and Related Intolerance, Preparatory Committee, "Documents Adopted by the Regional Conference of the Americas, Held in Santiago de Chile, Chile from 5–7 December 2000," Geneva, January 15–16, 2001, articles 103–19 "Peoples of African Descent."

70. Centro Cultural Afro-Ecuatoriano, *Congresos de cultura negra de las Americas* (Quito: Centro Cultural Afro-Ecuatoriano, 1989). Earlier phases of communication between the African-descent populations of the Americas emerged from networks created by individual travelers, communities of migrant laborers, and local black newspapers that featured international coverage.

the diaspora had well-established relationships with specific African nations and governments, the OAU provided a venue for continent-wide initiatives.

In 1999, Leon Sullivan of the Congressional Black Caucus in the United States convened the first of what became known as the Sullivan Summits aimed at directing diaspora support for African development. Representatives from the OAU participated in these meetings. As the OAU prepared for its transition to the African Union, it convened two Civil Society meetings in 2001 and 2002, the second of which included representatives of the diaspora. That meeting resulted in the election of a working group that included two regional diaspora representatives for Europe and the Western Hemisphere, respectively.

An African Union–Western Hemisphere Diaspora Forum was convened in Washington, DC in December 2002 "to empower the Diaspora to become more associated with AU objectives, growth and development so they can contribute effectively to the realization of its goals." The group also explicitly stated that the new relationship was to be "sustained and reciprocal."[71] The Western Hemisphere African Diaspora Network was established as a result of this meeting to support AU programs in a broad range of fields through permanent working groups of experts and resource people. It was the first formal administrative framework between the diaspora (or at least one significant segment) and the continent.

Nonetheless, any significant relationship with the diaspora required a far more comprehensive network than that represented by WHADN. Toward that end, in June 2004, the AU sponsored a meeting in Trinidad of experts from the continent and the diaspora to define the African diaspora. They were unable to craft a definition acceptable to the AU Executive Council, which wanted to include consideration of more recent diasporas and an express "commitment to the African cause."[72] In April 2005, experts from thirty AU member nations convened to formalize a definition of the diaspora with the following considerations:

a. the bloodline and/or heritage. The Diaspora should consist of people living outside the continent whose ancestral roots or heritage are in Africa;

b. migration: The Diaspora should be composed of people of African heritage, who migrated from or are living outside the continent. In this context, three trends of migration were identified—pre–slave trade, slave trade, and post–slave trade or modern migration;

c. the principle of inclusiveness. The definition must embrace both ancient and modern Diaspora; and

---

71. African Union Executive Council, "The Development of the Diaspora Initiative within the Framework of the OAU/AU," Third Extraordinary Session, May 21–25, 2003, Sun City, South Africa, available on-line at www.whadn.org (last accessed October 10, 2006).

72. African Union, "Report of the Meeting of Experts from Member States on the Definition of the African Diaspora," Addis Ababa, Ethiopia, April 11–12, 2005.

d. the commitment to the African course. The Diaspora should be people who are willing to be part of the continent (or the African family).[73]

One of the central objectives of the new definition was to organize the diaspora as the sixth region of the African Union, with the possibility of their participation in the work of its formal entities. The meeting concluded with adoption of the following definition: "The African Diaspora consists of peoples of African origin living outside the continent, irrespective of their citizenship and nationality and who are willing to contribute to the development of the continent and the building of the African Union.[74]

While smaller diasporas are recognized to exist within Africa, the AU definition established the framework for metalevel organization, with the entire continent positioned as "homeland." It remains to be seen how this metadiaspora concept will coexist with minidiaspora realities.

Conclusion

As diasporas mature, subsequent migratory waves may lead to multiple diasporas sharing an ancestral root that is no longer the most immediate or significant homeland orienting their activities. This is especially the case when diasporas span radically different historical eras. For the African diaspora, two significant segments now overlap and interact with each other in shared destinations abroad. The first of these was created during the slave trade, with their homelands either destroyed or colonized and their fates marked by racialized exploitation. The second is a more recent diaspora associated with the quest for new opportunities and flight from local problems as African nations have moved toward independence and reorganization. Once in the diaspora, African descendants with presumed commonalities confront the realities of social communities configured along other lines. To work together as *the* African diaspora is a political project that must be conceived and nurtured. Both political institutions and popular culture are essential to that project.

Each segment of the diaspora has its own strengths (and weaknesses) that interact with each other. To the extent advocates of the diaspora are aware of this dynamic, such interactions may lead to the strategic deployment of proven initiatives. It is useful to call attention to cross-influences within the diaspora as a focus of diaspora studies because they have an impact on the development and direction of diaspora consciousness and politics. To cite one example, the surge in research and institutional investment in African diaspora studies has created a platform for further attention to the Indian Ocean branch of the slavery-era dispersals. In January 2006, a major conference on the African diaspora in Asia set in motion a host of new research initiatives, including participation in an

---

73. Ibid.

74. Ibid. The text notes that one delegation advocated strongly for the inclusion of the word "permanently" before living outside the continent."

Asian division of the UNESCO Slave Routes Project. At the meeting, it became apparent that the scholars and the Siddi (Indians of African descent) delegates had arrived with differing agendas. The Siddis framed their struggles primarily within national contexts vis-à-vis the Indian government, whereas the scholars opened the possibility of situating those issues within the larger diaspora framework. The Siddis ultimately took a central role in forming TADIA, The African Diaspora in Asia. As one observer noted, "Participation in a conference on the African diaspora in Asia no doubt invites expressions of 'diasporic identity.'"[75] The Siddis may well take advantage of the successful strategies of their Western-branch counterparts as leverage in their mobilization for better conditions at home.

Moments of pandiaspora political mobilization remain ephemeral. One significant development for the African diaspora is the increasing involvement of individual African nations and the collective African Union with the diaspora, especially with regard to formal policy. Considerations such as voting, economic opportunities and entitlements, residency, and property law will affect and channel metadiaspora activities. Political involvement with diasporas is an increasingly important dimension of national governments; the African Union initiative is the first attempt at such policies at a continental diaspora level.

The struggles for liberation from slavery and colonialism mobilized pan-Africanist politics in the past. Today, new issues are arising that will challenge the metadiaspora to coordinate creatively and effectively. Reparations for the devastation visited upon Africans, their descendants, and the continental homeland is a potent political issue requiring distinct, but coordinated strategizing based upon the contextual location of each complainant. For example, the former British West Indies may articulate a legal case against the government of Britain and major investors supporting its slave economy, whereas national governments in Africa may sue for the restoration of historical artifacts from European museums and collectors. African-descent communities living as minorities face different challenges to effecting reparations policies.[76] All these causes, however, are interrelated and represent new opportunities for a metadiaspora politics in which the local and transnational work together symbiotically. It also remains to be seen how and to what extent the African Union may deploy diaspora resources to address such critical issues as health and warfare that are broadly affecting the continent.

The political science of diaspora is of critical importance insofar as diaspora is invoked primarily as a political strategy. Jana Evans Braziel and Anita Mannur caution that "diaspora studies will need to move beyond theorizing how diasporic identities are constructed and consolidated and must ask, how are these diasporic identities practiced,

---

75. Ineke van Kessel, "Goa Conference on the African Diaspora in Asia," *African Affairs* 105, no. 420 (2006): 461–64.

76. See, for example, Ali A. Mazrui and Alamin M. Mazrui, *Black Reparations in the Era of Globalization* (Binghamton, NY: Institute of Global Cultural Studies, 2002).

lived and experienced?"[77] Rather than assume an idealized notion of the structure of diasporas, we cannot move forward unless we understand the complex and often contradictory interactions of diaspora groups within metadiasporas.

Bibliography

African Diaspora Community Forum. "Report of the Proceedings." Ottawa, April 25, 2005.

African Union. "Report of the Meeting of Experts from Member States on the Definition of the African Diaspora." Addis Ababa, Ethiopia, April 11–12, 2005.

——, Executive Council. "The Development of the Diaspora Initiative within the Framework of the OAU/AU." Third Extraordinary Session, May 21–25, 2003, Sun City, South Africa. Available on-line at http://www.whadn.org.

Alpers, Edwards A. "The African Diaspora in the Indian Ocean: A Comparative Perspective." In *The African Diaspora in the Indian Ocean.* Edited by Shihan de S. Jayasuriya and Richard Pankhurst. Trenton, NJ: Africa World Press, 2003.

Black, Richard. "Working Paper C6: Migration and Pro-Poor Policy in Africa." Sussex Centre for Migration Research, Development Research Centre on Migration, Globalisation and Poverty, 2004.

Blakely, Allison. "Blacks in the Dutch World: The Evolution of Racial Imagery in a Modern Society." Bloomington: Indiana University Press, 1993.

Braziel, Jana Evans, and Anita Mannur. "Nation, Migration, Globalization: Points of Contention in Diaspora Studies." In *Theorizing Diaspora: A Reader.* Edited by Jana Evans Braziel and Anita Mannur. Malden, MA: Blackwell, 2003.

Bruner, Edward. "Tourism in Ghana: The Representation of Slavery and the Return of the Black Diaspora." *American Anthropologist* 98, no. 2, (1996): 290–304.

Butler, Kim D. "Defining Diaspora, Refining a Discourse." *Diaspora,* 10 no. 2 (2001): 189–219.

——. *Freedoms Given, Freedoms Won: Afro-Brazilians in Post-Abolition São Paulo and Salvador.* New Brunswick, NJ: Rutgers University Press, 1998.

Campt, Tina. *Other Germans: Black Germans and the Politics of Race, Gender, and Memory in the Third Reich.* Ann Arbor: University of Michigan Press, 2004.

Centre on Migration, Policy, and Society (COMPAS). "The Contribution of UK Based Diasporas to Development and Poverty Reduction." Oxford, April 2004.

---

77. Jana Evans Braziel and Anita Mannur, "Nation, Migration, Globalization: Points of Contention in Diaspora Studies," in *Theorizing Diaspora: A Reader,* ed. Jana Evans Braziel and Anita Mannur (Malden, MA: Blackwell, 2003), 9.

Chikezie, Chukwu-Emeka. "Accountability, Africa and Her Diaspora," www.openDemocracy.net.

Cohen, Robin. "The Diaspora of a Diaspora: The Case of the Caribbean." *Social Science Information* 31, no. 3 (1992): 159–69.

Department of City Planning, Population Division, City of New York. *The Newest New Yorkers: Immigrant New York in the New Millennium.* New York: Department of City Planning, 2004.

Desch-Obi, M. Thomas J. "Engolo: Combat Traditions in African and African Diaspora History." Ph.D. diss., University of California, Los Angeles, 2000.

Diallo, Kadiatou, and Craig Wolff. *My Heart Will Cross This Ocean: My Story, My Son, Amadou.* New York: Ballantine, 2003.

Edwards, Brent. *The Practice of Diaspora: Literature, Translation, and the Rise of Black Internationalism.* Cambridge, MA: Harvard University Press, 2003.

Eltis, David, Stephen Behrendt, David Richardson, and Herbert S. Klein. *The Trans-Atlantic Slave Trade: A Database on CD-ROM.* Cambridge: Cambridge University Press, 1999.

Falola, Toyin, and Matt D. Childs. *The Yoruba Diaspora in the Atlantic World.* Bloomington: Indiana University Press, 2004.

Frederickson, George M. *Black Liberation: A Comparative History of Black Ideologies in the United States and South Africa.* New York: Oxford University Press, 1995.

Ghana Homecoming Queen Web site, 2007, http://www.ghanahomecomingqueen.com.

Goodfriend, Joyce D. "Black Families in New Netherland." *Journal of the Afro-American Historical and Genealogical Society* 5 (1984): 94–107.

Gordon, Edmund T., and Mark Anderson. "The African Diaspora: Toward an Ethnography of Diasporic Identification." *Journal of American Folklore* 112/445 (Summer 1999): 282–96.

Hall, Gwendolyn Midlo. *Afro-Louisiana History and Genealogy Database.* Baton Rouge: Louisiana State University Press, 2000.

Hamilton, Ruth Simms, ed. *Routes of Passage: Rethinking the African Diaspora.* Vol. 1, part 1. East Lansing: Michigan State University Press, 2007.

Harris, Joseph E. "The African Diaspora in World History and Politics." In *African Roots/American Cultures: Africa in the Creation of the Americas.* Edited by Sheila Walker. Lanham, MD: Rowman and Littlefield, 2001.

——. *The African Presence in Asia: Consequences of the East African Slave Trade.* Evanston, IL: Northwestern University Press, 1971.

Helg, Aline. *Our Rightful Share: The Afro-Cuban Struggle for Equality, 1886–1912.* Chapel Hill: University of North Carolina Press, 1995.

Heywood, Linda, ed. *Central Africans and Cultural Transformations in the African Diaspora.* Cambridge: Cambridge University Press, 2002.

Hintzen, Percy Claude, and Jean Muteba Rahier. "From Structural Politics to the Politics of Deconstruction: Self-Ethnographies Problematizing Blackness." In *Problematizing Blackness: Self-Ethnographies by Black Immigrants to the United States.* Edited by Percy Claude Hintzen and Jean Muteba Rahier. New York: Routledge, 2003.

Holt, Thomas C. "Slavery and Freedom in the Atlantic World: Reflections on the Diasporan Framework." In *Crossing Boundaries: Comparative Histories of Black People in Diaspora.* Edited by Darlene Clark Hine and Jacqueline McLeod. Bloomington: Indiana University Press, 1999.

Jackson, Jennifer V., and Mary E. Cothran. "Black Versus Black: The Relationships Among African, African-American, and African Caribbean Persons." *Journal of Black Studies* 33, no. 5 (May 2003): 576–604.

Jayasuriya, Shihan de S., and Richard Pankhurst, eds. *The African Diaspora in the Indian Ocean.* Trenton, NJ: Africa World Press, 2003.

Kasinitz, Philip. *Caribbean New York: Black Immigrants and the Politics of Race.* Ithaca, NY: Cornell University Press, 1992.

Koser, Khalid, ed., *New African Diasporas.* London: Routledge, 2003.

Lake, O. "Toward a Pan-African Identity: Diaspora African Repatriates in Ghana." *Anthropological Quarterly* 68, no. 1 (January 1995): 21–51.

Manuh, Takyiwaa. "'*Efie*' or The Meanings of 'Home' among Female and Male Ghanaian Migrants in Toronto, Canada and Returned Migrants to Ghana." In Koser, ed., *New African Diasporas*, 140–159.

Meade, Teresa, and Gregory Alonso Pirio. " In Search of the Afro-American 'Eldorado': Attempts by North American Blacks to Enter Brazil in the 1920s." *Luso-Brazilian Review* 25, no. 1 (1988): 85–110.

Minority Rights Group. *No Longer Invisible: Afro-Latin Americans Today.* London: Minority Rights Group, 1995.

Mintz, Sidney, and Richard Price. *The Birth of African-American Culture: An Anthropological Perspective.* Boston: Beacon Press, 1992.

Mohamoud, A. A. "Mobilizing African Diaspora for the Promotion of Peace in Africa." Policy Report for the Netherlands Ministry of Foreign Affairs, Sub-Saharan Department. Amsterdam, May 2005.

Moore, Robin. *Nationalizing Blackness: Afrocubanismo and Artistic Revolution in Havana, 1920–1940.* Pittsburgh: University of Pittsburgh Press, 1997.

Morrison, Toni. "On the Backs of Blacks." In *Time*, special issue, Fall 1993, p. 57.

Noguera, Pedro A. "Anything but Black: Bringing Politics Back to the Study of Race." In *Problematizing Blackness: Self-Ethnographies by Black Immigrants to the United States.* Edited by Percy Claude Hintzen and Jean Muteba Rahier. New York: Routledge, 2003.

Nwolise, O. B. C. "Blacks in the Diaspora: A Case of Neglected Catalysts in the Achievement of Nigeria's Foreign Policy Goals." *Journal of Black Studies* 23, no. 1 (September 1992): 117–34.

Office of the Attorney General, State of New York, Civil Rights Bureau. "Report on Stop and Frisk." December 1, 1999.

Palmer, Colin. "Defining and Studying the Modern African Diaspora." *Perspectives* (newsletter of the American Historical Association) (September 1998): 22–25.

Pérez, Louis A. "Politics, Peasants and People of Color: The 1912 'Race War' in Cuba Reconsidered." *Hispanic American Historical Review* 66 (August 1986): 509–39.

Pérouse de Montclos, Marc-Antoine. "A Refugee Diaspora: When the Somali Go West." In Koser, ed., *New African Diasporas*, 37–55.

Pierre, Jemima. "Race Across the Atlantic: Mapping Racialization in Africa and the African Diaspora." Ph.D. diss., University of Texas at Austin, 2002.

Pires-Hester, Laura. "The Emergence of Bilateral Diaspora Ethnicity among Cape Verdean-Americans." In *The African Diaspora: African Origins and New World Identities*. Edited by Isidore Okpewho, Carole Boyce Davies, and Ali A. Mazrui. Bloomington: Indiana University Press, 1999.

Possar, Patricia R., and Pamela M. Graham. "Dominicans: Transnational Identities and Local Politics." In *New Immigrants in New York*. Rev. ed. Edited by Nancy Foner. New York: Columbia University Press, 2001.

Riccio, Bruno. "More Than a Trade Diaspora: Senegalese Transnational Experiences in Emilia-Romagna (Italy)." In Koser, ed., *New African Diasporas*, 95–110.

SAHAN Wetenschappelijk Adviesbureau. "Mobilizing African Diaspora for the Promotion of Peace in Africa." Policy report for the Netherlands Ministry of Foreign Affairs, Sub-Sahara Department. Amsterdam, May 2005.

Shepperson, George, "The African Abroad or the African Diaspora." In *Emerging Themes of African History: Proceedings of the International Congress of African Historians*. Edited by T. O. Ranger. London, Heinemann Educational, 1969.

St. Louis, Brett. "The Difference Sameness Makes: Racial Recognition and the 'Narcissism of Minor Differences.'" *Ethnicities* 5, no. 3 (2005): 343–364.

Stein, Judith. *The World of Marcus Garvey: Race and Class in Modern Society*. Baton Rouge: Louisiana State University Press, 1986.

Torres-Saillant, Silvio. "The Tribulations of Blackness: Stages in Dominican Racial Identity." *Latin American Perspectives* 25, no. 3 (1998): 126–46.

Totoricagüena, Gloria. *Identity, Culture, and Politics in the Basque Diaspora*. Reno: University of Nevada Press, 2004.

Turner, J. Michael. "Les Brésiliens: The Impact of Former Brazilian Slaves upon Dahomey." Ph.D. diss., Boston University, 1975.

Van Haer, Nicolas. *New Diasporas: The Mass Exodus, Dispersal, and Regrouping of Migrant Communities.* Seattle: University of Washington Press, 1998.

———, Frank Pieke, and Steven Vertovec; with the assistance of Anna Lindley, Barbara Jettinger, and Meera Balarajan. A Report by the ESRC Centre on Migration Policy and Society (COMPAS), University of Oxford, for the Department for International Development, April 2004.

Van Kessel, Ineke. "Goa Conference on the African Diaspora in Asia." *African Affairs* 105, no. 420 (2006): 461–464.

Van Sertima, Ivan. *They Came before Columbus.* New York: Random House, 1976.

Vickerman, Milton, "Jamaicans: Balancing Race and Ethnicity." In *New Immigrants in New York.* Rev. ed. Edited by Nancy Foner. New York: Columbia University Press, 2001.

Warner-Lewis, Maureen. *Central Africa in the Caribbean: Transcending Time, Transforming Cultures.* Barbados: University of the West Indies Press, 2003.

Waters, Mary C. *Black Identities: West Indian Immigrant Dreams and American Realities.* New York: Russell Sage Foundation, 1999.

———. "Ethnic and Racial Ideologies of Second Generation [Jamaicans]." In *The New Second Generation.* Edited by Alejandro Portes. New York: Russell Sage Foundation, 1996.

Wilder, Craig S. *A Covenant with Color: Race and Social Power in Brooklyn.* New York: Columbia University Press, 2000.

World Conference against Racism, Racial Discrimination, Xenophobia and Related Intolerance, Preparatory Committee. "Documents Adopted by the Regional Conference of the Americas, Held in Santiago de Chile, Chile from 5–7 December 2000." Geneva, January 15–16, 2001.

Wright, Michelle. *Becoming Black: Creating Identity in the African Diaspora.* Durham, NC: Duke University Press, 2004.

The Making of "Modern" Diasporas: The Case of Muslims in Canada

By NERGIS CANEFE

> Man is after all not a tree and humanity is not a forest.
>
> —Emmanuel Levinas, *Totality and Infinity*.

Liberal democratic citizenship has become the commonplace and yet decidedly challenged motto in every Western political system in the twenty-first century.[1] It was meant to symbolize respect for difference, institutionalized tolerance for disagreement, and legal protection of freedoms of expression and choice. Canada constitutes no exception in terms of the formal embrace of this rendition of citizenship. In effect, many believe that compared with its southern neighbor, with its current conservative and xenophobic presidential regime, or compared with the equally xenophobic and anti-immigration reflexes of European governments, Canada is apt to become the home guard for such a conception.[2]

I am thankful to my graduate students Lina Nadar and Nadia Turk for the stimulating debates we had on Muslim minorities in Canada during the preparation of this manuscript. I also learned a lot from Samy Shavit Swayd and his graduate students during my visit to the UCLA Center for Near Eastern Studies as a guest speaker for their Muslim Diasporas seminars in 2006. Finally, I would like to thank Mina Sharifi-Funk and Patrice Brodeur for their valuable feedback on my work during the various workshops we shared a table at in Toronto, Waterloo, and Ottawa between 2005 and 2007. The epigraph is from Emmanuel Levinas, *Totality and Infinity*, trans. Alfonso Lingis (Pittsburgh, PA: Duquesne University Press, 1969), 41.

1. Richard Falk, "The Decline of Citizenship in an Era of Globalization," *Citizenship Studies* 4, no. 1 (2000): 5–17.

2. Liza Schuster and John Solomos, "Rights and Wrongs across European Borders: Migrants, Minorities and citizenship," *Citizenship Studies* 6, no. 1 (2002): 37–54.

Meanwhile, from within Canada, the picture looks somewhat different. More and more Canadians who either recently acquired citizenship or assumed landed immigrant status are finding themselves at a crossroads: They have skills to offer, they have a significant range of legal membership rights, and yet they seem to be not on an even playing field with others who have become "Canadians" before they did or who belong to the Northern European and/or Francophone backbone of traditional Canadian society.[3] An invisible line divides recent immigrants from other Canadians when it comes to opportunities for stable, rewarding, and status-bearing jobs and for accessing public goods such as quality education, adequate housing, and amenities and opportunities in life beyond the basic means of survival, amenities that render us not just part of the working population feeding capitalist free-market economies, but humans in our full potential. Moreover, that line divides recent immigrants from other Canadians when it comes to political representation beyond group rights and to both the public images and private descriptions of what constitutes a Canadian. To put it bluntly, there are enough indicators to suggest that there exists a threshold that separates those who can *in principle* have it all and those who are kept back—via delay, caution, and interrogation—from full and acknowledged participation in Canadian social, political, and economic life.

Furthermore, contrary to the Marxist adage that long dominated discussions of "structural exclusion," what troubles the new immigrants does not appear to be strictly a class issue.[4] Private businesses, the surviving parts of the legendary activist Canadian state, pressure groups, many organs of the Canadian civil society, and even the Canadian intellectual and political elite all prove to be partners in this crime of omission, which somewhat defies definition. We are often all too keen to act as if in Canada, all is now in order, since the Canadian Charter of Rights and Freedoms (Part I of the Canadian Constitution Act) came into effect in 1982.[5] Accordingly, many believe, if there remains unequal access or differential utilization of our clearly spelled-out rights, it must be just a lag in the political culture of the larger society in terms of catching up with our state-of-art legal-institutional framework.[6] The Canadian state, civil society, and all Canadian institutions are expected to guide this change with expediency. In short, legal liberalism—hand in hand with the entrenched belief in the possibility of the realization of liberal democratic citizenship—runs deep and strong in the Canadian psyche as the be-all and end-all

---

3. Michael D. Behiels, *Canada's Francophone Minority Communities: Constitutional Renewal and the Winning of School Governance* (Montreal: McGill-Queens University Press, 2005); Martin Loney, *The Pursuit of Division: Race, Gender and Preferential Hiring in Canada* (Montreal: McGill-Queens University Press, 2003); Charles Taylor, et al., *Multiculturalism: Examining the Politics of Recognition* (Princeton, NJ: Princeton University Press, 1994).

4. Adrian Favell and Andrew Geddes, eds., *The Politics of Belonging: Migrants and Minorities in Contemporary Europe* (Brookfield, VT: Ashgate Publishing, 2003).

5. The full text of the charter can be found via http://www.efc.ca/pages/law/charter/charter.text.html (last accessed December 1, 2007).

6. Harry Arthurs and Brent Arnold, *Does the Charter Matter?* Unpublished draft paper, 2005, and Harry Arthurs, *The New Economy and the Demise of Industrial Citizenship* (Kingston, ONT: IRC Press, 1997).

solution to racism, sexism, xenophobia, Islamophobia, anti-Semitism, and any other, newer forms of exclusion in the offing.

What is overlooked in this grand scheme of institutional reform and political optimism is that changes in what is often cited as the "citizenship contract" in any given society have always been made within the context of existing norms of sociopolitical membership. In other words, they take place with direct reference to already-determined criteria for qualifications regarding full membership, the legal process of naturalization being the tip of the iceberg.[7] Thus, one can argue that there is a starting line in each society cum political community regarding the minimums of acceptance for full participation with protected rights, and, by default, regarding the agreed-upon principles of exclusion. It is those baselines that are the hardest to change, or even to question. Such changes have been observed, for instance, in cases whereby the ethnically based and/or monist understanding of citizenship was undone to accommodate multiethnic, multireligious, or multiracial dimensions. However, more often than not, integration or assimilation—depending on the steepness of the citizenship regime's expectations for the ordinance of full and formal membership—forces immigrants into conforming to "national stereotypes" developed to depict the core characteristics of "those who are one of us." In Canada, these include, but are not limited to obeying the law, paying taxes, and not becoming a burden upon the relatively generous public purse, educating and reeducating yourself and your family to remain as productive citizens in this age of the global economy while living at the core of it, and avoiding public displays as well as private embraces of emotive, charged, and what is often deemed archaic modes of discontent concerning your fellow citizens based on your or their religion, race, ethnicity, language, and other ordinary divides that traditionally define communal boundaries at the expense of a national sense of unity and principled pride.

These criteria on their own are inclusive enough to welcome cohorts of strangers to Canadian soil as potential citizens. In other words, the problems identified throughout this paper arise not from them per se, but in terms of their potential applicability. Some immigrants, including both would-be and recent Canadians, seem to be deemed categorically unable to satisfy fully the aforementioned criteria due to some "inherent" impediments attributed to their original citizenship and thus to their membership in a previous political community.[8] In this sense, the original, ethnoracially and religiously

---

7. Engin Isin and Bryan Turner, *Handbook of Citizenship Studies* (London: Sage Publications, 2002), and Engin Isin, *Being Political: Genealogies of Citizenship* (Minneapolis: University of Minnesota Press, 2002).

8. This is a judgment that needs further proof in terms of in-depth studies of the Muslim diaspora's standing in the society at large and its sense of self. However, there is at least a small set of reliable studies indicating that such an observation is not at all off the mark. This paper is not assigned to the task of exemplifying whether Muslims in Canada structurally suffer from specific kinds of segregation. Rather, it is an exercise in making sense of the already existing signs of differential treatment and how to engage in a debate that can underline the causes and effects of such engagements between diasporas and the Canadian mainstream and establishment. For further debate on the status and treatment of Muslims in Canada, see Cecile Laborde, "Secular Philosophy and Muslim Headscarves in Schools," *The Journal of Political Philosophy* 13, no. 3 (2005): 305–29; Yvonne Haddad Yazbeck and Jane Smith, eds., *Muslim Minorities in the West: Visible*

coded blueprint of who could qualify to become a Canadian—though no longer the actual qualifications of citizenship themselves—continues to haunt the Canadian society and its near-perfect model of liberal democratic citizenship.

This paper is dedicated to the discussion of a group of cases in which the effects of this lingering heritage of the past are most pronounced. These indicate that at this latest stage of the history of "Canadian society," religion—and in particular, the Muslim religion, especially when combined with ethnicity, race, and class—constitutes a key component of the silent barrier that separates those who categorically qualify for becoming a "true Canadian" and those who, at best, can approximate Canadianness. Religion, in this sense, and in particular, the religion of Islam, has been reinstated as a powerful force of demarcation in the New World in which immigrants arrive, just as it has been and continues to be in the Old Worlds from which they depart, albeit with somewhat different articulations of this infamous practice. In the end, it is fair to suggest that all the rhetoric of liberal democratic citizenship does not suffice to carry the weight of religious difference: the "veil of ignorance" that was to bring us the promised land of equality in difference cannot be fully donned due to fear, prejudice, and mistrust.[9] The belief that "Canada is for immigrants," that it embraces all newcomers who will subscribe to the citizenship contract of the society, stands in destructive tension with an older, more pernicious belief—that immigrants who are not demonstrably "for Canada" should be excluded from that contract.

Limits of Acceptability in the Case of Muslim Immigrants and Refugees

The observation that there is a presumed clash between Canadian liberal democratic ethics of citizenship and belonging and Muslim individual and communal identity might appear to be heavily influenced by the events of 9/11 and the backlash they created in terms of the perception and treatment of Muslim minorities in both North America and Europe.[10] However, I have other and more pressing reasons for turning my attention to the case of Muslim immigrants in the West, and in particular in Canada. To start with, the sheer numbers and migratory trends indicate that Muslim immigrants and refugees became the new force of challenge and change in contemporary Canadian society during

---

and Invisible (Walnut Creek, CA: Altamira Press, 2002); Syed Serajul, "Crisis of Identity in a Multi-cultural Society: The Case of Muslims in Canada," *Intellectual Discourse* 8, no. 1 (2000): 1–18; and Abdullah Hakim Quick, "Muslim Rituals, Practices and Social Problems," *Polyphony* (The Multicultural History Society of Ontario) 12: 120–124, whose full text can be accessed under "Articles" at http://epe.lac-bac.gc.ca/100/205/301/ic/cdc/magic/mhome.html (last accessed on December 4, 2007).

9. "Veil of ignorance' is the term used by liberal theorist John Rawls to describe the possibility of reaching a common ground despite our different perceptions of the good in the public realm. Once the veil of ignorance is put in effect, one supposedly becomes blind toward one's own prejudices, as well as others', and can reach a level of understanding that is rightful and transparent for all concerned. For further debate, see John Rawls, *A Theory of Justice* (Boston, MA: Harvard University Press, 1971).

10. Disha Ilir, *Location and Patterns of Anti-Arab and Anti-Muslim Hate Crimes* (Charlotte, NC: Southern Sociological Society Publications, 2005).

the last two decades.[11] Furthermore, this phenomenon is not unique to Canada. In stark terms, across the contemporary Anglo-American world, Muslims are now the second largest religious group.[12] Especially in the North American context, this development pushed Jews as the traditional "religious minority" into third and sometimes fourth place, thus rendering Muslims more of an *immediate* target for racial and ethnoreligious profiling and prejudice. Also, Muslims constitute sizeable, rather than symbolic minorities.[13] Following Great Britain and the United States—the latter being a home to in excess of ten million Muslims—according to the Statistics Canada Census 2001 results, Canadian Muslims constitute approximately 2 percent of the total Canadian population.[14] Finally, the rate of Muslim immigration to Canada has been steadily increasing since the 1970s, at this point further aided by American Muslims moving north for less institutional and societal discrimination or, at the very least, to avoid compulsory registration imposed by the current American government since 2002.

In terms of actual numbers, according to the 1981 census, there were 98,165 Muslims in Canada, accounting for less than 0.5 percent of the total population, compared with an estimated 33,000 in 1971. The 1991 census then counted 253,000 Canadians reporting affiliation with Islam. Statistics further suggest that their population figures increased by 128.9 percent between 1991 and 2001, reaching the number of 579,640 in 2001. Today, Canadian Muslims are estimated to have reached a population of roughly seven hundred and fifty thousand.[15] By the end of the decade, if the present demographic trend continues, Islam will firmly establish its status as the second principal religion in the country. This dramatic increase in Muslim immigration during the last two to three decades—in spite of the cumbersome selection and vetting process imposed by the Canadian point system—is to be accounted for by the influx of Muslims from the whole range of former British colonies, including, but not limited to, South Asia, Africa, and the Middle East.

A second phenomenon of interest for me is the destination of settlements entertained by Muslim immigrants and refugees to Canada. These are not at the periphery or in the distant agricultural hinterlands. On the contrary, they are situated right at the center of Canadian political and economic landscape, Ontario being the heartland of it all. Needless to say, the picture in this regard is not all that different from what applies to other

---

11. Haddad and Smith, eds., *Muslim Minorities in the West.*

12. Birgit Schaebler and Leif Stenberg, eds., *Globalization and the Muslim World: Culture, Religion, and Modernity* (Syracuse, NY: Syracuse University Press, 2004); Yvonne Yazbeck Haddad, *Muslims in the West: From Sojourners to Citizens* (Oxford: Oxford University Press, 2002).

13. Yvonne Yazbeck Haddad, Jane Smith, and John Esposito, eds., *Religion and Immigration: Christian, Jewish, and Muslim Experiences in the U.S.* (Walnut Creek, CA: Altamira Press, 2003).

14. See Quick, "Muslim Rituals, Practices and Social Problems."

15. The key organizations and news groups I examined that speak on behalf of Muslims in Canada, Canadian Muslims, and Muslims in North America include, but are not limited to, Dhimmi Watch, the Canadian Islamic Congress, the Muslim Chronicle, the Muslim Canadian Congress, and the Canadian Council on American-Islamic Relations (CAIR-CAN).

incoming ethnoreligious minorities. In general, the urban, cosmopolitan setting proves more welcoming and less exclusive than the white, Christian, agricultural, or resource-economy hinterlands. Of the thirteen Canadian provinces, Ontario thus hosts more than half of Canadian Muslims—their estimated number was 352,500 in 2001. More to the point, 5 percent of the Toronto population is counted as Muslim, rendering Toronto a city with the highest concentration of Muslims in North America. In sum, Muslim immigrants constitute concentrated and visible minorities in Canada.[16]

Equally crucial is the fact that, as the statistics prove, Muslims in Canada are not an aging group. Since the median age of Muslims in Canada is cited as 28 years, one can comfortably conclude that this is indeed a markedly young population. Compared to the Jewish and Roman Catholic populations, whose median age is 41.5 and 37.8 years old, respectively, as well as with the median age for the total Canadian population, which is 37, there is a significant difference in terms of the demographic composition and needs of this group of new Canadians. Further underlining this point, according to the community's own estimates, 91 percent of Muslims in Canada are first generation, 7.7 percent are second generation, and only 0.9 percent are third generation and over. Meanwhile, roughly 68 percent of Muslims in Canada are estimated to have Canadian citizenship. This leaves a hefty portion of the population as immigrants without Canadian passports and, concomitantly, without the enjoyment of full-fledged rights of formal citizenship. It is also important to note that although there are an estimated 6,310 Muslims with a Ph.D. degree in Canada, Muslims have the second-highest unemployment rate applicable to identifiable immigrant categories in the country, with 14.4 percent of the population unemployed, compared with a 7.4 percent national unemployment rate.

Why do Muslims immigrate to Canada in such increased numbers, despite the fact that on the whole, there doesn't seem to be a marked success rate, either in terms of economic or sociopolitical integration and acceptance? In terms of the histories of immigration, just like other migrants, Muslims have emigrated and continue to migrate to Canada for a variety of reasons. Economic reasons, including higher education, constitute only one incentive. Significant numbers came to Canada to reunite with their families, while others arrived in Canada as refugees and self-exiled people who left their homelands for political reasons. Contrary to popular perceptions, Muslim immigrants do not arrive solely from Somalia, Pakistan, or the Arab Middle East. Of the total world population of Muslims, the majority live in Asia and Africa, and only a much smaller portion reside in the Middle East. Reflecting this global geography of dispersion, Muslims have immigrated to Canada not just from the Arab world (Lebanon, Egypt, Palestine, Syria, Morocco, Tunisia, and Algeria), but also from Iran, Pakistan, India, Afghanistan, Turkey, Africa, Eastern Europe, the Caribbean, and South and Central America. As a result, Muslims living in Canada represent

---

16. For a full list of operating mosques in Canada, see http://en.wikipedia.org/wiki/List_of_mosques#Canada (last accessed December 4, 2007).

different ethnic backgrounds and races, as well as different nationalities, languages, and cultures. Again according to the community's own estimates, 37 percent of the Muslim population in Canada is of South Asian descent, 21 percent is of Arab and Middle Eastern descent, 14 percent is of West Indian descent, and the remaining 28 percent is made up of many other ethnicities such African, Chinese, and so on. On the whole, however, the majority of the Muslims in Canada qualify as members of "racial" minorities.[17] Combined with their minority status in terms of religion and ethnicity, the racial component of their difference further accentuates their standing apart from the rest of settled Canadian population. However, they blend with other recent immigrant groups, because white, European-descent, and Christian immigrants increasingly have become a minority. In other words, whatever kind of racial prejudice is involved, Muslim immigrants share that with other immigrants of different religious backgrounds. The question is whether their religious identity and practices worsen their case and heightens their status as the "temporarily suspended" members of the Canadian society.

In general terms, as with Jews, the preservation of religious belief, ritual, and practice remains key to the maintenance of Muslim identity in Canada, especially in the context of being a minority community with multiple candidates for the position. To this end, it is no surprise that there are more than eighty established mosques in the country, four of which are located in Ottawa itself. There are also numerous locations in most Canadian cities where space (*musallah*) is structurally set aside for prayer purposes. This is in addition to a diverse map of Islamic centers, associations, and educational institutions funded and utilized by various and often overlapping Muslim communities of different ethnolinguistic backgrounds.

In this context of organized religious practice and teaching, some of the commonplace practices widespread in Canadian society are considered to be in direct conflict with the religious boundaries deemed crucial for the sustenance of Muslim identity by its dominant schools of thought. For instance, the social and economic dictates of the religion require abstinence from consuming alcohol and other intoxicants, eating pork and pork products, and engaging in economic activities that are usury-based, such as mortgages, bonds, and interest-based transactions, gambling, as well as unattended courtship and sexual activities outside the bonds of marriage. However, contrary to common assumptions that all those in Canada who are practicing Muslims or have Muslim heritage agree with the currency of these judgments, it is yet to be determined what percentage of this group of people concur with them and abide by them. The number of immigrants who continue to identify themselves as Muslims, even though they may be secular, not observant, or choose to ignore the counter-Islamic practices in the society at large as impediments to their lifestyles, remains equally understudied as a phenomenon.

---

17. Serajul, "Crisis of Identity in a Multi-cultural Society."

The Status of Muslim Immigrants in Canada: Four Episodes

Four specific clusters of cases have preoccupied the Canadian public regarding the status of Muslim immigrants during the last decade or so. These are the female genital mutilation (FGM) debate, the headscarf issue in Canadian and in particular in Quebecois public and private schools, the Maher Arar case of unlawful extradition to abroad via United States, and the Shari'a courts case in Ontario. My goal in attending to each of these episodes is to spell out the premises according to which Muslims in Canada may have been deemed to be unwilling, incognizant, or incapable of understanding the fundamental codes of civil conduct and democratic membership in a liberal democracy. In the case of Muslims, as perhaps could be argued in the case of other once unwanted minorities, the fundamental premise does not seem to be "Canada is for immigrants," but immigrants must be "for Canada." These immigrants and refugees are not only expected to learn and follow the rules of political membership in contemporary Canadian society, they are also expected not to challenge them, since the legal-institutional model of liberal democratic citizenship is by now believed to be at a perfect state. If and when they fail to be satisfied with their current status, the onus is thus put on their shoulders—whoever may constitute that "they"—in terms of failing to understand what the requirements of living as a full member in Canada are.

The first case in hand, female genital mutilation (FGM) comprises the whole range of procedures involving partial or total removal of the external female genitalia or other injuries to female genital organs for nontherapeutic reasons. Commonly know as female circumcision, it is an invasive practice that is usually performed on girls before puberty. The immediate and long-term health consequences of FGM vary according to the type and severity of the operation performed.[18] Contrary to the common belief that it is a widespread Muslim practice, however, FGM is performed among both Christian and Muslim families who have emigrated from African countries, Indonesia, and the Middle East (Yemen, in particular), where FGM is regarded as an essential social tradition. Its supporters consider the practice to be a mixture of religious duty, social custom, and a necessary operation for presumed health reasons. In the West, on the other hand, FGM is considered and treated as a cruel mutilation of a female child or an adolescent girl in order to reduce or totally suppress her sexual desire after puberty for purposes of social control. Consequently, since the late 1980s, it has been outlawed in Britain, Canada, France, Sweden, Switzerland, and the United States. In fact, U.S. representatives to the World Bank and similar financial institutions are required to oppose loans to countries where FGM is prevalent and in which there are no anti-FGM educational programs.

---

18. Immediate complications include severe pain, shock, hemorrhage, urine retention, ulceration of the genital region, and injury to adjacent tissues. Long-term complications include recurring urinary tract infections, pelvic infections, infertility scarring, difficulties in menstruation, fistulae (holes or tunnels between the vagina and the bladder or rectum), painful intercourse, sexual dysfunction, and problems in pregnancy and childbirth related to the need to cut the vagina to allow delivery, often compounded by restitching.

In Canada, the Criminal Code of Canada is used as a direct means to address the issue of FGM. Also, since the early 1990s, Canada has recognized fear of gender persecution as a ground for claiming refugee status. As a result of the growing recognition of FGM as a violation of human rights in Canada, in 1994, the Ministry of the Solicitor General and Correctional Services issued a memorandum to all chiefs of police and the commissioner of the Ontario Provincial Police emphasizing that FGM is a criminal offence. The same year, the Ministry of the Attorney General also sent a memorandum to all crown attorneys on the prosecution of charges related to FGM.[19] In May 1997, the federal government amended the Criminal Code and included the performance of FGM as aggravated assault under section 268 (3). Under the Criminal Code, any person who commits an aggravated assault is guilty of an indictable offence and liable to imprisonment for a term not exceeding fourteen years. A parent who performs FGM on his or her child may also be charged with aggravated assault. Where the parent does not commit the act, but agrees to have it performed by another party, the parent can be convicted as a party to the offence under section 21(1) of Criminal Code Bill C-33. Finally, Section 273.3 of the Canadian Criminal Code protects children who are ordinarily resident in Canada as citizens or landed migrants from being removed from the country in order to be subjected to FGM.

Under these circumstances, in both the United States and Canada, the small percentage of Muslims who wish to continue the practice find it impossible to find a doctor who will perform the operation. The operation may then be performed illegally in the home by poorly trained persons and without adequate sterilization or medical attention. Under the current circumstances, legislation against FGM may thus prove to be counterproductive in some cases. It might discourage young women from seeking medical care out of fear that their parents might be charged for criminal conduct. Similarly, if the operation is blotched, the parents may be reluctant to take the child to a hospital out of fear of being criminally charged with child abuse. Equally important is the lack of public education campaigns to challenge the commonplace assumption that all Muslim families would resort to FGM if given the chance and that it is a practice inherent to Islam as a religion. Neither those who traditionally felt obliged to practice FGM nor those who have nothing to do with the practice despite being Muslim are shielded from the societal judgments at large that there is something inherently barbaric about Islam, in particular where the treatment of women and young girls is concerned.

The second case I will discuss also relates to the non-Muslim understandings of treatment of women according to Islamic teachings. In the 1990s, a convoluted debate erupted over the expulsion of Muslim Quebec high-school students who refused to remove their headscarves and of non-Muslim teachers who refused to cover their heads in a private Muslim school. The issue of the right of Muslim students to wear a hijab (Islamic

---

19. Ontario Human Rights Commission. *Policy on Genital Female Mutilation*, available on-line at http://www.ohrc.on.ca/english/publications/fgm-policy.shtml under "Publications" (last accessed on August 21, 2007).

headscarf) in Quebec's public schools was eventually settled, along with the 1995 ruling concerning the latter case. Specifically, the Quebec Human Rights Commission decided that a requirement imposed by a private Montreal Muslim school that all female teachers, including non-Muslims, wear the hijab as a condition of employment was discriminatory and contravened human-rights legislation. Then came the 2003 appeal regarding the expulsion of a Muslim female student from a secular private school for wearing the hijab. In 2005, the Quebec Human Rights Commission again stepped in to end the debate by settling the case regarding Irene Waseem and by setting a precedent affecting all practicing young Muslim girls who go to private schools in Canada. The commission concluded that College Charlemagne was wrong to forbid Waseem to wear her hijab to class when she was a student at the Pierrefonds high school two years previously.[20] At the time of her expulsion, several human rights organizations, including the Canadian Jewish Congress and the League for Human Rights of B'nai Brith, condemned the student's expulsion. According to the commission's president, Pierre Marois, both private, not-for-profit schools and the public schools in Quebec have the obligation to make "reasonable accommodation" for their students' religious beliefs. Meanwhile, religious groups will not be able to use the ruling to force sweeping changes in the ways schools operate or to place undue burden on the staff and the general student body. For instance, they won't be able to demand prayer rooms in secular schools or separate boys' and girls' pools in coeducational ones. Similarly, schools with a specific vocation to serve a particular religious, ethnic, or language group, such as Catholic schools, will in principle continue to have the right to favor members of that group. With its precedent ruling in 1995 and its role as the watchdog of human rights in Quebec, the Human Rights Commission indeed acted as a successful arbiter between the secularist politics of Quebec and minority communities demanding what the Canadian Charter of Rights and Freedoms dictates as fundamental human rights. Some thus argue that in both the Quebecois and Canadian society, the hijab issue has come to a close. I would beg to differ.

In fact, my observations are to the contrary and indicate that the issue is far from being fully resolved. Covered Muslim women in Canada report that they are often told off by non-Muslim Canadians.[21] They are reminded that this is Canada—it is a secular country and one does not *have to* wear a hijab. The common response of devout, practicing Muslim women who wear the headscarf, the veil, or the hijab to such criticism has been that it is a dictate of their belief, and not of any state or of the men in their families.[22]

---

20. Editorial, "Canada: Wise Decision on Right to Wear Hijabs," *Montreal Gazette*, June 16, 2005, available on-line at http://www.montrealmuslims.ca/Article1475.html (last accessed December 4, 2007).

21. Between 2002 and 2005, I conducted several interviews with Muslim Canadian students and assigned student essays in my classes at York University discussing the particular issue of how wearing the hijab effects their lives or their families' lives. I would like to thank them for their views, observations, and opinions. The names of the students will remain anonymous to protect their privacy.

22. Katherine Bullock, a convert to Islam since 1994, published her interview findings in the March–April 1998 issue of *Islamic Horizons* magazine. Her findings are similar to mine in terms of the unease experienced by these educated and adult women who feel that they are forced to defend themselves and their beliefs. Some of her work can be found at www.

When asked to explain why they are covered, they claim that the Muslim way of dressing symbolizes not oppression, but purity and modesty in accordance with a woman's Islamic identity. They also emphasize the belief that Muslim women and men are brothers and sisters in faith and belief. Thus, they believe it is their duty not to distract men from practicing their faith.

The counterargument to theirs is that whether it is covering girls' and women's heads and bodies, or regarding Muslim women as bastions of sexual virtue in general, these rigid differences between the sexes negatively influence the performance and life chances of Muslim women in Canadian society. This concern is addressed by practicing Muslims who support wearing the hijab by noting that the principal definition of equality in Islam is how human beings are regarded in relation to God and that the Qur'an unequivocally states that men and women are equal in the eyes of God. Accordingly, both sexes are individually responsible and accountable for their actions. In summary, the women in question do not believe the hijab or the veil hinders their freedom or constitutes an imposition on them.[23] On the contrary, covering a woman's body as an act of modesty is regarded as a device to facilitate Muslim women's movements outside their home in greater comfort, curtailing unwanted male gazes. The veil and the hijab are thus often linked with increased self-esteem, because not the body, but the soul and personality of the covered women are considered to be paid attention to in the society.

In contrast, the non-Muslim Canadian understanding of the covered Muslim women remains by and large synonymous with the oppression of women and the violation of their human rights. It also often represents to them the authoritarian and autocratic uses of political power in non-Western societies. Furthermore, since the events of 9/11, there is a direct association made between Islam, extremism, terrorism, fundamentalist politics, and the veil and hijab. Given these negative readings and attributions, some Muslims try to hide their Islamic identity to the point of changing their last names, not mentioning their religious affiliation in public, and refraining from carrying any observable signs associated with Islam. Muslim women who cover themselves thus take the risk—like Orthodox Jewish or Sikh men—of being identified immediately as members of a religious minority that is at the very least seen as problem-laden and at the very worst as a threat to the whole society. The agency of the women in question, their reasons for choosing or adhering to the principle of being veiled, and their activities and life stories regardless of the veil become subject to a widespread disregard.

Meanwhile, it is not only the Muslim women whose membership status in Canadian society has been rendered questionable due to their lifestyle choices in particular and ethnoreligious background in general. Muslim men, and more so Arab Muslim men, are

---

islamfortoday.com/hijabcanada.htm and at www.themodernreligion.com/women/hijab-canada.htm (both last accessed on August 23, 2007).

23. This belief was clearly stated in numerous autobiographical essays I collected for the Islam and Modernity fourth-year and Masters classes I taught at York University between 2002 and 2005.

increasingly portrayed as either potential or actual terrorists among us. A poignant case in point—that of Maher Arar—constitutes the third episode in this present discussion concerning what Muslims in Canada presumably lack in terms of fulfilling their obligations as citizens in a liberal democracy.

Maher Arar is a Canadian citizen of Syrian birth and a practicing Muslim. He first entered Canadian public debates in relation to his treatment by the American, Jordanian, and Syrian authorities, which constituted a devastating exposure of the new methods that Washington began to employ in its officially declared war against terrorism after 9/11.[24] It has become public knowledge that Arar was deported by the American government to Syria via Jordan with the understanding that the Syrian authorities would question him on Washington's behalf, even though there was no credible evidence linking him to any terrorist organization. However, much more relevant for Canadian society are the questions his case raised regarding the role that the Canadian government and its police and intelligence agencies played in delivering Canadian citizen Maher Arar into the hands of non-Canadian authorities and thus initiating the series of events that led to Arar's illegal detention and torture.[25]

In the absence of his lawyer or a Canadian consular representative, an immigration hearing was held at which Arar was told he was being expelled to Syria. Arar spent a total of ten months in captivity in Syria. For much of this time, he was held in solitary confinement in a special cell, three feet wide and six feet deep, with no light. Throughout the entire duration of Arar's detention and captivity, neither the American nor the Canadian authorities proved a connection to terrorists or laid formal charges against him.

Why does Arar's story matter? There are many angles that can be taken for discussing his treatment by both Canadian and American authorities, though here, I will emphasize only one. Given the fact that at present, 20 percent or more of Canadian citizens were born outside of Canada or the United States, Arar's case signals that the

---

24. Keith Jones, "The Maher Arar Case: Washington's Practice of Torture by Proxy," WSWS: News & Analysis: North America, November 18, 2003, available on-line at www.wsws.org/articles/2003/nov2003/arar-n18.shtml (last accessed on August 23, 2007).

25. In summary, the thirty-three-year-old computer and telecommunications technician was detained by U.S. immigration officials at New York's JFK Airport in September 2002 while returning to Canada from Tunisia, where he was visiting his wife's family. For the first five days of his subsequent twelve-day interrogation by U.S. immigration officers, New York City Police, and the FBI, Arar was not permitted to see a lawyer or inform anyone, including his family or the Canadian consulate, about his whereabouts and condition. He was told that he had no right to a lawyer, since he was not an American citizen. This is despite the fact that Arar had frequently traveled to the United States for his work and only a few months earlier had had his U.S. work permit extended. The reason for Arar's detention appears to be that he is an acquaintance of another Syrian-Canadian who is believed to know an Egyptian-Canadian whose brother was purportedly mentioned in an al-Qaeda document. When he realized he might be deported to Syria by the U.S. authorities, he protested as a former citizen of Syria who had left that country without performing the compulsory military duty and who had had family members jailed there for alleged ties to the Muslim Brotherhood. Nonetheless, U.S. authorities did not accede to Arar's request that he be deported to Canada, the country where he had resided for most of the past fifteen years, where his wife and two children live, and on whose passport he was traveling. Indeed, U.S. government officials stated that it was on the basis of intelligence supplied by Canadian police and security agencies that they acted against Arar. Consequently, the U.S. authorities rendered him to Syria, where he could be detained indefinitely without trial and his interrogators could use methods of interrogation that are not sanctioned in North America.

Canadian-U.S. border has become a site of a differential treatment for Canadian citizens that is actually endorsed by Canada. Furthermore, of that 20 percent, 5 percent or so are estimated to be of Muslim origin and many also fit the criteria for racial profiling—all too common a practice for both American and Canadian security establishments, especially since 9/11. To this end, it is apt to call the Arar case a direct assault against democracy from within Canada, irrespective of the American involvement in his unfair and illegal treatment. Are Muslims in Canada, citizen, immigrant, worker, or refugee, by definition suspected of criminal activity? Are they guilty until proven innocent, and if nothing else, by association, by ethnoreligious descent, by politics, by racial attributes? These are the kinds of questions that the Arar case brought to the fore above and beyond the issue of American supremacy over Canadian sovereignty.

The last case to which I will draw attention in this paper is Premier Dalton McGuinty's rejection of the use of Islamic Shari'a law as a basis for arbitration in Ontario, Canada.[26] In September 2005, the premier made the decision that there will be *no* religious arbitration in Ontario and only one law for all "Ontarians."[27] Furthermore, McGuinty announced that all existing private religious courts were to be outlawed. Some, such as Homa Arjomand, who is the coordinator of the International Campaign against Shari'a Courts in Canada, were delighted with this decision, because they share McGuinty's views that religious arbitrations threaten the "common ground" that ties Canadians of different origins together.[28] Meanwhile, others, such as Joel Richler—the Ontario region

---

26. Mainstream Islam distinguishes between *fiqh*—the understanding the details and inferences drawn by religious scholars, and *shari'a*, referring to the principles that lie behind *fiqh*. Shari'a is composed of laws that are regarded as divinely ordained, concrete, and timeless for all relevant situations (for example, the ban against drinking liquor as an intoxicant). It also contains laws that are extracted based on principles established by Islamic lawyers and judges over the centuries. In deriving Shari'a law, Islamic lawmakers attempt to interpret divine principles. Therefore, although Shari'a in general is considered divine, a lawyer's or judge's extraction or opinion on a given matter is not accepted as such. For Sunni Muslims, the primary sources of Islamic law are the Qur'an, the Hadith, or directions of the Islamic prophet Muhammad, the unanimous decisions of Muhammad's disciples on a certain issue (*ijma*), and *qiyas* which is to draw analogies from the essence of divine principles. The consensus of the community or people, public interest, and others is also accepted as a secondary source where the first four primary sources allow. For Shia Muslims, on the other hand, Shari'a corresponds to the Imami-Shia law, and its sources are the Qur'an, anecdotes of the Prophet's practices, and those of the twelve Shia imams and the intellect (*aql*). Finally, the practices called Shari'a today in various parts of the world also have roots in local customs. Fur further discussion, see YvonneYazbeck Haddad and Barbara Freyer Stowasserm eds., *Islamic Law and the Challenges of Modernity* (Walnut Creek, CA: Altamira Press, 2004).

27. Keith Leslie, "McGuinty Rejects Ontario's Use of Shari'a Law and All Religious Arbitrations, *Canadian Press*, Sunday, September 11, 2005. Full text of this and similar articles can be found at www.nosharia.com (last accessed on August 23, 2007).

28. The International Campaign Against Shari'a Courts in Canada started in Toronto in October 2003 with a handful of supporters, and it gradually grew into a coalition of eighty-seven organizations from fourteen countries with over one thousand activists. Its leading cadres in Toronto were human-rights activists who were forced to flee Iran during and after the 1989 Islamic Revolution. Their stance was later supported by organizations such as the Progressive Muslim Union (PUM). This latter organization is the result of extensive collaboration between a group of North American Muslims who state that they are committed to representing and renewing the Muslim community in all its social, ideological, and political diversity. PMU members range from deeply religious to totally secular, sharing a commitment to learning, political and social empowerment, justice and freedom, and a stated concern and love for the Muslim community. Further information can be found at their Web site www.pmuna.org (last accessed on December 14, 2007).

chairman of the Canadian Jewish Congress—expressed disappointment and shock over McGuinty's decision. This was due to the fact that the current system of arbitration has been in place since 1992, it has reportedly worked well, and there was no obvious or documented reason for it to be changed for either desiring Jewish or other communities.

In this context, the two questions that remain to be answered are the following: Who was demanding that Ontario should become the first Western jurisdiction to allow the use of a set of religious rules called Shari'a law to settle Muslim family disputes, and who else in general demands that religious arbitrations be allowed in a country with established liberal democratic and secular traditions? In addition, on the second front, why was it not deemed enough to have the right to seek advice, including religious advice, on matters of family or trade, rather than having separate bodies undertaking religion-based arbitration? Interestingly, contrary to the decision reached by McGuinty, as recently as December 2004, a report from the former New Democratic Party attorney general, Marion Boyd, recommended that the province should allow and regulate Shari'a arbitrations in much the same way it has been handling Christian and Jewish tribunals. Which constituency and stated interests led to the conclusions reached by Boyd, and which supported the McGuinty decision?

A key part of the answers to these questions lies in the nature of the allowances made by Ontario's Arbitration Act of 1991 (S.O. 1991, Chapter 17).[29] Until it was amended in 2006, the act allowed civil disputes ranging from custody and support to divorce and inheritance to be resolved through an independent arbitrator if both parties agreed. Catholics, Mennonites, Orthodox Jews, aboriginal Canadians, and Jehovah's Witnesses, among others, often used the act to settle family law questions without resorting to the governmental courts. Meanwhile, those who opposed permitting Shari'a family arbitration—though not necessarily the act itself—argued that the extension of the act to Muslim communities would have given legitimacy to a legal code they believe is not only unfair to women, but also inimical to the Canadian Charter of Rights and Freedoms. Similarly, McGuinty argued that the debate around Shari'a gave his government the chance to reconsider the merits of the original decision to allow religious arbitrations in Ontario. He also noted that seventeen women in his Liberal Party caucus strongly urged him to reject the idea. In addition, a very influential group of [non-Muslim] Canadian women, including author Margaret Atwood, activist Maude Barlow, writer June Callwood, and actresses Shirley Douglas and Sonja Smits issued an open letter to the premier on behalf of the No Religious Arbitration Coalition.[30] This was then followed up by the rows of angry demonstrators outside the Ontario legislature likening McGuinty to Afghanistan's former extremist Taliban leaders for even considering Shari'a. Similar rallies were also held in Ottawa, Montreal, and Victoria, while smaller protests were held abroad

---

29. The full text of the act can be found via http://www.e-laws.gov.on.ca (last accessed on August 23, 2007).

30. The organization's press release can be read at www.owjn.org/issues/mediatio/legislation.htm (last accessed on August 23, 2007).

in London, Amsterdam, Paris, and Dusseldorf. Yet the most recognizable support for McGuinty's decision came from Tarek Fatah, head of the Muslim Canadian Congress. As part of the congress's demand for reforms within Canada's more traditional Muslim organizations, Fatah judged McGuinty's surprise announcement a great victory for all Canadians, but particularly for Muslims in Canada, because it was also to be considered a defeat for Islamic fundamentalists and those who are preaching Islamic fundamentalism in Canada.[31]

Here, one of the big questions lurking behind the scenes is that of how to live as a Muslim in a non-Muslim, and in particular, in a secularized liberal democratic state and society where laws are not encoded according to religious principles.[32] The supporters of the Shari'a courts suggest that because God's name is mentioned in the preamble of the Constitution, the Canadian state is bound to allow space for religious law as long as it does not curtail the functioning of the society as a whole. In this regard, the easiest issue to be argued involves Muslim personal family law as it pertains only to Muslims who choose to resort to it. Again, the supporting argument is that if Muslims are prevented from implementing and adhering to such laws even in the private sphere, they are then prevented from freely pursuing and committing themselves to their religious tradition in the public sphere, where democracy unfolds. Because Muslim personal law was never incorporated into the Canadian legal system, and because Muslims now constitute the largest religious minority in the country, the question is thus posed as why they are denied the right to govern their personal lives in accordance with the Muslim personal and family law injunctions. Since Muslim clergy are not able to take part in the secular court system, they cannot effect decisions in the Canadian courts' arbitration of property matters and divorce. In summary, the comprehensive body of Islamic jurisprudence regarding inheritance, custody, access to children, and other rights upon marital breakdown cannot be implemented in Canada, and that is considered by some groups, such as the Canadian Society of Muslims and the Islamic Congress of Canada, to be a breach of constitutional rights protected by the Charter of Rights and Freedoms itself.

According to this point of view, Muslims in Canada are living at the mercy of a secular court system that they would not have chosen otherwise, and as such, they are

---

31. Tarek Fatah's views can be read at the online magazine, MuslimWakeup.Com as well as the Web page www.muslimcanadiancongress.org (last accessed August 23, 2007). He is a founding member of the Muslim Canadian Congress and lives in Toronto, Canada. Born in Pakistan, Tarek Fatah was a student leader in the 1960s and early 1970s, twice imprisoned by successive military governments in Pakistan. A biochemist by education, he started his career as a journalist with the Karachi *Sun* in 1970. After another coup in 1977, Fatah and many of his colleagues were fired by the military junta and had to leave the country. Since coming to Canada in 1987—after a ten-year stay in Saudi Arabia—he has been active in politics, running for the Ontario legislature in 1995. He has been the host of the *Muslim Chronicle* TV show since 1996 and has written for the *Toronto Star*, the *Globe and Mail*, and the *TIME Magazine*. He was a founding member of the Muslim Canadian Congress after 9/11 to counter the growing influence of fundamentalist Muslim organizations. The MCC is a grassroots organization of activist Muslims in Canada who believe that the "gender apartheid" practiced by some Muslims should end and that separation of religion and the state is a necessity, including in Muslim countries.

32. David Lyon and Marguerite Van Die Lyon, eds., *Rethinking Church, State and Modernity: Canada between Europe and the United States* (Toronto: University of Toronto Press, 2000).

portrayed as not acting of their own volition and free will. The only recourse available for the believer in Islam appeared to be the Ontario Arbitration Act, which provided that the parties to a dispute may appoint an arbitrator by mutual consent and instruct him or her to apply the rules of law designated by the parties. It is on this basis that the Canadian Society of Muslims decided to inaugurate the Islamic Institute of Civil Justice and the Muslim Court of Arbitration as an alternative dispute resolution system. The idea was that Canadian Muslims could then resolve their family law disputes in conformity with the customs, traditions, and rules of their own communities. Again, the assumption here is that secular Canadian courts would serve only the interests of people of non-Muslim background, and Muslims would not be able to benefit fully from the law under such conditions. The judges in the Canadian legal system are deemed to be lacking the qualifications, training, and experience to understand the fine points, sensitivities, and nuances of particular cultural and religious problems specific to communities such as those of Canada's Muslims. The strife-ridden parties are thus believed to suffer from trying to explain and resolve their differences before a non-Muslim, rather than a coreligionist legal authority.

What this argument overlooks is the fact that decisions made by any existing or future court of arbitration could not be in conflict with the stipulations and basic tenets of civil, family, contract, or criminal law in the Canadian legal code. For instance, if a custody arrangement violates the principles of equal access and responsibility for the children upon the dissolution of a marriage, it cannot be upheld in Canadian courts based on reasons of religious exception. Similarly, inheritance laws in Canada cannot endorse a practice whereby siblings are given differential treatment based on their gender. Only by operating pursuant to Ontario and Canadian law could the Islamic tribunals have offered an alternative for the Muslim community, or parts of it.

Furthermore, because contemporary Islam is practiced according to the principles of not just one, but a number of schools and sects, which rendition of Shari'a law was to be used and who would make that decision in the Canadian setting was a debate that was put aside before making a demand to institutionalize Shari'a through courts of arbitration. Finally, the argument for the establishment of Shari'a courts stipulated that parties seeking recourse from a Muslim court are more likely to be inclined toward compromise and reconciliation, because the decision of such a court is bound to be viewed as "their own," rather than emanating from a judge who derives his authority and training from an outside source. This claim by Canadian Muslims creates a much-resented image of believers of Islam as a society unto themselves, cut off from all other groups and traditions to the point that even the arbiter of legal conduct and the binding premises of Canadian society are reacted against as having been imposed on Muslims by "outsiders." Accordingly, this image is seen as symbolizing a yearning for a world where Christian laws should be for Christians, Jewish laws for Jews, and Muslims laws for Muslims, instead of one law applying to all in this mixed and largely secular society.

In light of these concerns, it is no wonder that the secular body of the Muslim Canadian Congress fiercely opposed the formation of Shari'a courts and publicly stated that it would lead to the ghettoization of Canadian Muslims, harming both the community and the society at large.[33] In addition, there was doubt that the Shari'a courts could uphold the core principles framing the Arbitration Act. These include the ruling that arbitration can apply only to civil matters, that participation in the arbitration—as opposed to the court system—must be voluntary, and that the secular courts have the right to intervene to prevent unequal or unfair treatment of the parties.

In effect, the major fear of feminist organizations in Canada and abroad was that decisions made in religious courts that might be weighted against women, although they would not be enforceable or could be overturned in the courts, might never come to Canadian courts if the women involved were isolated, did not know their rights within the Canadian legal system, or came under familial and communal pressure. One answer to this problem would have been to insist on mandatory pretribunal counseling so that participants fully understood their rights in the larger, Canadian legal context. In this sense, there was no reason to expect that the Islamic Institute or the proposed tribunals would have been run as if the Taliban had set up shop in Ontario. Those who fear fundamentalism regard committed religious belief necessarily as a sign of militancy or extremism, and that remains as a problem-laden issue after the McGuinty decision as much as, if not more than, before. The price for these fears is now to be paid not only by Muslims who believe in channeling their private conduct according to religious principles, but by all other religious minorities who also entertain similar dispositions.

Whether banning arbitration altogether will bring these communities back into the Canadian mainstream or whether it will further alienate them is to be seen only in time. However, across the Atlantic Ocean, the examples set by staunch secularist policies with no compromise are not that encouraging. In late October and November 2005, during several weeks of extensive rioting, Paris was burning.[34] Furthermore, it is not the first time for such outrage to engulf a metropolitan capital in the West, and neither is it likely to be the last.[35]

The State as the "Custodian" of Minority Access to Rights in the Diaspora: Problems and Concerns

Taking a step back from the status, treatment, and perception of the rights of Muslims in Canada, let us now look at the codification and practice of these rights in general. My

---

33. For further debate, see the Toronto *Globe and Mail*, "An Islamic Court? Here? Why Not?" August 28, 2004, Opinion page. The full text can be accessed at http://muslim-canada.org/globeboydaug2822004.html/ (last accessed on August 23, 2007).

34. A detailed timeline of the riots between October 25th and November 14th, 2005 can be found at http://news.bbc. co.uk/1/hi/world/europe/4413964.stm (last accessed on August 23, 2007).

35. Paul Silverstein, *Algeria in France: Transpolitics, Race, and Nation* (Bloomington: Indiana University Press), 2004.

reason for this detour is to determine whether the Canadian belief in the merits of the legal liberalism is reciprocated in the fields of human-rights and citizenship studies. One of the most critical facets of the debate regarding citizenship, minority, and refugee rights, including the negotiation of ethnoracial and ethnoreligious difference, indeed concerns what we can expect from the *state* and its legal-institutional establishment. Is the state to be accepted as the principal custodian of human rights, including minority and group rights? Can the state be regarded as neutral in its perception and treatment of rights? Is it an arbiter of change in its own right, or is it simply an institutional means to deliver the message of what is deemed rightful in the society?

Contemporary Canadians seem to be rather extreme in their views in regard to these questions. Worldwide, not everyone believes to the same extent in the merits of the liberal democratic state in its moral interventionist form. Notwithstanding its pivotal role in sustaining rights-based politics, the common agreement among human-rights scholars, for instance, indicates that historically, the nation-state has also been the greatest enemy of a transnational or supranational human-rights regime.[36] This is not only due to the fact that often states fail in their role to protect or to promote human rights. They actually engage in acts that clearly violate human-rights principles and often provide justifications or cover-ups for these violations, whether in the name of national security, protection of the public good, political peace, or economic survival. Thus, there exists an inherent tension between universal aspirations for justice articulated by what may be called the "rights discourse" and, national, regional, and international politics, a tension that deters the advancement of a global or at least transnational network of protection for those who are vulnerable in terms of their civil membership status, as well as for those limited in their enjoyment of rights ordinarily associated with citizenship.[37]

History has proven time and again that practical techniques of "managing difference" within national polities cannot easily avoid the deep-seated effects of this tension. Nationalist resistance to international migration is just one of them. Repeated waves of widespread xenophobia with changing targets is yet another.[38] Practical solutions to problems such as systemic exclusion based on ethnoracial or religious identity may indicate that radical changes in law would, in principle, provide the required remedy. What really needs to emerge, however, is not just a system of legal constraints and rearrangements,

---

36. Howard Hensel, ed., *Sovereignty and the Global Community: The Quest for Order in the International System* (Aldershot, UK: Ashgate, 2004); Joanne van Selm and Edward Newman, eds., *Refugees and Forced Displacement: International Security, Human Vulnerability, and the State* (Tokyo: United Nations University Press, 2003); Kurt Mills, *Human Rights in the Emerging Global Order: A New Sovereignty?* (New York: St. Martin's Press,1998); Mortimer Sellers, ed., *The New World Order: Sovereignty, Human Rights, and the Self-determination of Peoples* (Oxford: Berg, 1996).

37. Ludger Pries, *Migration and Transnational Spaces* (Aldershot, UK: Ashgate and the Danish Centre for Migration and Ethnic Studies, 1998); Yasemin Soysal, *The Limits of Citizenship: Migrants and Postnational Citizenship in Europe* (Chicago: University of Chicago Press, 1994).

38. Veit Bader, "Democratic Institutional Pluralism and Cultural Diversity," in *The Social Construction of Diversity: Recasting the Master Narrative of Industrial Nations*, ed. Danielle Juteau and Christiane Harzig (Oxford: Berghan, 2003), 131–67; Veit Bader, "Religious Diversity and Democratic Institutional Pluralism," *Political Theory* 31, no. 2 (2001): 265–94.

but a widespread civic ethic to ensure that the citizens of liberal democracies are not just caricaturelike embodiments in the flesh of the "jealous warrior-citizen personality fierce in the defense of [only] his or her or their rights,"[39] They need to have a sense of what others' rights may be, as well.

Here we face the difficulty of all difficulties. From city-state to nation-state and in all that lies in between, citizenship has always been assumed to be derived from and in return to feed into a set of civic virtues associated with a shared identity. Disparate parts of a political community are presumed to have come together to create a whole larger than the sum of its parts through this sense of common devotion.[40] Whether it is possible to have a "cosmopolitan" version of this particular virtue is a debate that falls beyond the scope of the present analysis.[41] Suffice it to say, though, this line of thought leads us straight into the thick of the field of nationalism. The repertoire of common signifiers such as flags, anthems, national schooling systems, national languages, national churches, and of course, common(alized) historical narratives function as containers for differences within the boundaries of a designated national polity. Our original question about rights could perhaps be reformulated as: What is to happen to those who do not "naturally" fit into this repertoire?[42] Muslims in Canada, in this sense, constitute a rather apt example for undertaking this inquiry.

As the four episodes I discussed in the previous section indicate, it is not the general state policies per se (except, of course, the security regime profiling Muslims as threats) or the Charter of Rights and Freedoms per se that lies at the foundation of the problems of alienation, mistrust, and prejudice. Instead, specific interpretations of both law and the principles of the liberal democratic social order lead to marginalization of this newly emerging diaspora.[43] At least in Canada, race and ethnicity may have already been removed from the registers of officialized discrimination via the institutionalization of legal corrections and protections. Religion, however, remains as a taboo. Very similar to what happens in the traditional identification of ethnoracial minorities *only* with reference to their "race" or "ethnicity," those who are not of a mainstream Christian background mainly seem to have the attributes associated with "religiosity." Among them, Muslims stand out, because their religion cuts across regions, languages, ethnoracial groupings, and, above all, colonial and postcolonial states. Their versatile identity ironi-

---

39. Stephen Castles and Alastair Davidson, *Citizenship and Migration: Globalization and the Politics of Belonging* (London: Routledge, 2000), 212.

40. David Miller, *Citizenship and National Identity* (Cambridge: Polity Press, 2000).

41. David Held and Mathias Koenig-Archibugi, eds., *Taming Globalization: Frontiers of Governance* (Cambridge: Polity Press, 2003).

42. Rainer Baubock, *Transnational Citizenship: Membership and Rights in International Migration* (Aldershot, UK: Edward Elgar, 1998); Rainer Baubock, *Blurred Boundaries: Migration, Ethnicity, Citizenship* (Aldershot, UK: Ashgate 1994).

43. Meanwhile, it should be noted that not all immigrant groups form diasporas. For an authoritative discussion on the subject, see Nicholas van Haer, *New Diasporas: The Mass Exodus, Dispersal, and Regrouping of Migrant Communities* (London: UCL/Routledge, 1998).

cally makes it possible for their characterization to be adequately elusive to feed any form of prejudice.

One way to deal with this issue of religious difference and what is attributed to it is has been to try to turn the clock back and to pressure immigrants and refugees with a Muslim background to assimilate without exception. Asking migrants to "forget" their cultural and ethnoreligious background on account of them becoming citizens in the Western *metropoles* of the world, which are incidentally the capitals of former or recent empires, is obviously not a novel strategy. In fact, perhaps somewhat surprisingly so from the liberal Canadian point of view, this drive remains in full swing across the European Union countries. Its chief executioner is the French state vis-à-vis its Maghrebi Muslim population.[44] Respecting the dignity and origins of others while adhering to a civic ethic that encompasses all concerned may be the alternative, Canadian ideal. Interestingly, it is the same ideal that also justifies state-level and societal practices questioning the eligibility of migrants and refugees for being granted full citizenship rights in the United States.[45] Furthermore, split realities and multiple belongings endemic to the condition of living "in the diaspora," combined with the rejection or problematized status of dual citizenship, render the stated goal of "inclusiveness" rather elusive, even in Canada.[46] Participation in the democratic selection of national or local representatives in political institutions or access to welfare, health-care, or educational benefits constitute only a part of the equation pertaining to full membership in a society. The expectation of adherence to predetermined common principles, as well as reasonable and lawful conduct, constitute the actual litmus test for those who formally qualify to become citizens.

Yet how do we define reasonableness? Does it come with a color code or a geographical tag attached to it, relating to one's country of origin? Does it indicate class and education? Are all members of the middle classes and educated elite in any given country regarded with the same degree of high expectations? Why are Canadian doctors who trained in Somalia, nurses who graduated from schools in Jamaica, engineers with years of work experience in Egypt, criminologists with an established history of employment in Ukraine, deemed less qualified in their training and experience than those qualified in Canada, the United States, or the British Isles? More to the point, why would we assume that Muslim immigrants and their children are less likely to become the future doctors, lawyers, bureaucrats, and engineers in Canadian society in comparison with

---

44. Michael Blohm and Claudia Diehl, "Rights or Identity? Naturalisation Processes among 'Labor Migrants' in Germany," *International Migration Review* 37, no. 1 (2003): 133–62; Riva Kastoryano, *Negotiating Identities: States and Immigrants in France and Germany* (Princeton, NJ: Princeton University Press, 2002); Alice Bloch and Carl Levy, eds., *Refugees, Citizenship, and Social in Europe* (Houndsmills, UK: MacMillan Press, 1999); Thomas Faist, "How to Define a Foreigner?: The Symbolic Politics of Immigration in German Partisan Discourse, 1978–1992," *West European Politics* 17, no. 2 (1994): 50–72; Rodgers Brubaker, *Citizenship and Nationhood in France and Germany* (Cambridge, MA: Harvard University Press, 1992).

45. Favell and Geddes, *The Politics of Belonging*; David Jacobson, *Rights across Borders: Immigration and the Decline of Citizenship* (Baltimore: John Hopkins University Press, 1997); Jeffrey Reitz and Raymond Breton, *The Illusion of Difference: Realities of Ethnicity in Canada and the United States* (Toronto: C. D. Howe Institute, 1994).

46. Falk, "The Decline of Citizenship in an Era of Globalization."

others? Why would we assume that qualified Muslims would first and foremost serve their own community and keep a closer eye on the interests of their own diaspora, rather than Canadian society in its totality? Why would we fear that Muslims, often silently compared to Jews, would always form clusters of interest and pressure groups and carve a niche for a distinctive lifestyle, perpetually keeping themselves separate from the rest? Is there something inherently isolating or orthodox in Islam that renders the adherents of that religion less willing to participate in the life of the larger society if and when it is not dictated by Islamic principles? What makes non-Muslim Canadians envisage that if possible, Muslim immigrants would establish little independent republics of Islamic rule in the midst of Canada and would willingly fail to negotiate with others in sustaining a common life of liberal democratic virtues? What renders the condition of Muslim immigrants and refugees so exceptional in comparison with all others whose origins are also different from those from the founding "nations"?

Some may fear that multiculturalism has gone too far in Canada and that group rights have given immigrants the wrong impression that they have no obligation to learn, to adjust, to compromise in their adopted new country. Others argue that since 1980s, the issuance of a right to "difference" such as was instituted in Canada led to compartmentalized injustice under the guise of sociocultural diversity. Needless to say, furthering communal rights has its dangers and limits. Yet the notion of community is not embraced only by immigrants and refugees who do so in order to make their own lives more humane and to render their differences more acceptable, or at least tolerable, by others. With an ironic twist, Jean-Marie Le Pen's neo-Fascist movement in France, the Reform movement in Canada, certain streams of the republican tradition in the United States, and the Lega Nord movement in Italy are all communal claims made on behalf of the majority for having the ultimate say in what defines who is a true citizen. In other words, there may be no simple institutional or legal solution to the problem of developing and sustaining a civic ethics that in turn could guarantee at least a minimum degree of "conviviality" and respect for difference in liberal democratic societies.

Furthermore, as I already argued, citizenship is often defined as a consensual agreement between people who are already members of a political community. Little or no allowance is made for those who may be joining in later. Indeed, traditional citizenship ethics going back to Pericles say very little about issues such as "social capital," which is essential to the condition of immigrants and refugees.[47] To avoid the sin of anachronism, I should explain that social capital refers to "ageless" phenomena such as the trust, norms, and associational networks that facilitate coordinated action in society.[48] All the more importantly, it signifies an at-large sense of reciprocity in the care of common principles

---

47. Derek Heater, *Citizenship: The Civic Ideal in World History, Politics and Education* (Manchester, UK: Manchester University Press, 2004).

48. David Halpern, *Social Capital* (Cambridge: Polity Press, 2005); Barry Ferguson and Lance Roberts, eds., *Social Capital and Community in Canada and Germany* (Winnipeg: St. John's College Press, 2004); Robert Putnam, ed., *Democracies in Flux: The Evolution of Social Capital in Contemporary Society* (New York: Oxford University Press, 2002).

and on account of long-term benefits. Therefore, it can be acquired and utilized by anyone who understands and appreciates the principles behind it. The core idea related to the concept of social capital is that if there is not a significant overlap of norms and networks of active civic engagement, the end result is a malfunctioning democracy and citizenship regime that only claims to be fully developed. Social capital, when taken as a valiant attempt at developing and sustaining a kind of *evolving* civic virtue that acknowledges difference as an integral part of politics, can thus lead to the establishment of a framework within which multidenominational, multiethnic, multiracial grids of belonging further exacerbated by class issues might be addressed openly and with some hope. Tolerance, in this context, requires more than putting up with difference within set limits and on pragmatic grounds.[49] It means negotiating with others who may challenge the status quo as newcomers. Hence, I believe it is apt to underline the fact that in the discussion pertaining to Muslims in Canada, precious little attention has been paid to the meaning of social capital, and the results of this gap—or lack—in attention are not admirable.

This brings us back to the basic premises informing anti-immigrant, antirefugee, antiminority, and anti-immigration movements. It is true that these movements, their followers, and precincts vary considerably in character from country to country. However, what is often overlooked is that they are not limited to the aggressive rhetoric of the British Conservative Party, the French Front National, the German Republikaner, the Deutsche Volksunion, the Ku Klux Klan in the United States, the One Nation Party in Australia, or the Reform Party in Canada. Racism, like fascism, is a societal phenomenon. Both of these largely function as enhancers of "superior" identities, which is a yearning endemic to any situation where there is a perceived threat to the networks of safety in a given society.[50] Therefore, it would be a mistake to identify Muslims in Canada as an exceptional case of immigrants suffering from undue prejudice. They are the latest link in a rather long chain.

The profile of the Muslim communities in Canada supports this observation. Muslims arriving in Canada during the 1950s were typically skilled workers and professionals who were brought to change the structure of the economy. This coincided with the inauguration of a program in Islamic Studies at McGill University in 1952 and a decade later at the University of Toronto, attracting both Muslim scholars and students from abroad. Bilingualism and multiculturalism also played a crucial role in the further establishment of a "Canadian Muslim" identity. The next phase of the Muslim migration to Canada was marked by the influx of teachers, technocrats, and, later, entrepreneurs. This began in the mid-1960s, with the replacement of immigration quotas on Asians and Africans by a more technocratic selection criterion based on education and skills.

49, Again, certain limits of toleration will have to remain, because repressing others' opinion, freedoms, or life chances could not be endorsed under the name of toleration, no matter what the circumstance may be. T. M. Scanlon, *The Difficulty of Tolerance: Essays in Political Philosophy* (Cambridge: Cambridge University Press, 2003).

50. Étienne Balibar and Immanuel Wallerstein, *Race, Nation, Class: Ambiguous Identities*, trans. of Etienne Balibar by Chris Turner (London: Verso, 1991).

Subsequently, many Muslims, most in the prime working age group, were admitted into the country based on their qualifications in keeping with the expanding labor market. As the spouses of these immigrants arrived, Muslim immigrants in Canada experienced their first baby boom.

Furthermore, there is little reason to suspect that, at least in the case of Canada, Muslim immigrants constituted an undue burden on the public purse, hence causing the emergent resentment. Since the majority of Muslims in Canada are in the prime labor force age group of twenty-five to forty-four years old, proportionally, they withdraw much less from the system and contribute much more to it than the Canadian population as a whole. According to the Muslim community's own estimates, Muslim families derive only 4 percent of their total income from social-security programs—including old-age pensions, unemployment-insurance benefits, family allowances, welfare payments, and so on. By comparison, this percentage for all families in Canada is 7 percent. The comparisons become even more striking with respect to the financing of the social safety net: While there are only five people working to support each one in retirement in the country as a whole, among Muslims, there are fifteen workers to support each retiree. Furthermore, Muslim immigrants participated in almost every major development throughout the economic history of Canada, and thus the xenophobic image of them keeping only to themselves or running small retail shops cannot be more inaccurate. They were part of the labor force building the Canadian Pacific railway in the late nineteenth century, and they were among the pioneers who opened up Alberta and Saskatchewan for cultivation and settlement in the beginning of the twentieth century. Skilled and professional Muslim immigrants were an integral part of the economic growth of the 1960s and 1970s. Muslim educators, doctors, and engineers responded to the need for new professionals as the baby boom children of the post–Second World War period entered into grade schools and universities. They have been in Canada long enough to be accorded the trust and acceptance to become full members of society, not only in formal, but also in normative terms. Consequently, their identification as the "Muslim diaspora" and thus the continual essentialization of their individual identities based on their communal and, above all, religious affiliation constitutes a major impediment in the way of the functional interpretation of the ideal of liberal democratic citizenship.

Conclusion

In contemporary Canadian society, marginalization is not suffered only by immigrants who are marked by their ethnoreligious and racial difference. Children, single parents, female heads of households, the disabled, the homeless, the minimum-wage worker, the Native Canadian, continue to experience it firsthand in its many disguises. Meanwhile, the connections made between class, race, gender, and ethnoreligious identity tend to stop short of allowing us to pay enough attention to the unmediated and subtle effects of the clash between insiders and newcomers, outsiders and denizens of Canadian society. In the context of Muslims in Canada, I have proposed that questions of identity, in particular, communal and/or diasporic identity, can be attended to only in the context of other questions. Among many, one specific inquiry stands out: How does one become what is defined as "Canadian" while remaining a unique individual with idiosyncratic, though politically meaningful choices? Incidentally, this was the old question that burdened both the creators and the condemners of Canadian multiculturalism.[51] In addition, where does communal identity end, where does individual identity start, and, what does citizenship entail with reference to each of these two ways of addressing membership? Canadian political philosophy has made noteworthy contributions in this field of interrogation.[52] In addition, scholars of diaspora, immigration, and refugee studies have endeavored to produce answers to the conundrums of what was hoped to be postnational citizenship in addressing these and similar tensions.[53] Often, these scholars have entertained the choice of supranational regimes of citizenship and transnational networks of rights as more relevant than the constricting and seemingly outmoded "national" context. This alternative framing of citizenship has delivered the message that national belonging, and especially its ethnoreligious and racial underpinnings, do not constitute the sine qua non of membership in a political community and acquisition of the rights thereof. Such counterintuitive flexing of muscles exists in its most developed form within the context of regional political organs such as the European Union, though whether agreements proposed EU Constitution or NAFTA (the North American Free Trade Agreement) qualify for lofty honors is open to much heated debate.

Furthermore, particularly in its European embodiment, the issue pertaining to qualification for citizenship rights continues to simmer beneath the polished surface of the EU rhetoric. Due to the limited political and civil rights of large numbers of settled immigrant workers and refugees who do not possess or could not acquire citizenship in a member state of the European Union, a "democracy deficit" seems to go hand in hand with xenophobia in the Old World.[54] The problem faced in Europe and elsewhere is not so much the management of differences in terms of starting points—that is, being born to parentage holding national citizenship, as opposed to arriving in a country from outside. What is at stake here is whether the supranational, cosmopolitan project of membership rights can indeed avoid the pitfalls of exclusivism that has historically been endemic to nationalism. The changed settings such as the EU or, indeed, the Canadian federal state, which are purportedly more democratic, more decentralized, and more open to changes, do not always deliver the Promised Land. As the case of Muslims in Canada illustrates, fear and lack of trust are not just tactics employed by far-right movements when it comes to how we treat strangers among us. Their expressions are manifold and leave an imprint

---

51. Charles Taylor, et. al., *Multiculturalism*.

52. Joseph Carens, *Culture, Citizenship and Community: A Contextual Exploration of Justice as Evenhandedness* (New York: Oxford University Press, 2000); Will Kymlicka, *Politics in the Vernacular: Nationalism, Multiculturalism and Citizenship* (Oxford: Oxford University Press, 2001).

53. Baubock, *Transnational Citizenship*; Soysal, *The Limits of Citizenship*.

54. Jamal Malik, *Muslims in Europe: From Margins to the Core* (Piscataway, NJ: Transaction Publishers, 2004); Blohm and Diel, "Rights or Identity?"

at every level of politics, from the local and the communal to the international and the supranational.

Since the time that the first mosque was built there, the hopes and aspirations of the Muslim communities in Canada underwent several transformations. The immigrants' and refugees' changing social and religious needs were in many ways directly related to the search for identity and a desire for a broader base of its acknowledgment in Canadian society. From self-preservation manifested in the early years, to the formation of local community associations, to an identity revolving around the mosque, Muslims in Canada gradually established themselves as a cohesive community. They are now aspiring to make claims and effect a difference in the country's educational, social, economic, and political institutions as a diaspora.[55]

The resurgence of Islam among young people of Muslim heritage and yet often born to secular parents—especially at a time when other young people are abandoning their forefathers' religions—is one of the most significant phenomena in Canadian religious history. It appears to be the case that the identity crises suffered by these youths is expected to be resolved via firm religious affiliation. If so, what kind of society have we created that forces people to claim a religion to have a recognized stake in our present and future? Political liberalism has been rather late in admitting that cultural and political tradition do not bias us, but actually position us. Because strength of conviction constitutes no substitute for the force of argument, liberalism has to provide evidence beyond belief in the possibility of neutral arbitration with regard to public reasoning. It is the recognition of this tension between reason and faith that provides a deeper understanding of the conditions under which the liberal democratic ideal is expected to work.

As things stand, the liberal democratic ideal is failing to create a New World. As the case of Muslims in Canada demonstrates, it clings onto Old World notions of essentialized difference, religion being the among the most potent and the most recent to come to the fore, in order qualify membership in the form of substantive, politically viable citizenship. The irony is that many who emigrated from these Old Worlds did not at first envisage the extensiveness of such rigid categorizations. And yet, they are given no choice but to act as Muslim immigrants and diasporas, because the society at large insists on classifying their claims for existence in such stark terms and almost at the expense of all else.

As an end note, it is important to underline the fact that Muslim diasporas in Europe are characterized by many as having a divided and relatively ineffective political voice.[56]

---

55. Daood Hassan Hamdani "Muslims and Islam in Canada," in *Muslims and Islam in the American Continent*, vol. 1 of *The Encyclopedia of Muslim Minorities in the World*, ed. Ali Kettani and M. M'Bow (forthcoming). The full text can be found via a search at http://www.muslim-canada.org (last accessed on August 24, 2007).

56. Steven Pfaff and Anthony Gill, "Will a Million Muslims March? Muslim Interest Organizations and Political Integration in Europe," Comparative Political Studies 39, no. 7 (2006): 803–28; Jytte Klausen, *The Islamic Challenge: Politics and Religion in Western Europe* (London: Oxford University Press, 2005); Joel S. Fetzer and J. Christopher Soper, *Muslims and the State in Britain, France and Germany* (Cambridge: Cambridge University Press, 2005); Pippa Norris and Ronald Inglehart, *Sacred and Secular: Religion and Politics Worldwide* (Cambridge: Cambridge University Press, 2004); Frank J. Buijs and Jan

This is despite the fact that the continent's polities have had direct dealings with Muslim minorities since 1960s. More specifically, Muslim interest organizations functioning in Western democratic politics are often seen as making collective action difficult and operating based on the logic of factional self-righteousness and small-scale interests. This is in part due to the fact that organizations representing conservative Muslim interests stand in direct opposition to those engaged in secular politics, treating Muslim identity not in terms of the sort of religious commitment common to many faiths, but in terms of ethno-racial markers and cultural heritage. Thus, centralization is not often possible or, indeed, desired. In the absence of a dominant culture marked by Islam or a state that embraces a chosen set of Islamic principles in jurisprudence or policies pertaining to social justice, European Muslim communities are thus seen as led by sectarian impulses in terms of their organizational structures. Religion is seen in this context as the main determinant of identity.

The remaining question is why religious organizations are the main vehicle for claims making and asserting interests in the case of immigrants with a Muslim background. What makes Islam into an ersatz homeland, even among the second-generation and third-generation immigrants in societies that preach principled toleration and, in many cases, multiculturalist inclusion policies? If public expressions of religious commitment continue to be portrayed and perceived as a sure sign of failure to integrate by the larger society, religious organizations may have no other option but to occupy the front lines of organized expressions of interest and concern, armed with the growing network of transnational Islamist networks. The mobilization achieved by Muslim organizations with a religion-related mandate does not necessarily exclude the communities represented by them from public affairs and regularized relations with secular democracies. Nonetheless, it does limit points of entry for the exchange to issues concerning religion. In this form, the interaction often inevitably takes the form of a clash between secular public norms and religious private interests. This form of narrow interest articulation then leads to the self-fulfilling prophesy of the perception of immigrants with Muslim heritage primarily in terms of their religion.

In this larger context, at present, at least, available data from both North America and Europe point to the fact that civic participation among Muslim immigrants is primarily linked to mosque attendance and involvement with religious organizations.[57] Muslim immigrants are currently more concerned with their own communities and rights issues than with larger and mainstream political matters in their adopted homes. This is no doubt subject to variations depending on the political involvement of community

Rath, *Muslims in Europe* (New York: Russell Sage Foundation, 2002); W. A. R. Shahid and P. S. van Koningsveld, eds., *Religious Freedom and the Neutrality of the State: The Position of Islam in the European Union* (Leuven, Belgium: Peeters, 2001).

57. Jamal Amaney, "The Political Participation and Engagement of Muslim Americans: Mosque Involvement and Group Consciousness," *American Politics Research* 33, no. 4 (2005): 521–44; Karen Isaksen Leonard, *Muslims in the United States: The State of Research* (New York: Russell Sage Foundation, 2003); M. Jones-Correa and D. Leal, "Political Participation: Does Religion Matter?" *Political Research Quarterly* 4 (2001): 751–70.

members in their home countries, their investment in transnational networks of activism, and the conditions pertaining to the internal and international status of the societies and states from which they immigrated. In addition to this qualifier, one should also note that mosques in Western democracies are linked to hubs of political activity, civic participation, and group consciousness. They have become "homes away from home" for at least some of the Muslim immigrants, a place where common problems affecting the communities are addressed and new forms of attachments are fostered.[58] However, to attribute this trend to Islam would be a grave mistake. How we deal with immigrants and refugees arriving from countries with Muslim majority populations has less to do with the ascendancy or rebirth of the mosque as the quintessential point of anchorage for an emergent Muslim diaspora and more to do with how the adopted homes of these communities treat difference.

Bibliography

Arthurs, Harry. *The New Economy and the Demise of Industrial Citizenship*. Kingston, Ont.: IRC Press, 1997.

——, and Brent Arnold. "Does the Charter Matter?" Unpublished draft paper, 2005.

Atkinson, Rowland, and Gary Bridge, eds. *Gentrification in a Global Context: The New Urban Colonialism*. London: Routledge, 2005.

Bader, Veit. "Democratic Institutional Pluralism and Cultural Diversity." In *The Social Construction of Diversity: Recasting the Master Narrative of Industrial Nations*. Edited by Danielle Juteau and Christiane Harzig. Oxford: Berghahn, 2003.

——. "Religious Diversity and Democratic Institutional Pluralism." *Political Theory* 31, no. 2 (2001): 265–94.

Balibar, Étienne, and Immanuel Wallerstein. *Race, Nation, Class: Ambiguous Identities*. Trans. of Etienne Balibar by Chris Turner. London: Verso, 1991.

Baubock, Rainer. *Blurred Boundaries: Migration, Ethnicity, Citizenship*. Aldershot, UK: Ashgate, 1998.

——. *Transnational Citizenship: Membership and Rights in International Migration*. Aldershot, UK: Edward Elgar, 1994.

Behiels, Michael D. *Canada's Francophone Minority Communities: Constitutional Renewal and the Winning of School Governance*. Montreal: McGill-Queens University Press, 2005.

Bloch, Alice, and Carl Levy, eds. *Refugees, Citizenship and Social Policy in Europe*. Houndsmills, UK: MacMillan Press, 1999.

---

58. Michael W. Suleiman, ed., *Arabs in America: Building a New Future* (Philadelphia: Temple University Press, 2000).

Blohm, Michael, and Claudia Diehl. "Rights or Identity? Naturalisation Processes among 'Labor Migrants' in Germany." *International Migration Review* 37, no. 1 (2003): 133–62.

Bramadot, Paul, and David Seljak. *Religion and Ethnicity in Canada.* Toronto: Pearson Longman Press, 2005.

Brubaker, Rogers. *Citizenship and Nationhood in France and Germany.* Cambridge, MA: Harvard University Press, 1992.

Buijs, Frank J., and Jan Rath, *Muslims in Europe: The State of Research.* New York: Russell Sage Foundation, 2002.

Canadian Center for Justice Statistics Series. *Religious Groups in Canada.* Ottawa: Statistics Canada, 2001.

Carens, Joseph. *Culture, Citizenship and Community: A Contextual Exploration of Justice as Even-handedness.* New York: Oxford University Press, 2000.

Castles, Stephen, and Alastair Davidson. *Citizenship and Migration: Globalization and the Politics of Belonging.* London: Routledge, 2000.

Faist, Thomas. "How to Define a Foreigner?: The Symbolic Politics of Immigration in German Partisan Discourse, 1978–1992." *West European Politics* 17, no. 2 (1994): 50–72.

Falk, Richard. "The Decline of Citizenship in an Era of Globalization." *Citizenship Studies* 4, no. 1 (2000): 5–17.

Favell, Adrian, and Andrew Geddes, eds. *The Politics of Belonging: Migrants and Minorities in Contemporary Europe.* Brookfield, VT: Ashgate Publishing, 2003.

Ferguson, Barry, and Lance Roberts, eds. *Social Capital and Community in Canada and Germany.* Winnipeg: St. John's College Press, 2004.

Fetzer, Joel S., and J. Christopher Soper. *Muslims and the State in Britain, France and Germany.* Cambridge: Cambridge University Press, 2005.

Haddad, Yvonne Yazbeck. *Muslims in the West: from Sojourners to Citizens.* Oxford: Oxford University Press, 2002.

———, and Barbara Freyer Stowasserm, eds. *Islamic Law and the Challenges of Modernity.* Walnut Creek, CA: Altamira Press, 2004.

———, and Jane Smith, eds. *Muslim Minorities in the West: Visible and Invisible.* Walnut Creek, CA: Altamira Press, 2002.

———, Jane Smith, and John Esposito, eds. *Religion and Immigration: Christian, Jewish, and Muslim Experiences in the U.S.* Walnut Creek, CA: Altamira Press, 2003.

Halpern, David. *Social Capital.* Cambridge: Polity Press, 2005.

Heater, Derek. *Citizenship: The Civic Ideal in World History, Politics and Education.* Manchester, UK: Manchester University Press, 2004.

Held, David, and Mathias Koenig-Archibugi, eds. *Taming Globalization: Frontiers of Governance*. Cambridge: Polity Press, 2003.

Hensel, Howard, ed. *Sovereignty and the Global Community: The Quest for Order in the International System*. Aldershot, UK: Ashgate, 2004.

Holton, John. *Liberalism, Multiculturalism, and Toleration*. New York: St. Martin's Press, 1993.

Ilir, Disha. *Location and Patterns of Anti-Arab and Anti-Muslim Hate Crimes*. Charlotte, NC: Southern Sociological Society Publications, 2005.

Isin, Engin. *Being Political: Genealogies of Citizenship*. Minneapolis: University of Minnesota Press, 2002.

———, and Bryan Turner. *Handbook of Citizenship Studies*. London: Sage Publications, 2002.

Jacobson, David. *Rights across Borders: Immigration and the Decline of Citizenship*. Baltimore: John Hopkins University Press, 1997.

Jamal, Amaney. "The Political Participation and Engagement of Muslim Americans: Mosque Involvement and Group Consciousness." *American Politics Research* 33, no. 4 (2005): 521–44.

Jones-Correa, M., and D. Leal. "Political Participation: Does Religion Matter?" *Political Research Quarterly* 4 (2001): 751–70.

Kastoryano, Riva. *Negotiating Identities: States and Immigrants in France and Germany*. Princeton, NJ: Princeton University Press, 2002.

King, Anthony D., ed. *Representing the City: Ethnicity, Capital and Culture in the 21st Century*. London: Macmillan, 1996.

Klausen, Jytte. *The Islamic Challenge: Politics and Religion in Western Europe*. London: Oxford University Press, 2005.

Klopp, Brett. "The Political Incorporation of EU Foreigners before and after Maastricht: The New Local Politics in Germany." *Journal of Ethnic and Migration Studies* 28, no. 2 (2002): 239–57.

Knox, Paul L., and Peter J. Taylor, eds. *World Cities in a World-System*. Cambridge: Cambridge University Press, 1995.

Kymlicka, Will. *Politics in the Vernacular: Nationalism, Multiculturalism and Citizenship*. Oxford: Oxford University Press, 2001.

Laborde, Cecile. "Secular Philosophy and Muslim Headscarves in Schools." *The Journal of Political Philosophy* 13, no. 3 (2005): 305–29.

Leonard, Karen Isaksen. *Muslims in the United States: The State of Research*. New York: Russell Sage Foundation, 2003.

Levinas, Emmanuel. *Totality and Infinity*. Translated by Alfonso Lingis. Pittsburgh, PA: Duquesne University Press, 1969.

Loney, Martin. *The Pursuit of Division: Race, Gender and Preferential Hiring in Canada.* Montreal: McGill-Queens University Press, 2003.

Lyon, David, and Marguerite Van Die Lyon, eds. *Rethinking Church, State and Modernity: Canada between Europe and the United States.* Toronto: University of Toronto Press, 2000.

Malik, Jamal. *Muslims in Europe: From Margins to the Core.* Piscataway, NJ: Transaction Publishers, 2004.

Mills, Kurt. H*uman Rights in the Emerging Global Order: A New Sovereignty?* New York: St. Martin's Press, 1998.

Miller, David. *Citizenship and National Identity.* Cambridge: Polity Press, 2000.

Norris, Pippa, and Ronald Inglehart. *Sacred and Secular: Religion and Politics Worldwide.* Cambridge: Cambridge University Press, 2004.

Ontario Human Rights Commission. *Policy on Genital Female Mutilation.* Available on-line at http://www.ohrc.on.ca/english/publications/fgm-policy.shtml under "Publications."

Pfaff, Steven, and Anthony Gill. "Will a Million Muslims March? Muslim Interest Organizations and Political Integration in Europe." *Comparative Political Studies* 39, no. 7 (2006): 803–28.

Pries, Ludger. *Migration and Transnational Spaces.* Aldershot, UK: Ashgate and the Danish Centre for Migration and Ethnic Studies, 1998.

Putnam, Robert, ed. *Democracies in Flux: The Evolution of Social Capital in Contemporary Society.* New York: Oxford University Press, 2002.

Quick, Abdullah Hakim. "Muslim Rituals, Practices and Social Problems." *Polyphony* (Multicultural History Society of Ontario) 12 (1990): 120–24.

Rawls, John. *A Theory of Justice.* Boston, MA: Harvard University Press, 1971.

Reitz, Jeffrey, and Raymond Breton. *The Illusion of Difference: Realities of Ethnicity in Canada and the United States.* Toronto: C. D. Howe Institute, 1994.

Sassen, Saskia. *Globalization and Its Discontents.* New York: New Press, 1998.

Scanlon, T. M. *The Difficulty of Tolerance: Essays in Political Philosophy.* Cambridge: Cambridge University Press, 2003.

Schaebler, Birgit, and Leif Stenberg, eds. *Globalization and the Muslim World: Culture, Religion, and Modernity.* Syracuse, NY: Syracuse University Press, 2004.

Schuster, Liza, and John Solomos. "Rights and Wrongs across European Borders: Migrants, Minorities and Citizenship. *Citizenship Studies* 6, no. 1 (2002): 37–54.

Sellers, Mortimer, ed. *The New World Order: Sovereignty, Human Rights, and the Self-determination of Peoples.* Oxford: Berg, 1996.

Serajul, Syed. "Crisis of Identity in a Multi-cultural Society. The Case of Muslims in Canada. *Intellectual Discourse* 8, no. 1 (2000): 1–18.

Silverstein, Paul. Algeria in France: *Transpolitics, Race, and Nation.* Bloomington: Indiana University Press, 2004.

Shahid, W. A. R., and P. S. van Koningsveld, eds. *Religious Freedom and the Neutrality of the State: The Position of Islam in the European Union.* Leuven, Belgium: Peeters, 2001.

Smidt, C. "Religion and Civic Engagement: A Comparative Analysis." *The Annals of the American Academy of Political and Social Science* 565 (1999): 176–92.

Soysal, Yasemin. *The Limits of Citizenship: Migrants and Postnational Citizenship in Europe.* Chicago: University of Chicago Press, 1994.

Statistics Canada. *1981 Census of Canada.* Volume 2, provincial series. Population, Economic Characteristics/Recensement du Canada de 1981. Volume 2, série provinciale. Population, caractéristiques économiqes. Ottawa: Statistics Canada, 1984.

Suleiman, Michael W., ed. *Arabs in America: Building a New Future.* Philadelphia: Temple University Press, 2000.

Taylor, Charles, et al. *Multiculturalism: Examining the Politics of Recognition.* Princeton, NJ: Princeton University Press, 1994.

Van Haer, Nicholas. *New Diasporas The Mass Exodus, Dispersal, and Regrouping of Migrant Communities.* London: UCL/Routledge, 1998.

Van Selm, Joanne, and Edward Newman, eds. *Refugees and Forced Displacement: International Security, Human vulnerability, and the State.* Tokyo: United Nations University Press, 2003.

Creolization and Diaspora: The Cultural Politics of Divergence and (Some) Convergence

By Robin Cohen

At first sight, creolization and diasporas are divergent forms of cultural politics with different sensibilities and different trajectories. The concept of creolization centers on the cross-fertilization between different cultures as they interact. When creolization occurs, participants select particular elements from incoming or inherited cultures, endow these with meanings different from those they possessed in the original culture, and then creatively merge these to create totally new varieties that supersede the prior forms. Creolization is thus a "here and now" sensibility that erodes old roots and stresses fresh growth in a novel place of identification. A diasporic consciousness, by contrast, generally reflects a degree of unease with cultural identities in the current location. A "homeland" or a looser notion of "home" is reconstructed and revalorized through fabulation, recovered historical memory, and social organization. The past provides a continuing pole of attraction and identification. By contrasting these two forms of cultural politics, I hope to illuminate both. Perhaps unexpectedly, there are also possibilities and examples of convergence, which I explore as well.

Fugitive Power

Melting Pot

Take a pinch of white man
Wrap him up in black skin
Add a touch of blue blood
And a little bitty bit of red indian boy
Oh like a curly latin kinkies

Oh lordy, lordy, mixed with yellow chinkies, yeah
You know you lump it all together
And you got a recipe for a get along scene
Oh what a beautiful dream . . .
We should all get together in a lovin machine . . .

(Lyrics from "Melting Pot," released November 15, 1969 by Blue Mink)

The lyrics of a 1960s popular song hardly form the basis of a serious social analysis, yet the very naiveté of the sentiments cannot but evoke some sympathy from those who are troubled by the destructive effects of a resurgent nationalism (for example in the United States), an unyielding ethnicity (as in the Balkans and Rwanda), and fundamentalist religious affinities (as in the Middle East). In the face of such experiences, which are hardly unusual, the reader might wonder, in evoking a song by Blue Mink, whether the author is still in the grip of a hallucinogenic haze lingering from an earlier era.

My response to claims about the current resurgence of nationalistic, ethnic, and religious absolutism is twofold. First, it is common to find such dogmatic assertions of identity in the face of a subterranean shift in reality. At a surface level, a resurgent and invincible U.S. nationalism seems to have been signaled with the invasion of Iraq in 2003 and the declaration of a "Long War" against terrorism, especially Islamic jihadists. Some of cracks in this seemingly impregnable surface emerge on closer examination. The United States is overextended militarily, its share of global GNP is declining, its erstwhile allies (such as Germany and Turkey) are not so compliant, its enemies (such as Iran and Venezuela) are openly defiant, its trade and fiscal deficits are massive, it is facing sustained resistance in Iraq, and it has lost the soft war (the power to persuade) in many parts of the world. U.S. nationalism is thus better understood as the thrashing about of a dinosaur, not the emergence of a new species. Similar arguments can be mounted in the cases of at least some other strident expressions of nationalism, ethnicity, and religious zealotry.

Second, by contrast, we easily miss subtle, discreet, but undeclared social changes that cumulatively, but slowly, generate major shifts in social behavior and consciousness. Behind the thunderous nationalist, fundamentalist, and monocultural noises are the soft, but pervasive sounds of diversity, complexity, and hybridity. This is akin to what Zygmunt Bauman has described as "the new lightness and fluidity of the increasingly mobile, slippery, shifty, evasive and fugitive power."[1] In contrast to the naked, brutal, heralded power (say, of the Pentagon), my notion of fugitive power stresses the hidden, subtle, subrosa, elusive (i.e., difficult to catch or to detect) forms of power found in collective shifts of attitudes and social behavior. Creolization is one form of fugitive power.

---

1. Zygmunt Bauman, *Liquid Modernity* (Cambridge: Polity Press, 2000), 14.

The Etymology and Implications of "Creole" and "Creolization"

The terms "creole" and "creolization" are used in many different contexts and generally in an inconsistent way. It is instructive to start with the origins of the root word. It was probably derived from the Latin *creara* ("created originally").[2] The most common historical use was the Spanish *criollo*, which described the children of Spanish colonizers born in the Caribbean. The Furetière dictionary (1690) uses the word *criole* in this way. The French transformed the word to *créole* and, Marie-José Jolivet has argued that it become synonymous with any white person born in the colonies.[3] However, the racially exclusive definition, which confined the term to whites, had been challenged as early as 1722, when in a four-volume travelogue by a French missionary, Father Labat, a distinction was drawn between "Créole slaves" and "traded slaves." "Creole corn" and "Creole livestock" soon followed.[4] The implication was clear: "Creole" referred to something or someone that had foreign (normally metropolitan) origins and that had now become somewhat localized. There is a further implication, though this was less explicit. There would have been no point in distinguishing a "Creole" from a "colonizer" if there were no perceived differences between the two. The Creole had become different, taking on some local "color," a word that I use deliberately to suggest a figurative and emotional relationship with the local landscape and a social and sometimes sexual relationship with the local people.

And who might those locals be? Ultimately, all of us are migrants. The DNA "architecture" revealed by the Human Genome Project conclusively situates the common origin of humankind in particular parts of Africa. Humans living elsewhere were subsequently dispersed by the disintegration of the continents or by relocation. Flight from natural disasters, adverse climatic changes, and competition from other species or communities, as well as practices such as transhumance—the herding of livestock to seasonal pastures— were common causes of movement. If they lived elsewhere for a long time or bonded emotionally with the local territory, people claimed autochthonous or indigenous status. They frequently ascribed divine properties to the earth, the fauna, the flora, the climate, and the geological features in their places of settlement.

You will notice we now have a trichotomy (and also an insufficient description, as we will see later, but it will do for now). First, we have the colonial, born in the metropole or anchored there psychologically and affectively. Next, we have the creole, born in a new place from foreign parents, who nonetheless identifies with his or her immediate surroundings or is so identified by others. Finally, we have the indigenous people whose had lived there for so long they are assumed to, or claim to, "belong" to the land.

---

2. Ernst Cashmore, *Dictionary of Race and Ethnic Relations*, 3rd ed. (London: Routledge, 2004), 94.

3. Marie-José Jolivet, *Jeux d'identités: Étude comparative à partir de la Caraïbe* (Paris: Harmattan, 1993); and Marie-José Jolivet, *La question créole: Esai de sociologie sur la Guyane française* (Paris: Editions de l'Office de la recherché scientifique et technique outré-mer, 1982).

4. Jolivet, *La question créole*.

Reexamining Mixed-Heritage Populations

Any full account of creolization would have to include discussion of creolized popular cultural practices (especially in food, music, and dancing), syncretic religions, and Creole languages. Whereas these have been studied for decades, new understandings of creolization have emerged more recently in sociology, anthropology, and the study and practice of cultural politics. This has led to a renewed interest in recognized Creole societies in countries as diverse as Sierra Leone, Nicaragua, the Guyanas, Cape Verde, the Caribbean islands, and coastal zones on the edge of the Caribbean Sea, Réunion, Mauritius, Seychelles, Liberia, and Nigeria. More ambitiously, the three examples that I discuss below—the substantial mixed-heritage populations in Brazil, South Africa, and the United States—also have been reexamined through the lenses of creolization.

Brazil: Official and Subversive Creolization

In the case of Brazil, Christopher Wagley maintained that "by the end of slavery the intermediate freeman class made up of people of Negroid, Indian and Caucasian racial stocks, and of a wide variety of *mestiços,* was numerically more important that the white elite or the Negro slaves."[5] Subsequent census data in Brazil use the categories *branca* (white), *preta* (black), *parda* (brown/*mestizo*), *amarela* (yellow/East Indian) and *indigena* (native/indigenous). In the 2000 census, 66 million (of the total of 169.7 million) described themselves as *parda* (39 percent) compared with 8.7 million categorized as *parda* in the total population of 41.2 million in 1940 (21.1 percent).[6]

Livio Sansone's innovative account of "blackness without ethnicity" in Brazil starts with the observation that many social scientists studying Brazilian society have been highly skeptical of the official, elite, and popular celebrations of hybridity and mixture—in which, in effect, creolization has been reconstituted as the national ideology. Such scholars are determined to reduce the Brazilian experience to the terrain of ethnic segmentation familiar to the pattern of Anglophone race relations. Brazilian society comprises, they say, Afro-Brazilians, Italian Brazilians, Japanese Brazilians, and so on. Such views, Sansone argues, are erroneous, because Brazilian forms of ethnicity are constructed only fitfully, episodically, and situationally. In Brazil, ethnicity is never "strong" or determinant and certainly never is primordial.

He also has reservations about the idea of a "pigmentocracy," a color continuum with many intervals, but with the high-ranking whites at the top and low-ranking blacks at the bottom. The statistics of self-identification still confirm a general aspiration to whiteness or lightness, but this does not mean that a positive idea, image, and imaginary of blackness in Brazil is not salient. Sansone suggests that in the past, blackness was associated with those locked into a diasporic tradition, asserting their African roots, and

---

5. Christopher Wagley, ed., *Race and Class in Rural Brazil* (Paris: UNESCO, 1952), 143.

6. Livio Sansone, *Blackness without Ethnicity: Constructing Race in Brazil* (New York: Palgrave Macmillan, 2003), 22–24.

"with closeness to nature, magical powers, body language, sexuality and sensuality."[7] Now, however, black Brazilian culture is reaching out to modernity and even to globalization via the intermediation of Jamaica, the United States, and rest of the "black Atlantic." (As the last expression indicates, Sansone is influenced by the work of Paul Gilroy, whom he acknowledges fulsomely.)[8] "Black" has become revalorized among the young, the better-educated, and those plugged into international youth and musical currents. Other affirmative aspects of black culture include the elaborate Angolan-derived martial art *capoeira*, the syncretic religion Candomblé, and the famous Carnival. These have all created "black spaces" that invert and subvert the pigmentocracy.

In short, if we return to our central concept of creolization, we can argue that creolization has developed in two directions—the first involving a state-led appropriation of "mixture" that is identified with the Brazilian national character and celebrated accordingly. The official tourist board, for example, suggests that while tourists think first of the country's natural beauty, they discover "such hospitality that they soon become enchanted with the mixture of colors, races and cultures of the people, as well."[9] The second version of creolization is more subversive. It rejects bland renditions of "mixture" and relies much less on a recovered memory of Africa by a relatively isolated population displaced by slavery. Instead, those who have been marginalized by poverty and cultural alienation have discovered new circuits of cultural capital that they can tap into to create alternative and dissident forms of "black" creolization.

South Africa: From Colored to Creole

A fundamental reassessment of mixed identities in South Africa has also taken place in the wake of political democratization. As is well known, South Africa has a large mixed population. In mid-2005, the "Coloured" population group (a first approximation of those of mixed heritage) numbered 4.1 million out of the total population of 46.8 million. At 8.8 percent of the total, the Coloured group is just below the proportion of whites in the population.[10] The attempt to enforce racial segregation had to await the coming to power in 1948 of the (white) Nationalist Party, the Population Registration Act, and the elaborated ideology of apartheid articulated notably by Hendrik Verwoerd.[11] The South African case was particularly absurd in that creolization had reached such a stage of maturity that the mixed population had to be recognized in itself as one of the primordial ethnic groups—so the South African apartheid regime distinguished between whites, Bantus (Africans), Asians, and Coloureds, the last rendered with a capital letter in order

---

7. Ibid., 12.

8. Paul Gilroy, *The Black Atlantic: Modernity and Double Consciousness* (London: Verso, 1993).

9. Available on-line at http://www.turismo.gov.br (last accessed September 2, 2007).

10. Statistics South Africa, *Mid-year Population Estimates, 2005* (Pretoria: Government of South Africa, 2005), 9.

11. See Robin Cohen, *Endgame in South Africa?: The Changing Structures and Ideology of Apartheid* (London: James Currey, 1986), 1–14.

to signify its supposed primordial status. In fact, of course, the colored community was none other than the creole community.

In common with the implacable refusal by many intellectuals and political activists in postapartheid South Africa to accept apartheid nomenclature, Zimitri Erasmus firmly rejects biological categories and insists that "colouredness must be understood as a creolized cultural identity,"[12] an identity, moreover, that is derived not merely from two "pure" traditions, African and European, but from multiple sources that themselves are impure and contingent:

> In re-imagining coloured identities we need to move beyond the notion that coloured identities are "mixed race" identities. Rather we need to see them as cultural identities comprising detailed bodies of knowledge, specific cultural practices, memories, rituals and modes of being. . . . The result has been a highly specific and instantly recognizable cultural formation—not just a "mixture," but a very particular "mixture" comprising elements of British, Dutch, Malaysian, Khoi and other forms of African culture appropriated, translated and articulated in complex and subtle ways. These elements acquire their specific cultural meaning only once fused and translated.[13]

Crain Soudien presents an even more ambitious proposition, suggesting that South Africa at its birth be "presented as an embrace of difference. Europe, Africa and Asia are figuratively assimilated, incorporated and naturalized on the rich soil of the Cape. There is in this figurative construction, in some senses, the notion of the African cradle of humanity receiving back its diasporic seed."[14]

Attentive readers will note that later in this paper, I will address the links and contradictions between creolization and diaspora more fully, but here, we can merely note that one possibility raised by Soudien is that a thoroughgoing creolization ends, or resolves, a diaspora. The spirit of reconciliation that marked the foundational moment of the new, postapartheid South Africa implied that backward glances toward culturally distinct roots were no longer appropriate or necessary. A creolized identity could thus be conceived as the embryonic form of a truly South African, perhaps even a tricontinental, identity. It transcended the claims for primacy, purity, and authenticity on the part of black and white South Africans and fatally undermined the racial categories inherited from the apartheid era.[15]

---

12. Zimitri Erasmus, "Introduction: Re-imagining Coloured Identities in Post-apartheid South Africa," in *Coloured by History, Shaped by Place: New Perspectives on Coloured Identities in Cape Town*, ed. Zimitri Erasmus (Cape Town: Kwela Books, 2001), 22.

13. Ibid., 21.

14. Crain Soudien, "District Six and Its Uses in the Discussion About Non-Racialism," in *Coloured by History, Shaped by Place: New Perspectives on Coloured Identities in Cape Town*, ed. Zimitri Erasmus (Cape Town: Kwela Books, 2001), 123.

15. I do not want to get too diverted into a rather local debate, but I need to qualify this celebration of the possibilities of a superseding form of creolization. It is not the case that Nelson Mandela himself, the architect of popular postapartheid ideology, ever advocated creolization. He preferred the language of a "rainbow nation"marked by respect for difference and equality of regard for all "peoples." Placing a reconstituted creolized identity at the foundation of the new South Africa would have been threatening to some (by no means all) African groups that retained strong ethnic identities (for example,

The United States: Heritage and New Multiracial Identities

In the United States, the South, and more particularly New Orleans, provides a rich array of contrasting experiences of creolization. There, from the eighteenth century on, people of mixed ethnic backgrounds maintained a precarious intermediate status, distancing themselves from the black parts of their origins, but not accepted by polite white society. In fact, the social struggle for status revolved precisely around the expression "Creole." Some whites determinedly continued to describe *themselves* exclusively as "Creole" and authenticated this claim by referring to the original sense of the word, that is, that they were proud descendants of French or Spanish settlers, but born in the New World. This claim, a form of heritage politics common in the United States, was reasserted as late as in M. H. Herrin's 1951 book titled *The Creole Aristocracy*.[16] The "white Creoles" sent their children to Paris to study, if they could afford it, continued to speak a version of French, and lionized French culture. However, their snobbery did not extend to their sexual practices, with many males finding black or so-called "light" or "yellow" mistresses, setting them up in the French Quarter of New Orleans in bijou houses of their own.

Descendants of such liaisons were Creoles, or "black Creoles," who were augmented by people of purer black origin who had nonetheless made a cultural shift into French New Orleans society. In New Orleans, there are both black and white Creoles and many who are somewhere between black and white. All "nonwhite" Creoles were under threat in the period after the Civil War, when the reactionary Jim Crow laws (exemplified in the Louisiana Legislative Code III) insisted that any person with the smallest amount of "black blood" was to be described as a Negro and to suffer the discriminatory consequences. This is described as the "one-drop" rule (or, more technically, "hypodescent").

It is noteworthy that the Creole imaginary was prevalent despite the ideological dominance of biological categories, Social Darwinism, and legal codes requiring that people be reduced to primordial "races" even where this was manifestly inappropriate. In the context of the United States, particularly the southern states, elaborated Creole cultures had already emerged, and white power holders, including the Ku Klux Klan, tried with considerable success to use the period after 1865 to force Creole peoples into the category of "Negro." Benjamin Ringer shows how Supreme Court decisions over a period of fifty years facilitated these assertions of white power.[17] The postbellum period "depended heavily on the coercive arm of the law and where necessary a vigilantism of community sentiment; it thereby sought to draw a sharp line between black and white without exception and spread the authority to maintain this line to a variety of public officials, bureaucrats, and ordinary white citizens."[18]

---

the Zulu Inkatha movement) and perhaps also to some whites. The African National Congress needed to keep both on board to ensure a minimum of violence.

16. M. H. Herrin, *The Creole Aristocracy: A Study of the Creole of Southern Louisiana* (New York: Exposition Press, 1951).

17. Benjamin Ringer, *"We the People" and Others: Duality and America's Treatment of Its Racial Minorities* (New York: Tavistock Publications, 1983), 215–384.

18. Ibid., 225.

In fact, people of mixed heritage seemed to get it in the neck from all sides. As David Pilgrim shows, in popular culture in the United States, the person of mixed origin, particularly if she was a woman, was depicted in tragic terms:

> Literary and cinematic portrayals of the tragic mulatto [*sic*; this should read mulatta] emphasized her personal pathologies: self-hatred, depression, alcoholism, sexual perversion, and suicide attempts being the most common. If light enough to "pass" as White, she did, but passing led to deeper self-loathing. She pitied or despised Blacks and the "blackness" in herself; she hated or feared Whites yet desperately sought their approval. In a race-based society, the tragic mulatto found peace only in death. She evoked pity or scorn, not sympathy.[19]

Such arguments were sustained with particular force around emerging iconic figures such as Billie Holiday—the great jazz singer—and Dorothy Dandridge, the star of the musical *Carmen Jones* (1954), who was the first Creole actress on the cover of *Life*. Both women committed suicide in despairing circumstances and were poignant instances of the tragedy of creoledom. While Hollywood often focused on the tragic, beautiful mulatta, it did not fail to remind us also of the case of male and child mulattos, as in the popular film *Angelo* (released in 1949), whose protagonist found it impossible to live "in a *white man's world*" (every emphasized word counts in this description).

As if this popular disdain of mixed-heritage people were not enough, black American attitudes were also often hostile. The black leader and founder of the Universal Negro Improvement Association, Marcus Garvey, was perhaps the most explicit:

> I believe in a pure black race just as how all self-respecting whites believe in a pure white race, as far as that can be. I am conscious of the fact that slavery brought upon us the curse of many colors within the Negro race, but that is no reason why we of ourselves should perpetuate the evil; hence instead of encouraging a wholesale bastardy in the race, we feel that we should now set out to create a race type and standard of our own which could not, in the future, be stigmatized by bastardy, but could be recognized and respected as the true race type anteceding even our own time.[20]

Though an extreme version, such attitudes were common among black leaders in the United States. Assertions of purity were also the focus of later political movements—such as the Black Panthers—and the more popular expressions of the day such as "black power," "black pride," and "black is beautiful."

This counterhegemonic expression of black self-regard rather than black self-hatred left little room for those who were phenotypically more ambiguous. Any demur was met by the charge that people of mixed ancestry who could not admit that they were black were experiencing denial and betraying their black brothers and sisters. Explanations for this position vary. They include hostility to those who were favored in the plantation

---

19. David Pilgrim, "The Tragic Mulatto Myth" (2000). Available on-line at: http://www.ferris.edu/HTMLS/News/jimcrow/mulatto, unpaginated (last accessed on September 3, 2007).

20. Marcus Garvey, *The Philosophy and Opinions of Marcus Garvey*, Vols. I and II, ed. Amy Jacques-Garvey (New York: Atheneum, 1977) 37.

system; the perverse influence of white racism, Social Darwinism, and Nazism; and complex psychological and gender tensions. Resolving this question is not particularly salient to my current argument. What is salient is that the effects of this hostility were to force those of visible mixed heritage into declaring their undivided loyalty to the black "race" or to join the white "race" by "passing."

It is difficult to date exactly at what point a third choice opened between these two paths, but one powerful symbolic moment was when the successful golfer Tiger Woods suggested on an Oprah Winfrey show in April 1997 that he was not an African American but a Cablinasian (a mixture of Caucasian, black, American Indian, and Asian). "I'm just who I am, whoever you see in front of you," he told the talk-show hostess. *Time* magazine recorded that the golfer's remark infuriated African Americans who saw him as a "sell-out," while no less a figure than the former general and secretary of state, Colin Powell, ticked Woods off by announcing that "in America, which I love from the depths of my heart and soul, when you look like me, you're black."[21]

Rainier Spencer, who alludes to this episode, argues that the debate around Tiger Woods's statement and other forms of recognition of mixture still often continues to use predictable racial categories, thereby falling into the trap of hypodescent.[22] Indeed, it is notable that discourse in the United States still centers on "bi*racialism*" and the "multi-*racial*" experience, rather than the superseding categories of "nonracialism" used in post-apartheid South Africa and of multiculturalism, hybridity, and creolization used there and elsewhere. While Spencer is correct in suggesting this is a real limitation on exploring the complexity of emerging identities in the United States, he cites a number of authors, including Kerry Ann Rockquemore and David L. Brunsma, who are developing racially neutral categories such as "border," "protean," "transcendent," and "traditional" identities.[23] Again, Spencer is somewhat scornful of the discovery in popular magazines of the new levels of biracialism in the United States, which accept current race labels as valid.[24] (*Time* and *Newsweek* both covered this issue at length.) He argues that if one were historically informed, "there are at least 30 million people of [mixed] African, Native American and European ancestry in the United States." However historically valid such statements may be, self-ascription remains a vital datum. In this respect, it is notable that census data show a quadrupling of children in self-identified "interracial" families over the period from 1970 to 1990 (from less than half a million to about two million). It also is significant that when given the chance to respond to a question about multiple origins in the 2000 census (for the first time), 6.8 million Americans availed themselves of this opportunity (see Table 1).

---

21. Gary Kamiya, "Cablinasian Like Me" (1997). Available on-line at http://www.salon.com/april97/tiger970430.html, unpaginated (last accessed December 14, 2007).

22. Rainier Spencer, "Assessing Multiracial Identity Theory and Politics: The Challenge of Hypodescent," *Ethnicities* 4, no. 3 (2004): 357–79.

23. Ibid., 360. See Kerry Ann Rockquemore, and David L. Brunsma, *Beyond Black: Biracial Identity in America* (Thousand Oaks, CA: Sage, 2002).

24. Spencer, "Assessing Multiracial Identity Theory and Politics," 374.

The U.S. figures thus show that though Blue Mink's "lovin machine" has barely got into its stride, in recent years, the number of people who identify themselves as of mixed origins is increasing substantially. This is merely an indicator and prelude to the possible emergence of new forms of creolization that may shape attitudes and social behavior. As I argue below, the Creole culture centered in New Orleans has both been challenged and grown new roots in the wake of hurricanes Katrina and Rita.

Table 1: U.S. Population by Number of Races Reported, 2000

No. of races	Number	% of total population	% of population (2 or more races)
Total population	281,421,906	100.0	—
One race	274,595,678	97.6	—
Two or more races	6,844,228	2.4	100.0
Two races	6,386,075	2.3	93.3
Three races	410,285	0.1	6.0
Four races	38,408	—	0.6
Fives races	8,637	—	0.1
Six races	823	—	—

Source: U.S. Census Bureau, 2003. *Census 2000*. Redistricting data (Public Law 94-171). Summary file. Table PL1.

Creolization as an Intellectual Movement

In my introduction, I alluded to the soft, but pervasive sounds of diversity, complexity, and hybridity, a subtle shift toward a new positive valorization of creolization. We have seen how this process has emerged and differed in three large societies—Brazil, South Africa, and the United States. However, much of the supporting theorization and defense of creolization has occurred elsewhere. First, I will discuss the development of a movement for Creolité in the Francophone Caribbean, a relatively small setting, but one that nonetheless has global implications and resonances. Second, I will consider the celebration of hybridity, or at least its recognition, by two eminent postcolonial writers, Salman Rushdie and V. S. Naipaul. (There are others, of course, but I refer here to two prominent examples.) Third, will I refer to the increasing recognition of mixed-identity categories among official statisticians and the call for the end of "raciology" by certain academics and intellectuals.

Creolité, Not Négritude

As I have indicated, self-hatred was one of the targets of early expressions of black pride and identity politics. It was at the heart of the Garveyite movement, which wanted black Americans to think of themselves as Africans. It also suffused the idea of Négritude, developed by the Caribbean and Senegalese intellectuals Aimé Césaire, Leon-Gontran Damas, and Léopold Senghor. As in the United States, the fear of the rejection of mixture seemed to underlie some of the Caribbean understandings of their own identities. Take the views of Frantz Fanon, himself born in Martinique of mixed origin and highly sensitive to the possibility of dismissal of "West Indians" by Africans. When this happened, Fanon claimed, "he [the West Indian] suffered despair. Haunted by impurity, overwhelmed by sin, riddled by guilt, he was prey to the tragedy of being neither white nor Negro."[25]

Fanon's insights were based on his background in the Caribbean and his experience in Africa and probably also carry some autobiographical imprint. While Fanon's diagnosis was accurate, it was left to others in the Caribbean to develop a fully formed alternative to the fear of rejection by those who claimed purer racial origins. Logically, this had to commence, as Richard D. E. Burton noted, with an attack on Négritude:

> Négritude may invert a stereotypical European definition of blackness and black culture, divesting it of its overly racist character and transforming the negative into the positive, yet the underlying structure of that definition is retained. Négritude in this view merely substitutes one alienating definition for another and, to that extent, enmeshes the black African or West Indians still more tightly in the assimilationist problematic or scheme of things even as it seems to release the repressed and repudiated black "essence" within him.[26]

As Burton comments, the appeals of Négritude in the context of the Caribbean were simply not convincing after three centuries of social and physical creolization. Créolité, a cultural and political movement articulated by a number of Caribbean intellectuals, became an explicit alternative. The proponents of Créolité are at pains to include all resident groups—African, European, Indian, Chinese, and Lebanese. The founders of the movement, Jean Bernabé, Patrick Chamoiseu, and Raphaël Confiant,[27] produced a compelling manifesto of the movement, arguing that "in multiracial societies, such as ours, it is urgent that we abandon the habitual raciological distinctions and that we resume the custom of designating the people of our country by the one term that, whatever their complexion, behooves them: Creole. Socio-economic relations within our society must henceforth be conducted under the seal of a shared creolity [Créolité] without that obliterating in any way whatsoever class relations and conflicts."[28]

Through such intellectual movements, creolization has escaped its colonial cage, a development that was signaled earlier in the work of the Martinican writer and cultural theorist Edouard Glissant. Glissant was strongly committed to the idea of creolization emanating from the situation of displaced African slaves having to rebuild their lives in new settings, and therefore he had some differences with the relaxed recognition of diversity promoted by his fellow-islanders. However, he too, saw the wider implications

---

25. Frantz Fanon, *Toward the African Revolution* (Harmondsworth, UK: Pelican, 1970), 35–36.

26. Burton, Richard D. E. "The Idea of Difference in Contemporary French West Indian Thought: Négritude, Antillanité, Créolité," in *French and West Indian: Martinique, Guadeloupe and French Guiana Today*, ed. Richard D. E. Burton and Fred Reno (London: Macmillan, 1995), 141.

27. See Jean Bernabé, Patrick Chamoisseau, and Raphaël Confiant, *Eloge de la créolité* (Paris: Gallimard, 1989).

28. Cited in Burton, "The Idea of Difference in Contemporary French West Indian Thought," 152.

of creolization, suggesting that "perhaps creolization is becoming one of our present day goals," not just "on behalf of the America but of the entire world." Further, Glissant asked, instead of perpetuating existing racialized identities, shouldn't we favor "an identity that would not be the projection of a unique and sectarian root, but of what we call a rhizome, a root with a multiplicity of extensions in all direction? Not killing what is around it, as a unique root would, but establishing communication and relation?"[29]

The universal virtues of Créolité as a form of cultural politics and creolization as a sociological category now become apparent. They allow us to include all population groups, including later immigrant arrivals in addition to the original trichotomy (the colonial, Creole, and indigene). They allow us also to escape the political cage and unscientific trap of racial, phenotypical, and biological categorizations, thereby avoiding such expressions as "colored," "half-caste," "mixed-race," "mixed-blood," "mestizo," "mulatto," "quadroon," "octoroon," "*gens de coleur*," "half-breed," "zambo," "griffe," and many other descriptions that are even less flattering, such as "baster" (South Africa), "dougla/h" (Trinidad), "mud people" (used by the Ku Klux Klan), or "ox head" (southern China).

Rushdie and Naipaul: Prophets of the Impure

The celebration of hybridity and mongrelism, together with the articulation of a distrust of traditional and ascribed social identities, has been Salman Rushdie's self-assigned task in much of his work, notably in *The Satanic Verses* (1988). Although the professed grounds for the fatwa directed at Rushdie after the publication of the book depended on a number of specific religious objections, the more general offence caused by the book among some Muslims was its explicit attack on authenticity, on singular and monochromatic identities, and on the ideas of a single Truth and a Pure Way. As Rushdie himself says of *The Satanic Verses*:

> Those who oppose the novel most vociferously today are of the opinion that intermingling with different cultures will inevitably weaken and ruin their own. I am of the opposite opinion. *The Satanic Verses* celebrate hybridity, impurity, intermingling, the transformation that comes of new and unexpected combinations of human beings, cultures, ideas, politics, movies, songs. It rejoices in mongrelization and fears the absolutism of the Pure. *Mélange*, hotchpotch, a bit of this and a bit of that is how newness enters the world. It is the great possibility that mass migration gives the world, and I have tried to embrace it.[30]

While Rushdie is optimistic about the impure and indeed celebrates it, as Thomas Hylland Eriksen suggests, a more complex reading of mixed identities is provided by the Trinidadian-born V. S. Naipaul:

---

29. Edouard Glissant, cited in Eve Stoddard and Grant H. Cornwell, "Cosmopolitan or Mongrel: Creolité, Hybridity and 'Douglarisation' in Trinidad," *European Journal of Cultural Studies* 2, no. 3 (1999): 349.

30. Salman Rushdie, *Imaginary Homelands: Essays and Criticism, 1981–1991* (New York: Viking, 1991), 394.

Shocked by India, alienated by England, aloof from the Caribbean, Naipaul became a writer about torn identities. Several of his mature, largely tragic novels, from *The Mimic Men* (1967) and *In a Free State* (1971) to *The Enigma of Arrival* (1987) and *Half a Life* (2001), are about men (and a few women) who try to be something that they are not, usually because they can see no alternative. It is the dark, unprivileged side of Rushdie's brave new world.[31]

There is a tragic quality to Naipaul's impossible search for belonging and rootedness, but, as Eriksen argues, despite his own pronouncements, which remain sardonic and gloomy, "it can also be said that the tragic grandeur of Naipaul's best books confirm an assumption, which he himself might reject, that exile and cultural hybridity are creative forces."[32] His poignant novel, which may also be his best, *A House for Mr. Biswas* (1961), is said to be based on his father. Biswas emerges as a sympathetic character, despite the author's mockery of Biswas's pathetic mimicry of European ways.

Statisticians and Intellectuals in the United Kingdom and the United States

As I suggested earlier, the categories "mixed race" and "mixed heritage" are increasingly recognized in census categories in the United States as numbers of citizens refuse to locate themselves in the rigid categories imposed in previous censuses. In the case of the United Kingdom, the public debate about "multiculturalism" as a way of understanding diversity in the UK has been led by the chairman of the Commission for Racial Equality, Trevor Phillips.[33] He has espoused a belief that the cultural segments of which British society is composed are no longer stable and that nothing should be done to make them more rigid. Although there is no unanimity on this question among academics, there has long been unease about how commonly deployed ethnic categories are being decomposed under the force of new patterns of social interaction, new sources of immigrants, and radical "refusals" by people of mixed heritage to identify themselves using particular ethnic labels. The augmentation of visible minorities (African, Indian, Bangladeshi, and black Caribbean) by other Asian and European immigration has generated a much more complex understanding of the nature of British identity. The UK 2001 census allowed the box "mixed" to be selected for the first time, which partly accounts for the proportion of minority ethnic groups moving from 6 to 9 percent of the population.[34]

Beyond such data about the rising levels of population mixture is a much more telling argument, namely, that at the level of popular discourse and practices, purity and authenticity have often been displaced by a suspicion of traditional and ascribed social

---

31. Thomas Hylland Eriksen, "Creolization and Creativity," *Global Networks* 3, no. 3 (2003): 226.

32. Ibid., 226.

33. *Times* (London), April 3, 2004.

34. UK National Statistics, *Census 2001: Ethnicity and Religion in England and Wales* (UK Government, London: Office of National Statistics, 2003), available on-line at: http://www.statistics.gov.uk/pdfdir/ethnicity0203.pdf (last accessed December 14, 2007).

identities among a significant UK minority. Even some of the historically "white" UK population is also beginning to reconstitute itself as "mixed" or "post-race."[35] Again, a number of writers and intellectuals have called for the end of racial categorization in social science in favor of more complex and overlapping social categories. Here are just three examples:

- For Stuart Hall complexity is found by defining "new ethnicities." As he puts it, "If the black subject and black experience are not stabilized by Nature or by some other essential guarantee, then it must be the case that they are constructed historically, culturally, politically—and the concept which refers to this is 'ethnicity.'"[36]

- For Paul Gilroy, "To comprehend the history of blackness' appeals to the future and how that history may contribute to the cultural dynamism and moral confidence of a cosmopolitan and hospitable Europe, we need to appreciate . . . phases in the process of dissent from raciology."[37]

- For Homi Bhabha, a dynamic "third space" both emerges from two original moments and recognizes that those moments are themselves unstable. Thus, "the act of cultural translation . . . denies the essentialism of a prior given or original culture" and allows us to see that "all forms of culture are in a continuous process of hybridity."[38]

Affirming Mixed Identities

I have sought to establish the heuristic potential of the expressions "Creole" and "creolization" used as sociological and cultural terms. While it is true to assert that creolization had its locus classicus in the context of colonial settlement, imported black labor, and often a plantation and island setting, by indicating that there are other pathways for creolization, I want to signify the potentially universal applicability of the term. To be a creole is no longer a mimetic, derivative stance. Rather, it describes a position interposed between two or more cultures, selectively appropriating some elements, rejecting others, and creating new possibilities that transgress and supersede parent cultures, which themselves are increasingly recognized as fluid. If this is indeed happening on a significant scale, we need to recast much traditional social theory concerning race and ethnic relations, multiculturalism, nation-state formation, and the like, for we can no longer assume the stability and continuing force of the ethnic segments that supposedly make

35. Suki Ali, *Mixed-Race, Post-Race: Gender, New Ethnicities and Cultural Practices* (Oxford: Berg, 2003); Miri Song, *Choosing Ethnic Identity* (Cambridge: Polity Press, 2003).

36. Stuart Hall, "New Ethnicities," in *'Race', Culture and Difference*, ed. James Donald and Ali Rattansi (London: Sage Publications in association with the Open University, 1992), 257.

37. Paul Gilroy, *Between Camps: Nations, Cultures and the Allure of Race* (London: Penguin, 2000), 339.

38. Homi K. Bhahba, "The Third Space: Interview with Homi Bhahba," in *Identity: Community, Culture, Difference*, ed. Jonathan Rutherford (London: Lawrence and Wishart, 1990).

up nation-states. Likewise, we cannot assume that the nation in international relations has a continuously uniform character. To accept the force of hybridity and creolization is also to accept that humankind is refashioning the basic building blocks of organized cultures and societies in a fundamental and wide-ranging way.

Mobile, transnational groups are themselves undergoing what has been described as "everyday cosmopolitanism," while dominant, formerly monochromatic cultures have themselves become crisscrossed and sometimes deeply subverted by hybridization and creolization. It is this last quality that lends credence to the notion, advanced by the Swedish social anthropologist Ulf Hannerz, that we live in "creolizing world."[39] In his discussion of the global ecumene, Hannerz argues that cultures are no longer as bounded or autonomous as they once were and that complex and asymmetrical flows have reshaped cultures that, given existing forms and meanings of culture, are not likely to result in global homogenization. He is clear that "emerging hybridized webs of meaning" are neither spurious nor inauthentic cultures.[40] While these creole cultures may be relatively unformed because they are recent, they can and do take on a complex character, often because the periphery is stronger than it may appear. As Hannerz maintains:

> Creolization also increasingly allows the periphery to talk back. As it creates a greater affinity between the cultures of the center and the periphery, and as the latter increasingly uses the same organizational forms and the same technology as the center . . . some of its new cultural commodities become increasingly attractive on a global market. Third World music of a creolized kind becomes world music. . . . Creolization thought is open-ended; the tendencies towards maturation and saturation are understood as quite possibly going on side by side, or interleaving.[41]

The creolization of the world in the sense described by Hannerz and other writers cited earlier has provided a space for many people to create a new sense of home, a locus to express their uniqueness in the face of cultural fundamentalisms and imperialism. Behind the strident assertions of nationalism, "old ethnicities," and religious certainties is an increasing volume of cultural interactions, interconnections, and interdependencies and a challenge to the solidity of ethnic and racial categories. These are the soft sounds of fugitive power, but you may need to have your ear cocked to the ground, or your finger on the pulse, if you are to hear them fully and discern their influence.

Social Constructionist Critiques of Diaspora

I suggested that creolization and diasporas are, at first sight, divergent forms of cultural politics with different sensibilities and different trajectories. However, two of the major building blocks defining diasporas, namely "homeland" and "ethnic community,"

---

39. Ulf Hannerz, "The World in Creolization," *Africa* 57, no. 4 (1987): 546–59.

40. Ulf Hannerz, *Cultural Complexity* (New York: Columbia University Press, 1992), 217–63, 264.

41. Ibid., 265–66.

have gradually been decomposed under the weight of social-constructionist critiques.[42] With apologies for returning to an earlier debate, this statement needs some background explanation.

One of the most influential statements marking the beginning of contemporary diaspora studies was William Safran's 1991 article "Diasporas in Modern Societies: Myths of Homeland and Return" in the opening issue of the then new journal *Diaspora*.[43] Safran was strongly influenced by the underlying paradigmatic case of the Jewish diaspora, but correctly perceived that many other ethnic groups were experiencing analogous situations due to the difficult circumstances surrounding their departure from their places of origin and their limited acceptance in their places of settlement. Arguably however, the Jewish experience continued to influence his view of the vital importance of "home*land*" in defining one of the essential characteristics of diaspora. Members of a diaspora were said to retain a collective memory of "their original homeland" and to idealize their "ancestral home," and they were seen as committed to the restoration of "the original homeland" and as continuing in various ways to "relate to that homeland."[44] While recognizing his path-breaking contribution, in my 1997 book, *Global Diasporas: An Introduction*, I was concerned about Safran's overemphasis on "homeland" and, in my extended list of a diaspora's common features, added "the possibility of a distinctive creative, enriching life in host societies with a tolerance for pluralism."[45]

While the decoupling of diaspora from homeland was merely one option among several in my 1997 book, this rupture had taken a more insistent turn in Avtar Brah's *Cartographies of Diaspora: Contesting Identities* (1996), where he dethroned the foundational idea of a homeland, arguing that "the concept of diaspora offers a critique of discourses of fixed origins, while taking account of a homing desire, which is not the same thing as a desire for 'homeland.'"[46] So, homeland had become a homing desire, and soon home itself became transmuted into an essentially placeless, though admittedly lyrical space. As Brah explains:

> Where is home? On the one hand, "home" is a mythic place of desire in the diasporic imagination. In this sense it is a place of no return, even if it is possible to visit the geographical territory that is seen as the place of "origin." On the other hand, home is also the lived experience of a locality. Its sounds and smells, its heat and dust, balmy summer evenings, or the excitement of the first snowfall, shivering winter evenings, sombre grey

---

42. I have used the expression "social constructionist" to signify a mode of reasoning, closely associated with post-modernism, that suggests that reality is determined by social interaction (or intersubjectivity), rather than by objectivity (a natural or material world) or by subjectivity (individual perceptions).

43. William Safran, "Diasporas in Modern Societies: Myths of Homeland and Return," *Diaspora* 1, no. 1 (1991): 83–99.

44. Ibid., 83–84.

45. Robin Cohen, *Global Diasporas: An Introduction* (London: UCL Press, 1997), 23, 26).

46. Avtar Brah, *Cartographies of Diaspora: Contesting Identities* (London: Routledge, 1996), 180.

skies in the middle of the day . . . all this, as mediated by the historically specific everyday of social relations.[47]

Through this and similar interventions, "home" became more and more generously interpreted to mean the place of origin; or the place of settlement; or a local, national, or transnational place; or an imagined virtual community (linked, for example, through the Internet); or a matrix of known experiences and intimate social relations (thus conforming to the popular expression that "home is where the heart is").

Floya Anthias upped the stakes further in an article titled "Evaluating 'Diaspora': Beyond Ethnicity" (1998) by criticizing a number of scholars (this writer included) for using what she described as "absolutist notions of 'origin' and 'true belonging.'" For her, scholars of diasporas showed insufficient attention to internal divisions with ethnic communities or to the possibilities of selective cultural negotiations between communities:

> the lack of attention given to transethnic solidarities, such as those against racism, of class, of gender, of social movements, is deeply worrying from the perspective of the development of multiculturality, and more inclusive notions of belonging. For a discourse of anti-racism and social mobilization of a transethnic (as opposed to a transnational) character, cannot be easily accommodated, within the discourse of the diaspora, where it retains its dependence on "homeland" and "origin," however configured.[48]

Two years later, in "Citizenship and Identity: Living in Diasporas in Post-War Europe?" (2000) Yasemin Nuhoḡlu Soysal amplified the charge. Despite the fact that notions of diaspora were "venerated," they inappropriately "privileg[ed] the nation-state model and nationally-defined formations when conversing about a global process such as immigration." Postwar developments, Soysal, maintained:

> render diaspora untenable as an analytical and normative category, and direct our discussion to new formations of membership, claims-making and belonging—which either remain invisible to the conventional conceptions of diaspora, or are frequently deemed insignificant in the face of its normative weight. . . . In this [erroneous] formulation, the primary orientation and attachment of diasporic populations is to their homelands and cultures; and their claims and citizenship practices arise from this home-bound ethnic-based orientation.[49]

After her initial critique of diaspora, Soysal attended to her case of European citizenship, but she returned with a vengeance to her dislike of the concept of diaspora in a postscript, maintaining that the idea "suspends immigrant experience between host and home countries, native and foreign lands, home-bound desires and losses—thus obscur-

---

47. Ibid., 192.

48. Floya Anthias, "Evaluating 'Diaspora': Beyond Ethnicity," *Sociology* 32, no. 3 (1998): 577.

49. Yasemin Nuhoğlu Soysal, "Citizenship and Identity: Living in Diasporas in Post-War Europe?" *Ethnic and Racial Studies* 23, no. 1 (2000): 1–3.

ing the new topography and practices of citizenship, which are multi-connected, multi-referential and postnational."[50]

It is doubtful whether the full weight of these critiques can be sustained in any close reading of work of the authors cited, but this is not the point. The crucial effect of these and similar appraisals of existing notions of diaspora was to force a larger and larger wedge between "diaspora," on the one hand, and "homeland," "place," and "ethnic community," on the other. Clearly for some authors—of whom Anthias and Soysal are good representatives—the concept of diaspora is irredeemably flawed. It simply cannot do what they wanted—in Anthias's case, it cannot produce a platform for a transethnic, gender-sensitive, antiracist movement, while, in Soysal's case, it cannot provide a means of understanding postnational citizenship in Europe.

"Diaspora," Your Flexible Friend

Perhaps the simplest response to such critiques of diaspora would be to regard them as misplaced, because they reflect political agendas that have little to do with the history and meaning of the term or the phenomena it sought to and continues to explain. As far as I can discern, the diaspora theorists that these critiques targeted made no claim to explain all forms of international migration, did not see their task as creating a progressive antiracist movement (desirable as that may be), and did not seek to describe patterns of sociality unrelated to some degree of prior kinship. Unlike fossil fuels, there is no worldwide shortage of concepts, and if diaspora does not work for any one purpose, my first impulse is to ask why other, more appropriate, concepts (such as multiculturalism, cosmopolitanism, interculturality, hybridity, or, perhaps, creolization) cannot be deployed instead.

However, this would be too cantankerous a reaction, and we are, in any case, locked into a paradox. The concept of diaspora has become so "venerated" (Soysal's expression), so fashionable, so "highly-favored"[51] so "hip" and so "in,"[52] that, like Procrustes, "diasporists" have had to stretch short people or cut off the limbs of long people so they can fit them all into the proverbial iron bed. Pioneering scholars such as Khachig Tölölyan, who more or less constructed the field of diaspora studies, thus have found themselves in a dilemma:

> Diasporists shaped by globalizing discourse describe genuine erosions of the link between a bounded place and a people, diagnose it as irresistible, and quickly affirm its contribution to a pluralistic, multicultural, hybrid world of which they approve. Diasporists like myself, who want to argue that attachment to place was indispensable to diasporic life and thought

50. Ibid., 13.

51. David Chariandy, "Postcolonial Diasporas," *Postcolonial Text* 2, no. 1 (2006), on-line journal, unpaginated, available at http://postcolonial.org/index.php/pct/article/view/440/159 (last accessed December 14, 2007).

52. Martin Sökefeld, "Mobilizing in Transnational Space: A Social Movement Approach to the Formation of Diaspora," *Global Networks* 6, no. 3 (2006): 265–84.

until very recently, and that despite its erosion it remains important today, must tread carefully in order to avoid the charge that we are either imitating discredited nationalist rhetoric about the link between land, people, and culture, or that we remain naïve about the global spaces that have opened up in the past several decades.[53]

Fortunately, the concept of diaspora seems much more of a flexible friend than Procrustes' guests proved. By way of illustration, let me provide three examples from recent work by William Safran, Martin Sökefeld, and David Chariandy.

De-Zionization

The first example of a more flexible use of conventional diasporic theory is by an established scholar of diasporas, Safran, whose work on the necessity of homeland to the concept of disapora has already been cited. Partly on the basis of recent attitudinal surveys, in "The Tenuous Link between Hostlands and Homeland: The Progressive De-Zionization of Western Diasporas" (2005), Safran now argues that in the case of Israel on the one hand, and European and American Jews on the other, the links between hostlands and homeland are becoming more tenuous.[54] Those in the Jewish diaspora experiencing a process of what he calls "de-zionization" include groups he designates as secularists, socialists, potential investors in Israel, nonorthodox believers, enlightened Western Jews, left-wing ideologues, academics, and others disillusioned with the expressions of Israeli state power. The other side of the coin is that (despite intermittent bursts of anti-Semitism) life in the diaspora is sufficiently attractive and sufficiently emotionally and physically secure not to prompt an invariable identification with Israel.

Intriguingly, proto-Zionists have also promoted summer camps where, in safe rural U.S. settings, virtual *aliya* (migration "up" to Israel) can take place, complete with Israeli flags, Hebrew lessons, religious rituals, imitations of life on a kibbutz, and access to other attractive aspects of Israeli popular culture.[55] As Safran himself recognizes, the harder notion of homeland has now yielded to softer notions of a found home in the diaspora and to a virtual home in a summer camp—perhaps augmented by occasional visits to Israel, rather than permanent settlement. I will add that the unexpected, but considerable flow of Israelis *to* the United States and Europe (which attracts strong disapprobation by Zionists) has also fundamentally changed the relationship between homeland and hostlands.[56]

---

53. Khachig Tölölyan, "Restoring the Logic of the Sedentary to Diaspora Studies," in *Les diasporas: 2000 ans d'histoire*, ed. Lisa Anteby-Yemeni, William Berthomière, and Gabriel Sheffer (Rennes: Presses Universitaires de Rennes, 2005), 138–39.

54. William Safran, "The Tenuous Link Between Hostlands and Homeland: The Progressive De-Zionization of Western Diasporas," in *Les diasporas: 2000 ans d'histoire*, ed. Lisa Anteby-Yemeni, William Berthomière, and Gabriel Sheffer (Rennes: Presses Universitaires de Rennes, 2005), 193–208.

55. Ibid., 199–200.

56. See Steven J. Gold, *The Israeli Diaspora* (London: Routledge, 2002).

Diasporas and Social Movements

My second example arises from Sökefeld's article "Mobilizing in Transnational Space: A Social Movement Approach to the Formation of Diaspora" (2006), where he, somewhat uncritically, accepts a number of the unsympathetic comments of the social construction-ists, but inverts their purpose. Instead of using intersubjectivity as a means for dethroning the concept of diaspora, he uses the same starting point for interrogating how diasporas can come into being and sustain themselves. He considers the formation of diasporas as "a special case of ethnicity." They are "imagined transnational communities which unite segments of people that live in territorially separated locations." Not all immigrants will cohere into communities, and not all immigrant communities will imagine themselves as transnational, thus it is a fundamental error to allow the use of diaspora as a synonym for all immigrants. A diasporic consciousness, moreover, has to be socially mobilized—that is, constructed. A significant number of social actors need to accept their collective self-definition as a transnational community, organize to spread this perception, and persuade others to participate in actions designed to cement their diasporic character and status.

Sökefeld then makes his most innovative theoretical intervention. While diasporas cannot simply be equated to social movements, there are sufficient parallels to use the social-movement literature to gather insights on the formation of diasporas. In particular, diasporas need: *opportunity structures*, such as an enhanced means of communication and a permissive legal and political environment; *mobilizing practices*, such as neighborhood asso-ciations, demonstrations, and fund-raising events; and *frames* that allude to an idea of roots or the importance of memory in history, ideas that feed into the collective imagination of the group concerned. In other words, Sökefeld moves away from assigning particular attributes to particular ethnic groups and instead asks questions such as: What events or developments propel a disaporic response? What agents undertake the dissemination of a diasporic discourse and foster a diasporic imaginary? What threats and opportunities unite people in transnational organizations? Through these means, Sökefeld has injected a necessary dose of social science into debates that arguably have been too dominated by historians, on the one hand, and cultural studies theorists, on the other.

Postcolonial Diasporas

My third and final example draws Chariandy's article "Postcolonial Diasporas" (2006). Like some of the earlier critics cited, Chariandy has great expectations for the concept of diaspora, but unlike them, has not abandoned hope that it can be used to illuminate con-temporary forms of progressive cultural politics. Although he recognizes that we are still "struggling to develop adequate terms for the profound socio-cultural dislocations result-ing from modern colonialism and nation building," he finds in the concept of diaspora the potential for showing how "historically disenfranchised peoples have developed tac-tics to challenge their subordinate status." Though initially assigning these aspirations to other scholars, it is clear that he, too, sees a rosy future for diaspora studies:

In the past fifteen years, "diaspora" has emerged as a highly favored term among scholars whom we might associate with contemporary postcolonial studies; and while there exists within the nebulous field of postcolonial studies no simple agreement on what diaspora is or does, scholars such as Paul Gilroy, Floya Anthias, Stuart Hall, Carole Boyce Davies, Rey Chow, Smaro Kamboureli, Diana Brydon, and Rinaldo Walcott all seem to share these hopes: that diaspora studies will help foreground the cultural practices of both forcefully exiled and voluntarily migrant peoples; that diaspora studies will help challenge certain calcified assumptions about ethnic, racial, and above all, national belonging; and that diaspora studies will help forge new links between emergent critical methodologies and contemporary social justice movements.[57]

In Chariandy's progressive ambitions for postcolonial diaspora studies, formerly designated "Third World" peoples can find some space to express their antinationalist and radical political preferences and can even prefigure a utopian future. Yet he is sufficiently self-critical and dialectical to understand that the cosmopolitan voices of Third World intellectuals may be somewhat self-serving and that "the virtues of fluid and border-crossing identities are endorsed not only by radical scholars, but, sometimes, ever more earnestly, by the powers that be." This last insight links the expression of a diasporic consciousness to the increased density and velocity of the circuits of capital (a process captured partly by the expression "globalization"), without, however, suggesting that in some crude way, diasporic intellectuals or communities are unwitting agents of capital.

As I have provided examples of the expanding use of the concept of diaspora, we have seen how it can be adapted to at least some of the features hitherto captured by concepts of creolization and cosmopolitanism. Let us consider the work, or more accurately, *the implications of the work*, of Safran, Sökefeld. and Chariandy in turn. If the Jewish diaspora is progressively becoming de-Zionized, it is, by the same token, finding links, affinities, and shared cultural and political associations in the hostlands. We could, of course, imagine pure enclave societies where diasporic groups were both de-Zionized *and* cut off from their surrounding communities. However, as is clear from Safran's comments about political participation and the growth of exogamy, many in the diaspora have adapted to a form of dual consciousness—poised between virtual Zionism and interculturality. For Sökefeld, diasporas have to be mobilized, so, by inference, there are periods when they are not mobilized or perhaps circumstances when they became demobilized. In these two last cases, forms of sociality with other communities are inevitable. Finally, for Chariandy, a diasporic consciousness represents but one form of mobilization in a wider struggle to attain global social justice. Again, the implication of crossover with other communities is clear, and, indeed, he perhaps goes furthest in suggesting that diaspora can be made compatible with a cross-ethnic cooperative struggle by progressive forces and Third World peoples of many different backgrounds.

---

57. Chariandy, "Postcolonial Diasporas" and personal correspondence. I have yet to examine the writing of all the authors mentioned by Chariandy, but as indicated earlier, I disagree with his portrayal of Floya Anthias, who does not, it seems clear to me, share his hopes for the library possibilities of the concept of diaspora.

While it is true that none of these three positions is an explicit endorsement of creolization (I do not think the word has issued from their word processors), they are all a long way from the idea that a diaspora is a single, endogamous ethnic group with a fixed origin, a uniform history, a lifestyle cut off from their fellow citizens in their places of settlement, and political aspirations wholly focused on their places of origin. Of course, any such notion was a caricature invented by the social constructionists in the first place. However, the constructionists' barbs have nonetheless been blunted by the apparently flexible character, rude good health, and continuing heuristic value of the concept of diaspora.

A Creole Diaspora: The Oxymoronic Case

For much of this paper I have suggested that a diasporic consciousness as classically conceived is tendentially opposed to the process of creolization. However, as I prepared this paper, I became more and more interested in what might be described as a Creole diaspora—an ostensibly oxymoronic category, given my earlier arguments. However, there are at least two cases where this seems to make some sense[58] and where (following Sökefeld's line of reasoning) there seems to be some mobilization of dispersed Creoles along diasporic lines.

The Indian Ocean Creole Diaspora

My first case focuses on the Indian Ocean islands of Mauritius (including its dependency Rodriques), Réunion, and the Seychelles. Mauritius is a Creole society par excellence insofar, as Megan Vaughan explains, all its inhabitants are newcomers:

> Without natives, the island's beginnings were necessarily the product of no one thing or people but of many, more or less foreign, more or less "naturalized." It has always been a Creole island. *Creole* is a notably slippery term, and its meaning in relation to Mauritius shifts historically, as we shall see. But here, by "creole," I simply mean that the island, without natives, has always been the product of multiple influences, multiple sources, which to differing degrees merge, take root, and "naturalize" on this new soil.[59]

As she later elaborates in her compelling account, Indo-Mauritians and Franco-Mauritians continued to retain a residual diasporic character, though the links with their homelands were attenuated by colonialism in the first case and the passing of the island to British control in the second. By contrast, those of African, Malagasy, and other origins were generally fully creolized, while *all* Mauritians were able to establish a distinctive lifestyle, popular musical idiom, and shared Creole language.

---

58. The Cape Verde islands, Sierra Leone, and other places may also be seen as having generated Creole diasporas, but space forbids extending my already too long paper even further.

59. Megan Vaughan, *Creating a Creole Island: Slavery in Eighteenth-Century Mauritius* (Durham, NC: Duke University Press, 2005), 2.

What happens, however, when in the late twentieth-century people from the named Indian islands start getting drawn into the global circuits of capital and labor mobility? A Creole identity is normally seen as an unstable, fluid, and contingent. However, their consciousness had by this stage become sufficiently set, fixed, and articulated that the inhabitants of the identified Indian islands had become, in effect, a Creole nation or nation in formation (if not quite an indigenous people). It is thus not at all surprising to find Web sites in Australia and elsewhere calling on the loyalties of Indian island Creoles to mobilize for common social, cultural, and political purposes. Here is one description by a Creole activist:

> The Creole Diaspora of Australia is composed mainly of those coming from Mauritius, the Seychelles and Rodrigues. There could be a handful coming from Réunion Island or other Creole islands of the Pacific like Haiti and the West Indies [*sic*]. . . . The Creoles in Australia through the years have kept strong ties with their motherland mainly because they still have relatives over there. It is also a fact that they have kept most of their traditions and culture as most of them came as adults. In view of this situation the children, even born in Australia, have naturally acquired most of the Creole way of life. The community-based activities like balls, fancy-fairs, sports, social gatherings, etc., have also helped to keep a strong support in this direction.[60]

Even though the author is apparently under the impression that Haiti and the West Indies are in the Pacific, this has not inhibited him from making links with the International Creole Organization, which promotes "the unity of Creoles all over the world and for the promotion of the Creole language and culture."[61]

The New Orleans Creole Diaspora

My second example is much closer to where we now sit and arises from the forcible displacement of the Creole community in New Orleans as a result of hurricanes Rita and Katrina. Much of the community is unlikely to return, given the adverse ecology of the city and the clear determination of the authorities to favor the high ground where the old tourist haunts and predominantly white society can be reconstituted. Although there has been a lively debate on the Internet about whether the expressions "refugees," "displacees." or "evacuees" are appropriate descriptions of those forced to leave New Orleans (the first is particularly resented), the notion of a "Creole diaspora" is increasingly being used to describe those dispersed to Houston (approximately a quarter of a million people) and to other areas of Louisiana, such as Baton Rouge and Cane River–Natchitoches, and to other states. Susan Saulny suggests about thirty to sixty thousand of the people of New Orleans considered themselves Creoles, excluding those who were strongly influenced by Creole cultural pursuits (such as Creole food, music, architecture,

---

60. Louis de Lamare, "The Creole Diaspora in Australia" (2006), unpaginated. Available on-line at: http://www.iocp. info/articles/The%20Creole%20Diaspora%20in%20Australia.htm (last accessed December 14, 2007).

61. Ibid.

and the Mardi Gras).[62] While the tone of many interviews is cast in tragic diasporic terms (stressing loss, exile, despair, suffering), the fate of those forced to leave New Orleans has also occasioned a strong degree of militancy from radical sympathizers. Here is one sample:

> New Orleans and the Gulf belong to its people, the Creole Diaspora and the survivors, not to an ideology or market. So much of what they owned has been destroyed or is now being taken away. They are our brothers and sisters, and they are beseeching us, crying for our help. That is not easy, they are proud people. Let's help them re-build the Big Easy and Gulf. Let's help them re-claim their home and hope. As the Commander Robert Gould Shaw said in the movie Glory, "We fight for men and women whose poetry is not yet written." This is a good fight, a fight for the future. We all own this fight.[63]

Conclusion

Can I be permitted to make an autobiographical intervention, which may clarify my position? For me, an interest in cosmopolitanism[64] and creolization was alternative and parallel to my earlier interest in diasporas. I was not particularly swayed by the negative comments of some of the social constructionists about the limits of the concept of diaspora, because I had always thought that a diasporic identity is one among several possible outcomes for those seeking to define or redefine their self-conceptions, cultural identities, or political trajectories in the face of the challenges arising from globalization and other rapid social changes. The five major possibilities are:

- A reaffirmation of felt (i.e., invented) primordial loyalties to *subnational units* such as a tribe, ethnicity, language group, region, or locality

- A recasting of *supranational identities* such as diasporas, world religions, and world language groups (for example, Francophonie)

- A revival of *nationalism,* particularly in the wake of the breakup of the Soviet Union, the fragmentation of the Balkans, and the appeals to national solidarity after the terrorist incidents of recent years

- A linking and blending with other groups through a process of *creolization*

- The development of a universal spirit that transcends any particularities and simply stresses the quality of being human—that is, the *cosmopolitan* possibility

---

62. Susan Saulny, "Cast from Their Ancestral Homes, Creoles Worry about Culture's Future." *New York Times,* October 11, 2005.

63. T. W. Croft, "Gulf Storms, Fables of Reconstruction and Hard Times for the Big Easy: The Wind Has Changed," *Counterpunch* (2005), e-newsletter available on-line at http://www.counterpunch.org/croft12302005.html (last accessed December 14, 2007).

64. Steven Vertovec and Robin Cohen, eds., *Conceiving Cosmopolitanism: Theory. Context, and Practice* (Oxford: Oxford University Press, 2002).

Of course, any notion that these are watertight logical alternatives is naïve, though I had to write this paper to see quite how naïve it is. Diaspora and creolization do tend in opposite directions, the one to a recovery of a past identity in reconstituting a transnational link, the other to a severance of past identities in the interests of establishing a new cultural and social identity. Having probed the contours and limits of a diasporic identity, I was attracted to the new challenge of examining "hybridized webs of meaning" (Hannerz's phrase), in which people are drawn together by common aspirations and situations, which tends to reduce their transnational ethnic identities and diasporic links with home. I therefore found it somewhat of a surprise to find that the concept of diaspora was being used for situations and socialities for which creolization (or perhaps hybridity) seemed to be more fit for the purpose.

In the course of writing this paper, I have somewhat changed my mind and see that discussions of diaspora and creolization can to some degree become compatible. In particular, I have been influenced by the flexible use of the notion of diaspora that has rendered it valuable for considering intermediate and more ambiguous forms of social mobilization. Despite this, the two concepts cannot be used interchangeably. In some settings, creolization has, in effect, triumphed over diaspora. I alluded to the case of South Africa,[65] referred to the virtually complete creolization of the Indian Ocean islands, and described the movement of Créolité in the Francophone Caribbean (which has eclipsed the diasporic Négritude movement). In other settings, there are simultaneous processes of creolization and diasporization. The relative strength of each will turn on external variables and the extent of mobilization of the group concerned toward one or the other trajectory. We can even imagine a situationalist logic where an oscillation between creolization and diaspora occurs according to context. Finally, I have shown that despite an initial incredulity at this possibility, Creoles seemingly can themselves form diasporas. "Creolistas" and "diasporists" also probably share something less tangible and more idealistic. They probably both believe that global justice requires that people's languages, religions, attitudes, behavior, and social conventions are respected and given space to develop. Where there is no self-expression, we have only a poverty of creativity and of the imagination. Expanded uses of diaspora, and certainly creolization, demonstrate that people thrive not by getting stuck in fixed quasi-racial identities, but at the nodes and connection points where new ideas and original inventiveness are developed. As Derek Walcott famously declared, "No nation, but the imagination."

Bibliography

Ali, Suki. *Mixed-Race, Post-Race: Gender, New Ethnicities and Cultural Practices*. Oxford: Berg, 2003.

---

65. Soudien, "District Six."

Anthias, Floya. "Evaluating 'Diaspora': Beyond Ethnicity." *Sociology* 32, no. 3 (1998): 557–80.

Bauman, Zygmunt. *Liquid Modernity.* Cambridge: Polity Press, 2000.

Bernabé, Jean, Patrick Chamoisseau, and Raphaël Confiant. *Eloge de la créolité.* Paris: Gallimard, 1989.

Bhahba, Homi K. "The Third Space: Interview with Homi Bhahba." In *Identity: Community, Culture, Difference.* Edited by Jonathan Rutherford. London: Lawrence and Wishart, 1990.

Brah, Avtar. *Cartographies of Diaspora: Contesting Identities.* London: Routledge, 1996.

Burton, Richard D. E. "The Idea of Difference in Contemporary French West Indian Thought: Négritude, Antillanité, Créolité." In *French and West Indian: Martinique, Guadeloupe and French Guiana Today.* Edited by Richard D. E. Burton and Fred Reno. London: Macmillan, 1995.

Cashmore, Ernst. *Dictionary of Race and Ethnic Relations,* 3rd ed. London: Routledge, 2004.

Chariandy, David. "Postcolonial Diasporas." *Postcolonial Text* 2, no. 1 (2006). On-line journal, unpaginated; http://postcolonial.org/index.php/pct/article/view/440/159.

Cohen, Robin. *Endgame in South Africa?: The Changing Structures and Ideology of Apartheid.* London: James Currey, 1986.

———. *Global Diasporas: An Introduction.* London: UCL Press, 1997.

Croft, T. W. "Gulf Storms, Fables of Reconstruction and Hard Times for the Big Easy: The Wind Has Changed." *Counterpunch* (2005). E-newsletter available at http://www.counterpunch.org/croft12302005.html.

Erasmus, Zimitri. "Introduction: Re-imagining Coloured Identities in Post-apartheid South Africa." In *Coloured by History, Shaped by Place: New Perspectives on Coloured Identities in Cape Town.* Edited by Zimitri Erasmus. Cape Town: Kwela Books, 2001.

Eriksen, Thomas Hylland. "Creolization and Creativity." *Global Networks* 3, no. 3 (2003): 223–37.

Fanon, Frantz. *Toward the African Revolution.* Harmondsworth, UK: Pelican, 1970.

Garvey, Marcus. *The Philosophy and Opinions of Marcus Garvey, Vols. I and II.* Edited by Amy Jacques-Garvey. New York: Atheneum, 1977.

Gilroy, Paul. *Between Camps: Nations, Cultures and the Allure of Race.* London: Penguin, 2000.

———. *The Black Atlantic: Modernity and Double Consciousness.* London: Verso, 1993.

Gold, Steven J. *The Israeli Diaspora.* London: Routledge, 2002.

Hall, Stuart. "New Ethnicities." In *'Race', Culture and Difference.* Edited by James Donald and Ali Rattansi. London: Sage Publications in association with the Open University, 1992.

Hannerz, Ulf. "The World in Creolization." *Africa* 57, no. 4 (1987): 546–59.

——. *Cultural Complexity.* New York: Columbia University Press, 1992.

Herrin, M. H. *The Creole Aristocracy: A Study of the Creole of Southern Louisiana.* New York: Exposition Press, 1951.

Jolivet, Marie-José. *Jeux d'identités: Étude comparative à partir de la Caräibe.* Paris: Harmattan, 1993.

——. *La question créole: Esai de sociologie sur la Guyane française.* Paris: Editions de l'Office de la recherché scientifique et technique outré-mer, 1982.

Kamiya, Gary. "Cablinasian Like Me." (1997). Available on-line at: http://www.salon.com/april97/tiger970430.html.

Lamare, Louis de. "The Creole Diaspora in Australia." (2006). Available on-line at: http://www.iocp.info/articles/The%20Creole%20Diaspora%20in%20Australia.htm.

Naipaul, V. S. *The Enigma of Arrival.* London: Viking, 1987.

——. *In a Free State.* London: André Deutsch, 1971.

——. *Half a Life.* London: Picador, 2001.

——. *A House for Mr. Biswas.* London: André Deutsch, 1961.

——. *The Mimic Men.* London: André Deutsch, 1967.

Pilgrim, David. "The Tragic Mulatto Myth" (2000). Available on-line at: http://www.ferris.edu/HTMLS/News/jimcrow/mulatto/.

Ringer, Benjamin. *"We the People" and Others: Duality and America's Treatment of Its Racial Minorities.* New York: Tavistock Publications, 1983.

Rockquemore, Kerry Ann, and David L. Brunsma. *Beyond Black: Biracial Identity in America.* Thousand Oaks, CA: Sage, 2002.

Rushdie, Salman. *Imaginary Homelands: Essays and Criticism, 1981–1991.* New York: Viking, 1991.

——. *The Satanic Verses.* London: Jonathan Cape, 1988.

Safran, William. "Diasporas in Modern Societies: Myths of Homeland and Return." *Diaspora* 1, no. 1 (1991): 83–99.

——. "The Tenuous Link Between Hostlands and Homeland: The Progressive De-Zionization of Western Diasporas." In *Les diasporas: 2000 ans d'histoire.* Edited by Lisa Anteby-Yemeni, William Berthomière, and Gabriel Sheffer. Rennes: Presses Universitaires de Rennes, 2005.

Sansone, Livio. *Blackness without Ethnicity: Constructing Race in Brazil.* New York: Palgrave Macmillan, 2003.

Saulny, Susan. "Cast from Their Ancestral Homes, Creoles Worry about Culture's Future." *New York Times,* October 11, 2005.

Sökefeld, Martin. "Mobilizing in Transnational Space: A Social Movement Approach to the Formation of Diaspora." *Global Networks* 6, no. 3 (2006): 265–84.

Song, Miri. *Choosing Ethnic Identity*. Cambridge: Polity Press, 2003.

Soudien, Crain. "District Six and Its Uses in the Discussion About Non-Racialism." In *Coloured by History, Shaped by Place: New Perspectives on Coloured Identities in Cape Town.* Edited by Zimitri Erasmus Cape Town: Kwela Books, 2001.

Soysal, Yasemin Nuho-lu. "Citizenship and Identity: Living in Diasporas in Post-War Europe?" *Ethnic and Racial Studies* 23, no. 1 (2000): 1–15.

Spencer, Rainier. "Assessing Multiracial Identity Theory and Politics: The Challenge of Hypodescent." *Ethnicities* 4, no. 3 (2004): 357–79.

Statistics South Africa. *Mid-year Population Estimates, 2005*. Pretoria: Government of South Africa, 2005.

Stoddard, Eve, and Grant H. Cornwell. "Cosmopolitan or Mongrel: Creolité, Hybridity and 'Douglarisation' in Trinidad." *European Journal of Cultural Studies* 2, no. 3 (1999): 331–53.

Tölölyan, Khachig. "Restoring the Logic of the Sedentary to Diaspora Studies." In *Les diasporas: 2000 ans d'histoire*. Edited by Lisa Anteby-Yemeni, William Berthomière, and Gabriel Sheffer. Rennes: Presses Universitaires de Rennes, 2005.

UK National Statistics. *Census 2001: Ethnicity and Religion in England and Wales*. UK Government, London: Office of National Statistics, 2003. Available on-line at: http://www.statistics.gov.uk/pdfdir/ethnicity0203.pdf.

U.S. Census Bureau. *Census 2000: Redistricting Data (Public Law 94-171)*. Summary file. Table PL1. Washington: U.S. Census Bureau, 2003.

Vaughan, Megan. *Creating a Creole Island: Slavery in Eighteenth-Century Mauritius*. Durham, NC: Duke University Press, 2005.

Vertovec, Steven, and Robin Cohen, eds. *Conceiving Cosmopolitanism: Theory. Context, and Practice*. Oxford: Oxford University Press, 2002.

Wagley, Christopher, ed. *Race and Class in Rural Brazil*. Paris: UNESCO, 1952.

In Search of the Basque American Diaspora

By William A. Douglass

Eusko Jaurlaritza, the government of Spain's Basque Autonomous Community, which encompasses the provinces of Bizkaia, Gipuzkoa, and Araba, calculates that there are nine million Basques worldwide. The count includes the populations of Navarra and Iparralde (or the French Basque Country), a procedure that places the population of the European Basque homeland at approximately three million persons—or about one-third of the world's Basques.

Even for the homeland, these seemingly straightforward numbers are nevertheless predicated upon a problematic assumption—that everyone residing in a Basque territory self-identifies as Basque.[1] In point of fact, nearly half of Euskadi's population is constituted by non-Basque migrants from other parts of Spain and their Euskadi-born descendants, immigrants from other European Union countries, as well as increasingly by legal and illegal aliens from Latin America and Africa. The large majority of Navarrese self-identify as Spaniards (and/or Navarrese), rather than as Basques. And although Iparralde's small population is predominantly Basque, ethnic activism there appeals only to a minority.

The six-million-persons figure for the Basque diaspora(s) is at best a loose approximation and includes the emigration from Navarra and Iparralde, as well. It is replete with definitional problems regarding the "Basque credentials" of its components, exacerbated by the individual censusing procedures of twenty or more recipient countries of Basque immigration. Of considerable obscuration, for example, is the fact that, as products of a substate European homeland, diasporic Basques have but rarely been censused as such. Rather, they tend to be reported as Spanish and French nationals. There is also the

---

1. Jacqueline Urla, "Cultural Politics in an Age of Statistics: Numbers, Nations, and the Making of Basque Identity," *American Ethnologist* 20, no. 4 (1993): 818–43.

problem of documentation (or lack thereof) regarding return migration. And, of course, over time in the host countries the cultural assimilation of Basque immigrants and the dilution of the ethnic awareness of subsequent generations of their descendants through intermarriage exacerbate the definitional questioning of the ethnic credentials (and self-identification) of hyphenated Basques. Taken together, these factors all but obviate the possibility of real statistical precision informing the assertion that there are six million persons in the global Basque diaspora(s).

The Imperial Census

The desire and imperative, particularly by government, to count people and property is evident throughout recorded history. Indeed, its earliest records are such lists, without which statecraft, if not impossible, was impaired. The most obvious purposes of censuses were to provide the state with taxes, labor corvees, and military conscripts. Therefore, from the standpoint of households, whole communities, and regions, there was considerable incentive not to be noticed by the census taker or, at the very least, to be undercounted. It is this overriding feature that calls into question the absolute and, in many cases, even the relative accuracy of the listings. While the same defensive dynamic is still apparent to this day, and particularly with regard to individual wealth, within the contemporary, populist welfare state (capitalist and socialist alike), there is also a discernible desire to be counted, or even overcounted, as the key to qualifying for the social benefits accorded to certain categories of citizens.

Census taking is never a neutral and/or entirely benign exercise. At one level, it is simply far too complex and expensive to undertake lightly. Censusing is intrinsically invasive; indeed, its very value to the state correlates with its capacity to be so. Hence, the more extensive or "better" the census instrument, the more likely it is to raise the level of apprehension and suspicion among those being counted. Furthermore, given near universal global migratory movement of both the legally sanctioned variety and a whole plethora of extralegal and illegal forms, there are those within every contemporary state who fear and avoid the process as a matter of personal survival. There are also the dangers of technical computational errors, which at times have proven to be considerable. Hence, despite the benefits of the impressive current technologies at the census takers' disposal, the results of contemporary population counts are both contestable and are regularly contested. It is therefore scarcely surprising that while all states effect censuses, they do so either sporadically or with relatively infrequent periodicity.

All of the foregoing regards census taking within homelands circumscribed by political boundaries and that enjoy the statehood that is requisite for initiating a "national" census in the first place. The value of some sort of count, however flawed, in order to collect revenue, implement social and economic policies, and defend the national territory is self-evident. Far less so is the need to count their expatriates, on the one hand, or their immigrant populations as such, on the other, that is, the very subject matter of diaspora studies. The issue is fundamental, since whether or not the world's census takers choose to disaggregate both their emigrants and immigrants according to "national origins," "ethnic groups," or some other such distinction, we students of transnational population transfers certainly do. The problem is exacerbated considerably when dealing with populations that claim and act out substate or stateless ethnic identities within their country of origin and/or their diasporic host countries. The Basques of both Spain and France provide a prime, although far from unique, example.

While a comparative study of how Basque emigrants have been counted (or not) in host countries—ranging from Argentina to Australia—would raise illuminating issues, I plan to sacrifice such breadth for the depth of documenting the single case study of the Basque Americans of the United States.

Configuring Basque Americans

The history of Basque settlement in the United States is reasonably well documented in narrative fashion.[2] For present purposes, certain features of Basque American historical demography may be underscored.

While some Basques participated in Spanish colonial and exploratory activities in what is today the American Southwest and Southeast, the historical baseline of the contemporary Basque Americans dates from the California Gold Rush of the mid-nineteenth century. Despite the initial attraction of fortune seeking, however, some Basques in the ranks of the so-called "Argonauts," many of whom had experience on the pampas of southern South America, abandoned mining for livestock raising, particularly as nomadic sheepmen on the vast open ranges of the public lands.

By the beginning of the twentieth century Basque sheepmen were present in all eleven states of the American West, with the largest concentration living in California, Idaho, and Nevada. Despite their relative ubiquity throughout the region, the Basque Americans were actually divided broadly into two distinct colonies corresponding to different immigratory pulses—an earlier French Basque one dating from the mid-nineteenth century and concentrated primarily in California and a subsequent Bizkaian influx near the end of the nineteenth century into northern Nevada and southern Idaho. The two colonies were largely isolated from and nearly unaware of each other's existence until after World War II.

But Basque Americans were as concentrated within a single "industry" writ large, sheep raising (as herders and ranchers and even hotel keepers for the transient sheepherder work force) as any other American immigrant group.

The typical Basque immigrant was a single male sojourner seeking a stake with which to return to Europe, rather than a permanent foothold in an adopted land. Consequently, although a few Basque women immigrated to serve as domestics in the hotels,

---

2. William A. Douglass and Jon Bilbao, *Amerikanuak: Basques in the New World* (1975; Reno: University of Nevada Press, 2005); William A. Douglass and Richard W. Etulain, *Basque Americans: A Guide to Information Sources.* Ethnic Studies Information Guide Series, vol. 6 (Detroit: Gale Research Company, 1981).

there was marked gender imbalance within the Basque American community until the latter half of the twentieth century—or after the era of the Basque sheepman was practically over and the residual Basque American community had matured by producing two or more generations of individuals born in the New World.

During the 1920s, the United States Congress passed immigration quotas that severely limited the entry of Spanish nationals while accommodating that of French ones. Consequently, while the French Basque colony of the American West continued to receive regular infusions of European immigrants throughout the twentieth century, the entry of Spanish Basques was initially all but interdicted. After World War II, the latter were able to enter under a contract labor program, but its terms limited their activity to herding and their stay to three years.

Given the relative instability of the Basque American community stemming from its gender imbalance, sojourner nature, and subsequent discriminatory legislation against its Spanish-national components, and despite more than a century and a half of Basque immigration, the 2000 census reported the entire Basque American population to be 57,793 persons. In 2000, collectively, California (20,868), Idaho (6,637), and Nevada (6,096) accounted for nearly 58 percent of all Basque Americans. Nevertheless, even in those states, Basques remained a tiny minority distributed sparsely over a vast territory—in no case did they constitute the majority of a particular community, the Basque ethnic neighborhood was rare, and there was nothing approximating a Basque ghetto to be found anywhere.

Consequently, while in recent decades Basque Americans have emerged in the media and popular awareness as one of the more prominent (and exotic) ethnic groups in at least certain communities of the American West (Boise, Reno, Elko, Bakersfield, etc.), throughout much of their history, they failed to elaborate (beyond certain rudimentary forms) the voluntary associations, internal business networks, ethnic churches, and ethnic press so characteristic of many other American immigrant groups.

Counting Basque Americans Before 1980

Prior to the decision of the U.S. Bureau of the Census to include "Basques," "Spanish Basques," and "French Basques" as ethnic categories within the 1980 census (and the two subsequent ones as well), Basque Americans nevertheless were identified and then counted in the United States in a number of ways and for a variety of reasons. We might reiterate that populations are rarely, if ever, censused by anyone as an abstract exercise. Rather, there is some clear purpose for the enumeration.

Such was the case when Martin Biscailuz, California-born, European-educated descendant of French Basques decided, in 1885, to found the Los Angeles periodical *Escualdun Gazeta* (Basque Gazette). It was not only the initial Basque-language newspaper in North America, it was the first anywhere—including the Basque homeland. Biscailuz noted that his initiative was inspired by the presence of two thousand Basques in Los

Angeles alone, a vast majority being French Basque and Navarrese. So far as we know, *Escualdun Gazeta* published but three issues before expiring.

Prior to Biscailuz's population estimate, our only others were the subjective statements in travel accounts from the California Gold Rush. The German Friedrich Gerstäcker noted, after visiting Murphys Camp in 1850, the presence there of "An immense number of French, a larger part of them Basques."[3] After a stay in a different camp in 1852, Canadian William Perkins described a Basque funeral and noted: "These Basques are strange people, and we have large numbers of them amongst us."[4]

In 1893, a French Basque journalist born in the Old World, José Goytino, founded his own newspaper in Los Angeles, *California-ko Eskual Herria* (California Basque Country). In it, he estimated the state's Basque population to be five thousand, again primarily French Basques and Navarrese.[5] While his periodical regularly published news of Latin American Basque colonies and the Basque Country itself, it all but ignored the more recently arrived Bizkaians of northern Nevada and southern Idaho.

Our next quantification of Basque Americans is even more partial. It was in 1917 that the entrepreneur Sol Silen published his fee-based vanity book of Basque American biographies. Despite its Spanish title of *La historia de los Vascongados en el oeste de los Estados Unidos* (History of Basques in the Western United States), the book's scope was limited geographically to northern Nevada and southern Idaho. It contains 131 biographies identifying 215 individuals, of whom more than 90 percent were Bizkaians (and a few Gipuzkoans).[6] While the introductory material was bilingual (Spanish and English), both its title and the sketches themselves were in Spanish. There is no estimate of the magnitude of the Basque American population in the subject region, but it is clear from the retrospective sketches that its Spanish Basque presence dated from at least 1890 and was well established by the turn of the century.

In 1955, Adrien Gachiteguy, a French Basque chaplain assigned by the bishop of Bayonne to minister to the Basques of the American West, published an overview of them in a work entitled *Les Basques dans l'ouest americain* (Basques in the American West).[7] It was based upon his intimate knowledge of his "parishioners"—not surprisingly, the French Basques (and Navarrese) of California and beyond. For our purposes, the strength of the work is its meticulous listing of the members of Basque American households constituting his far-flung parish, as well as their endogamy. Unfortunately, Gachiteguy's population statistics are far from comprehensive, since they encompass only the communities on his circuit, as well as within them the literal communicants.

---

3. Friedrich Gerstäcker, *Califorsche Skizzen* (Leipzig: Arnold, 1856), 160.

4. William Perkins, *Three Years in California: William Perkins' Journal of Life at Sonora (1849–1852)* (Berkeley: University of California Press, 1964).

5. *California-ko Eskual Herria*, May 18, 1895, 1.

6. Sol Silen, *La historia de los Vascongados en el oeste de los Estados Unidos* (New York: Las Novedades, 1917).

7. Adrien Gachiteguy, *Les Basques dans l'ouest americain* (Belloc: Éditions Ezkila, 1955).

In 1959, there was another attempt to identify (if not necessarily to census) Basque Americans. It was initiated by a committee based in northern Nevada engaged in organizing what was to be the first National Basque Festival. The makeup of the committee, which included French Basques and Bizkaians, those born in both the Old World and the United States, extended its purview to all Basque Americans. Nor were they forced to create their data base ex nihilo. By then, there were Basque clubs in Boise and port of entry New York City, as well as ones in Northern and Southern California. The French Basque chaplain provided his list of addresses. But the real resource was the letter file of one committee member, Robert Laxalt, who two years earlier had published his best-selling book *Sweet Promised Land* (1957).[8] In rich and poignant detail, it narrated his father's story as an immigrant sheepherder, converting Laxalt into the literary spokesman of the Basque American experience. He had received hundreds of letters of gratitude from his fellow ethnics.

The Sparks event was a huge success, bringing together an estimated five thousand to six thousand Basque Americans while nurturing their ethnic pride. It was a combined coming-out party and staging of roots that established the model for subsequent Basque festivals, celebrated to this day in several communities throughout the American West, while stimulating the founding of Basque clubs in many of them.

The last initiative I will consider was my own. In 1967, I was hired by the Desert Research Institute of the University of Nevada System to start a Basque Studies Program (BSP) within its Center for Western North American Studies. The first summer, I attended many festivals throughout the American West to announce the BSP while conducting the initial interviews for its prime research priority—a historical and social-anthropological overview of the region's Basque American community. It was my belief that for the BSP to succeed, it would need to distribute some kind of newsletter, both to keep Basque Americans informed of our activities and to facilitate access to them for research purposes. Consequently, for about three years during my perambulations throughout much of the American West, it was my nightly ritual in some modest motel room to read through a purloined copy of the local telephone directory to underscore the quite distinctive Basque last names for our growing mailing list back in Reno.

The exercise was neither perfect nor comprehensive. Not every Basque is distinctively surnamed, nor is every Basque-surnamed individual necessarily culturally Basque. For example, Aguirre is a Basque surname and, if encountered in the Boise telephone directory, in all probability its bearer is Basque. Conversely, in the Los Angeles phone book, there were several pages of Aguirres, almost all of whom are most certainly Mexicans or Chicanos centuries removed from their Basque legacy, if any. I could, however, count upon a Hirigoyen, the distinctively French Basque spelling of the less reliably Basque (in Los Angeles) Spanish Basque surname Irigoyen. Needless to say, in Southern California, I ignored "Aguirre" and "Irigoyen," but harvested "Hirigoyen." Despite such

---

8. Robert Laxalt, *Sweet Promised Land* (New York: Harper and Row, 1957).

caveats, I managed to compile the names and addresses of approximately five thousand Basque American households throughout the American West.

Counting on the U.S. Census

Actually, it is an exaggeration to regard the U.S. censuses prior to 1980 as totally worthless from the perspective of Basque American scholarship. Indeed, when Jon Bilbao and I first published *Amerikanuak: Basques in the New World*, in 1975, we actually made certain assumptions that admitted some use of the earlier censuses. Again to cite California, the standard census question regarding foreign nationality, derived from either one's own birthplace, if a nonnative, or that of one's parents, if first-generation progeny of an immigrant, was truly useless, since Basques constituted a (unquantifiable) minority of the state's Spanish and French nationals. However, in Idaho, Basques seemed most certainly to represent the vast majority of Spanish nationals, as did they Wyoming's French ones (given the largely French Basque colony of Buffalo).

There was, of course, the possibility of going beyond the population summaries of a particular census to examine the actual forms filled out by the census takers. Indeed, such an approach was employed by Iban Bilbao and Chantal de Eguiluz and reported in their work *Vascos en el censo de la población del oeste americano 1900* (Basques in the 1900 Population Census of the American West). Unfortunately, the exercise did more to clarify methodological and other difficulties than to elucidate a statistical overview of the Basque Americans at the turn of the century. California was excluded initially from consideration, and the exercise was further limited to investigation in the other ten Western states to counties with a significant ranching dimension. Even then, there were many ambiguous cases stemming from illegibility or inclusion of the occasional non-Basque-surnamed Spanish or French national sheepherder. Bilbao and de Eguiluz therefore qualified their findings by referring to "possible Basques" in their study area. Nevertheless, they were able to document only 289 individuals residing in the four states of Nevada (179), Idaho (61), Oregon (26), and Arizona (23). They failed to find a single Basque reported in what seemed the most probable districts of Colorado, Montana, New Mexico, Utah, Washington, or Wyoming.[9]

Bilbao and de Eguiluz subsequently published an analysis of the California census for 1900 and were able to identify only 726 possible Basques in it. Of particular interest, however, was their ability to discern a maturing of the California colony. Nearly half of its identified Basques were American-born.[10]

Since this general paucity of western North American Basques was counterintuitive, given the testimony of oral historical evidence and some published reports of a more significant Basque American presence throughout the region by 1900 (both the Biscailuz

---

9. Iban Bilbao and Chantal de Eguiluz, *Vascos en el censo de población del oeste Americano 1900* (Vitoria-Gasteiz: Diputación Foral de Alava, 1981).

10. Iban Bilbao and Chantal de Eguiluz, *Vascos en el censo de población de California 1900* (Vitoria-Gasteiz: Diputación Foral de Alava, 1982), 83.

and Goytino estimates for California, for example), the authors speculated about the probable causes of such significant undercounting. They noted that many Basques were itinerant sheepmen without a home base, ranging as nomads across the public lands and hence elusive targets for the census taker. Furthermore, the count was effected in May, or during shearing and lambing in many areas of the Great Basin, a time when even settled Basque Americans were likely to be in the sheep camps helping out, rather than at home awaiting the census taker's visit. It was also the immediate aftermath of the Spanish-American War, a time in which a Spanish national was likely to strike the lowest possible profile. And so forth.[11]

In 1986, the attempt to examine turn-of-the-century questionnaires for U.S. census for California in particular was extended by Marie-Pierre Arrizabalaga to the 1910 enumeration. She utilized the 1900 figures provided by Bilbao and de Eguiluz as her baseline in determining the magnitude of increase in Basque settlement in the three key states of California, Nevada, and Idaho by 1910. Although she underscored the familiar reasons for suspecting an undercount, she was able to document a truly dramatic increase in the magnitude of the Basque colonies of the three states: in California, from 745 Basques in 1900 to 6,267 in 1910; in Nevada, from 180 to 971; and in Idaho, from 61 to 999. She was also able to document a growing trend during the decade of Spanish Basque immigration into the San Francisco Bay Area.[12]

It should be noted that the selection of the 1900 and 1910 censuses as objects of the foregoing analyses was determined by the delayed access by investigators to the actual census forms imposed by the U.S. government in the interest of citizens' privacy. The mandated time lag is seventy-two years.

The Pivotal 1980 Census

There were, however, significant developments afoot during the mid-1970s as the U.S. government prepared for the 1980 census exercise. Given the discontent of minority groups who felt that they had been undercounted in previous censuses (and thereby deprived of their fair share of the population-determined, federally dispensed social largesse), the Bureau of the Census was under considerable pressure to include an ethnicity question in the next census.[13] The most vocal voice of discontent stemmed from the nation's "Hispanics," particularly Mexican Americans.[14] After many confrontational

---

11. Ibid., xi–xiii.

12. Marie-Pierre Arrizabalaga, "A Statistical Study of Basque Immigration into California, Nevada, Idaho, and Wyoming, 1900–1910," master's thesis, University of Nevada, Reno, 1986, 40, 44.

13. Ian I. Mitroff, Richard O. Mason, and Vincent P. Barabba, eds., *The 1980 Census: Policy-making Amid Turbulence* (Lexington, MA: Lexington Books, 1980); Margo A. Conk, "The 1980 Census in Historical Perspective," in *The Politics of Numbers*, ed. William Alonzo and Paul Starr (New York: Russell Sage Foundation, 1987); William Alonso and Paul Starr, eds., *The Politics of Numbers* (New York: Russell Sage Foundation, 1987).

14. Harvey M. Choldin, "Statistics and Politics: The 'Hispanic Issue' in the 1980 U.S. Census," *Demography* 23, no. 3 (1986): 405–9.

meetings between an Hispanic Advisory Committee and bureau officials, it was decided to allow one in six respondents in 1980 to self-identify ethnically by opting for one or more possibilities provided in a list to be prepared by the bureau. The results of such a sample would then be extrapolated to the population as a whole.

It was a compromise that failed to satisfy either ethnic activists and some scholars, who were demanding greater comprehensiveness, or the censusing professionals, who shuddered at the effort and cost of collating and reporting the information.[15] Both factions struggled with the definitional challenges—just what subcategories of "Hispanic" to include in the survey.[16] However flawed,[17] the ethnicity question was nevertheless approved and subsequently implemented in the 1980 census.[18]

At some point during this process, I received a call from Edward Fernandez, the person at the Bureau of the Census charged with dealing with the sensitive Hispanic issue.[19] What could I tell him about Basques? He was including Old World Spaniards within the Hispanic rubric (obviously defined in the broadest possible terms), but what to do with the Basques? Were they Spanish, French, both, or should they be assigned a separate ethnic category?

Not only did I argue for the last alternative, I insisted that it should be disaggregated into Spanish Basques, French Basques, and "just" Basques (since I knew at least some U.S.-born Basque Americans increasingly perceived their ethnic heritage in generic terms). Fernandez's initial response to my tripartite proposal was to reject it out of hand. Each distinction would cost an impressive amount of effort and money to implement. But as we continued the conversation, he softened his position. Would I provide him with contacts within the Basque American community so he could call them himself rather than rely exclusively upon an academic's interested representations of their realities? Of course.

Several months later, I heard back from Fernandez. The decision had been made to include on the census form the possibility of self-identifying as "Spanish Basque," "French Basque," and (generic) "Basque"! At a stroke, Basques had gone from being one of America's most obfuscated ethnic groups within the census to, arguably, its best-

---

15. Kenneth Darga, *Sampling and the Census: The Case against the Proposed Adjustments for Undercount* (Washington, DC: The AEI Press, 1999).

16. Choldin, "Statistics and Politics"; Charlotte A. Redden, "Identification of Spanish Heritage Persons in Public Data," *Public Data Use* 4 (1976): 3–11.

17. William Petersen doubted that it is even possible to frame an unambiguously meaningful ancestry/ethnicity question. See William Petersen, "Politics and the Measurement of Ethnicity," in *The Politics of Numbers*, ed. William Alonzo and Paul Starr (New York: Russell Sage Foundation, 1987).

18. Edward W. Fernandez, *Comparison of Persons of Spanish Surname and Persons of Spanish Origin in the United States*, U.S. Bureau of the Census Technical Papers no. 38 (Washington, DC: U.S. Government Printing Office, 1975); Clara E. Rodríguez, *Changing Race: Latinos, the Census, and the History of Ethnicity in the United States* (New York: New York University Press, 2000).

19. While Choldin, in "Statistics and Politics," suggests that bureau officials were reluctant players, my experience would suggest the opposite, as will become apparent.

documented one. Basque Americans were now not only able to self-identify as such, but could parse their identity in three different fashions. To place this in perspective, one might contrast the situation of the 38,838 Basques listed in the 1980 census (the sum of all three subcategories)[20] with that of the millions of self-conscious Sicilian Americans who were allowed only to self-identify as "Italian."[21]

Not only had Basque Americans achieved the status of recognized ethnic group, they also qualified as a minority. For a brief period in the early 1980s, as director of the Basque Studies Program, I was required to provide an annual enumeration of employees of Basque descent (as well as all females) for inclusion within the university's affirmative action report to the federal government. Then, without explanation, I was told to desist because Iberian-born (or Iberian-descended) persons no longer qualified for minority status.[22]

The ancestry/ethnicity exercise has not been without its academic critics. In retrospect, the fashion in which the question was framed in the 1980 census was critiqued by M. Mark Stolarik.[23] Specifically, respondents had been asked to specify "What is this person's ancestry?" and, as an illustration: "For example: Afro-Amer., English, French, German, Honduran, Hungarian, Irish, Italian, Jamaican, Korean, Lebanese, Mexican, Nigerian, Polish, Ukrainian, Venezuelan, etc."[24] With the exception of "Afro-American" and (at the time) "Ukrainian," the list of suggestions still parsed the world by sovereign nationalities. Stolarik, executive director of the Balch Institute for Ethnic Studies, wrote in a letter to the director of the Bureau of the Census:

> The question the Census Bureau *should* have asked is the following: "What is your ethnic heritage?" As an illustration your staff might have written "For example, Afro-Amer.,

---

20. The reported 1980 estimate of 43,140 Basque Americans was flawed by miscoding in the Midwestern part of the United States. The actual figure should have been more like 38,838. See the explanatory note to Table 1 for exposition of the reasoning. For present purposes, I will employ the recalculated figure, rather than the official one when referring to 1980.

21. Reporting of French ancestry now carries the proviso "excluding Basques." Curiously, the same is not true of the category "Spaniard."

22. I subsequently learned that the decision regarding the minority status of Iberians stemmed from the protests of Luso Americans. Unlike peninsular Spaniards in the United States, who have little sense of their ethnic distinctiveness, let alone their own ethnic organizational infrastructure, Portuguese Americans constitute a highly self-aware group in both New England and parts of the American West. By 1980, they had their ethnic associations, annual festivals, and so on. Once the Hispanic minority-status designation was extended to Spaniards, it in effect opened the door to a similar claim by Luso Americans. However, unlike for the passive Spaniards, the designation became a contentious issue among Portuguese Americans. Some were prepared to accept the opportunities afforded by affirmative-action programs for minorities. However, others were offended and made the argument, including in testimony before the U.S. Congress, that Luso Americans are good, hardworking, and economically successful (not to mention Caucasian) Americans in little need of federal largesse. The latter viewpoint prevailed, and the Portuguese Americans were reclassified, an outcome seemingly extrapolated to all Iberians and their descendants.

23. M. Mark Stolarik, "Director's Corner: The Not-So-Accurate 1980 Census," *New Dimensions* (Spring 1984).

24. Bureau of the Census, U.S. Department of Commerce, *Twenty Censuses: Population and Housing Questions, 1790–1980* (Washington, DC: U.S. Government Printing Office, 1979), 82.

Appalachian, Basque, Chinese, English, French-Canadian, German, Gypsy, Hutterite, Jewish, Mormon, Norwegian, Puerto Rican, Scotch-Irish, etc."

The illustration would have made it clear that one's ethnicity is *not* necessarily tied to the country of one's ancestors. Ethnicity *may* arise from country of origin; it *may* be tied to language. But it can also arise from one's religion (Jews, Hutterites, Mormons); it can arise from the region one grows up in (Appalachian); or it can result from one's status as an outcast people (Gypsy). The point is that ethnicity is much more complicated than simply the country of origin of one's ancestors.[25]

In response to such criticism, in the 1990 census, the illustration was modified to read: "For example: German, Italian, Afro-Amer., Croatian, Cape Verdean, Dominican, Ecuadorian, Haitian, Cajun, French Canadian, Jamaican, Korean, Lebanese, Mexican, Nigerian, Irish, Polish, Slovak, Taiwanese, Thai, Ukrainian, etc."[26]

Clearly, this example, while still ignoring regional (e.g., "Appalachian") and religious (e.g. "Mormon") configurations of ancestry, moves away from "nationality." Gone are such major categories in the 1980 prompt as "English" and "French," though not "German," "Italian," and "Irish." No longer do the examples flow in strict alphabetical order, although there is one abortive reflection of it ("Afro-Amer." through "Haitian"), and the exercise ends on an alphabetical note ("French Canadian"and so on). The persistence of the nationality bias is still evident in that fourteen of the twenty-one examples refer to the nationalities of countries with seats in the United Nations in 1990. It might be further noted that there is some redundancy in that question four elicits race, question seven seeks to profile persons of Spanish/Hispanic origin separately, and question eight asks the country of birth of the foreign born.[27]

While the foregoing may strike some as scholastic hairsplitting of nomenclature, in fact, the influence of such categorical designations and shifts upon outcomes can be profound. Recently, James P. Allen analyzed the "For example" factor upon the responses and concluded,

> Examples listed under the ancestry question have occasionally had powerful effects on ethnic group numbers. For example, over 49 million people reported an English ancestry in 1980 when "English" was shown beneath that question as illustrative of ancestry. In 1990, "English" was no longer listed, and only 33 million Americans reported English ancestry. Similarly, in 1980, when "French" was third on the list of ancestry examples, 934,000 people in Louisiana claimed it while only about 7,700 people in that state reported an Acadian or Cajun ancestry. In 1990, however, "Cajun" replaced "French" in the list of

25. Stolarik, "Director's Corner," 5.

26. Bureau of the Census, U.S. Department of Commerce, *Measuring America: The Decennial Censuses from 1790–1990* (Washington, DC: U.S. Government Printing Office, 2002), 91.

27. Ibid., 92.

illustrative ancestries, prompting some 432,000 Louisiana people to claim Cajun ancestry, with only 550,000 still reporting French.[28]

In the 2000 census, the illustration to question ten that now asked "What is this person's ancestry or ethnic ancestry" (rather than "ancestry" alone) was: "For example, Italian, Jamaican, African Am., Cambodian, Cape Verdean, Norwegian, Dominican, French Canadian, Haitian, Korean, Lebanese, Polish, Nigerian, Mexican, Taiwanese, Ukrainian, and so on."[29] No longer were respondents prompted with *either* a "French" or a "Cajun" example. As a consequence (surprise!), only 44,960 Louisianans claimed Cajun ancestry/ethnicity while 545,429 self-identified as "French."[30]

Counting Basques in the 1980, 1990, and 2000 U.S. Censuses

Before considering the actual reported totals in the censuses in question, certain caveats are in order regarding the possible undercounting *and* overcounting of Basque Americans. Given the dramatic effects of inclusion or exclusion of "French" within the illustrative example of ethnicity provided in the census schedule, the fact that "Basque" was never listed explicitly as an ethnic alternative in any of the three censuses alone suggests possible undercounting of Basque Americans. Conversely, while the long form of the census that included the ancestry question was applied to approximately one in six households in each of the three censuses, with the estimates for a particular ethnic group then being extrapolated by multiplying the actual responses by six, the long form was actually applied to half of the households in census divisions with fewer than 2,500 persons. Given the concentration of a significant segment of the Basque American community in the sparsely settled ranching districts of the American West, there is likely some resultant overcounting of them vis-à-vis more urbanized ethnic groups.

Another source of error regards sample size. Obviously, the statistical unreliability (the parameter of error) is far greater when extrapolating a total from the 16 percent of respondent households of a small population (e.g., Basques) than is the case regarding larger ones. Thus, when first reporting the estimated figure for Basques in the 2000 census at 57,232 individuals, the U.S. Census Bureau placed the "lower bound" at 45,331 and the upper one at 69,133, a range of error approximating 20 percent! Regarding the estimated 20,575,998 Irish, however, the lower parameter is 20,381,493 and the upper one 20,770,503, a swing from the estimate on the order of but 1 percent.[31] The sampling error for small groups is exacerbated by the fact that it is the ethnic identity of the head

28. James P. Allen, "Measuring Ethnic Trends with Recent U.S. Census Data: Some Cautionary Notes," *The Immigration and Ethnic History Newsletter* (November 2001), 9.

29. Bureau of the Census, *Census 2002*, Summary File 3, Matrices PCT15 and PCT18, Ancestry Code List (PDF 35 KB), "Louisiana," 2002, 101.

30. Ibid.

31. This was initially reported on the Bureau of the Census Web site (2001) and was subsequently removed.

of household alone that is being recorded and then extrapolated, rather than that of each of its members.

It should also be noted that respondents could ignore the question altogether, opt simply for "American," and claim multiple ancestries. Each of these possibilities obfuscates the results. We have no way of quantifying how many persons with Basque genealogical credentials chose to ignore the fact.

There is also the issue of identity prioritization and privileging. In answering the ancestry question in the three censuses, respondents were allowed to list multiple identities, although only the first two were calculated for reporting purposes (additional ones had to be written in). In the results of the 1980 census, 18,911 of the 38,838 Basque Americans gave "French Basque," "Spanish Basque" or "Basque" as their *sole* identity.[32]

The 1990 census did not distinguish between those claiming a single ancestry, but did list prioritization. Thus, of the 47,956 Basque Americans in the nation, 37,842 (or 78.9 percent) listed some variation of Basque as their first choice (a category that would include those claiming it as their sole ethnic identity), while 10,114 respondents invoked Basqueness as their second identity.[33]

Table 1 (see p. 132) details the Basque totals by state in the last three U.S. censuses. Perhaps the best way to understand the profound impact of the new configuration of the schedules is to consider the status of our anecdotal impression of Basque American demographics prior to 1980. It was then believed that Basques were distributed sparsely and mainly throughout the 11 Western states. To the extent that there were concentrations at all, they were in the open-range ranching districts (and their servicing centers), where Basques, since the latter half of the nineteenth century, had worked as the ubiquitous sheepherders. The existence of urban colonies in the greater San Francisco and Los Angeles areas was also known. The states of Idaho, Nevada, and California were believed to have the largest Basque populations, but their absolute numbers, and even their relative ranking, remained uncertain. New York City, as the major port of entry, and Miami, as the focus of both the Basque ball game jai alai and post-Castro Cuban refugee resettlement (including Basques), were also known to have Basque colonies. Mildly surprising, then, was the presence of at least some Basques in all fifty of the United States.

In certain respects, the 1980 census confirmed the foregoing impressions while fleshing them out. Prior to 1980, at least some scholars and many Basque Americans privileged Idaho with the distinction of likely having more Basques than any other state. In retrospect, it is now apparent that this was due to several factors. There was Idaho's "Bizkaian factor." That is, as earlier noted, even prior to 1980, scholars could be relatively certain that the state's reported total among the foreign-born of "Spanish nationals"

32. Bureau of the Census, U.S. Department of Commerce. *Ancestry of the Population by State: 1980* (Washington, DC: U.S. Government Printing Office, 1981), 12.

33. Bureau of the Census, U.S. Department of Commerce, *1990 Census of the Population, Detailed Ancestry Groups for States* (Washington, DC: U.S. Government Printing Office, 1992), 13.

regarded Basques exclusively and Bizkaians in particular. There was but a handful of non-Basque Spaniards in the state. Then, too, Boise and its hinterland constituted the epicenter of Basque settlement in Idaho. The Bizkaian subethnic heterogeneity of the area's Basques facilitated their activism. By the mid-twentieth century, Idaho's capital city had a Basque club with its own physical Basque center and dance group that performed frequently (both in and out of state) and even represented Idaho at the Seattle World's Fair (1962), the New York World's Fair (1964), the Smithsonian's National Folk Festival (1968), and Expo '70 in Montreal. Such activity, emanating from the capital city of a state whose overall population was miniscule, gave Idaho Basques a high public profile well before those of other Western states were even noticed, let alone acknowledged. In sum, the evident significant population of foreign-born Basques in Idaho, in combination with vague calculations of the number of their descendents in light of the historical depth of its Basque American community, as well as its ethnic activism, led to some estimates of Idaho's Basque population that ranged into the low tens of thousands.

Therefore, the actual reported total of 4,332 Idaho Basques in the 1980 census was a bit startling. By comparison, California's 15,530 Basques, roughly three and a half times more than Idaho's total, were not even a blip on that populace state's demographic radar screen. Furthermore, California Basques encompassed greater Old World Basque regional heterogeneity, a fact that did not preclude (but neither did it facilitate) collective action. Finally, and utilizing 1990 totals, while Idaho's Basques were concentrated in the Snake River drainage (4,099) and with an epicenter in the Ada County (or Boise) area (2,242 persons), California's Basque Americans had southern (6,201 individuals in the greater Los Angeles area) and northern (4,200 persons in the San Francisco Bay area) epicenters that were quite distant from one another, as well as a Central Valley corridor of dispersed (yet relatively significant) Basque colonies in Kern (1,351), Fresno (987), and Sacramento (709) Counties. San Diego County (1,449) had its own considerable Basque American contingent.[34]

Even after purging the totals of a coding error, in 1980, nationally, more respondents claimed French Basque identity than did those opting for Spanish Basque. While this subsequently shifted somewhat in 1990 and 2000, the figures remain disproportionate when compared with Old World Basque demographic reality, where Spanish Basques outnumber their French counterparts by about fourteen to one. They are, however, reflective of the somewhat differing histories in the United States of the respective subethnic groups.

---

34. Figures for Idaho are derived from Bureau of the Census, U.S. Department of Commerce, *1990 Census of Population: Social and Economic Characteristics, Idaho* (Washington, DC: U.S. Government Printing Office, 1993) and for California from Bureau of the Census, U.S. Department of Commerce, *1990 Census of Population: Social and Economic Characteristics, California*, vol. 1 (Washington, DC: U.S. Government Printing Office, 1993). The Snake River drainage figure includes results from Ada, Canyon, Elmore, Gooding, Owyhee, and Twin Falls Counties. The Greater Los Angeles figure incorporates the totals for Los Angeles, Orange, Riverside, San Bernardino, and Ventura Counties. The San Francisco Bay Area figure includes those from the Counties of Alameda, Contra Costa, Marin, San Francisco, San Mateo, Santa Clara, Sonoma, and Solano.

As we have seen, French Basques had longer involvement in the region, and their access to it was less affected by restrictive national origins' U.S. immigration legislation.

Utilizing the sanitized total of 38,838 Basque Americans in the 1980 census, the increase in the self-reported Basque American population between 1980 and 1990 was on the order of 19 percent, which is nearly identical to the growth rate between 1990 and 2000. Taken together, California, Nevada, and Idaho host well over half of the Basque American community in all three censuses—60 percent in 1980, 62 percent in 1990, and 58 percent in 2000. Between 1980 and 2000, at times, all three were among the nation's fastest-growing states. In the 1980–1990 intercensal period, their combined growth rate of 25.8 percent surpassed that of the Basque American community of the United States. However, between 1990 and 2000, while the rate of increase in Idaho (28.5 percent) and Nevada (66.3 percent) remained robust, that of California dropped to a more modest 13.8 percent, considerably less than that of the nation's Basque American community. During the same decade, California's Basque American population grew by 9.2 percent, less than 1 percent annually and less than half the growth rate of the nation's Basque Americans. Throughout both intercensal periods, percentagewise, Nevada was the fastest-growing state in the United States. Between 1980 and 1990, its Basque American community increased by 43.3 percent; from 1990 to 2000, the growth rate held at 26 percent. Nevertheless, the growth remained below that of the state's population as a whole. At 29 percent, growth was robust among Idaho's Basques during the first intercensal period, particularly in light of the state's modest 6.7 percent total population increase. During the second intercensal period, at 18.8 percent, the increase in Idaho's Basques was respectable, although less than that of the nation's Basque American community and the growth in the state's overall population (28.5 percent).

By 2000, then, Nevada's Basque population (6,096) was beginning to challenge Idaho's (6,637) status as the second largest in the nation. It is perhaps indicative that there is now a Basque festival in Las Vegas, the fastest-growing city in the United States, but far removed from Nevada's "traditional" area of Basque settlement (the ranching districts several hundred miles to the north). By 2000, Clark County had 713 Basques, up from 341 in 1990.[35]

There is also an urban immigration effect evident in several states. Indeed, the attraction of Seattle in Washington, Salt Lake City in Utah, Denver in Colorado, Phoenix in Arizona, Atlanta in Georgia, several metropolitan areas in Texas, Chicago in Illinois, and Miami in Florida seems to account for the increases in the respective Basque populations of those states during the last two decades of the twentieth century (see Table 2, p. 133). This likely reflects both the growth in individuals born in the New World within the Basque American community and their progressive generational distancing from

---

35. Bureau of the Census, U.S. Department of Commerce, *Census of Population: Social and Economic Characteristics, Nevada* (Washington, DC: U.S. Government Printing Office, 1993), 159.

their immigrant roots. Increasingly, Basque Americans pursue higher education, with the attendant mobility (physical and social) that it implies.

Another development worthy of speculation is the marked shift between 1980 and 1990 in the way that some Americans claimed Basque descent. In 1980, 22,686, or 58 percent of the respondents opted for a "Basque" identity, meaning that 42 percent chose to specify a "French Basque" or "Spanish Basque" ethnic heritage, instead. However, by 1990, fully 72 percent of Basque Americans listed generic "Basque" as their ethnic identity, which then increased to 74 percent in the 2000 census. Between 1990 and 2000, there was an increase in all three categories, yet more than seven thousand of the nearly ten-thousand-person increase in the Basque American community opted for the generic Basque identity—its total in 2000 (41,811) had surpassed that of all Basque Americans (38,838) in 1980. To appreciate the significance of this trend, as well as the conundrum that it poses for the scholar of Basque American society, it is necessary to consider both Old World and New World political and cultural developments.

The twentieth century was a period of marked ethnonationalism in the Basque homeland. However, its effects differed in Iparralde (the French Basque area) and Hegoalde (the three Spanish Basque provinces and Navarra). Basque nationalism has never garnered more than single-digit electoral support in Iparralde. Consequently, for its inhabitants, "Basqueness" is more of a cultural than political phenomenon. Conversely, in Hegoalde, during the first third of the twentieth century, Basque nationalism emerged as a significant political force that constituted its own independent state (briefly) during the early phase of the Spanish Civil War. Throughout the Franco years (1939–75), Basque nationalists remained a formidable political force in parts of the Basque diaspora (although not in the United States), as well as clandestinely within the Spanish state. The willingness of one sector of the movement to respond to Franco's oppression with violence gave rise to ETA, thereby triggering Western Europe's second-most virulent and deadly (after Ulster) post–World War II ethnonationalist conflict.

In the aftermath of Franco's death, the Basques refused to ratify the proposed Spanish Constitution, but then approved a Statute of Autonomy that constituted Eusko Jaurlaritza, the autonomous region of Euskadi overarching the three provinces of Araba, Gipuzkoa, and Bizkaia. While not endowed with full political sovereignty, Eusko Jaurlaritza has its own president and parliament, as well as broad powers in domestic and fiscal matters. Throughout its existence, it has been dominated by the Basque Nationalist Party, usually as the dominant partner within a ruling coalition.

Eusko Jaurlaritza has a Ministry of External Affairs with a section charged with diasporic matters. Gloria Totoricagüena's paper in this volume deals with much of the detail. For my purposes, suffice it to say that Eusko Jaurlaritza now proffers various forms of outreach and assistance to the Basque clubs of the American West, including those with large French Basque contingents. In short, the activities of Eusko Jaurlaritza in the United States are framed in terms of a common generic Basque identity.

The twentieth century also witnessed a major development within the Basque cultural scene. Under the aegis of Euskaltzaindia, the Basque Language Academy, there was a serious effort to unify the several dialects of spoken (and written) Basque into a single language. Euskara Batua now dominates the media and educational system of Euskadi. While it has not entirely supplanted the dialects and is arguably more dominant in Hegoalde than in Iparralde, it both nourishes and facilitates a common Basque identity.

The influence of the foregoing upon the self-identification of Basque Americans to the census taker is difficult to ascertain with precision. The majority of Basque Americans are descended from immigrants who entered the United States as young bachelors from rural origins, with modest educational backgrounds and political formation, and at a time when Basque nationalism in Spain was still in its formative phase. It is scarcely an exaggeration to state (with some exceptions) that even Basque Americans descended from Hegoalde have been unresponsive to Old World Basque politics (except to abhor the label of "terrorists" facilely associated with "Basque" in the international media), while Basque Americans descended from Iparralde are positively indifferent, when not hostile, to Basque nationalism. Nor has Euskara Batua enjoyed a great deal of success in supplanting the dialects among the minority of Basque Americans still fluent in the language.

In short, while we can demonstrate that the decade of the 1980s was a significant one in the evolution of Basque political and cultural consciousness in Hegoalde, its impact upon Basque Americans was minimal, although not altogether absent. How, then, can we explain the pronounced shift toward a generic Basque identity among Basque Americans? I would be inclined to ascribe it mainly to what might be called the "NABO effect." That is, by the decade of the 1980s, NABO (North American Basque Organizations, Inc.), founded in 1972 as an overarching association of Basque American social clubs, was hitting its stride. Virtually all of the Basque clubs of the United States had joined, and NABO was facilitating the organization of new ones. It was hosting annual summer music camps where Basque American children from throughout the American West were brought together to learn songs and dances and to play traditional instruments. NABO was also sponsoring the U.S. tours of Old World Basque performing artists and an annual "national" *mus* (a Basque playing card game) elimination to determine the U.S. representative team to the annual international *mus* championship. NABO also interfaced with Eusko Jaurlaritza regarding the latter's efforts to stimulate Basque culture throughout the diaspora. From the outset, NABO's mission and activities have proclaimed that Basque Americans are simply "Basque," irrespective of Old World regional distinctions.[36]

---

36. This may account in some small measure for the decline during the 1980–1990 intercensal period in Idaho's (overwhelmingly Bizkaian) population from 600 to 353 persons who self-identified as "Spanish Basque," whereas simply "Basque" went from 3,511 to 5,068 persons, or an increase of 44.3 percent. This may also be reflected in the California totals. During the 1980–1990 intercensal period, the reported numbers of French and Spanish Basques declined but slightly, yet the total of persons claiming solely a "Basque" identity increased by 51 percent, from 8,098 to 12,227 individuals.

Finally, there is the question of the vigor or stability of their ethnic identity among Basque Americans. Basques are unlike most other long-standing European immigrant groups within American society that are manifesting declining or static numbers of persons claiming an ancestral identity.[37] As noted earlier, there has been an increase in the estimated Basque American population on the order of 20 percent since 1980 from one census to another. In sum, despite the paucity of Basque immigration in the United States during the last two decades of the twentieth century, the Basque American community has expanded at a vigorous pace.

Conclusion

In order to illuminate better the complex interplay of fragmentary purpose and even aleatory elements that inform the censusing of any population, I have limited my substantive treatment to but one strand of the Basque diaspora. Nevertheless, I do so in the belief that such analysis underscores several object lessons for the scholar of *any* diaspora. Our common conundrum is to ask who is counting whom and for what purposes. Since it is virtually impossible for the individual scholar of diasporic outcomes to effect a comprehensive census of her own, there is therefore inevitable recourse to the clearly flawed and often near irrelevant statistics generated by others—and particularly the censuses conducted by the emigrants' sending and receiving countries. Since we all suffer from similar inadequacies in this regard, there is a certain laissez faire acceptance among diaspora studies researchers of each other's guesstimates regarding subject population. In short, we seldom question one another's definitions and methodology out of subliminal uncertainty regarding our own. It is far easier to accept that there are nine million Basques in the world than to ask who was being counted (if at all), how, why, and by whom.

I have no methodological panacea to offer other than to note that the problem can be dealt with only incrementally. The first step is clearly to recognize, rather than simply to finesse, the shortcomings of our databases. At that point, it may be possible if not to effect our own censuses, then to affect the official census takers themselves by influencing the assumptions that inform their questions. I have considered the example of how Basque Americans have gone from being one of the worst-documented to one of the best-documented ethnic groups within American society, albeit through no fault of their or my own. The current improved state of affairs proved possible once late twentieth-century census takers in the United States became sensitized to the need (for public purposes, rather than academic ones) for better understanding of the country's ethnic makeup.[38]

---

37. For example, between 1990 and 2000, the percentage of persons opting for Belgian ancestry declined by 8.4 percent, German Americans by 26.1 percent, English Americans by 24.9 percent, Finnish Americans by 5.4 percent, Irish Americans by 21.2 percent, French Americans by 26.1 percent, Welsh Americans by 13.8 percent, Scottish Americans by 9.3 percent, and so on. Bureau of the Census, U.S. Department of Commerce, *Ancestry: 2000* (Washington, DC: U.S. Government Printing Office, 2004), 4–5.

38. In justifying specification of ancestry in the 2000 census, the Bureau of the Census noted, "Information about ancestry is required to enforce provisions under the Civil Rights Act that prohibit discrimination based upon race, sex,

The same tendency is clearly apparent in Canada, Australia, and Great Britain—that is, pretty much throughout the Anglo-configured world—and is not entirely missing elsewhere.[39] Nevertheless, while it is a vast improvement from the perspective of a student of Basque American reality, I find the present approach far from perfect.[40]

Improving the numbers, of course, is only a part of the challenge, since refining our understanding of them is clearly of greater importance. It is at this juncture that we enter the messy realm of identity formation—possibly the most active interdisciplinary concern at present in most of the social sciences (excluding economics) and several of the humanities. I believe that it is particularly incumbent upon scholars of immigrant diasporas to refine our subject matter. For in addition to our flawed statistics, our other little secret is how we massage their components.

To cite the Basque American example, should I include a person with impeccable genealogical credentials (four Basque grandparents), born in the United States, who cares not one whit about ethnic heritage and ignores, rather than avoids eating in the local Basque restaurant, attending the local festival, and joining the local Basque club? Conversely, do I accord full status in the category "Basque American" to the person with a single Basque great-grandparent who self-identifies, that is, fills in the blank, as "Basque" in the U.S. census questionnaire? Framed somewhat differently, what do I do with the individual born of Galician parents, born in the Basque Country and emigrated from the port of Bilbao to Buenos Aires, who then joins that city's Spanish club, but none of its Basque associations? It would seem that for certain purposes he or she might be counted "Galician" (a viable ethnic distinction within Argentine society), "Basque," "Spanish," or even all three, but only insofar as I became quite explicit regarding the terms and purposes of my analysis. Such are but some of the more obvious challenges to the configuration of the Basque diaspora, as well as any other.

---

religion, and national origin. More generally, these data are needed to measure the social and economic characteristics of ethnic groups and to tailor services to accommodate their cultural differences." Ibid., 9.

39. Heather Booth, "Which 'Ethnic Question?': The Development of Questions Identifying Ethnic Origin in Official Statistics," *Sociological Review* 32 (1985): 254–74; David I. Kertzer and Dominique Arel eds., *Census and Identity: The Politics of Race, Ethnicity, and Language in National Censuses* (Cambridge: Cambridge University Press, 2002).

40. Regarding the counting of Basque Americans prior to 1980, there is a promising development to report. In 2005, the Nevada State Legislature appropriated $250,000 during the biennium for creation of a genealogy initiative within University of Nevada, Reno's Center for Basque Studies. As of this writing, a team of seventeen persons, including fifteen extractors based at Center for Family History and Genealogy at Brigham Young University, have begun searching the 1880, 1900, 1920, and 1930 U. S. censuses for Basques throughout the American West. The purview is being extended to Social Security Administration records, the military conscription files for World War I, the Ellis Island passenger lists, and selected state and county vital records.

William A. Douglass

TABLE 1

Basque Population of the United States, as Reported
by the U.S. Bureau of the Census, 1980, 1990, and 2000.

STATE	Basques, French		Basques, Spanish		Basques, n.e.c.		Total Basques		
	1980	1990	1980	1990	1980	1990	1980	1990	2000
Alabama	36	24	0	44	46	14	82	82	107
Alaska	10	37	33	38	62	170	105	245	276
Arizona	152	53	199	298	749	965	1,100	1,316	1,655
Arkansas	34	20	0	21	39	63	73	104	71
California	3,619	3,387	3,813	3,508	8,098	12,227	15,530	19,112	20,868
Colorado	341	148	168	110	446	679	955	937	1,674
Connecticut	36	22	64	64	120	233	220	319	262
Delaware	18	0	0	7	3	6	21	13	12
Dist. of Columbia	22	0	12	16	29	21	63	37	180
Florida	201	117	315	334	343	738	859	1,189	2,127
Georgia	87	11	59	27	77	90	223	128	282
Hawaii	10	19	4	29	55	121	69	169	175
Idaho	221	166	600	353	3,511	5,068	4,332	5,587	6,637
Illinois***	422	49	66	75	165	321	654*	445	533
Indiana***	94	55	48	0	18	135	160	190	168
Iowa***	260	20	24	8	40	31	324	59	50
Kansas ***	92	10	18	24	50	36	160	70	146
Kentucky***	81	11	15	15	36	68	132	94	55
Louisiana	133	73	57	38	65	115	255	226	354
Maine	22	2	0	21	28	13	50	36	57
Maryland	51	60	48	45	148	163	247	268	339
Massachusetts	34	37	80	73	187	227	301	337	383
Michigan***	145	7	28	47	158	162	331	236	306
Minnesota***	110	24	8	15	102	91	220	130	195
Mississippi	7	4	2	0	20	24	29	28	64
Missouri***	164	27	18	10	61	114	243	151	180
Montana	116	66	6	46	268	357	390	469	564
Nebraska***	2,707	0	6	0	41	45	2,754	45	85
Nevada	371	472	915	776	2,092	3,592	3,378	4,840	6,096
New Hampshire	3	0	0	0	29	53	32	53	158
New Jersey	98	72	134	143	265	319	497	534	643
New Mexico	87	63	83	61	291	378	461	502	600
New York	202	131	508	242	716	927	1,426	1,300	1,252
North Carolina	57	16	48	6	31	97	136	119	330
North Dakota***	25	0	0	0	0	11	25	11	39
Ohio***	207	33	31	15	85	155	323	203	230
Oklahoma	21	0	5	23	84	82	110	105	126
Oregon	369	172	224	298	1,660	1,787	2,253	2,257	2,627
Pennsylvania	138	23	14	13	68	214	220	250	278
Rhode Island	5	0	44	0	40	24	89	24	23
South Carolina	24	4	31	14	14	30	70	48	76
South Dakota***	50	0	7	8	5	22	62	30	64
Tennessee	34	2	4	14	16	75	54	91	145
Texas	159	98	170	238	558	912	887	1,248	1,691
Utah	129	148	134	261	610	1,013	873	1,422	1,361
Vermont	0	0	0	0	28	2	28	2	34
Virginia	168	19	72	59	112	325	352	403	575
Washington	124	145	306	154	704	1,471	1,134	1,770	2,665
West Virginia	78	0	5	0	23	9	106	9	8
Wisconsin	189	8	5	8	49	85	243	101	98
Wyoming	155	146	103	21	241	435	499	602	869
TOTALS	11,918	6,001	8,534	7,620	22,686	34,315	43,140	47,956	57,793**

N.B. The source for 1980 and 1990 is the Census Bureau's own published statistics, Bureau of the Census, U.S. Department of Commerce, *1990 Census of the Population, Detailed Ancestry Groups for States* (Washington, DC: U.S. Government Printing Office, 1992), 13. The results for all Basque Americans in 2000 were released initially by state, but without distinguishing among the three subcategories of Basques. It was not until April 2006 that the subcategories were released, but only on the Census Bureau's Web site and in national aggregate format. Unfortunately, at this time, there is no plan to disaggregate and report by state the distribution of the three subcategories of Basque Americans in the 2000 census. This, of course, impairs our capacity to effect longitudinal analysis of the trends in Basque American self-identification.

* There is a compiler's discrepancy of one French Basque in the 1980 Illinois count.

** Includes 187 Basques in Puerto Rico. It was not until the 2000 census that Puerto Rican ancestry totals were reported within the overall national count.

*** States with likely overcounts of French Basques in 1980. The figures for the 1980 census include a coding error that has never been corrected. In the Midwestern United States a different group (undetermined) was being coded wholly or partially as "French Basque." The total French Basque population of the states identified in Table 1 with a triple asterisk is 4,546 individuals, versus 244 reported in 1990. Nebraska provided the most egregious example. The 1980 census reports 2,707 French Basques in the state, whereas there is not a single one in the 1990 count! Consequently, I have "sanitized" the national totals of French Basques and all Basques in 1980 by subtracting the 1990 figure for French Basques in the thirteen Midwestern states with likely coding errors from their reported 1980 outcomes. In this fashion, the 1980 national total for French Basques is 7,617 (rather than 11,919) and for all Basque Americans is 38,838 (rather than 43,140). The former figure has been used in the text when stating totals for all and subcategories of Basque Americans in 1980 and the percentage of the subsequently demographic evolution of the Basque American community.

TABLE 2
Basques Residing in Selected Metropolitan Areas, 1990 Census

State	Number of Basques	Metropolitan Area	Number of Basques	Metropolitan Area as Percentage of State Total
Arizona	1,316	Phoenix	628	47.7
Colorado	937	Denver	296	31.6
Florida	1,189	Miami	376	31.6
Georgia	128	Atlanta	103	80.5
Illinois	445	Chicago	331	74.4
New York	1,300	New York City	838	64.5
Oregon	2,257	Portland	658	29.2
Texas	1,248	Metropolitan*	833	66.7
Utah	1,422	Salt Lake–Ogden	1,105	77.7
Washington	1,770	Seattle-Tacoma	789	44.6

* Dallas–Fort Worth, El Paso, Houston, and San Antonio.

Bibliography

Allen, James P. "Measuring Ethnic Trends with Recent U.S. Census Data: Some Cautionary Notes." *The Immigration and Ethnic History Newsletter* (November 2001).

Alonso, William, and Paul Starr, eds. *The Politics of Numbers.* New York: Russell Sage Foundation, 1987.

Arrizabalaga, Marie-Pierre. "A Statistical Study of Basque Immigration into California, Nevada, Idaho, and Wyoming, 1900–1910." Master's thesis, University of Nevada, Reno, 1986.

Bilbao, Iban, and Chantal de Eguiluz. *Vascos en el censo de población de California 1900.* Vitoria-Gasteiz: Diputación Foral de Alava, 1982.

———. *Vascos en el censo de población del oeste Americano 1900.* Vitoria-Gasteiz: Diputación Foral de Alava, 1981.

Booth, Heather. "Which 'Ethnic Question?': The Development of Questions Identifying Ethnic Origin in Official Statistics." *Sociological Review* 32 (1985): 254–74.

Bureau of the Census, U.S. Department of Commerce. *Ancestry of the Population by State: 1980.* Washington, DC: U.S. Government Printing Office, 1981.

———. *Ancestry: 2000.* Washington, DC: U.S. Government Printing Office, 2004.

———. *Census of Population: Social and Economic Characteristics, Nevada.* Washington, DC: U.S. Government Printing Office, 1993.

———. *Census 2000: Ancestry First-Reported Universe Total Population.* PCT024, 2001.

———. *Census 2002,* Summary File 3, Matrices PCT15 and PCT18, Ancestry Code List (PDF 35 KB), "Louisiana," 2002.

———. *Measuring America: The Decennial Censuses from 1790–1990.* Washington, DC: U.S. Government Printing Office, 2002.

———. *1990 Census of the Population, Detailed Ancestry Groups for States.* Washington, DC: U.S. Government Printing Office, 1992.

———. *1990 Census of Population: Social and Economic Characteristics, California.* Vol. 1. Washington, DC: U.S. Government Printing Office, 1993.

———. *1990 Census of Population: Social and Economic Characteristics, Idaho.* Washington, DC: U.S. Government Printing Office, 1993.

———. *Twenty Censuses: Population and Housing Questions, 1790–1980.* Washington, DC: U.S. Government Printing Office, 1979.

Choldin, Harvey M. "Statistics and Politics: The 'Hispanic Issue' in the 1980 U.S. Census." *Demography* 23, no. 3 (1986): 403–17.

Conk, Margo A. "The 1980 Census in Historical Perspective." In *The Politics of Numbers.* Edited by William Alonzo and Paul Starr. New York: Russell Sage Foundation, 1987.

Darga, Kenneth. *Sampling and the Census: The Case against the Proposed Adjustments for Undercount.* Washington, DC: The AEI Press, 1999.

Douglass, William A., and Jon Bilbao. *Amerikanuak: Basques in the New World.* 1975; Reno: University of Nevada Press, 2005.

———, and Richard W. Etulain. *Basque Americans: A Guide to Information Sources.* Ethnic Studies Information Guide Series, vol. 6. Detroit: Gale Research Company, 1981.

Fernandez, Edward W. *Comparison of Persons of Spanish Surname and Persons of Spanish Origin in the United States.* U.S. Bureau of the Census Technical Papers no. 38. Washington, DC: U.S. Government Printing Office, 1975.

Gachiteguy, Adrien. *Les Basques dans l'ouest americain.* Belloc: Éditions Ezkila, 1955.

Gerstäcker, Friedrich. *Californsche Skizzen.* Leipzig: Arnold, 1856.

Kertzer, David I., and Dominique Arel, eds. *Census and Identity: The Politics of Race, Ethnicity, and Language in National Censuses.* Cambridge: Cambridge University Press, 2002.

———. "Censuses, Identity Formation, and the Struggle for Political Power." In *Census and Identity: The Politics of Race, Ethnicity, and Language in National Censuses.* Edited by David I. Kertzer and Dominique Arel. Cambridge: Cambridge University Press, 2002.

Kurlansky, Mark. *The Basque History of the World.* New York: Walker and Co, 1999.

Laxalt, Robert. *Sweet Promised Land.* New York: Harper and Row, 1957.

Mitroff, Ian I., Richard O. Mason, and Vincent P. Barabba, eds. *The 1980 Census: Policy-Making amid Turbulence.* Lexington, MA: Lexington Books, 1980.

Perkins, William. *Three Years in California: William Perkins' Journal of Life at Sonora (1849–1852).* Berkeley: University of California Press, 1964.

Petersen, William. "Politics and the Measurement of Ethnicity." In *The Politics of Numbers.* Edited by William Alonzo and Paul Starr. New York: Russell Sage Foundation, 1987.

Redden, Charlotte A. "Identification of Spanish Heritage Persons in Public Data." *Public Data Use* 4 (1976): 3–11.

Rodríguez, Clara E. *Changing Race: Latinos, the Census, and the History of Ethnicity in the United States.* New York: New York University Press, 2000.

Silen, Sol. *La historia de los Vascongados en el oeste de los Estados Unidos.* New York: Las Novedades, 1917.

Stolarik, M. Mark. "Director's Corner: The Not-So-Accurate 1980 Census." *New Dimensions* (Spring 1984).

Urla, Jacqueline. "Cultural Politics in an Age of Statistics: Numbers, Nations, and the Making of Basque Identity." *American Ethnologist* 20, no. 4 (1993): 818–43.

Diasporic Politics in the European Union: Paris's City Hall and the Jewish Quarter

By Michel S. Laguerre

The study of European neighborhoods as "global ethnopolises" or "global chronopolises" can be used to understand the internal organization of the globalization process within the European Union.[1] This "globalization from below" complements the "globalization from above" of international politics and of trading practices between states. It is an intrinsic component of European globalization because of its distinctive contributions to the process. In other words, these local places are being transformed into operative global sites that, in their own different ways, link the local to the global, rearticulate the global with the local at the local level, and rearticulate the local with the global at the global level.

The social integration of European neighborhoods has taken place at the same time the countries in which they are located are being integrated into the European Union. This manifests itself in the double adaptation of these neighborhoods—at the country level in terms of the urban policies of city hall, and at the level of the European Union in terms of immigration policy, since the European Parliament can overrule local practices.[2] The reengineering of local practices is being carried out at the same time as diaspor-

I want to thank Jais Avi Bitton, Michel Kalifa, and Claude Dubois for discussing these issues with me while I was conducting the research in Paris, Bud Bynack for editorial assistance, and Gloria Totoricagüena for the invitation to read this paper at the Center for Basque Studies Conference. This essay will also appear in my new book entitled *Global Neighborhoods: Jewish Quarters in Paris, London, and Berlin* (Albany: State University of New York Press, forthcoming).

1. For definitions of "ethnopolis" and "chronopolis," see Michel S. Laguerre, *The Global Ethnopolis: Chinatown, Japantown and Manilatown in American Society* (New York: Macmillan, 2000), and Michel S. Laguerre, *Urban Multiculturalism and Globalization in New York City* (New York: Palgrave Macmillan, 2003).

2. Judith Allen, "Europe of the Neighborhoods: Class, Citizenship and Welfare Regimes," in *Social Exclusion in European Cities*, ed. Ali Madanipour, Goran Cars, and Judith Allen (London: Routledge, 2000).

ic residents of these neighborhoods are entertaining transnational relations with their homelands and other diasporic sites where their compatriots have resettled, thereby adding another layer of complexity to the globalization process.

This essay examines the relations of Paris's city hall with the city's Jewish quarter. The city administration has been studying the best way to intervene and renovate the Jewish quarter. It has argued that this area needs to integrate with the larger modernization plan for the city being implemented by the mayor's office. This controversy has created a messy situation in the neighborhood due to the merchants' association's protests against such urban renovation, since they believe it will lead to the extinction of many shops and the eventual disappearance of the Jewish quarter itself. What follows analyzes the controversy and explains what is at stake for both sides.

The relations of the neighborhood with city hall are a pivotal issue to analyze in order to understand the Jewish quarter's manifold globalization. These relations have a global content, and their outcome shapes some aspects of neighborhood globalization. This is so because city hall has more than just the well-being of the neighborhood in mind in developing the municipality's urban policies.

The local government must think globally, that is, not only in terms of articulating the Jewish quarter with the rest of the city, but also in terms of increasing profit by opening it up to tourists from around the world and therefore enhancing the tax base and improving the local economy. Globalization is also a factor when this issue is seen from the residents' standpoint. These relations, among other things, are evaluated in terms of the residents' ability to maintain ties with the homeland and with other diasporic sites through the maintenance and reproduction of their way of life and cultural traditions, which are also what attracts tourists to their businesses.

While city hall has the tourist trade in general in mind, the residents think more specifically in terms of Jewish tourists, that is, Jews who come to visit and buy things from the merchants, to attend synagogue services and other cultural events, or simply to eat at the local restaurants. The residents' strong opposition therefore tended to focus on the mayor's proposals to renovate, modernize, and reshape the look of the streets and redirect traffic routes inside the Jewish quarter.[3] The views of the residents, of course, were not homogeneous. Those opposing the initiative were to be found mostly among local merchants who wanted to protect the integrity of their niche market and among religious Jews who depended on the shops in the quarter for the purchase of religious books, cultic objects, and kosher food. Nevertheless, the controversy over the renovation of the Jewish quarter evolved out of two different approaches to city planning, two dif-

---

3. The Jewish quarter has been the subject of several studies, including Nancy Green, *Les travailleurs immigrés juifs à la Belle Epoque, Le Pletzl de Paris* (Paris: Fayard, 1985); Sylvia Ostrowetsky, "La puissance des disposifs spatiaux," in *Formes architecturales, formes urbaines* (Paris: Anthropos, 1994); Marie-Helene Poggi, "Le quartier du Marais, le mélange et le feuillete," in *Pour une sociologie de la forme* (Paris: L'Harmattan, 1999); Lorenza Mondada, "Un sescripteur contesté: Le ghetto," in *Décrire la ville* (Paris: Anthropos, 2000); Jane Brody, "Le quartier de la Rue des Rosiers, ou l'histoire d'un cheminement," in *Les cheminements de la ville* (Paris: Editions CTHS, 1985); Bernadette Costa, *Je me souviens du Marais* (Paris: Parigramme, 1995); and Paul E. Hyman, *The Jews of Modern France* (Berkeley: University of California Press, 1998).

ferent perceptions of the problem that the ethnic neighborhood faced, and two different ways of stabilizing the Jewish character of the site—a top-down approach taken by city hall, and a bottom-up approach taken by advocates for preserving the ethnic character of the neighborhood. Ironically, it was the neighborhood's opposition to the plan that was reinforced by globalized local resources against the efforts of city hall to implement the French national ideal of equality, of treating everyone the same, rather than conserving ethnic differences. The renovation controversy thus provides an example of a site where the global not only meets the local, but also complicates the local resolution of the problem.

In the winter of 2004, while conducting field research in the Jewish neighborhood in Paris, I became aware of this boiling opposition to the mayor's plan to refurbish the site and the Jewish merchants' association's plan to stop the implementation of what they considered to be an ill-advised initiative.[4] I went to the mayor's office to interview a high-ranking municipal official so as to have a better sense of the rationale behind this new urban planning project, including what was to be remodeled and the time-table contemplated for implementation. I interviewed the point person of the mayor in charge of the Jewish quarter dossier, who both advised the mayor, Dominique Bertinotti, and coordinated her relations with the Jewish neighborhood in matters related to local democracy.

Well-informed on the position of the dissident group of merchants and other residents, this municipal official briefly explained to me that the plan of renovation was in line with the Plan Malreaux, in which the former minister of culture elaborated and promulgated a national agenda for the renovation of French cities. So far, this national plan had been implemented almost everywhere in Paris except in the Jewish quarter. The Jewish quarter initiative was an offspring of this larger plan and had been elaborated, according to this official, taking into consideration the views of the residents and the needs of the municipality. In the mayor's view, the outcome of renovation would be good for both the neighborhood and the city in terms of revenue maximization, the facilitation of traffic, and the modernization of the streets.

Neighborhood Renovation and Globalization

Although the ethnic character of the neighborhood existed prior to the existence of France as a nation-state, the politics of the city vis-à-vis its renovation must be seen in light of the current assimilation policy of the municipal government. Various aspects of French urban policy vis-à-vis ethnic neighborhoods have emphasized the notion of social

---

4. Elaine Sciolino, "Jewish District Rallies to Save Its Soul from Renovation," *New York Times*, Monday, April 5, 2004; Cecilia Gabizon, "Polémique sur l'aménagement de la Rue des Rosiers," *Le Figaro*, Monday April 6, 2004; Francoise Chirot, "Controverse autour de la "piétonnisation" du quartier juif de Paris," *Le Monde*, Friday, November 21, 2003; Aurélie Sarrot, "Consultation prolongée pour la Rue des Rosiers," *MétroParis*, Monday, February 9, 2004; Christophe de Chenay, Les Parisiens veulent préserver l'originalité de leurs quartiers," *Le Monde*, Friday, November 28, 2003; Eric Le Mitouard, "Les 10 vérités sur la future Rue des Rosiers," *Le Parisien*, Tuesday, December 2, 2003.

and ethnic balance to prevent the spatial concentration of immigrants, the ghettoization of their residential space, and the polarization of ethnic communities in order to enhance their incremental integration in French daily life. The French municipal government sees ethnic enclaves as impeding assimilation and as potential sources of conflict. Therefore, the municipality sees the role of the state as upholding the common good in its planning policy above the ethnic good.[5] While some analysts view the housing market as the main catalyst of integration, others point to ethnic commerce as the vector along which the ethnic enclave interacts with city officials.[6] Others stress the unanticipated consequences of urban reorganization or argue that urban renewal has been undertaken with the intent of transforming Paris into the cultural capital of the European Union.[7]

From the standpoint of the nation-state, renovation is meant to modernize the locale by alleviating the plight of the residents, refurbishing the infrastructure, and preventing all the negative aspects of ghettoization, such as segregation, juvenile delinquency, unemployment, and poverty in general. The sociological literature on French urban policy concerning neighborhood renovation addresses these various aspects of the issue and derives from the French ideology of citizenship, in which ethnicity is viewed as a secondary factor. In this context, neighborhood renewal in the Jewish quarter simply meant the harmonization of the site with the rest of the city to enhance the quality of life in the neighborhood and to enhance its ability to produce tax revenues. In contrast, the Jewish neighborhood was concerned with strengthening the ethnic identity of the site while also enhancing the ability of the stores to increase profits by luring more clientele to shop in the neighborhood and with enhancing the quality of life by receiving more services from the city, such as street cleaning, garbage collection, and crime prevention.

City hall and the Jewish residents also possessed two different views of the role that globalization ought to play in the renovation of the neighborhood. While for city hall, renovation was to create a global destination that would bring in more tourists and more expensive stores that would cater to tourists' needs, thereby contributing positively

---

5. Annick Tanter and Jean-Claude Toubon, "Mixité sociale et politiques de peuplement: Genèse de l'ethnicisation des opérations de réhabilitation," *Sociétés Contemporaines*, no, 33/34, (1999): 59–86; Catherine Rhein, "Globalization, Social Change and Minorities in Metropolitian Paris: The Emergence of New Class Patterns," *Urban Studies* 35, no. 3 (1998): 429–47; James W. White, "Old Wine, Cracked Bottle? Tokyo, Paris, and the Global City Hypothesis," *Urban Affairs Review* 33, no. 4 (1998): 451–77; Edmond Préteceille, "Division sociale de l'espace et globalisation: Le cas de la métropole parisienne," *Sociétés Contemporaines* no. 22/23 (1995): 33–67.

6. Martine Berger, "Trajectories in Living Space, Employment, and Housing Stock: The Example of the Parisian Metropolis in the 1980s and 1990s," *International Journal of Urban and Regional Research* 20, no, 2 (1996): 240–54; Emmanuel Ma Mung, "Territorializzazione commerciale delle identita: I Cinesi a Parigi," *La Critica Sociologica* no. 117/118 (1996): 64–77; Vasoodeven Vuddamalay, Paul White, and Deborah Sporton, "The Evolution of the Goutte D'Or as an Ethnic Minority District in Paris," *New Community* 17. no. 2 (1991): 245–58.

7. Sue Collard, "Politics, Culture and Urban Transformation in Jacques Chirac's Paris, 1977–1995," *French Cultural Studies* 7, no. 1 (1995): 1–32; H. V. Savitch, "Reorganization in Three Cities: Explaining the Disparity Between Intended Actions and Unanticipated Consequences," *Urban Affairs Quarterly* 29, no. 4 (1994): 565–95; Jean-Paul Alday, "L'aménagement de la région de Paris entre 1930 et 1975: De la plannification à la politique urbaine," *Sociologie du Travail* 21, no. 2 (1979): 167–200; Alain Cottereau, "Les débuts de plannification urbaine dans l'agglomération parisienne, *Sociologie du Travail* 12, no. 4 (1970): 362–92.

to the revenue of the city, the Jewish merchants saw the neighborhood as an already existing global site because of the extraterritorial relations it has always maintained with other Jewish sites. They saw uncontrolled renovation as undermining the infrastructure through which they expressed their identity because of the inevitable flight of the residential population as a result of potentially higher rents and real-estate speculation of all kinds. In what follows, I examine how, in this case, ethnic neighborhood renovation was negotiated at the interface of the local with the global. Furthermore, it shows how the dynamic of globalization from below and globalization from above affect the decision-making process in urban planning.

The City Hall Plan for the Neighborhood

The controversy over the mayor's proposal to modernize the Jewish quarter hinged on two main arguments. The proponents of the plan, the city hall officials, claimed that the quarter should match the reality of the rest of Paris. The opponents of the plan, the Jewish quarter residents and merchants, believed that it was important to preserve the villagelike life that had provided a protective niche for the maintenance of their culture. From the viewpoint of city hall, the plan called for minimal change, while local Jewish merchants saw it as a major intervention that would destroy the last bastion of Jewish life in Paris.

On June 24, 2003, in a public meeting attended by local government officials, supporters of the plan, and members of the merchants' association and others opposed to the implementation of the initiative, the mayor explained the changes that would be made and the rationale for the proposal. After recognizing the well-deserved international reputation of the Rue des Rosiers—the street targeted for remodeling—she mentioned the enduring problems of the street related to loitering, overcrowding, lack of security, noise, and automobile traffic. She then framed the issue by stating: "How can we offer business a better environment by reducing the presence of cars, bicycles, motorcycles, and mopeds, reducing the overflowing crowds, while also facilitating a new environment for the local residents' daily activities? This is the goal of the renovation planned for the Rue des Rosiers." In the following statement, she explained how her administration intended to resolve the issue.

> The first action must be to increase pedestrian space. However, because firemen need 3.5 meters of open space [in the street], and with more than 3.5 meters people will try to park their cars, the only way to improve pedestrian life is to transform the Rue des Rosiers (and therefore the Rue des Ecouffes and perhaps the Rue Duval) into a semipedestrian street without sidewalks and where pedestrians have priority, but where cars can go under fifteen kilometers per hour. There will be a central lane of 3.5 meters with flowers and trees planted on the north side (facing south) and decorations on the south side (potted plants, streetlights, stone boundaries). . . . The primary goal is to avoid easy and multiple points of access to the Rue des Rosiers and then to avoid the traffic congestion along the Rue des Rosiers. To do that, it is necessary to reverse the direction of the Rue Duval and the last

section of the Rue du Roi de Sicilie (between the Rue Duval and the Rue Malher) for the south side of the Rue des Rosiers. North of the Rue des Rosiers it is necessary to reverse the last section of the Rue des Hospitallières Saint-Gervais before the Rue des Francs-Bourgeois.

The second action will be to reduce the size of trucks allowed to drive on the Rue des Rosiers. . . . The third action will be to reduce and better organize the types of parking allowed: allowing deliveries, but limiting them from stopping in the middle of the street, and covering four distinct zones that satisfy the various businesses on the Rues des Rosiers, Ecouffes, Duval, and Hospitallières.

The Rue Pavée is the only entrance to the Rue des Rosiers, which gives an easy option for establishing a barricade on Sundays between 2:00 P.M. and 7:00 or 8:00 P.M. . . . This barricade will allow firemen, ambulances, and local residents with proper identification [to enter the street]. No motorcycles, mopeds, or bicycles will be allowed on the road Sunday afternoon.

We will be opening one or more gardens. . . . There will also be plantings of trees and borders from the Rue Malher to the Rue Duval. Then, up to the Rue Vielle du Temple, there will be space for flowers (primarily roses) that will produce a beautiful botanical promenade. . . . Other plants will supplement roses, especially for the winter season. . . . Finally, several small trees will be carefully planted between the Rue Duval and the Rue Vielle du Temple. . . .

Due to their liveliness, as well as their contribution to the monitoring of public space, businesses improve public space and limit destructive behavior, for example, illegal parking. (e.g. the pastry shop at the corner of the Rue des Ecouffes, the bookstore, the restaurant on the Rue des Hospitallières, etc.). However, use and development of public space must be done cooperatively with the rest of the street. Not all businesses provide the same benefits, and some provide nuisances (bad odors, garbage in the streets, garish signs, and unattractive terraces . . .).

To improve the public space, one must limit terraces from overcrowding the street, and they must be well constructed, with the Rue Cloche Perce as an example. Garbage cans must be installed. There will also be a quality standard proposed to the business people concerning the appearance of storefronts, further allowing our project to have positive impact.

The new direction of traffic will no longer allow the juvenile high jinks that currently block traffic on narrow streets. Better use of space, the revitalization of space, the plantings, decorations, the presence of pedestrians in the center of the road, will all remove the open, casual atmosphere of streets conducive to speeding. In addition, parking spaces for motorcycles, bicycles, and mopeds will be between the Rue du Roi de Sicilie and the Rue de Rivoli, at the entrance to Rues Malher, Pavée, Duval, and des Ecouffes. As a result, the parking for motorcycles, bicycles, and mopeds will be banned on the Rue des Rosiers, the Rue des Ecouffes, and the Rue Ferdinand Duval.

Open spaces are subject to crowding. Once present, crowds tend to grow and inspire acts of incivility, which together with traffic congestion negatively impact the Rue des Rosiers. It is therefore necessary to fill the space, especially at the corners of Ecouffes and Duval, with tall plantings (primarily roses), half-grown trees propped up by metal grills, a small fountain, border decorations.

The broader view concerning the initiative was expressed by a high-ranking employee in the following interview, which places the issue in a historical, sociological, and political context and explains the projected outcome of the plan and how it would benefit the residents, the city, and incoming tourists.

The maintenance of the Jewish character is not only for tourists, but for the residents—because there are residents on the Rue des Rosiers, and those residents suffer because there are very narrow roads, which are not easy to endure on a daily basis, because there are narrow sidewalks that do not facilitate the mobility of pedestrians or deliveries and encourage traffic jams and honking. We support the restoration of the neighborhood for the residents (so as to respond to the expectations of the residents) and those who like the neighborhood, who come to visit, but not only for those people. This is the reason why we have elaborated the project. . . .

You have here the narrow part, the historical part of the Rue des Rosiers, with very small sidewalks with borders on both sides. Our project is to end walking on the sidewalk in order to permit a more simple passage between the street and the sidewalk. The sidewalk is so narrow that one cannot stay on it all of its length. At the widest part, we will widen the sidewalks a little in order to plant a few trees. All of this has been part of long deliberations with the residents, the city's technical infrastructure, and the urban infrastructure.

Some people have talked about two false things: "Pedestrianization" [*piétonisation*]. It was never a plan to make the Rue des Rosiers a pedestrian street, except on Sunday afternoons. That means that on Sunday afternoons, the Rue des Rosiers will be reserved for pedestrians, given that there is a considerable influx of people on that day and that cohabitation with cars is very dangerous. We hope that between 2:00 P.M. and 8:00 P.M., the Rue des Rosiers will be closed to cars—only deliveries and the residents can come by car, and for all other people, it will be impossible to come by car to the Rue des Rosiers on Sundays. At all other times in the week, the Rue des Rosiers will remain accessible to cars. So there is no "pedestrianization" going on. On the contrary, a complete pedestrianization of the neighborhood would risk distorting [*dénaturer*] the Rue des Rosiers and mostly serve the interests of tourists. That would break the equilibrium between the residents, the traders, and the tourists. We wish for an equilibrium between all the components that would permit everyone to live a certain quality of life, as legitimately expected with trade, for the possibility of functioning with tourists and the people who come to shop and take walks in the neighborhood—and to do so in good condition. But one component should especially not be emphasized to the detriment of the other. So we maintain that equilibrium [between interest groups].

Some opponents have said that the project of urban development (restructuring of the sidewalks) is an attack against the Jewish heritage of the neighborhood. We find this really insulting and very dangerous, because when one makes this argument, the next step is pretty clear. Some people did not hesitate to talk about anti-Semitism on the part of municipal authorities, which is really entirely false. I could give you an example of when in the gay neighborhood, when there was this same question of restructuring of the streets, Mrs. Bertinotti was called homophobic. Here again, the refusal of communitarianism is justified if we begin to make this mistake, and it's particularly the very strong and dangerous arguments that are out of line.

This initiative of city hall for the remodeling of the Rue des Rosiers was opposed by the association of merchants (Association des Commerçants, Habitants, Propriétaires et Copropriétaires du IVème Arrondissement) and those it represents. Here, this dissident body presented the nature of its objections and the empirical basis upon which they had made their argument. They reminded the local administrators that such a policy had already been implemented elsewhere in Paris, and it had not produced the desired outcome from the perspective of the residents of these neighborhoods.

> We believe that such actions, as in other Paris neighborhoods where they were tried, will lead to a change in business conditions on the street: Some businesses will disappear, especially traditional ones, and new businesses will enter the street, which will lead to tension among local residents. We have seen this in other neighborhoods and heard from residents of the 4th Arrondissement, who have already lived through such turmoil. Furthermore, you, Ms. Mayor, are aware of these conflicts, for example, the very strong opposition of business people and residents of the Rue des Francs-Bourgeois to the experiment of semipedestrian-only status for the Rue des Francs-Bourgeois.
>
> We would like to add that the traditional businesses that will be harmed by the changes are part of the history and culture of a neighborhood with a very strong cultural identity. These businesses are the bedrock of our community, and their commercial energy, along with increased traffic in the neighborhood, is in sync with and announces Jewish holidays.
>
> *We must remember that the streets under consideration are part of the oldest Jewish neighborhood in the city, dating back almost ten centuries. Each year, about 100,000 people from all over the world meditate in these historic sites to pay homage to those who have gone before. This very identity is being challenged.* **This is the crux of the debate.**
>
> Even if one experiments with "semi"-pedestrian-only streets, it does no good to remove the sidewalks. First of all, to remove the sidewalks signifies that the decision is irreversible. But also, previous experiences have shown that sidewalks offer safety for the pedestrian and their absence produces disorder, as one can see at Les Halles or St.-Séverin.

Each camp recruited people to its side. Certain neighborhood organizations supported the mayor's office, while religious residents who have gone to these shops for kosher food supported the dissenting merchants. A Chinese individual who operated a nutrition store in the Jewish quarter, for example, sided with the position of city hall:

> I think that the pedestrianization is a very interesting idea because it will lead to a new type of environment. Already certain business owners imagine cafes with patios laden with trees. One can imagine the interaction that will take place. I am somewhat doubtful, though. It must be said that the concerns of the local residents are controlled by certain political parties. We encounter diverse interests, more or less drawn on [*tiré*] by the political parties (socialist, rightist). It's a little complicated. Honestly, pedestrianization does not cause problems. I don't see how one can distort a neighborhood by making it a pedestrian neighborhood.

In contrast, a young Jewish lawyer who lived in the neighborhood and purchased his kosher meat from one of the shops sided with the merchants' association.

> One can estimate that half of the Jewish community in France lives in the Parisian region, and there are not a lot of kosher things sold in the city. Le Marais is the only neighborhood where there are many kosher groceries, butcher shops, etcetera. Jews from far away come to shop in those stores. They come by car. It's not just people who live in the neighborhood who will be affected. There are some of the clients who live in the neighborhood who come on foot, but one can estimate that half of the clientele comes from other Paris arrondissements or from the Parisian suburbs.
>
> If tomorrow the town hall project is achieved and the streets are turned into pedestrian zones and access to cars is forbidden, those people will no longer come. They will say, "It is difficult to park, I am forced to park farther away. I'm forced to go into a parking lot and pay." So they will tell themselves that instead of going to Le Marais, they should go to other places. They will go to other places. There is a butcher shop here and another one there. Jewish shops are pretty few and far between. It's pretty spread out. But we will go somewhere else. The profits of Jewish business owners will start plummeting. In addition, the owners of buildings who rent space to shopkeepers, they will say, "The sector is pedestrianized and, according to the law, it's a factor of commercialization; that means normally it should bring more clients, so I, the owner, should be able to raise the rent." Those businesses will lose clients and at the same time their rents will increase. Also, there are big fashion stores like Gucci, etcetera, that will see those stores and tell them, "Me, I'd like to buy your business." As you can see, all around the Jewish neighborhood, there are many big fashion designers. And if you add those three factors that I've just told you: decrease of profits, increase of rent, and mouthwatering offers from the big brands, those shopkeepers will give up in the end and will sell their businesses. What will happen? The small food businesses will close.
>
> The people who live in the neighborhood, why did they move into the neighborhood? Me, why did I come into the neighborhood? It's because there are these Jewish stores, because I don't have to go to other places to find things I need. As soon as those kosher businesses leave, Jews will desert the neighborhood. And if the Jewish residents leave the neighborhood, there are synagogues that will close. There are Jewish schools that will close. And little by little, the Jewish neighborhood will disappear. That's why when we tell town hall that pedestrianization endangers the Jewish identity of the neighborhood, it's not accusations of anti-Semitism, it's the truth. If the project is achieved, the historically Jewish neighborhood of Paris will disappear. There are hundreds of streets in Paris. There are perhaps thousands. I don't know the exact number. Of all those streets, there are three that constitute the Jewish neighborhood. It's those three streets that town hall wants to pedestrianize. However, us, what we ask: "We have three streets. Leave us those streets. If you want to pedestrianize somewhere else, pedestrianize. But if you pedestrianize our streets, it will be the disappearance of the Jewish neighborhood on the island of Paris."

The Virtual Globalization of the Conflict

On-line, both French residents and foreign Jews debated the issue of the renovation of the Jewish quarter. These virtual discussions attest to the diasporic inscription of the neighborhood in the transnational network of Jewish sites and the interest of overseas residents in the issue. Of course, this virtual debate was supposed to influence the policy outcome of city hall one way or another.[8] The following messages posted on http://www.quartierrosiers.org/soutien/ or on http://www.antisemitisme.info/phpBB2/viewtopic.php?t=15&start=0&sid=483e46cbd give a glimpse of the content of the virtual debate:[9]

> I can no longer adapt to the constant noise of honking every morning in my street (I work at home). If the renovation of the quarter, by transforming certain streets for use only by pedestrians leads to ending this noise (a source of sound pollution), I am in favor of such a project. (Male, Paris, posted on 12/18/2003)
>
> I could not imagine a better solution to resolve all the problems of my street. The renovation project can do nothing but good. You must not forget that there is nothing in the Torah that says "you must make a lot of noise with your car while you are trying to break the legs of passersby," "destruction of the Jewish memory of the quarter." Okay. Why haven't you said anything when the Jewish baths of the twelfth century were being destroyed so that a parking garage could be constructed? Thanks, I am waiting with impatience to see you all in a quiet and green street. (Male, the Rue des Rosiers, Paris, posted on 12/17/2003)
>
> Residents of Quarter! I am for the project of renovation of the quarter. Thanks for your actions in this direction. (Male, the Rue des Ecouffes, Paris, posted on 12/16/2003)
>
> As one who often visits the Rue des Rosiers, I would like to see a convivial, warm, clean, pleasant street and not to have to experience this feeling of aggressiveness. (Female, St. Maur, France, posted on 12/14/2003)
>
> I am a resident of this neighborhood. I have to approve of the project for the renovation and beautification of the Rue des Rosiers and cross streets: less noise, more green, more comfort on Sunday: What more can we ask for? (Female, Paris, posted on 12/4/2003)
>
> I reside on the Rue Ferdinand Duval, and I totally endorse the project, which visibly will turn my quarter into a more pleasant and attractive place. I cannot see how less traffic would impact the authenticity of the Rue des Rosiers? I would like for both the Rue Ferdinand Duval and the Rue des Ecouffes to be open only to pedestrians. (Chinese female, Paris, posted on 12/3/2003)
>
> "Yes" for a pedestrian street and "no" to the infernal noise made by visiting vagabonds on scooters with their prolonged honking. It is an exaggeration to say that the small shops will be negatively affected by this project, since they depend on pedestrian tourists for their survival. Only these little junkies who circulate with speed on Sunday on their scooters in

---

8. For a discussion of "virtual diaspora" and "virtual diasporic public sphere," see Michel S. Laguerre, *The Digital City: The American Metropolis and Information Technology* (New York: Palgrave Macmillan, 2005), and Michel S. Laguerre, *Diaspora, Politics and Globalization* (New York: Palgrave Macmillan, 2006).

9. The first of these Web sites was last accessed on December 23, 2003 and is no longer available. The second was last accessed on December 7, 2007, but the content has changed.

the neighborhood and bring out the raw nerves of everyone will be forced to change their destination. (Female, the Rue des Rosiers, posted on 12/5/2003)

On October 23, 2003, will the Council of Paris decree the expulsion of Jews from the Rue des Rosiers? . . . The Council of Paris is about to decree and organize the destruction of the Jewish Quarter in downtown Paris, an exceptional neighborhood that dates back to the medieval era, often referred to as "Pletzl" or "St. Paul," with an international reputation. . . . To save the Rue des Rosiers, to save an emblematic site of French Judaism, to save an essential element of the memory of all the Parisians, we must organize, protest, and defend our patrimony. (Posted from Israel on 10/15/2003)

Hello, I could not find the Forum! Effectively we must save the Rue des Rosiers. I am not from Paris. (Posted from the Bahamas on 10/15/2003)

Hearing about the proposed destruction of the Jewish Quarter makes me sick. Every time I am in Paris or waiting for a plane, I always stop by my root quarter, his king of falafel, Finkelstajn, the old Goldenberg, and others. (Posted from Aden, Yemen, on 10/16/2003)

Although the conflict began as an off-line interaction between city officials and some members of the neighborhood, it later became extended to such on-line discussions, clarifications, and protests. Both sides had their Web sites or chat rooms where adherents and opponents explained their positions and criticized the other side. With this on-line interaction, the debate acquired a global identity. Whether they sided with the mayor's office or with the local merchants who spearheaded the opposition, some of the participants did not live in the neighborhood, some were not even Jewish, and some were foreign Jews.

Arguments presented off-line were scrutinized and rejected on-line, thereby providing new ammunition for interface interactions. Some ideas that had been rejected off-line began a life of their own on-line; some ideas were discussed only on-line and never made it off-line because they were only reactions to on-line opinions, while some ideas expressed off-line never made it on-line because they were not controversial propositions and were accepted by both camps.

The on-line public sphere thus did not coincide with the off-line public sphere in this debate. One was neighborhood-based, while the other covered a global arena. Each influenced the content of the other. One was made of people who knew or could know each other directly, while the other was made of strangers who lived in different places. While those off-line spoke about how their daily experiences would be affected, those on-line tended to talk about past history, reminiscences of the neighborhood, and why it was important to leave it as it was so that memories of the site as a heritage place could be revived.

Each camp followed the virtual debate of the other side to gauge their standing or to prepare counterarguments to be presented off-line. The on-line debate thus fed the off-line debate. It is fair to say that these two dimensions complemented each other and that one cannot understand the effect of one without reference to the other.

Foreign Jews intervened in the debate not as outsiders offering a balanced and cautionary argument to help moderate a difficult situation, but because they saw the quarter as part of the Jewish transnation. Some did it because they once resided there, others because it is the place they visited when they came to Paris, and still others because a portion of the memory of their family was buried there. Virtuality has made it possible for all of these individuals to be on the same page discussing one of the diasporic sites of the transnation. This shows one of the ways in which transglobal diasporic urbanism is constituted and explains the rationale used to justify the intervention of foreigners in the politics of a local place.

A Top-Down Approach to Urban Renewal

The various people interviewed at city hall made it clear that their approach was the opposite of what is being done by urban administrators in the United States—that is, facilitating the growth of "ethnic neighborhoods." In their top-down approach, all neighborhoods are theoretically to be treated the same way and are seen through the same prism, and in turn, the general rules of neighborhood renovation developed by the city are to apply to all areas equally. For example, the same architectural constraints define what is allowed regarding the preservation of the cultural heritage of the buildings. One municipal official interviewed explained that "as soon as you want to modify a window, you have to ask for permission first in order to maintain the cultural heritage aspect. . . . All this tells you that there is no desire to go at it alone . . . to make of it a sort of recreational park that would be Jewish, homosexual, or Chinese, etcetera. . . . Not at all." To reinforce that the modifications are about a team approach, and not the mayor's personal agenda, he added that "as soon as one touches something in the arrondissement, the architect of the buildings of France, who is the person in charge of making sure the salvaging project is respected, gives his opinion. If that person agrees, it happens, if she doesn't agree, it doesn't happen."

The difference of opinion between city hall and its opponents on what effect the project would have on the neighborhood was not simply a difference of perception, but rather was a conflict over whether the renovation would be more advantageous for tourists or residents. As a city hall administrator put it:

> There is a strong will in the Fourth Arrondissement, where we have Notre Dame, Le Marais, Bobourg, the Place des Vosges, the Jewish quarter, city hall, etcetera, to have tourism under control and to maintain residential life in the center of Paris. It's really true. But we have the will to maintain residential life and to conciliate tourism, commerce, and recreation, and we try to be careful that it doesn't happen at the expense of residential life.

City hall's strategy of implementing a policy that benefited the common good over the needs of an ethnic neighborhood was applied not only to urban issues, but also to social, environmental, and cultural issues. An advisor to the mayor said that "the mayor is opposed to any 'ethnic policy' that favors the survival of separate ethnic enclaves in the borough and prevents assimilation to French daily life. So nothing is done to create an ethnic neighborhood next to another ethnic neighborhood or to treat the question of urban renewal through a 'Jewish angle,' and next to it through a 'homosexual angle,' etcetera."

Both sides recognized that neighborhood change had been brought about by real-estate speculation. The merchants believed this speculation was caused or enhanced by the policies of city hall, which they thought aimed to transform the neighborhood into a museum. For city hall, it was purely and simply a case of the free market at work. According to a city hall official:

> We have one difficulty in Paris—maybe it's the same thing in other capitals. It's that one notices the progressive disappearance of corner stores: That is, as soon as a business is sold, it is often bought by Chinese traders or others. This is less the case when it comes to us. It's even stronger in other arrondissements or through big fashion billboards etcetera that have the means to acquire real estate in the center of Paris. The result is that we have a lot more difficulty finding a butcher or a baker. The problem is the same for the Jewish neighborhood, and for several decades, we have noticed the progressive disappearance of otherwise historical businesses, which constituted the particularity of the Rue des Rosiers and the surrounding neighborhood. There are fewer than before. What response can the municipality adopt with regard to this matter? It's a difficult situation because in France, constitutionally, it's part of the liberty of trade. One cannot prevent a Jewish trader from settling in a certain place. If you want to put thirteen identical businesses next to each other, that's possible. As a municipality, we cannot forbid it. Either the city buys the buildings and rents them to whomever it wants, or the law of free markets is applied here in the same way that it is applied everywhere else. And this permits us to have a certain amount of control in the matter. It's a difficulty. We cannot, as a municipality, say that Jewish businesses will remain in the Jewish neighborhood. If tomorrow there is a Syrian or an Arab who wants to settle there, he can. There was a big polemic five or six years ago when McDonald's wanted to settle in the Rosiers neighborhood. And it was not city hall that opposed this, because it did not have the means—it was the residents. And after the polemic, which included the petitions and support of certain elected persons, such as Dominique Bertinotti, who was in the opposition and supported the residents, McDonald's was not able to settle there.

To gain a foothold in the community, the mayor created her own association with members of the neighborhood who supported her project. They posted fliers on their doors and maintained a Web site to recruit sympathizers. It was an attempt at neutralizing individuals and groups who were against the urban renewal project and to sway neighborhood opinion to welcome the renovation policy.

A Bottom-Up Approach to Urban Renovation

The bottom-up approach to the renovation in this case was more static, because it argued that the change proposed by city hall was likely to cause imbalance in the neighborhood and ultimately would lead to the death of the Jewish quarter. In the residents' view, renovation would accelerate the invasion of the bohemian and tourist crowds, the replacement of the population, and the disappearance of the mom-and-pop shops that characterized the identity of the ethnic neighborhood. As the president of the merchants' association put it:

> It's not only tourist-centered businesses that one must make of us. One should not make museums of us, where people come to see where nobody lives any longer. . . . The [restoration] work that they are proposing reflects the authorities' desire, not the population's. The semipedestrianization that they are proposing to us is, in fact, a real pedestrianization that they want to give us, because when the sidewalks are removed and a central sewer [*canivau*] is put in place and we have smelly streets, and it is us that are going to live on them. Mrs. Bertinotti will benefit from a project that is hers, and not ours. And tomorrow that will bring advantages and inconveniences. We are only told about the advantages, that flowers will be planted on the street, but we are not told what tomorrow's problems will be: Monoactivity [*monoactivité*], drugs, thieves, squatters, people in the streets, bars, restaurants, noise—all things that people do not want. It is the people who live on top that must decide now. Now we are going to live in streets that will no longer belong to us. We have chosen to live in the Fourth Arrondissement for its conviviality, its proximity, not for the difficult situation that we have today. All of our street parking spaces will be taken away. Our clients will not be able to come buy their merchandise. Our people want to enter commercial activity—there are not only butcher shops, there are bookstores, [money] lenders, deli owners [*charcutiers*]—all of this will be modified. So Jewish shopkeepers will also be negatively affected. They are chased away, forced to leave, offered gold hens. However, there is a quality of life today. The Fourth is being "pushed up" because of the terrible real-estate speculation.

To give more weight to their argument, some longtime residents compared their experience in the neighborhood with that of city hall bureaucrats, who come and go. As one resident put it, "We are both interested in the same subject, but for Mrs. Bertinotti, it's not a subject that she lives. On her part, it's a technical intervention. For us, it's our life. It's our neighborhood." They saw the plan as reflecting the wishes of city hall employees more than the desires of the Jews. In fact, the mayor's office did not dispute that.

It's absolutely normal that city hall and the merchants would propose two conflicting approaches to the problem, top-down and bottom-up. City hall clearly said that they were not taking a communitarian approach because if they did, other ethnic groups would say "that's what we want." They didn't want to enter the game where the community indicates what it wants and defines the politics of city hall. As soon as things were put under the rubric of immediate experience, however, the variables changed. The Jewish merchants were more capable of projecting the future ramifications and consequences of such a project. To corroborate this point, the president of the merchants' association said:

> We have been living on this street for forty years. We know its logic. Her [the mayor], she's been here for one year, and she wants to change everything. . . . She is not interested in her reelection, because she's aiming for the senate. No answer. But we have places of worship [*lieux de culte*] here. If tomorrow nobody comes to the neighborhood, our ceremonial areas

will disappear, our soul will disappear, and so will our religion. It's a historic part of the city of Paris. It's one of the historical landmarks of the city of Paris. It's been here for more than one thousand years. It was named Rebeka Street [the Rue des Rosiers]. The Rue Ferdinand Duval used to be named the Rue aux Juifs. There was the Hotel aux Juifs. Today, if you pass the first part of the Rue des Rosiers, where there used to be food stores, now clothing stores have settled in. This enabled certain older populations to retire, since they were offered more money than they would have ever earned in their lifetime for their businesses, and this induced them to leave. They were offered a million francs. They would never have made this much money. The businesses that took their place have closed. The businesses have changed hands eleven times. The clothing stores are not surviving. They cannot survive alone. The Jewish food businesses, for their part, can survive. If the Jewish part leaves, what will remain on this street? If there isn't this Jewish atmosphere, what will remain here? Franchise stores and bars. We won't be able to have terraces.

The plan's opposition could not provide an alternative plan. Rather, they could only stress the potential negative consequences of the mayor's initiative. They believed that the stores they operated would be the first to be eliminated and that this would necessarily lead to the disappearance of synagogues and oratories and eventually the last vestiges of the Jewish quarter. A young Jewish lawyer who visited the quarter once a week to purchase kosher meat said the following:

The Paris town hall has a vision: It's to turn the neighborhood into a museum, to bring tourists to the area. In their statements, they say that that's not what they're doing, but in practice, it's the result that one must take into account. In practice, it's exactly what's needed. But, sir, when you close the roads to vehicles and when you prevent life from entering the streets, parking zones are suppressed. Who are those roads made for? They are for the people who like to walk, or go out. It's going to be areas for going out, for pleasure, for extranormal life. It's going to be for night, but not for the day. And all of the factors involved in the commercializing of the street will change. Life will begin at ten in evening and end at three in the morning, and people will no longer want to live on top of stores, because people will say that it's even noisier than before. The first trashcan is for boxes, the second trashcan for the dogs' waste, and the third for the bottles. Parisians will come play music, accordion, knives, bells, and the streetwalkers and everyone [else] will bring their nuisances. And to think there are those who believe that a pedestrian street is for serenity and tranquility! They say no cars, no horns. But there will be other things that are even worse than cars and horns: nuisances, drugs, security problems, all incidents caused by a population that is not of the neighborhood who will come from the other areas and leave right away after doing damage. Who will suffer from this change? History will be marked by making the neighborhood or its soul disappear in the interest of turning it into a museum, a "touristification" of sorts. They will have the benefit of having changed the neighborhood, and we will have disappeared.

Such dissidents conceived of urban renovation as a "euphemism for gentrification,"[10] and the opposition of the Jewish merchants to renovation must be seen in the light of the fast-paced gentrification they had been observing in the neighborhood. There had been both commercial gentrification, with the establishment of stores that catered to a non-Jewish population, which transformed the Jewish business corridor into a multicultural business agglomeration with Chinese, French, Indian, Sephardic, and Ashkenazi stores, and demographic gentrification, with the encroachment of the gay neighborhood of Paris into the Jewish quarter. The gentrification of the neighborhood had been an ongoing occurrence that indeed had undermined the Jewish character of the site. Juliet Carpenter and Loretta Lees note that "postwar outmigration to the suburbs [means that] in Le Marais the working classes were moving to suburban public, rather than private, housing."[11] It was therefore not in dispute that there had been a disappearance of Jewish business and shops and the gentrification of the quarter. How to renovate without accelerating this double movement was the troubling question that generated much passion from both sides of the debate.

"Regulative" versus "Generative" Planning

Urban planning seldom meets the approval of all of the concerned population, but more often than not it is the result of the decision of the city government—it is "regulative," imposed from above on the neighborhood community, not "generative," motivated from within that community. The coalition of grassroots associations that spoke on behalf of the community had to transform themselves into a parapolitical organization to enhance their effectiveness and to oppose the renovation of the neighborhood because of the projected negative effects it would have.[12] This form of grassroots activism was marked by an effort to develop coalitions that sought the aid of public intellectuals, former members of the neighborhood who lived abroad, politicians who supported the cause, and foreign journalists who might influence public opinion, further giving this local issue a global voice.[13]

However, the data indicate that urban planning most often is imposed from above, and the process is justly referred to as "coercive."[14] In the controversy analyzed here, a

---

10. James C. Fraser, Edward L. Kick, and J. Patrick Williams, "Neighborhood Revitalization and the Practice of Evaluation in the United States: Developing a Margin Research Perspective," *City and Community* 1, no. 2 (2002): 217–36.

11. Juliet Carpenter and Loretta Lees, "Gentrification in New York, London and Paris: An International Comparison," *International Journal of Urban and Regional Research* 19, no. 2 (1995): 268–303.

12. Gary McDonogh, "Discourses of the City: Policy and Response in Post-Transitional Barcelona," *City and Society* 5, no. 1 (1991): 40–63.

13. Ariadne Vromen, "Community-Based Activism and Change: The Cases of Sydney and Toronto," *City and Community* 2, no. (2003): 47–70.

14. Donald V. Kurtz, "Regulative and Generative Planning: Provocative Themes and Future Research," *City and Society* 5, no. 1 (1991): 3–9, 1991. Anne C. Kubisch, Karen. Fulbright-Anderson, and James P. Connell, "Evaluation Community Initiatives: A Progress Report," in *New Approaches to Evaluating Community Initiatives*, vol. 2., *Theory, Measurement, and Analysis*, ed. Anne C. Kubisch, Karen Fulbright-Anderson, and James. P. Connell (Washington DC: Aspen Institute, 1998).

classic case of regulative, top-down versus generative, bottom-up, or "community-driven" planning,[15] the predictive value of previous studies is confirmed: Despite the protests registered by the Jewish merchants and religious Jews to preserve the memory and ethnic identity of the place, in January 2005, the mayor of the Fourth Arrondissement began the first phase of the implementation of the renovation plan. The public-works projects necessary to complete the construction scheme were supposed to be completed in two years.

Global Inscription

The inscription of the global in this local site was achieved through the participation of overseas people in the debate, through the expansion of the network by including outsiders to support the cause, through on-line communication generated by this controversy, through the tourists who were affected one way or the other, through overseas Jewish communities and organizations that remained abreast of developments and that offered their moral support, and through reportage published in foreign daily newspapers such as the *New York Times* and monthly newspapers published in various diasporic sites.

The interest of the Jewish diaspora in the resolution of this problem attests to the way in which this neighborhood has been inscribed in the network of Jewish sites as something that belongs as much to the greater diasporic network as it does to the city. Renovation indirectly affected not only the local people, but also people overseas whose memories valorized the site because they or their parents once lived there. Not only did city hall and the neighborhood residents view the effects of renovation differently, but they also constructed the global public that was affected by it differently, as well. For city hall, the global public was reduced mostly to the tourists the site would attract in the future, while for the residents, it was both the tourists and the Jewish diasporic communities dispersed throughout the globe. Nevertheless, in this instance, the values and interests of the nation-state, as represented by metropolitan institutions and politicians, prevailed over the efforts of the globalized local ethnic community. Despite the globalization of the local in defense of its uniqueness, the local here was inexorably being assimilated into the matrix of metropolitan Paris.

Bibliography

Alday, Jean-Paul. "L'aménagement de la région de Paris entre 1930 et 1975: De la plannification à la politique urbaine." *Sociologie du Travail* 21, no. 2 (1979): 167–200.

---

15. Douglas Uzzell, "Dissonance of Formal and Informal Planning Styles, or Can Formal Planners Do Bricolage?" *City and Society* 4, no. 2 (1990):114–30.

Allen, Judith. "Europe of the Neighborhoods: Class, Citizenship and Welfare Regimes." In *Social Exclusion in European Cities*. Edited by Ali Madanipour, Goran Cars, and Judith Allen. London: Routledge, 2000.

Berger, Martine. "Trajectories in Living Space, Employment, and Housing Stock: The Example of the Parisian Metropolis in the 1980s and 1990s." *International Journal of Urban and Regional Research* 20 no. 2 (1996.): 240–54.

Brody, Jane. "Le quartier de la Rue des Rosiers, ou l'histoire d'un cheminement." In *Les cheminements de la ville*. Paris: Editions CTHS, 1985.

Carpenter, Juliet, and Loretta Lees. "Gentrification in New York, London and Paris: An International Comparison." *International Journal of Urban and Regional Research* 19, no. 2 (1995): 268–303.

Chenay, Christophe de. "Les Parisiens veulent préserver l'originalité de leurs quartiers." *Le Monde*, Friday, November 28, 2003.

Chirot, Francoise. "Controverse autour de la "piétonnisation" du quartier juif de Paris." *Le Monde*, Friday, November 21, 2003.

Collard, Sue. "Politics, Culture and Urban Transformation in Jacques Chirac's Paris, 1977–1995." *French Cultural Studies* 1, no. 19 (1995): 1–32.

Costa, Bernadette. *Je me souviens du Marais*. Paris: Parigramme, 1995.

Cottereau, Alain. "Les débuts de plannification urbaine dans l'agglomération parisienne." *Sociologie du Travail* 12, no. 4 (1970): 362–92.

Fraser, James C., Edward L. Kick, and J. Patrick Williams. "Neighborhood Revitalization and the Practice of Evaluation in the United States: Developing a Margin Research Perspective." *City and Community* 1, no, 2 (2002): 217–36.

Gabizon, Cecilia. "Polémique sur l'aménagement de la Rue des Rosiers." *Le Figaro*, Monday, April 6, 2004.

Green, Nancy. *Les travailleurs immigrés juifs à la Belle Epoque, Le Pletzl de Paris*. Paris: Fayard, 1985.

Hyman, Paul E. *The Jews of Modern France*. Berkeley: University of California, 1998.

Kubisch, Anne C., Karen Fulbright-Anderson, and James. P. Connell. "Evaluating Community Initiatives: A Progress Report." In *New Approaches to Evaluating Community Initiatives*. Vol. 2. *Theory, Measurement, and Analysis*. Edited by Anne C. Kubisch, Karen Fulbright-Anderson, and James. P. Connell. Washington DC: Aspen Institute, 1998.

Kurtz, Donald V. "Regulative and Generative Planning: Provocative Themes and Future Research." *City and Society* 5, no. 1 (1991): 3–9.

Laguerre, Michel S. *Diaspora, Politics, and Globalization*. New York: Palgrave Macmillan, 2006.

——. *The Digital City: The American Metropolis and Information Technology.* New York: Palgrave Macmillan, 2005.

——. *The Global Ethnopolis: Chinatown, Japantown, and Manilatown in American Society.* New York: Macmillan, 2000.

——. *Urban Multiculturalism and Globalization in New York City.* New York: Palgrave Macmillan, 2003.

Le Mitouard, Eric. "Les 10 vérités sur la future Rue des Rosiers." *Le Parisien,* Monday, December 2, 2003.

Ma Mung, Emmanuel. "Territorializzazione commerciale delle identita: I Cinesi a Parigi." *La Critica Sociologica,* no. 117/118 (1996): 64–77.

McDonogh, Gary. "Discourses of the City: Policy and Response in Post-Transitional Barcelona." *City and Society* 5, no. 1 (1991): 40–63.

Mondada, Lorenza. "Un descripteur contesté: Le ghetto." In *Décrire la ville.* Paris: Anthropos, 2000.

Ostrowetsky, Sylvia. "La puissance des disposifs spatiaux." In *Formes architecturales, formes urbaines.* Paris: Anthropos, 1994.

Poggi, Marie-Hélène. "Le quartier du Marais, le mélange et le feuilleté." In *Pour une sociologie de la forme.* Paris: L'Harmattan, 1999.

Preteceille, Edmond. "Division sociale de l'espace et globalisation: Le cas de la métropole parisienne." *Sociétés Contemporaines,* no. 22/23 (1995): 33–67.

Rhein, Catherine. "Globalization, Social Change and Minorities in Metropolitian Paris: The Emergence of New Class Patterns." *Urban Studies* 35, no. 3 (1998): 429–47.

Sarrot, Aurélie. "Consultation prolongée pour la Rue des Rosiers." *MétroParis,* Monday, February 9, 2004.

Savitch, H. V. "Reorganization in Three Cities: Explaining the Disparity between Intended Actions and Unanticipated Consequences." *Urban Affairs Quarterly* 29, no. 4 (1994): 565–95.

Sciolino, Elaine. "Jewish District Rallies to Save Its Soul from Renovation." *New York Times,* Monday, April 5, 2004.

Tanter, Annick, and Jean-Claude Toubon. "Mixité sociale et politiques de peuplement: Genese de l'ethnicisation des opérations de réhabilitation." *Sociétés Contemporaines,* no. 33/34 (1999): 59–86.

Uzzell, Douglas. "Dissonance of Formal and Informal Planning Styles, or Can Formal Planners Do Bricolage?" *City and Society* 4, no. 2 (1990): 114–30.

Vromen, Ariadne. "Community-Based Activism and Change: The Cases of Sydney and Toronto." *City and Community* 2, no. 1 (2003): 47–70.

Vuddamalay, Vasoodeven, Paul White, and Deborah Sporton. "The Evolution of the Goutte D'Or as an Ethnic Minority District in Paris." *New Community* 17, no. 2 (1991): 245–58.

White, James W. "Old Wine, Cracked Bottle? Tokyo, Paris, and the Global City Hypothesis." *Urban Affairs Review* 33, no. 4 (1998): 451–777.

Democracy, Pluralism, and Diaspora Identity: An Ambiguous Relationship

By William Safran

Diasporas may grow or shrink, maintain themselves, disappear, or be newly created. The origin of a diaspora is normally found in a particular homeland, but its survival depends on the conditions prevailing in the host country. Persons leaving their homeland and settling in another country may adapt to the latter in a variety of ways. As Gabriel Sheffer has put it, "After migrants make initial adjustments and solve the immediate problems involved in settling down in a host country, their main dilemma is whether to opt for eventual assimilation or maintain their ethno-national identity."[1] This, as Sheffer notes, requires tactical decisions based on the migrant's expectations. But such decisions are not made by the migrant alone; they evolve gradually, often based on the conditions of the host country.

The survival of a diaspora depends on many factors: its size, its duration, the thickness of its culture and its attractiveness in comparison with that of the host society, the prestige and efficacy of its leadership, the degree of its unity, the extent of its internal organization, and the nature of its relationship to the homeland. It is my contention that the collective identity of a diaspora and its long-term prospects depend above all on the political context of the host country and, albeit to a lesser extent, on conditions in the homeland.

My approach to diasporas is based on a definition of this condition in terms of a relationship between the host country and a (real or imaginary) anterior homeland. Unless that relationship is taken into account, diaspora becomes a metaphor for virtually any kind of divergence from the prevailing social norms. Diaspora identity, then, is not just a

---

1. Gabriel Sheffer, "Defining Ethno-National Diasporas," *Migration* 33/34/35 (2002): 81.

condition of "otherness" or a narrative about this condition. It is about a concrete social and political reality of "here" and "there." And this complex reality is best apprehended in institutionalist terms.

The question that concerns this paper is: What are the specifically political conditions of the hostland and the homeland that make for the maintenance, perpetuation, or weakening of diasporas? Does regime type make a difference? What is the relative importance of the structure of society and the nature of the dominant ideology in shaping diaspora identity? What are the institutional and other facilitators for assimilation and homeland orientation?

In order to address these questions, one must make a distinction between authoritarian and democratic regimes. An authoritarian regime may impede the free articulation as well as the institutional expression of diaspora identity so that it gradually weakens to the point of disappearance, but such a regime may be so oppressive that the "imagined" homeland becomes more attractive, and diaspora identity is sharpened. In Czarist Russia and Nazi Germany, conditions were such as to exacerbate the diaspora consciousness of Jews. In the former they were deprived of their legal rights and/or their residence permits in various parts of the country, so that they were effectively reduced to the status of barely tolerated outsiders. In the latter, they were excised from the body politic. While limiting the expression of subcommunities against the government and holding back the development of an autonomous civil society, an authoritarian regime may import ethnic minorities—that is, *create* diasporas—and encourage the maintenance of diaspora identities among selected communities in order to contribute to interethnic conflict for purposes of *divide et impera* and economic exploitation, as the British did in Burma and South Africa and the Dutch in Indonesia.[2]

Democratic Structures: Facilitators or Hindrances?

Most diasporas exist or are newly established in democratic countries because they are the preferred destination of people in search of economic opportunity and/or political freedom. This is true even of Africans, many of whom want to migrate to these countries despite the latter's histories of slavery.[3] The ideal-typical democracy has an open society, allows the unfettered expression of minority culture, and does not interfere in the relationship between the homeland and its kin in the hostland—all of these being conditions making the maintenance of a diaspora possible. But it can also be argued that democracy may have the opposite effect. Although the creation of new diasporas in industrialized democracies is often the result of the importation of scab labor from the Third World,

2. See the discussion of a "plural society" by John S. Furnivall, who coined the term. John S. Furnivall, *Netherlands India: A Study of Plural Economy* (Cambridge: Cambridge University Press, 1944) and *Colonial Policy and Practice: A Comparative Study of Burma and India* (Cambridge: Cambridge University Press, 1956). A plural society consists of a number of parallel subcommunities, most of them imported, who meet in the marketplace but do not merge and do not become integrated components of the host society.

3. Lydia Polgreen, "Ghana's Uneasy Embrace of Slavery's Diaspora," *New York Times*, December 27, 2005.

the freedoms that exist in these polities are soon used to create pressures for economic, social, and political benefits that contrast favorably with the conditions in countries of origin. This is especially true if the homeland is not free or independent. Once the homeland (re)gains freedom or independence, the expatriated ethnic minority's interest in it is revived, and diaspora identity is revived as well. This happened to the Armenian, Jewish, Croatian, and Ukrainian diasporas when their respective homelands became sovereign states.[4] But soon enough these homelands began to be judged critically against the positive features of the host country, especially by second-generation and third-generation descendants of immigrants who were well assimilated and whose connection with their ethnoreligious community had become tenuous.[5] In the Polish case, the restoration of homeland independence came too late—by the end of World War I, the descendants of the Polish diaspora, especially in France and the United States, had melted into the majority.

The favorable social, economic, and political conditions prevailing in democratic host countries benefit all minorities in one way or another, including immigrants and diasporas. But not all democratic polities provide an identical context for diasporas. Jacobin, centralized, and monochromatic regimes, committed to statism and a policy of cultural integration and homogenization, tend to speed up the assimilation process, which makes it difficult for ethnocultural minorities to maintain themselves, whereas in decentralized and pluralistic regimes, a tradition of polyarchy and cultural pluralism and a relatively autonomous civil society create opportunity structures for the maintenance of diasporic identities and institutions.

Some form of institutional backing of an ethnic or religious minority seems to be necessary for the maintenance of diasporic identity, but such backing requires a sufficiently large number of people, an ethnic (or religious) elite that has a stake in the continuation of the diaspora, a degree of rootedness that is, by definition, not present in a relatively transient minority community, and an overall political context that facilitates the building of autonomous nongovernmental organizations. Such a context tends to exist in democratic polities, which are characterized by robust civil societies that provide opportunity structures in the form of private spheres in which ethnic and/or religious minorities may maintain their own institutions that enable them to influence the public authorities.

The universe of democratic regimes includes not only "nation-states" but also multinational states. In the latter, there tends to be a habitual institutionalized commitment to ethnic pluralism, marked by accommodation policies or power-sharing schemes—by means of federalism (e.g., in Canada, Switzerland, India, and [gradually] Spain), or consociation, patronage, local options, or functional (or personal) autonomy (e.g., in the Low

---

4. Although not the country of proximate origin for the Jewish diaspora, the state of Israel is still their presumed historic homeland.

5. Daphne Winland, "'We Are Now an Actual Nation': The Impact of National Independence on the Croatian Diaspora in Canada," *Diaspora* 4, no. 1 (1995): 13–14.

Countries and increasingly in Great Britain)—that are set up for the benefit of indigenous ethnic and/or religious communities (e.g., in the Low Countries). These states, in which lobbying is a constitutional right of ethnic minorities, make it easier for immigrants to maintain their cultural or emotional identities without incurring the charge of dual political allegiance. These immigrants "may never identify with their adopted country in terms of exclusive cultural, linguistic, and even political loyalty, and hence [one uses] the term 'diaspora,' which implies a certain degree of social distance between the migrant community and the receiving country."[6] Nevertheless, the immigrants will gradually become habituated to their hostland and regard it as a "home away from home."

The degree of acceptance and the possibilities of assimilation of a transnational community into a host society depend on the nature of its collective identity. Ruud Koopmans et al. have listed five types of collective identity of transnational communities: foreigners, minorities, immigrants, and asylum seekers; racial groups, for example, blacks and Asians; religions; ethnic groups, for example, Turks, Algerians, Pakistanis, and Arabs; and hybrid identities, such as Armenians, Jews, and Sikhs.[7] The continued diaspora identity of a particular group depends also on the dominant collective identity of the host society. The more similar it is to the hostland majority in terms of these identities, the easier it is for a transnational community to choose both "voice" *and* "exit," to express its particular community concerns and to opt out of the community.[8]

In the United States, it is easier for Jews to be part of society than it is in France or Germany, because Judaism is considered one of the "constitutive" American religions. In France, once regarded as "the eldest daughter of the [Catholic] Church," Protestants have been considered as constitutive elements of national society for the past two centuries, and more recently and hesitantly, Jews, as well, but not Muslims. In post-Nazi Germany, Jews are publicly considered "our fellow citizens," but it is doubtful whether they are genuinely so regarded by the majority of the population. Such less than full acceptance of a categoric ethnoreligious group serves to perpetuate diaspora identity. In concrete terms, however, such perpetuation depends also on the political and social context of the hostland. In democratic and pluralistic countries, diasporas are free to maintain autonomous institutions and to articulate their specific diasporic concerns. They are permitted to develop institutions in civil society, to communicate freely with homelands, to send emissaries and remittances to them, and to lobby on their behalf. Above all, they enjoy the freedom to articulate and to commemorate.

Articulation has meant not merely the publication of nostalgic homeland narratives, but also the expression of themes forbidden in a homeland whose freedom had been

---

6. Sarah Wayland, "Diaspora Engagement in Homeland Conflict: A Case Study of Sri Lankan Tamils in Toronto," paper delivered at Immigration Seminar, Center for European Studies, Harvard University, September 2, 1998.

7. Ruud Koopmans, Paul Statham, Marco Giugni, and Florence Passy, *Contested Citizenship: Immigration and Cultural Diversity in Europe* (Minneapolis: University of Minnesota Press, 2005), 114–24.

8. Albert O. Hirschman, *Exit, Voice, and Loyalty: Responses to Decline in Firms, Organizations, and States* (1970; Cambridge, MA: Harvard University Press, 1981).

extinguished. Examples include the literary production by German, Russian, Spanish and Basque intellectuals exiled respectively from of Nazi Germany, Stalinist Russia, Franco Spain, and more recently Tibetans from Communist China. While preserving the best of homeland culture, this production also served to buttress diaspora identity in democratic hostlands.

Commemoration has included Holocaust memorials. Such memorials have been built in the United States, Canada, France, Germany, and other Western democratic countries, but they were not permitted in the Soviet Union, and they have been constructed in East-Central European countries only in the post-Communist period. In Russia, the Armenian genocide was officially recognized only in 1995. In recent years, the French Parliament formally acknowledged the historicity of the Armenian genocide, and at this writing, a memorial to that genocide is being built in Lyon, largely as a result of pressures by the Armenian diaspora community. Concurrently, pressures are also being brought to bear on the French Parliament to make the public denial of the Armenian genocide a felony, analogous to the existing legislation regarding the denial of the Shoah.

Not all democratic countries are "pluralist" in the ethnic or cultural sense, and these make it difficult for diasporas to maintain themselves as such. Thus, the Poles who settled in France in the nineteenth century lost their diaspora identities not only because they lacked the requisite population density and ethnic entrepreneurs, but also—and perhaps primarily—because the Jacobin republican culture of the hostland discouraged the perpetuation of ethnic minority communities. In terms of the "civic" (or functional) definition of membership in the community of French republics—a major element of Jacobinism—culture, nation(ality), and political community are conflated, so that parallel or supplementary cultural or emotional orientations (as reflected in ascriptive or "organic" communities) are suspect. The suspicion that has traditionally applied to indigenous minorities (e.g., Alsatians, Basques, Bretons, and Corsicans) is magnified in the case of diasporas to the extent that their orientations are transpolitical, so that diasporas are considered subversive almost by definition.

A democratic regime that has an open society, that allows the free expression and retention of minority culture, and that does not interfere with a reciprocal relationship between the homeland and its expatriated kin is clearly conducive to the maintenance of diaspora identity. Yet it can also be argued that democracy may have precisely the opposite effect. A tolerant, pluralistic, and polyarchically structured regime may be so attractive as to co-opt ethnic minorities and in so doing make the continuation of diasporic sentiment (one based on perceptions of "relative deprivation") unnecessary. A democratic regime is a responsive one, a fact that is often reflected in the welfare state. Such a regime does not make it easy for diasporas to maintain their identities. If the welfare state connotes a set of genuinely redistributive policies, ethnic minorities are less dependent on their own communal resources and hence are less likely to retain diaspora identities. This was the effect of the policies of the New Deal, which were inclusive and embraced especially the urban poor, many of whom were immigrant ethnoreligious minorities. Their dependence on their own communal resources had served to preserve their diasporic identities, but now that the public authorities became concerned with their economic integration, they gradually became part of the socioeconomic system of the host country, and their diasporic identities weakened. This can be clearly demonstrated in the case of the Irish, Italian, Jewish, and Polish immigrants. Indeed, their respective religions, too, became indigenized in that Judaism as well as ethnicity-based Catholicism became part of the "American" religion.[9] This explains why Tibetan nationalists do not encourage the migration of Tibetans to the Western world, where communal "border patrolling" such as the avoidance of intermarriage is more difficult than in the Asian countries bordering the homeland.[10] It also explains why the Jewish *pieds noirs* retained their ethnic identity much better in Algeria than they have since they "repatriated" to France, but managed to preserve it well enough to contribute to the reethnification of Ashkenazi Jews.

Hostland Public Policy and Diaspora Identity

One of the elements of the institutional approach to understanding the maintenance, perpetuation, or weakening of diasporas is public policy. The depth and persistence of diasporic identity is strongly affected by the domestic policies of the host country, such as immigration, naturalization, elite co-optation, integration, and the legitimation of the specific cultural and/or religious claims of immigrants. Many of the policies adopted in Western democracies have been inclusive and have helped to bring ethnic and or religious minorities into conformity with the social and cultural norms of the dominant majority in the hostland, thereby reducing inequalities based on minority status and weakening collective diaspora consciousness. These policies have included equal access to education, employment, and other economic opportunities; racial equality; legal equality between native (natural-born) and naturalized citizens;[11] separation of religion and the state and equality of religions; and freedom of ethnoreligious diasporas to foster their culture, articulate their differences, and form voluntary associations.

The dilution of diaspora identity is also a consequence of the internal evolution of a diaspora as it adapts to the customs and values of the host society but this development must be facilitated by hostland institutions and policies. In the domain of culture, this adaptation is reflected in the perpetuation of ethnic literature printed in the hostland language and, in the domain of religion, in sermons delivered in the language of the hostland, in the architectural styles of churches, gurdwaras, mosques, and synagogues increasingly resembling those of the hostland, and even in the selective adaptation of

---

9. Will Herberg, *Protestant, Catholic, Jew: An Essay in American Religious Sociology* (Garden City, NY: Doubleday, 1955). Caryn Aviv and David Shneer, in *New Jews: The End of the Jewish Diaspora* (New York: New York University Press, 2005), argue that the "indigenization" process has gradually been extended to Jews in some other democracies, for example, France, where there is increasing reference to the "Judeo-Christian civilization."

10. Dibyesh Anand, "A Contemporary Story of Diaspora: The Tibetan Version," *Diaspora* 12, no. 2 (2003): 215.

11. In the United States, only "natural-born" citizens may become president, whereas in France, a law enacted in 1981 makes it possible for naturalized citizens to occupy the highest office of the republic.

ritual to that of the dominant religion.[12] Even if the architecture in the synagogues of the United States and France retained their "exotic" (e.g., Moorish) styles, this did not suggest that the people frequenting them retained their cultural exoticism.

This dilution may also occur when a discriminatory hostland policy coincides with cultural features of an immigrant ethnic group. For example, the "national-origins" quota legislation enacted in the United States in 1924, by limiting immigration, dried up ethnic replenishment, thereby weakening diaspora links to the homeland. The Italian American community, in contrast to the Jewish community, did not develop sufficient internal ethnic cultural or philanthropic institutions to compensate for this. Nathan Glazer and Daniel Patrick Moynihan report that the *prominenti* of the Italian diaspora in the United States concentrated, not on building institutions, but on grandiose projects—such as monuments to Columbus, Verdi, and Garibaldi—that did little for the preservation of a durable diaspora culture.[13] The political culture of "amoral familism" of Italian immigrants, especially from the Mezzogiorno region, should have reinforced diaspora identity, but that identity was weakened because the focus on the family was not extended to the ethnic community at large and thus impeded diaspora institution building and facilitated assimilation. The assimilation of the Irish immigrants and the weakening of the Irish diaspora's identity did not result from problems of replenishment, but from the fact that the majority of the Irish—as opposed to what Glazer and Moynihan refer to as "the Wild Irish"—had become so thoroughly a part of the American institutional context that Irish identity was no longer meaningfully homeland-oriented and certainly not concerned with the "Irish cause."[14] Irish identity was diffused into a more general Catholic identity, so that the assertions of John F. Kennedy and Ronald Reagan about their "Irishness" had neither a diasporic nor a specific cultural connotation.

Host countries, whether democratic or authoritarian, may instrumentalize the homeland orientations of their diasporas for their own foreign-policy purposes. During the Cold War, the United States mobilized its Baltic and Polish diasporas to exert pressure on the Soviet Union, mobilized Tibetan exiles in its conflict with China and had the CIA train a number of them for guerrilla warfare.[15] and has been using Cuban exiles on its soil in its campaign against the Castro regime. The reaction to this instrumentalization is not without ambivalence, however. Whereas older Cuban refugees in the United States resented its support of homeland dictators, which caused them to leave their homeland, members of the Cuban diaspora dating from the Castro revolution appreciate the U.S. fight against Castro, but, while appreciating the welcome extended to them by the host-

---

12. Some of these adaptations are compelled by the hostland government, for example, in the Code Napoléon, which obligated rabbis to deliver their sermons in French, instead of Yiddish.

13. Nathan Glazer and Daniel P. Moynihan, *Beyond the Melting Pot*. 2nd ed. (Cambridge MA: MIT Press, 1970), 192–93.

14. Ibid., 262–87.

15. Pankaj Mishra, "The Restless Children of the Dalai Lama," *New York Times Magazine*, December 18, 2005, 58–63.

land, they also resent the fact that they are ineligible for work permits and social-welfare benefits.[16]

In their struggle against global Communism, host countries such as the United States and, secondarily, the German Federal Republic often welcomed expatriate "freedom fighters," who were marked by a "pathological anticommunism" and whose democratic credentials were questionable.[17] The majority of members of diasporas in Western host countries have been democratically oriented, but what is significant is the fact that "the membership of even the biggest [diaspora] associations is shockingly small, a mere sliver of the diaspora as a whole. "[18]

Nevertheless, diasporas can also be influential actors in shaping hostland foreign policy and even in long-distance nation building, that is, in creating or recreating a homeland. This is particularly true of diasporas in democratic host countries, because these serve more effectively than authoritarian states as training grounds for political ideas transmitted to homelands. Eamon de Valera, who was to become the first president of independent Ireland, grew up in New York, and Thomas Masaryk imbibed democratic values in the United States, which were reflected in his politics when his Czechoslovakian homeland became independent. Similarly, Chaim Weizmann's constitutional liberalism in Israel was doubtlessly influenced by his long residence in England, and Sun-Yat-sen of China and Mikheil Saakashvili of post-Soviet Georgia attended college in the United States. George Soros, a native of Hungary, used his immense fortune to implant democratic ideas in East-Central Europe during both the Communist and post-Communist periods, with prospects of democratization obviously much greater during the latter.

In many cases, the linkages between homeland and host country have become institutionalized. This is attested by the Jewish Agency for Israel, which has been active in matters of immigration and immigrant absorption in that country, and India's High Level Committee on the Indian Diaspora, which is charged with developing "mutually beneficial relationship with Persons of Indian Origin and Non-Resident Indians in the context of constitutional provisions, Laws and rules applicable both to India and the countries of their residence."[19] In these relationships, the diasporas in prosperous democratic host countries can make the most positive contributions to the homeland—not only in terms of remittances, but, more important, in influencing the institutional development of homelands. American Jews have tried to influence Israel to adopt selected American political values, African Americans have been instrumental in getting South Africa to abandon apartheid, and Armenians, Cubans, Poles, and Haitians in these diasporas have

---

16. Holly Ackerman, "A Comparison of Features in Two Diaspora Communities: Cubans in Miami and Venezuela," paper presented at meeting of the International Studies Association, Washington, DC, February 16–20, 1999.

17. Paul Hockenos, *Homeland Calling: Exile Patriotism and the Balkan Wars* (Ithaca, NY: Cornell University Press, 2003), 10–11.

18. Ibid., 7.

19. L. M. Singhvi, *Report of the High Level Committee on the Indian Diaspora, Ministry of External Affairs*, August 18, 2000.

exerted pressures on homeland governments in favor of democratic reforms, often using institutional patterns in the their hostlands as models.[20]

In South Africa, the acceptance of pluralism and of the cultural and political demands of the Indian diaspora were achieved as a consequence of external pressures. This does not always work, as attested by the failure of the Chinese and Tibetan diasporas in getting China to move toward greater democracy. But in this case, the diaspora effort is hampered by the host country's foreign-policy considerations. Similarly, the remittances sent by sub-Saharan African diasporas in North America and Western Europe to their homelands, while crucial in the survival of individual villages, have not spilled over into democratic reforms in the recipient countries.[21]

Nation Building, Nationalism, and the Fate of Diasporas

The process of dissolution of diasporic identity is most evident in host countries that are in process of nation building. In the nineteenth century, both authoritarian and democratic countries, fired up by nationalist fervor and engaged in the process of national consolidation, had little patience with ethnic minorities, and they exerted pressure upon them to give up their diaspora identities. They were particularly successful with Armenian, Jewish, and Polish immigrants, for the simple reason that these had no politically independent homelands to relate to or to back them up.

After the French Revolution, and more specifically under Napoleon, Jews in France were transformed from members of the *nation juive* to individual and unmediated members of the French nation and, from the Orléanist régime to the end of the Second Empire, to *Juifs d'État*.[22] In the nineteenth century, Jews in Germany, in process of gaining civil and political rights, came to regard themselves as "German nationals of the Jewish faith" and classical Reform Judaism abandoned its millennial orientation toward "Zion." As Abraham Geiger, one of the reformers, put it, "Jerusalem is a noble memory from the past and the cradle of our religion; but it holds no hope for the future. No new life can begin there. Let us not disturb its rest."[23] Accordingly, the reformers abandoned prayers for a restoration of Temple service in Jerusalem and for an ingathering of exiles. According to Walter Rathenau, German Jews had become a German tribe, just like Saxons and Bavarians.[24] The process of assimilation of the Jews in France and Germany was so rapid that, according to a wide consensus among historians, their community would have been

---

20. Nina Glick-Schiller, Linda Basch, and Cristina Szanton-Blanc, eds. *Towards a Transnational Perspective on Migration: Race, Class, Ethnicity, and Nationalism Reconsidered* (New York: New York Academy of Sciences, 1992); Khachig Tölölyan, "Rethinking Diaspora(s): Stateless Power in the Transnational Moment," *Diasporas* 5, no. 1 (1996): 3–36.

21. Philippe Bernard, "L'argent renvoyé au pays: Une manne," *Le Monde*, April 11, 2005.

22. Pierre Birnbaum, *Les fous de la République: Les Juifs d'État de Gambetta à Vichy* (Paris: Fayard, 1992).

23. Cited in Amos Elon, *The Pity of it All: A History of Jews in Germany, 1743–1933* (New York: Metropolitan Books, 2002), 288.

24. Ibid.

almost completely melted into the mainstream of society within a few generations had it not been for certain unforeseen events.

In the authoritarian Russian Empire, in contrast, the nation-building process did not significantly threaten the continuation of the Jewish diaspora, nor did the Ottoman Empire. There was no serious effort to assimilate that diaspora. On the contrary, there was an institutionalized pattern of excluding it or subjecting it to legal disabilities, which only strengthened diasporic identity. (The situation in Austria-Hungary was more ambiguous: Assimilation was significant among the Jewish bourgeoisie in Budapest and Vienna, but not in the provincial non-Germanic and non-Magyar hinterlands, especially among the poor.)

After Poland ceased to exist as an independent state, a romantic longing for the homeland lingered among exiles, in particular the intelligentsia, the gentility, and the military,[25] and it was sustained for two or three generations by nationalist rebellions. By the beginning of the twentieth century, however, this longing had died out, especially among the large mass of Polish working-class immigrants to France and the United States, whose descendants have forgotten the Polish language, have largely intermarried, and have kept only Catholicism and parts of the Polish cuisine. A new Polish diaspora was created during World War II and the Cold War and the post–Cold War period; but it does not seem to have resulted in a "rediasporization" of the descendants of the older Polish immigrants.

Images of Hostland and Homeland

It may be argued that not all diasporas are affected by political developments in an equal measure. If the diaspora identity of a community is strengthened by its relationship to a homeland, if not defined altogether by it, and if homelands are manifested in the international system as states, then stateless diasporas, such as those of the Kurds, Tibetans, and Palestinians, are at a disadvantage: They have trouble asserting themselves effectively unless, as in the case of the Palestinians, their efforts are supported by other states or by international institutions.[26]

Diaspora images of the homeland reflect its institutional structures and its policy orientations. Just as a positive image of the homeland (relative to that of the hostland) serves to perpetuate a diaspora's identity, a negative image is conducive to severing its links with the homeland and ultimately eliminating a diaspora's identity. This is illustrated by experiences of the Huguenots in Germany and elsewhere outside France. During the years immediately following the revocation of the Edict of Nantes, "endogamy was the rule among them and the French language was jealously preserved."[27] A century

---

25. The Polish national anthem, "Jeszcze Polska nie zgyniela" (Poland Is Not Yet Lost), was composed by an expatriate legionary serving in Italy after the third partition of Poland in 1795.

26. Anand, "A Contemporary Story of Diaspora," 217.

27. Philippe Joutard, "La diaspora des Huguenots," *Diasporas* 1, 2nd semestre (2002): 115–21.

later, with the outbreak of the French Revolution, the Constituent Assembly declared that any descendant of a person expatriated for reasons of religion could automatically regain French nationality upon returning to France. But owing to their opposition to the policies of Napoleon, most Huguenots in Berlin decided to Germanize their names and those in London to Anglicize them.[28] Until the end of the nineteenth century, there were still Huguenots in the United States and elsewhere who preserved the French language, especially in their prayers, but their number has declined into insignificance. Moreover, their French had become quite different from that spoken in the homeland. The majority, however, while still adhering to the Huguenot rite, used the hostland language in their liturgy.

During the interwar period, the brutalities of the Nazi regime had made many members of the German diaspora reluctant to identify with their homeland, just as in our day, the deteriorating images of Maoist China, Croatia under Franjo Tudjman, and Serbia under Slobodan Milosevic have been a source of embarrassment to the respective diasporas of these countries. Israel's official treatment of non-Orthodox Judaism and its policies vis-à-vis the Palestinians have tarnished the image of that country in the eyes of many Jews in Western democracies.[29] Many members of the Armenian diaspora in the West have a less than positive image of the contemporary Armenian republic, whose political leadership is often considered corrupt. A similar deteriorating image of Iran under the ayatollahs can be observed among their respective diasporas in democratic host countries. Today, many Iranian immigrants do not consider the Islamic republic "as part of their imagination of Iran"; an increasing number use the label "Persian," rather than "Iranian" in referring to themselves; and more than a third of Iranian Americans surveyed spoke of having become accustomed to the comforts and freedoms of the United States and of not ever wanting to live in Iran.[30] Given the relative freedoms existing in India, few Tibetans born in that country, although regarded as stateless people, want to return to Tibet, which they consider to be under brutal occupation.[31] In short, a negative or deteriorating image of the homeland leads to a gradual alienation from and disidentification with it and eventually to dediasporization. This process is speeded up if the hostland is a welcoming place and encourages assimilation.

Conversely, if political conditions in the host country deteriorate and ethnic, religious, or racial minorities are persecuted, the (real, remembered, or imagined) homeland becomes more attractive, and minorities in the process of assimilation may become

---

28. Ibid.

29. William Safran, "The Tenuous Link between Hostlands and Homeland: The Progressive De-Zionization of Western Diasporas." In *Les diasporas: 2000 ans d'histoire*, ed. Lisa Anteby-Yemini, William Berthomière, and Gabriel Sheffer (Rennes: Presses Universitaires de Rennes, 2005); Bernard Wasserstein, *Vanishing Diaspora: The Jews in Europe Since 1945* (London: Penguin, 1997).

30. Laleh Khalidi, "Mixing Memory and Desire," May 13, 1998. Available on-line at http://www.iranian.com/Features/May98/Iranams/index.html (last accessed December 10, 2007).

31. Mishra, "The Restless Children of the Dalai Lama."

rediasporized. Thus, Jews were transformed from "German Citizens of the Jewish Faith" (as they had identified themselves upon being granted full citizenship in the nineteenth century) to "Jews living in Germany" when the Nuremberg racial laws effectively turned them into internal exiles and Jews in France were transformed from purely cultic *Juifs d'État* of the Orléanist regime and the Second Empire to the diasporic ethnic Jew after World War II. The diasporization of Jews in Germany became official toward the end of the 1930s, when the Nazi government changed the name of their central organization from "Reich Association of German Jews" to "Association of Jews Living in Germany" (Reichsvereinigung der Juden in Deutschland), and its leaders were chosen by the police. The experience of the Holocaust transformed many survivors into Zionists and "reethnified" Jewish identity. When the U.S. government sent Japanese Americans into internment camps during World War II, it did not deprive them of citizenship, yet it is unclear to what extent this treatment produced a diasporic identity. Whatever homeland nostalgia still existed was probably eclipsed by a negative image of an autocratic and imperialistic Japan. Several years after the war, the federal government officially apologized for the deportation. By that time, the descendants of the internees had become so thoroughly Americanized that they no longer regarded themselves as a diaspora.

Legitimating Measures

Legitimation of diasporas in democratic countries takes place by means of a variety of measures. Some of these imply that members of diasporas are entitled to the same rights as indigenous members of society, while others reflect an acceptance of a continued connection with the homeland. The first group includes the issuing of work permits; due-process protection; entitlements to education, minimum wages, and social-security protections; the freedom to choose one's residence and to travel; and the right to organize and lobby. The second group includes dual citizenship, the use of homeland teachers and clerics in hostland schools (as in the case of Muslims in France and Germany), and the right to vote in homeland elections. (It is unclear to what extent such measures will be reexamined as a consequence of growing international terrorism.) In 1981, the creation of voluntary associations of immigrants was officially permitted in France and at the end of in 2005, following the riots in suburban ghettos, an organization was established representing blacks, both indigenous French citizens (primarily from the overseas departments that are part of France) and immigrants and their descendants. This organization, the Conseil Représentatif des Associations Noires (CRAN), an umbrella for about sixty different groups, hopes to address itself to "the need of recognition and memory" of slavery and colonialism and to become an official interlocutor with the public powers.[32] In the Federal Republic of Germany, this response has even been formalized on the subnational level. Thus, in Frankfurt, an elective body, the Local Foreigners' Representative Board,

---

32. Blandine Grosjean, "Les Noirs de France solidaires montent un Cran." *Libération*, November 28, 2005.

was set up by the city council "to represent the interests of the foreign inhabitants" and to advise the various local authorities concerning them.[33] India, another federal state, has permitted exiled Tibetans to organize and has become the refuge of the Dalai Lama. In sum, such institutional developments suggest that one does not have to relinquish one's homeland citizenship in order to participate the political process of the host country.

Despite pressures by the political authorities in Latvia toward unilingualism as an element of "exclusionary nationalism," the "beached" Russian diaspora in that country[34] is able to maintain its connection with its neighboring homeland because Latvia and other Baltic countries are officially committed to democracy and the freedom of organization and expression implicit in it.[35] But this freedom of organization and action is not absolute, for the governments of these countries may limit or forbid the political activities of diaspora groups that tend to provoke internal violence or create difficulties in diplomatic relations. Nor is formal democracy enough: In Finland, the Kurdish diaspora has had difficulty organizing because of the geographic dispersal of its members and problems of funding,[36] and in Turkey, their relationships with other ethnic Kurds outside Turkey are seen as a threat to its territorial integrity. Nevertheless, the "democratizing" incentive of future membership in the European Union has led to a greater recognition of Kurdish cultural-linguistic demands, which, in turn, tends to facilitate transpolitical relations.

The discussion above suggests that pluralism, which makes possible the articulation of ethnic minority identities, is found today in democratic states of all kinds, including Jacobin centralizing ones. Here, the question arises to what extent the strength of the state itself affects the fate of diasporas. A strong state has the power to do with diasporas most of what it pleases: to constrain their activities, make the articulation of their cultures and orientations difficult or impossible, close their institutions, ban their contacts with homelands, expel them, and exterminate them. A state that is weak cannot do these things easily. However, a state that is strong enough can afford to tolerate diasporas and their transnational outlooks, whereas a weak state often finds its unity and coherence threatened by them. Thus, the United States is culturally self-assured and secure in its statehood and hence relatively relaxed about the presence of diasporas on its soil, whereas France is uncertain about its sovereignty and insecure about its national culture, which seems to be buffeted from all sides. This is reflected in its attitude toward the languages of ethnic minorities. In the nineteenth century, France suppressed ethnoregional languages in the name of nation building; today, it fears the spread of languages other than French because of the decline of the global position of French, which it attributes to

---

33. Joel S. Fetzer and J. Christopher Soper, *Muslims and the State in Britain, France, and Germany* (Cambridge: Cambridge University Press, 2005), 124.

34. This label has been used by David Laitin in *Identity in Formation: The Russian-Speaking Populations in the Near Abroad* (Ithaca, NY: Cornell University Press, 1998), 29.

35. Mark A. Jubulis, *Nationalism and Democratic Transition: The Politics of Citizenship and Language in Post-Soviet Latvia* (Lanham, MA: University Press of America, 2001),163–226.

36. Östen Wahlbeck, *Kurdish Diasporas* (London: Macmillan, 1999), 154–55.

the cultural imperialism of the Americans. The language that is making the greatest gains in France is Arabic, the most widely used diaspora language, but there are limits to the government's ability to suppress that language, limits imposed both by domestic considerations (the growing electoral importance of the Muslim community) and foreign-policy realities (dependence on Arab oil).

The British and German cases are more complex. The United Kingdom has for many years been favorably disposed toward pluralism, but recently, doubts have arisen about its integrative capabilities. Germany has traditionally been hostile to ethnic, religious, and racial minorities, but has been forced into a "multiculturalist" mode and a maximum possible openness to pluralistic collective identities by way of atoning for its recent history. To be sure, the public authorities have recently stressed the need of immigrants to conform to the dominant culture (*Leitkultur*), but the application of this notion has remained controversial and flexible. Compared with France, with its strong centralizing tradition, both Britain and Germany are *structurally* weak states because of the relative autonomy of their subnational authorities. The distinction between strong and weak states, however, may be challenged, because today, owing to globalization, the sovereignty of all states has declined, and transnational actors of all kinds, including diasporas, are less subject to control by the political authorities of a host country. Some transactions associated with technological modernization, such as cyberdriven communications among diasporas and between them and homelands—are virtually unstoppable. Transnational relations have even become legitimate—a development attested to not only by a widening of the notion of citizenship, but by the growing visibility and dynamic institutional development within diaspora communities.

Language Policy and Diaspora Identity

The effect of language policy on diaspora identity is a matter of controversy. In a number of democratic countries, culturally homogenizing educational elites have attempted to discourage, if not to forbid, the teaching of minority languages in order to weaken diasporic identity. But such a policy may be useless, if not counterproductive. It is true that the perpetuation of a language associated with an anterior homeland plays a role in the retention of diaspora cultural identity and that members of an ethnic minority who wish to rediscover their roots in order to mark their difference from the majority of the host society try to learn their ethnic language. But in most cases, it is a vain effort, because most members of diasporas—at least of the second generation—have been irreversibly assimilated linguistically. This is especially the case in modern host countries that provide compulsory education by means of a national school system in which the dominant language of the country is the medium of instruction.

Moreover, diaspora identity, which also includes affective elements not related to language, can often be inculcated and cultivated more effectively in the hostland language than in that of the homeland. The "ethnic revival" of several regional minorities in France that took place after the 1960s occurred when most of the members of the ethnic groups in question (including their elites) had long since gotten used to speaking nothing but French (a language, incidentally, in which modern ethnonationalism can be expressed much better than in Breton or Alsatian). As a Reform rabbi in nineteenth-century Germany was said to have remarked, "As long as they wrote in Hebrew, the Zionists were not dangerous; [but] now that they write in German, they must be resisted."[37] Today, Jews in the diaspora are more ethnically assertive than they had been earlier, while their competence in their respective ethnoreligious languages has declined. There are few Armenian diasporans who have been learning Armenian, even among those who proclaim their Armenian identity, and the revival of interest in Yiddish in the United States is confined to a small minority of Jewish college students in a sociological context that is no longer appropriate. This applies in growing measure to the Maghrebi diaspora as well. The threat that the Maghrebi Muslims in France are believed to pose to French institutions, in particular to republicanism and *laïcité*, comes not from language, but from religion, and explains the recent legislation against wearing of the hijab in public-school classrooms. Incidentally, the religions of the Muslim, Jewish, Sikh, and other diasporas are increasingly taught in the languages of the various host countries.

Economic Conditions and the Persistence of Diasporas

There is equal ambiguity about the effect of economic status on diasporas. John Furnivall, Ted Gurr (selectively),[38] and others (especially Marxists) have dealt with ethnic minority groups as "ethnoclasses" and as products of capitalism. To be sure, there are economic explanations for the slavery that created a black diaspora on the American continent; trade and commerce contributed to the creation of a Chinese diaspora in Southeast Asia; and the middleman occupations of Jews, Armenians, Indians, and Greeks in various parts of the world reinforced the diaspora consciousness of these communities and facilitated their transpolitical relationships. It is also true that Chinese and Italians were brought into the United States and Indians into South Africa as menial or indentured laborers in the nineteenth century, but their descendants have long since ceased to regard themselves as members of diasporas. The ambiguity of the economic explanation is suggested by the fact that diasporas have served both as the vanguard of economic imperialism and as buffers against the economic difficulties of hostlands. Nevertheless, the economic dimension, which cannot be fully dealt with here, does not provide a full explanation for the diaspora phenomenon.

Diasporas grow with economic development. The need for capital leads to a search for an innovating commercial class that is not rooted in a particular country and that has global connections, that is, a diaspora of commercial intermediaries, a category dis-

---

37. Werner E. Mosse, and Arnold Paucker, eds., *Juden im Wilhelminischen Deutschland, 1890–1914* (Tübingen: Mohr, 1998), 654.

38. Ted Robert Gurr, *Minorities at Risk* (Washington, DC: United States Institute of Peace, 1993).

cussed at length by John A. Armstrong, Robin Cohen, and Gabriel Sheffer.[39] In turn, the development of industries fuels a demand for cheap labor, which leads to the growth of immigrant labor diasporas. But both capitalist and proletarian diasporas weaken after a certain time. What, then, keeps them going? As I have argued above, the political-institutional context is of primary importance, as is the complex of public policies that contribute to making immigrants and their descendants feel "at home abroad" (as Gabriel Sheffer has aptly put it). David Laitin has argued that, from a rational-choice (or instrumentalist) perspective, the achievement of material satisfaction will make descendants of immigrant minorities forget their diaspora identity sooner or later.[40] One may, however, posit a counterargument: that freedom from quotidian worry about meeting economic needs permits individuals to focus on "postmaterialist" interests, such as cultural and genealogical ones. The rediscovery of their roots and the jogging of their memories may lead them to a renewed interest in their ethnic antecedents and identities and to a retrieval of their diasporic sensitivities. But for most of those who have reached this postmaterialist status, it is probably too late, because they tend to be the most assimilated (assuming that the features that once differentiated them from the dominant majority of the hostland society, such as language and religion, have been overcome), and their ethnic interests are not likely to entail more than the acquisition of trinkets and a superficial embrace of homeland ethnosymbols such as Saint Patrick's or Columbus Day parades, Chinese cuisine, dirndl dresses, or the playing of tunes from *Fiddler on the Roof.* Some of these ethnosymbols have become transethnic and indigenized. In any case, this is a moot point, because the vast majority of diasporans have not yet attained a postmaterialist status.

What about the wealth of a host country as an overall systemic context? Gabriel Sheffer is correct in pointing out that "despite societal and governmental opposition, in some poorer non-democratic host countries the existence of ethnic diasporas may help to pave the way toward legitimized pluralism, and the existence of ethnic diasporas in modern rich societies contributes to the emergence of multiculturalism."[41] But such emergence is not a foregone conclusion. France and Germany have been the host countries of as many diasporas as Britain, the United States, or Canada, yet multiculturalism, whether defined as cultural pluralism or preferential policies vis-à-vis ethnic minorities (affirmative action), has begun to take hold only recently, reluctantly, and incompletely in the former two countries. In South Africa, the existence of the Indian diaspora contributed neither to the development of cultural pluralism nor to the end of apartheid.

---

39. John A. Armstrong, "Mobilized and Proletarian Diasporas," *American Political Science Review* 70, no. 2 (1976): 393–403; Robin Cohen, *Global Diasporas: An Introduction* (Seattle: University of Washington Press, 1997); Gabriel Scheffer, *Diaspora Politics: At Home Abroad* (Cambridge, MA: Cambridge University Press, 2003).

40. Laitin, *Identity in Formation*, chapter 1. The instrumentalist perspective is never "pure," as illustrated in the case of Holocaust survivors, whose condition in host countries may range from total assimilation to permanent outsider identity, depending on cultural background, personal opportunity, age, peer influences, and so on.

41. Sheffer, *Diaspora Politics*, 94.

Similarly the presence of a significant Palestinian diaspora in Kuwait has not led to the development of pluralism or democracy. The causal relationship is even more problematic in Turkey, where ethnic pluralism was more legitimate under the Ottoman regime than it has been since the inauguration of the Kemalist polity, and whatever progress is made in the direction of legitimizing the cultural claims of the Kurds (who are an indigenous minority, rather than a diaspora) is likely to depend largely on pressure from the European Union.

Conversely, there is a clear parallel between the treatment (and behavior) of indigenous ethnic regionally concentrated minorities and nonterritorial and regionally dispersed ones, including diasporas, such as the Armenian, Jewish, Gypsy, Kurdish, Maghrebi, and the more recently settled East Asian. In France, for example, the increasingly open articulation of diaspora identities is a spillover from the growing acceptance and legitimation of the cultural demands of indigenous minorities.[42]

Who Is a Citizen? Defining Membership in the National Community

Definitions of citizenship are an important part of the political context. "Civic" nations such as the American, Australian, Brazilian, and Canadian, which are based on *jus soli*, that is, birth in the country, naturalization, or a commitment to the state's institutions and values, make it relatively easy for immigrants to become permanent members of the political community. "Ethnic" nations, such as those of Japan, Israel, and Switzerland, which are based in large measure on *jus sanguinis*, that is, kinship, tend to regard foreigners in their midst as temporary residents (or "guest workers") who are expected eventually to return to their homelands unless they share kinship ties with the host society. Germany (which regarded itself as an ethnic nation until the mid-1990s) used to make distinctions between *Volkszugehörigkeit* and *Staatsangehörigkeit*,[43] but it no longer does. The persistence of *jus sanguinis* in homelands, as in Switzerland, Japan, and a number of other states, serves to perpetuate a legal connection between emigrants and their ancestral homes and thus to foster a diaspora identity. Even in Germany and Israel, where the acquisition of citizenship by naturalization is possible, descent continues to figure in determining entitlement to citizenship. That entitlement may even extend to protection against criminal prosecution by the host country of naturalized citizens, as in the cases of Japan welcoming Alberto Fujimori, the former president of Peru; Israel providing haven to Jews indicted for criminal acts in Western Europe and the United States; and Austria harboring Nazi war criminals who have returned from exile. In the United States, a clear distinction is made between citizenship, which refers to political status, and nationality,

---

42. William Safran, "The French State and Ethnic Minority Cultures: Policy Dimensions and Problems," in *Ethno-Territorial Politics, Policy, and the Western World*, ed. Joseph R. Rudolph and Robert J. Thompson (Boulder, CO: Lynne Rienner, 1989); Cohen, *Global Diasporas*, 115–57.

43. William Safran, "Citizenship and Nationality in Democratic Systems: Approaches to Defining and Acquiring Membership in the Political Community," *International Political Science Review* 18, no. 3 (1997): 313–35.

which simply refers to a vague kind of identity that is based on ancestral background but that has no legal relevance and often no particular cultural or affective meaning. In French republics, the difference between *nationalité* and *citoyenneté* is obscured, at least in theory, so that no immigrant, and certainly no descendant of immigrants born abroad, needs to feel herself as being in a diaspora.

There is a direct relationship between a community's perception of being accepted by the host country as part of its political community and the weakening of homeland orientations, that is, of diaspora identity. A study by Koopmans and Statham points to an increasing acceptance of immigrant minorities in Britain and Germany, although there are differences: In Germany, minorities "enter the public sphere" as Turks, Kurds, Bosnians, or Iranians, rather than as Muslims, whereas the opposite is true in Britain, where Pakistanis and Bangladeshis make their claims as Muslims.[44] The situation in France (which is not examined in that study) is more complex: Under Jacobin dogma, French citizens are citizens *tout court* and are not broken down into subcategories. In fact, there has been no religious, ethnic, or racial census in that country since 1872. While in the United States, "immigration remains an essential part of the culture's self-definition . . . and [the] census [asks] questions about ethnic origin [in France] there [has been] no equivalent to the American notion of second-generation Italian Americans or Irish Americans."[45] In Britain, which, at least in principle, accepts the idea of a multicultural society, one habitually refers to citizens of non-European origins as "Asians" or "Indians." It has been remarked that the "British authorities have reproduced vis-à-vis the minorities their colonial model by co-opting as interlocutors notables who are charged with administering and controlling the [ethnoreligious] community. These are for the most part men and first-generation immigrants."[46] These minorities are regarded as diasporas because they are "postcolonial" victims of the old colonial system. (Postcolonial diasporas are by and large voluntary diasporas, compared with colonial diasporas, who were sent against their will to another country as indentured servants.)

Whatever the state dogma or legal definition regarding immigrants and/or other minorities, social reality does not always conform to it. Individuals are categorized by *society* selectively in terms of their origins as outsiders, for example, "Français d'origine algérienne, d'origine grecque," "d'origine israélite," "d'origine arabe," or "immigré de la deuxième génération"—sometimes referred to as "postcolonial natives." In contrast, there are hardly any references to "Français d'origine catholique," "d'origine italienne," or "d'origine portugaise." The emphasis on foreign origins, and sometimes even their mere mention, evokes a suspicion of "double allegiance." Political leaders themselves

---

44. Ruud Koopmans and Paul Statham, "Migration and Ethnic Relations as a Field of Political Contention: An Opportunity Structure Approach," in *Challenging Immigration and Ethnic Relations Politics*, ed. Ruud Koopmans and Paul Statham (Oxford: Oxford University Press, 2000).

45. Julian Jackson, "Historians and the Nation in Contemporary France," in *Writing National Histories*, ed. Stefan Berger, Mark Donovan, and Kevin Passmore (London: Routledge, 1999), 245.

46. Marc Semo, "Le royaume-uni en crise existentielle," *Libération*, August 13, 2005.

reflect such categorization. Thus, President Jacques Chirac (in an interview on July 17, 2004), deploring racism, referred to "nos compatriotes juifs, musulmans, et tout simplement parfois des Français" (Jews, Muslims, and sometimes simply French compatriots). These minorities are officially candidates for naturalization and are in fact easily naturalized, but society may be uncomfortable with their presence because they are widely considered to be people who do not quite belong because, as Chirac put it when he was mayor of Paris, of their "noises and odors." Such discomfort extends a fortiori to members of diasporas, insofar as they are defined as having supplementary (or complementary) transnational orientations. But it may also extend to those who are indigenous (or long-indigenized) members of the French nation, but who are becoming alienated as a consequence of their treatment by the hostland majority. This is reflected in the recent formation of CRAN mentioned above. In this respect, the situation in France resembles that of the United States, where African Americans are increasingly "diasporized" with a growing perception that, owing to their skin color, they are not fully accepted by the majority, despite an official government commitment to equal rights and opportunities.

The success or failure of social integration depends not only on the behavior of society at large, but also on the specific condition of an individual member of an ethnic minority, including a descendant of immigrants. A study of the Vietnamese diaspora showed a continuum of diaspora identities, ranging from "Vietnam, c'est tout, la France, c'est rien" (Vietnam is everything, France is nothing) to "total indifference, if not resistance, to their culture of origin."[47]

The triumph of social norms over state institutional decisions in regard to diasporas can be seen also in the case of the Gypsies in Hungary. During the Communist regime and to some extent also under the current post-Communist system, it had been official policy to end their diaspora condition by means of dispersal and sedentarization, but local bureaucrats nullified this policy by confining them in ghettos on the edge of villages. The local bureaucracy was pressured by social customs that were so pervasive as to be institutionalized.[48]

The French and German concerns with cultural-linguistic homogenization and their impatience with the cultural exceptionalism of minorities can be explained by the fact that (in contrast to the situation in the United States and Britain) culture has traditionally been part and parcel of their governments' structure of public policies. But the German and French exclusionary attitudes are undergoing change. The acceptance of *jus soli* in Germany in the 1990s has opened the door to naturalization, and a growing number of Turkish "guest workers" have acquired citizenship and even adopted the prevailing German culture and language. There is also anecdotal evidence that the collective diasporic identity has begun to weaken. In France, attitudes have changed as well: The increasing tolerance of ethnic identity is reflected in the statement by an official government

---

47. Marie-Paule Ha, "Vietnamese Diaspora in France," *Contemporary French Civilization* 27, no. 3 (2003): 269.

48. Michael Stewart, *The Time of the Gypsies* (Boulder, CO: Westview Press, 1997), 126–27.

commission that French people of foreign origin do not have to "efface the traces of their previous ethnicity"[49] and in the periodic acceptance of the existence of an emotional attachment of Jews to Israel and of Muslims to their various Arab homelands. It is also reflected in the selective toleration of cultural practices that are "un-French" (e.g., polygamy, female circumcision, and arranged marriages). Moreover, the acceptance of ethnic identity in general and of diaspora identity specifically is also attested by a continuing relationships of immigrant minorities to the homeland (e.g., remittances to families in Maghreb countries) and may be countenanced as a matter of realpolitik, as is the maintenance of the Institut du Monde Arabe with support from Arab countries.

Globalization

A major factor in the growing phenomenon of expatriation has been globalization. There is no doubt that it has altered the institutional context of relations between states and the peoples who inhabit them. Its effect on diasporas, however, has been ambiguous. On the one hand, it is generally admitted that globalization contributes to the massive movement of populations from their homeland to a hostland. As minority communities in host countries are enlarged by new waves of immigrants, a gradually waning diaspora identity among earlier immigrants may be resuscitated. Moreover, the permeability of borders and the ease of communication and transportation make it easier for expatriate ethnonational groups to keep in close touch with the homeland and periodically to replenish its cultural resources. Since globalization tends to aggravate the economic exploitation of the unskilled, the poor, and the powerless, it may accentuate diasporization insofar as many immigrant societies fall into these categories, rediasporize immigrant communities in process of assimilation, and create new diasporas. On the other hand, the diaspora identity of new immigrants may fail to develop if they are in close contact with well-assimilated fellow ethnics who had immigrated several generations earlier. Moreover, globalization contributes to secularization and to the development of a transnational mass culture. The one would leave less room for religious diversity (or for religion as a marker of collective identity) and the other for cultural diversity. It is true that the revolution in communications makes it easier for diaspora communities to be in constant cultural contact with their homelands and thus facilitates the use of the homeland language, but globalization also has a cultural spillover effect in the sense that a linguistic homogenization process is going on,[50] which makes the retention of ethnonational identities of all sorts more difficult than it had been in the past. In short, globalization has a homogenizing impact on all cultures, so that the homeland and hostland cultures are no longer as distinct as before.

One of the consequences of globalization is neoliberalism, which tends to undermine the welfare state, reverse the economic co-optation process, degenerate into Social

49. "Lutter contre les discriminations," *Regards sur l'Actualité* no. 256 (December1999): 35–47.

50. The rapid inroads of English and Yiddish into the Hebrew language attest both to a globalization *and* diasporization process taking place in the homeland itself.

Darwinism, and exacerbate the overinstitutionalization and impersonality of a mere *Gesellschaft*-based social order "where one is always dealing with strangers."[51] For many years, diasporas sought relief from this impersonality in religion, but owing to rapid secularization, religion is no longer as effective a focus around which to rally the majority of diasporas as it was in the past, and they try to compensate by a search for their ethnic roots as a basis for building an affectivity-based *Gemeinschaft*. This applies to expatriate minority communities such as the Armenians, Hindus, Jews, Sikhs, and Tibetans. They and their descendants, no longer held together by materritorial spiritual bonds, rediscover an anterior homeland, which functions as a substitute and reinvigorates their diaspora identities. It is no coincidence that the weakening of social protections, the underfunding of municipal housing projects, and a growing neglect of public schools in the United States and selected West European states has been accompanied by the growth parochial schools, including ethnoculturally oriented ones, which serve to sustain diaspora identities.

Postnational Citizenship

The galloping global mobility of people and the permeability of national boundaries has led to a modification of an exclusivist view of view of membership in the political community, as attested by an ever more generalized acceptance of dual citizenship. This development serves to legitimate diasporas officially by regarding a concurrent hostland and homeland identity as normal. It is reflected, inter alia, in members of a diaspora voting in homeland elections, for example, in those of Afghanistan, Bosnia, Croatia, East Timor, Kosovo, Ukraine, and elsewhere. In Croatia and Italy, expatriates have even been allocated seats in parliament. In the United States, voting centers were set up in Nashville, Tennessee, to enable Iraqi Kurds, who make up a significant part of the population, to vote in the recent Iraqi elections with the permission, and even encouragement, of the hostland government, without such voting infringing on the prospects of their naturalization.[52] It is reasonable to assume that this institutionalized involvement of the diaspora in homeland politics implies a transmission of the host country's democratic ideas—a process that is not always welcome in the homeland, especially if it is not democratic, and not always appreciated by the host country if, for reasons of its own national interest, it prefers to deal with a nondemocratic homeland.

The embrace of a broader view of membership in the sociopolitical community has been reflected in a revisiting of the concept of citizenship that has minimized the distinction between indigenous and diaspora status. Traditionally, the concept of citizenship

---

51. Khalidi, "Mixing Memory and Desire."

52. Ben Goldsmith, "Out-of-Country Voting in Post-Conflict Elections," *Democracy at Large* 1, no. 4 (2005): 30–33. This openness represents a change from previous official attitudes in the United States, whose government had attempted to deprive a naturalized citizen of his citizenship because he had voted in an Israeli election. But the U.S. Supreme Court (in *Afroyim v. Rusk* [1967]) held that under the Fourteenth Amendment to the Constitution this could not be done.

was purely national and political, and one could not be both a foreigner and a citizen. Some years ago, however, there appeared references by German politicians to "unsere ausländischen Mitbürger" (our foreign fellow citizens), a term often applied to Turkish guest workers and their descendants.[53] The notion of "foreign fellow citizens" is not the oxymoron it appears at first glance. The status of citizenship in a broader sense—that is, of membership in a supranational political community—is evinced in the right of noncitizens to vote in urban elections in member countries of the European Union countries. As Nicolas Sarkozy, the French president, argued when he was minister of the interior, "It is not abnormal that a foreigner who is [a legal] resident who pays his taxes and has lived in France for at least ten years could vote in municipal elections."[54]

The disjunction of citizenship and nationality that has been taking place in connection with the development of European supranational institutions has been accompanied by an expanded approach to citizenship that envisages a continuum of communities ranging from the "primordial" and local to the "functional" and transnational and that includes the state, the ethnocultural community, the province and municipality, and the professional/occupational community.[55] This would accommodate diasporas, whose members may belong to any or all the above. These "postnational" citizenships imply certain entitlements, such as social insurance, minimum wages, housing, and education. These forms of citizenship, which apply to members of diasporas whether or nor they are national citizens, help to remove the impediments to maintaining connection with an anterior homeland, such as charges of dual loyalty. Most importantly, however, they help diasporas to achieve three important aims: visibility, resonance, and legitimacy.[56] Although some elements of such a citizenship are conceivable for both democracies (such as Germany, France, Britain, and the United States) and authoritarian countries (such as South Africa during apartheid and Kuwait), others (such as the right to organize and entitlement to due process) are not usually granted in nondemocratic regimes. Nevertheless, the long-term effect on diaspora identity is unclear. On the one hand, the various postnational entitlements make it easier to maintain diaspora institutions, but on the other, they create an appreciation of the political context of the host country and have a co-optative and assimilative effect tending to dilute diaspora consciousness.

The above indicates that diasporas benefit from the inclusionary institutions provided by democracies. Yet it does not fully answer this recurrent question: Does a politics of inclusion of immigrants and their descendants secure the maintenance of diaspora *identity*, or does it distill and weaken such an identity? The evidence is ambiguous. If inclusion and incorporation persist through several generations, diaspora identity disappears,

---

53. *Deutschland-Nachrichten,* June 4, 1993, and September 30, 1994.

54. Alain Auffray, "Le ministre de l'intérieur relance la polémique qui court depuis 1981m" *Libération,* October 11, 2005.

55. Safran, "Citizenship and Nationality in Democratic Systems," 328–29.

56. Koopmans and Statham, "Migration and Ethnic Relations as a Field of Political Contention," 36–37.

but it may be revived as a result of a number of circumstances—institutional, relational, and contingent—or, more specifically, by changes in regime structure; a domestic policy of discrimination and exclusion; global realities, such as the growing pressure of Islam and dependence on Middle Eastern oil, both of which have generated responses such as increasing hostland accommodation to Muslim diasporas and their continuing relations with their hostlands (as in the case of the use by France and Germany of imams and religious teachers periodically imported from Arab countries and Turkey respectively, which keeps them tied to their homelands or home regions);[57] and "intervening variables": unforeseen events that serve as tipping points at which the process of dediasporization is arrested. Examples include the Holocaust and the influx of Jewish survivors after World War II into Palestine and various host countries, both serving to trigger diasporic solidarity and a reethnification and mobilization of the Jewish diaspora in Western countries; the earthquake in Stepanakert, in Armenia and the consequent burst of solidarity in the Armenian diaspora; the imprisonment of Abdullah Öcalan in Turkey and the active response among diaspora Kurds; Hitler's rise to power and his initial victories, which generated a revival of pan-Germanic sentiment among German Americans; the establishment of Israel and the revival of the diaspora identity of Jews in the Soviet Union; and the attack on the Golden Temple in Amritsar and the growth of Sikh diaspora nationalism. These facts do not constitute proofs about the relationship between regime type and the revival of diaspora orientations. But they do suggest that while this revival may be independent of regime type, its effective *articulation* is more likely to occur in democratic systems, although the precise form may vary from one country to another.

Orientation toward a Homeland

In the present paper, the specific features of what we call a diaspora are distinguished from ethnoreligious minorities in general whose ancestors had come from someplace else, but who no longer have a relationship with or even a consciousness of that ancestral homeland. As I have argued elsewhere,[58] a diaspora refers not merely to the fact of belonging to or descending from a group of people who could trace their origins to another country and who had once been dispersed. In short, the fact of having originated in country A and living in country B does not ipso facto constitute a diaspora. If it did, most people would be classifiable as members of diasporas, simply because migrations have been taking place for hundreds of years.[59] To cite just two examples: The descendants of the Germans who had migrated to Norway as part of the Hanseatic colony in Bergen (Bryg-

---

57. Note that imams and religious teachers sent to serve the Turkish community in Germany are paid by the Turkish government.

58. William Safran, "Deconstructing and Comparing Diasporas," in *Diaspora, Identity, and Religion*, ed. Waltraud Kokot, Khachig Tölölyan, and Carolin Alfonso. (London: Routledge, 2004), 14–15.

59. William Safran, "Diasporas in Modern Societies: Myths of Homeland and Return," *Diaspora* 1, no. 1 (1991): 83–99; idem, "Deconstructing and Comparing Diasporas."

gen) several hundred years ago were a cohesive German-speaking community with clear commercial and cultural connections to their homeland, but no trace is left of this, and they can no longer be distinguished from other Norwegians. Likewise, the Afrikaans-speaking descendants of Huguenots and Dutch Calvinists who live in South Africa today have no memories of, relations with, orientations toward, or even interest in the homeland of their ancestors, and except for their surnames and physical features, "they did not continue to live as a separate, clearly identifiable subcommunity. Already early in the eighteenth century they were assimilated by the rest of the population at the Cape as a result of both political measures and their minority numbers."[60] (They supported Calvinism, but so did their Dutch compatriots.) If the Huguenots are considered a diaspora, then we must regard the entire white population—and perhaps a good part of the African population—of South Africa as a diaspora. It follows that, contrary to the opinion of Paul Gilroy,[61] some sort of transpolitical relationship, preferably toward an anterior homeland, is an element of diaspora identity. This seems to be implied in Nina Glick-Schiller's approach to "transnationalism."[62] Clearly, such a relationship is easier in countries such as Britain, Canada, and the United States, where the existence of ethnocultural subcommunities is more readily accepted than in France, where "communautarisme" is considered un-French, if not subversive. That does not mean that communitarianism exists in the Anglo-Saxon countries in fully institutionalized political form, as the French frequently and falsely insist, for in none of these countries do diasporas (or any other ethnic minorities) have formal collective representation in decision-making institutions. It does mean, however, that these countries openly acknowledge the reality and legitimacy of complex multiple identities, including those of members of diasporas who are politically loyal to their host countries, but maintain a complementary cultural-affective relationship with their anterior homelands.

Conclusion

Ceteris paribus, diasporas have different destinies in prenationalist and predemocratic states, in democratic nation-building states, in authoritarian nation-building states, and in postnational democracies. All states, whether authoritarian or democratic, that seek to modernize their economies need both capital and technological expertise, and they frequently appeal to outsiders to provide both. These outsiders are members of diasporas, and, as such, they may not be fully a part of the host country in the view of the host society, their own view, or both. Nevertheless, their sense of belonging is variable. The

---

60. H. C. Viljoen, "The Contribution of the Huguenots in South Africa." *Huguenot Society of South Africa*, available on-line at http://www.geocities.com.sa_stamouers/huguenots.htm (last accessed December 10, 2007).

61. Paul Gilroy, "It Ain't Where You're From, It's Where You're At: The Dialectics of Diasporic Identification," *Third Text* 13 (Winter 1991): 3–16; James Clifford, *Routes: Travel and Translation in the Late Twentieth Century* (Cambridge, MA: Cambridge University Press, 1997), 267–69.

62. Glick-Schiller et al., *Towards a Transnational Perspective on Migration*.

extent and duration of diaspora identity are heavily influenced by the concrete political context of host countries as manifested in institutions and public policies. Diasporas that benefit from a favorable environment are easily motivated to adapt to the customs and values of the host society so that they gradually lose their collective consciousness of being outsiders. Such adaptation is reflected in the replacement of the homeland language by that of the host country and the adoption of the religion of the majority, or at least the adaptation to selected elements of it. One common adaptation is the change of the family name, but its retention is by no means an indicator of diasporic self-identification. Dwight Eisenhower was never considered a member of the German diaspora in the United States, nor Caspar Weinberger and John Kerry of the Jewish diaspora, and the Poniatowskis and Sanguinettis have not been members, respectively, of the Polish and Italian diasporas in France. Conversely, however, a change of name does not necessarily constitute proof of the abandonment of diaspora identity.

Anecdotal evidence suggests that in the democratic societies of Western Europe and North America, a significant number of descendants of ethnic minorities (other than those based on race) have abandoned their diasporic identities. I distributed a questionnaire to faculty and staff members with "ethnic" names to ask the following questions: Do you identify primarily as an American, or as a member of an ethnic group? If the latter, which group, specifically? Were you born in the United States? Where were your parents born? Do you consider yourself as being in a diaspora? The sample—117—was too small to be conclusive. Nevertheless, it was clear that a majority (82 percent) of the 102 American-born respondents identified primarily as Americans—as did 37 (85 percent) of the 42 who said that one or both parents were born outside the United States. Next came those who identified in ethnic or "hyphenated" terms—12 percent. But only 3 percent considered themselves as living in a diaspora.

The arguments in this paper illustrate the importance of the institutional context. Yet many of the points presented here, although based on factual evidence, are subject to debate. They can be substantiated or falsified by research that traces the fate of diasporas across time and space. They need to be revisited, supplemented, and revised by means of a systematic examination of the indicators of the rise and decline of ethnoreligious identity and homeland connections, among them the following: visits to the homeland, economic and diplomatic support, marriage patterns, religious syncretism and conversions, the survival of the ancestral language, the retention of homeland-related ethnosymbols, institution building and dismantling, and schooling in homeland-related history, culture, and values that contribute to substantive elements of a homeland connection beyond merely the "diasporic imagination" and that are crucial in the intergenerational transmission of diaspora identity.

Measuring these indicators requires both qualitative and quantitative approaches, the one calling for both in-depth study of a significant number of diasporas as well as homeland and the other the construction of data sets. The latter would imply a mixed "field" approach, for example, attitude surveys (based on questionnaires) and interviews with leaders of ethnoreligious minority communities, including diaspora elites and "entrepreneurs," and the use of studies of single cases as models or building stones for a systematic comparative study.

Bibliography

Ackerman, Holly. "A Comparison of Features in Two Diaspora Communities: Cubans in Miami and Venezuela." Paper presented at meeting of the International Studies Association, Washington, DC, February 16–20, 1999.

Anand, Dibyesh. "A Contemporary Story of Diaspora: The Tibetan Version." *Diaspora* 12, no. 2 (2003.): 211–29.

Armstrong, John A. "Mobilized and Proletarian Diasporas." *American Political Science Review* 70, no. 2 (1976): 393–403.

Auffray, Alain. "Le ministre de l'intérieur relance la polémique qui court depuis 1981." *Libération*, October 11, 2005.

Aviv, Caryn, and David Shneer. *New Jews: The End of the Jewish Diaspora*. New York: New York University Press, 2005.

Bernard, Philippe. "L'argent renvoyé au pays: Une manne." *Le Monde*, April 11, 2005.

Birnbaum, Pierre. *Les fous de la République: Les Juifs d'État de Gambetta à Vichy*. Paris: Fayard, 1992.

Clifford, James. *Routes: Travel and Translation in the Late Twentieth Century*. Cambridge, MA: Cambridge University Press, 1997.

Cohen, Robin. *Global Diasporas: An Introduction*. Seattle: University of Washington Press, 1997.

Deutschland-Nachrichten, June 4, 1933 and September 30, 1994.

Elon, Amos. *The Pity of it All: A History of Jews in Germany, 1743–1933*. New York: Metropolitan Books, 2002.

Fetzer, Joel S., and J. Christopher Soper. *Muslims and the State in Britain, France, and Germany*. Cambridge: Cambridge University Press, 2005.

Furnivall, John S. *Colonial Policy and Practice: A Comparative Study of Burma and India*. Cambridge: Cambridge University Press, 1956.

———. *Netherlands India: A Study of Plural Economy*. Cambridge: Cambridge University Press, 1944.

Gilroy, Paul. "It Ain't Where You're From, It's Where You're At: The Dialectics of Diasporic Identification." *Third Text* 13 (Winter 1991): 3–16.

Glazer, Nathan, and Daniel P. Moynihan. *Beyond the Melting Pot*. 2nd ed. Cambridge MA: MIT Press, 1970.

Glick-Schiller, Nina, Linda Basch, and Cristina Szanton-Blanc, eds. *Towards a Transnational Perspective on Migration: Race, Class, Ethnicity, and Nationalism Reconsidered.* New York: New York Academy of Sciences, 1992.

Goldsmith, Ben. "Out-of-Country Voting in Post-Conflict Elections." *Democracy at Large* 1, no. 4 (2005): 30–33.

Grosjean, Blandine. "Les Noirs de France solidaires montent un Cran." *Libération*, November 28, 2005.

Gurr, Ted Robert. *Minorities at Risk.* Washington, DC: United States Institute of Peace, 1993.

Ha, Marie-Paule. "Vietnamese Diaspora in France." *Contemporary French Civilization* 27, no. 3 (2003): 253–76.

Herberg, Will. *Protestant, Catholic, Jew: An Essay in American Religious Sociology.* Garden City, NY: Doubleday, 1955.

Hirschman, Albert O. *Exit, Voice, and Loyalty: Responses to Decline in Firms, Organizations, and States.* 1970; Cambridge, MA.: Harvard University Press, 1981.

Hockenos, Paul. *Homeland Calling: Exile Patriotism and the Balkan Wars.* Ithaca, NY: Cornell University Press, 2003.

Jackson, Julian. "Historians and the Nation in Contemporary France." In *Writing National Histories.* Edited by Stefan Berger, Mark Donovan, and Kevin Passmore. London: Routledge, 1999.

Joutard, Philippe. "La diaspora des Huguenots." *Diasporas* 1, 2nd semestre (2002): 115–21.

Jubulis, Mark A. *Nationalism and Democratic Transition: The Politics of Citizenship and Language in Post-Soviet Latvia.* Lanham, MA: University Press of America, 2001.

Khalidi, Laleh, "Mixing Memory and Desire," May 13, 1998. Available on-line at http:// www.iranian.com/Features/May98/Iranams/index.html.

Koopmans, Ruud, and Paul Statham. "Migration and Ethnic Relations as a Field of Political Contention: An Opportunity Structure Approach." In *Challenging Immigration and Ethnic Relations Politics.* Edited by Ruud Koopmans and Paul Statham. Oxford: Oxford University Press, 2000.

——, Marco Giugni, and Florence Passy. *Contested Citizenship: Immigration and Cultural Diversity in Europe.* Minneapolis: University of Minnesota Press, 2005.

Laitin, David. *Identity in Formation: The Russian-Speaking Populations in the Near Abroad.* Ithaca, NY: Cornell University Press, 1998.

"Lutter contre les discriminations." *Regards sur l'Actualité* no. 256 (December 1999): 35–47.

Mishra, Pankaj. "The Restless Children of the Dalai Lama." *New York Times Magazine*, December 18, 2005, 58–63.

Mosse, Werner E., and Arnold Paucker, eds. *Juden im Wilhelminischen Deutschland, 1890–1914.* Tübingen: Mohr, 1998.

Polgreen, Lydia. "Ghana's Uneasy Embrace of Slavery's Diaspora." *New York Times,* December 27, 2005.

Safran, William. "Citizenship and Nationality in Democratic Systems: Approaches to Defining and Acquiring Membership in the Political Community." *International Political Science Review* 18, no. 3 (1997): 313–35.

——. "Deconstructing and Comparing Diasporas." In *Diaspora, Identity, and Religion.* Edited by Waltraud Kokot, Khachig Tölölyan, and Carolin Alfonso. London: Routledge, 2004.

——. "Diasporas in Modern Societies: Myths of Homeland and Return." *Diaspora* 1, no. 1 (1991): 83–99.

——. "The French State and Ethnic Minority Cultures: Policy Dimensions and Problems." In *Ethno-Territorial Politics, Policy, and the Western World.* Edited by Joseph R. Rudolph and Robert J. Thompson. Boulder, CO: Lynne Rienner, 1989.

———. "The Tenuous Link between Hostlands and Homeland: The Progressive De-Zionization of Western Diasporas." In *Les diasporas: 2000 ans d'histoire.* Edited by Lisa Anteby-Yemini, William Berthomière, and Gabriel Sheffer. Rennes: Presses Universitaires de Rennes, 2005.

Semo, Marc. "Le royaume-uni en crise existentielle." *Libération,* August 13, 2005.

Sheffer, Gabriel. "Defining Ethno-National Diasporas." *Migration* 33/34/35 (2002): 69–90.

——. *Diaspora Politics: At Home Abroad.* Cambridge, MA: Cambridge University Press, 2003.

Singhvi, L. M. *Report of the High Level Committee on the Indian Diaspora, Ministry of External Affairs,* dated August 18, 2000. Available on-line at http://indiandiaspora.nic.in/contents.htm.

Stewart, Michael. *The Time of the Gypsies.* Boulder, CO: Westview Press, 1997.

Tölölyan, Khachig. "Rethinking Diaspora(s): Stateless Power in the Transnational Moment." *Diasporas* 5, no. 1 (1996): 3–36.

Viljoen, H. C. "The Contribution of the Huguenots in South Africa." *Huguenot Society of South Africa.* Available on-line at http://www.geocities.com/sa_stamouers/huguenots.htm.

Wahlbeck, Östen. *Kurdish Diasporas; A Comparative Study of Kurdish Refugee Communities.* Houndmills, Basignstoke, Hampshire, UK: Macmillan, 1999.

Wasserstein, Bernard. *Vanishing Diaspora: The Jews in Europe Since 1945.* London: Penguin, 1997.

Wayland, Sarah. "Diaspora Engagement in Homeland Conflict: A Case Study of Sri Lankan Tamils in Toronto." Paper delivered at Immigration Seminar, Center for European Studies, Harvard University, September 2, 1998.

Winland, Daphne. "'We Are Now an Actual Nation': The Impact of National Independence on the Croatian Diaspora in Canada." *Diaspora* 4, no. 1 (1995): 3–29.

The Diaspora Phenomenon in the Twenty-First Century: Ideational, Organizational, and Behavioral Challenges

By Gabriel Sheffer

As is quite widely known and recognized, at the beginning of the twenty-first century, the general phenomenon of the diaspora is far from disappearing or losing its considerable significance. Quite the contrary. Again, as is well known, the numbers of diasporas and diasporans are growing. Though governments, especially the governments of richer and more developed states, attempt to restrict immigration into their countries so that increases in the numbers of diasporas and diasporans may be restricted or diminished, the growth of diasporas cannot be stopped. By the same token, as a result of current, somewhat more favorable cultural, social, political, and economic processes occurring in various states, it seems that the influences and effects of diasporas and diasporans on their homelands, hostlands, and the international system are increasing. Hence, despite some negative reactions, mainly generated by hostland governments and various social groups in these countries, the capabilities and influences of disaporas and diasporans will only continue to increase.

This does not mean, however, that diasporans are totally free to develop their entities and behave strictly according to their own or their homelands' inclinations and interests. Like other nondiasporic minorities, they are under a range of pressures that affect diasporas, diasporans, homelands, hostlands, and other actors. As a result, there is an on-going need to reevaluate the present and future situation of the entire phenomenon. Doing so is the main goal of what follows.

Some politicians and academics have realized that this phenomenon is highly intricate, that it is becoming even more complicated, and that consequently the challenges facing the various existing and emerging diasporas are mounting, too.[1] Yet the general tendency revealed in the more theoretical and general studies of the phenomenon is to treat all migrants and diasporas as one uniform phenomenon and lump all of them together, thus making it difficult to asses the challenges facing these entities. This is particularly evident in the academic literature that has been written according to the transnational approach.[2]

More specifically, most of these academic observers have not paid sufficient attention to the fact that not all "others" in hostlands actually constitute diasporas and that there are differences in various aspects of migrants' and diasporans' existence, needs, interests, and behavior. It is definitely the case that such clear distinctions are essential for a better understanding of the various challenges confronting diasporas at the beginning of the twenty-first century.

In fact, all such "others" in hostlands fall into six categories: tourists, refugees and asylum seekers, legal and illegal nonorganized newly arrived migrants, irredentist groups, and members of two types of diasporas that will be more fully categorized and analyzed below. Unlike most members of those other groups, who are temporary residents in hostlands, the latter two types of entities are composed of persons who permanently dwell in host countries.

As noted, the first group is that of tourists. After accomplishing the preplanned purposes of their trips to other countries, most tourists return to their countries of origin or move to other receiving countries. Only some of the persons belonging to this category stay for longer periods or try to settle permanently in host countries with the hope of becoming citizens there. Though tourists who stay for longer periods may establish contacts with local diasporans and diasporic entities, if these exist there. Like other migrants, they actually join such entities only after becoming acquainted with the situation in the receiving states, overcoming migration traumas, making autonomous decisions about

---

1. Robin Cohen, *Global Diasporas: An Introduction* (Seattle: University of Washington Press, 1997); Jana Evans Braziel and Anita Mannur, eds., *Theorizing Diaspora: A Reader* (Oxford: Blackwell, 2003); Gabriel Sheffer, *Diaspora Politics: At Home Abroad* (Cambridge: Cambridge University Press, 2006).

2. On the concept of transnationalism in general and on its applications to transnational diasporas in particular see, for example, Anthony Smith, *The Ethnic Origins of Nations* (Oxford: Basil Blackwell, 1986); Nina Glick-Schiller, Linda Basch, and Christina Blanc-Szanton, "From Immigrant to Transmigrant: Theorizing Transnational Migration," *Anthropological Quarterly* 68 (1995): 48–63, and Nina Glick-Schiller, Linda Basch, and Christina Blanc-Szanton, "Towards a Transnational Perspective on Migration," *Annals of the New York Academy of Science* 645 (1992): 1–24; James Clifford, "Diasporas," *Cultural Anthropology* 9, no. 3 (1994): 302–38; John Lie, "From International Migration to Transnational Diaspora," *Contemporary Sociology* 24, no. 4 (1995): 303–6; Floya Anthias, "Evaluating 'Diaspora': Beyond Ethnicity," *Sociology* 32, no. 3 (1998): 557–80; Steven Vertovec and Robin Cohen, eds., *Migrations, Diasporas, and Transnationalism*, The International Library of Studies on Migration (Cheltenham, UK: Edward Elgar, 1999); Stanley J. Tambiah, "Transitional Movements, Diaspora, and Multiple Modernities," *Daedalus* 129, no. 1 (2000): 163–94; Ewa Morwaska, "Immigrants, Transnationalism, and Ethnicization: A Comparison of This Great Wave and the Last," in *E Pluribus Unum? Contemporary and Historical Perspectives on Immigrant Political Incorporation*, ed. Gary Gerstle and John Mollenkopf (New York: Russell Sage Foundation, 2001); Roger Waldinger and David Fitzgerald, "Transnationalism in Question," *American Journal of Sociology* 109, no. 5 (2004): 1177–95; Steven Vertovec, *Trends and Impacts of Migrant Transnationalism*, COMPAS Working Paper WP-04-03. Oxford: Centre on Migration, Policy and Society of the University of Oxford, 2004; and Rogers Brubaker, "The 'Diaspora' Diaspora," *Ethnic and Racial Studies* 28, no. 1 (2005): 1–19.

their futures, and becoming permanent citizens in these countries. Tourists who illegally stay in host countries for longer periods may maintain continuous contacts with their brethren's diasporic entities. Nevertheless, since they may be deported by the hostland authorities or may autonomously change their minds and return to their countries of origin, it is difficult to regard them as fully fledged diasporans.

The second group is that of refugees and asylum seekers. According to the United Nations High Commissioner for Refugees (UNHCR), more than twenty million people fall into these categories. Whereas about twelve million qualify as refugees, the remaining eight to nine million are asylum seekers and returnees to their homelands that have not been fully reintegrated into their original societies. Eventually, some of the asylum seekers may acquire citizenship in their hostlands and either join or form diasporas, but only a few refugees succeed in obtaining citizenship in their hostlands, and thus they must return to their homelands. Also, a majority of these persons are internally displaced in their homelands, a factor that makes it inappropriate to regard them as diasporans. Again according to the UNHCR, the main countries hosting refugees fleeing from hardships and difficulties in their homelands are Syria, Burundi, Sudan, Somalia, Angola, Sierra Leone, Eritrea, Congo, Liberia, Rwanda, Lebanon, and Jordan. All these are countries that have experienced internal turmoil, insurgency, or terrorism. The actual political, social, economic, and cultural situation in most of these countries is very far from being favorable for the establishment of active diasporic entities.[3]

The third category of others is that of legal and illegal nonorganized newly arrived migrants. The persons in this category are mostly guest workers or students. Though most, but not all host countries can and do record the numbers and identities of newly arrived legal migrants, which globally number tens of millions, nevertheless, no reliable figures exist about illegal migrants. Problematic cultural, social, political, and economic conditions in homelands and favorable conditions in hostlands lead most of these migrants to try to head to mostly developed and democratic countries, including most of Western European states, the United States, Canada, Australia, and Japan. Following the terrorist attacks on September 11, 2001 in the United States, a number of host countries have attempted to limit and control the flow of such migrants to prevent both terrorism and worsened economic conditions. Nevertheless, most borders, especially in the European Union and the United States, are porous, and such traffic hardly can be fully controlled. In this respect, democratic and democratizing states are of course disadvantaged, because they encounter immense ideological, legal, and practical inhibitions when handling immigration of various kinds. As a result, many terrorist, criminal, and other illegal activities have been carried out by members of this category of people in more developed democratic states. As the cases of Mexican and Latino legal and illegal migrants to the United States and Canada and Africans to France have been showing

---

3. United Nations High Commissionner for Refugees (UNHCR), Fifty-Sixth General Assembly, Third Committee, November 19, 2001.

quite clearly, among these persons, the demand for staying for longer periods or permanently in their new hostlands is substantial.[4] Indeed, many of these migrants succeed in
doing so. Thus, more than the others in the previously mentioned migrants' categories,
this category contributes many persons to various types of diasporas.

While these migrants in hostlands are unlikely to constitute diasporas in and of
themselves, two other groups of "others" clearly do so. The fourth category of others
in their host states is that of organized transstate ethnonational diasporas.[5] These are
dispersed persons in various host states. The members of these entities are of the same
ethnic and national origins, they are permanently residing in their host countries, and
while they are not assimilated, they are integrated into their host societies to different
degrees. These unassimilated persons form the cores and the peripheries of these entities. Usually, core members are organizing or organized. Either directly or through these
diasporic organizations, they maintain contacts with their homelands. According to current estimates, there are more than 300 million such people worldwide.[6]

Some of these organized diasporas are veteran "historical" established dispersals—
the Jewish, Armenian, Greek, Indian, and Chinese are obvious examples of the entities
in this subcategory. Some should be regarded as "modern" diasporas, which means that
they are relatively new and were established mainly in the nineteenth and early twentieth centuries—for instance, the Italians, the Irish, and the Polish fit into this subcategory.
And finally, some are incipient diasporas—that is, these are entities in the early stages of
formation and organization. In this subcategory are, for example, the Moroccans, the
Ghanaians, the Chechens, and the twenty-five million Russians in the former Soviet
empire.[7]

The final category should be labeled cultural and religious transnational dispersals.[8]
Similarly to the members of the transstate diasporas category, these are dispersed persons permanently residing out of their homelands. They share the same cultures, often
including the same languages, religions, beliefs, and ideologies. Yet, as will be noted
below, in fact, each of these groups is composed of persons from different ethnic and
national backgrounds. Examples of these dispersals are the "Muslim," "African," and

---

4. John García, *Latino Politics in America: Community, Culture, and Interests* (Lanham, MD: Rowman and Littlefield, 2003); Khalid Koser, ed., *New African Diasporas* (London: Routledge, 2003).

5. Gabriel Sheffer, "Defining Ethno-National Diasporas." *Migration* 33/34/35 (2002): 69–92, and Sheffer, *Diaspora Politics*.

6. Sheffer, *Diaspora Politics*, ch. 4.

7. Paul Kolstoe, *Russians in the Former Soviet Republics* (London: Hurst, 1995) Charles King and Neil Melvin, *Nations Abroad: Diaspora Politics and International Relations in the Former Soviet Union* (Boulder, CO: Westview Press, 1998); Rogers Brubaker, *Accidental Diasporas and External "Homelands" in Central and Eastern Europe: Past and Present*, Political Science Series no. 71 (Vienna: Institute for Advanced Studies, 2000); Michael Mandelbaum, *The New European Diasporas: National Minori-ties and Conflict in Eastern Europe* (New York: Council on Foreign Relations Press, 2000); Rainer Münz and Rainer Ohlinger, eds., *Diasporas and Ethnic Migrants: Germany, Israel, and Post-Soviet Successor States* (Portland, OR: Frank Cass, 2003).

8. Chantal Saint-Blancat, "Islam in Diaspora: Between Reterritorialization and Extraterritoriality," *International Journal of Urban and Regional Research* 26, no. 1 (2002): 138–51.

"Latino" persons scattered around the world. As a result of terrorist activities launched by al-Qaeda and other dispersed Sunni and Shiite Muslim transnational groups and organizations, observers have referred to these groups as homogeneous transnational diasporas. In reality, though, the latest waves of terrorism and other violent actions have been carried out not by highly organized and homogeneous "Muslim," "Arab," or "North African" diasporas, but separately and autonomously by migrants belonging to the various groups mentioned earlier and members of different older organized and incipient transstate ethnonational diasporas whose members' only common characteristic is that their religion is Islam. Indeed, much closer attention should be paid to the motivations and purposes of the actual members various Muslim, Latino, and African groups, whose origins are in different nation-states. Various analysts doubt whether indeed there are such transnational diasporas.[9]

When focusing on the abovementioned diasporas, it should be realized that the distinctions between the historical, modern, and incipient diasporas,[10] the distinction between state-linked and stateless diasporas, and the existence or nonexistence of transstate and transnational diasporas are overlapping characterizations. However, these characterizations should be applied differently in regard to each diaspora. Thus, for example, while the Jewish diaspora should be typified as a "historical state-linked transstate diaspora," the dispersed Palestinians should be typified as a "modern stateless transstate diaspora," and as mentioned before, according to some politicians, journalists, and academics, the worldwide dispersed Muslims should be viewed as forming a "historical transnational diaspora."

Similarly, it should be strongly emphasized that none of the diasporas are homogeneous entities. In this respect and as far as the diasporans themselves are concerned, a critical distinction should be made between core and peripheral members of such entities. Core members are all those who emotionally and cognitively cling to the general inherent identity characterizing their entire ethnonational group, including, of course, the segments living in their actual or imagined ethnonational homeland, who regard themselves and are regarded as members of such entities, and who, whenever it is needed, publicly identify with the entire entity in their hostlands, homelands, and various dispersals. Peripheral members are those who have been fully or partly integrated, but not assimilated, into their hostland societies, but still maintain their "original" identity and some contacts with the organized part of their diaspora. This significant distinction should also be carefully considered when analyzing the entire diasporic phenomenon and the challenges facing the phenomenon at large and specific entities in particular.

---

9. On the critics of the attribution of such a concept to these groups see, for example, Emanuel Sivan, *Clash Inside Islam* [in Hebrew] (Tel Aviv: Am Oved, 2005).

10. Cohen, *Global Diasporas*; Robert Smith, "Diasporic Memberships in Historical Perspective: Comparative Insights from the Mexican, Italian, and Polish Cases," *International Migration Review* 37, no. 3 (2003): 724–59; Sheffer, *Diaspora Politics*.

The Different Types of Diasporas

When discussing the main issues and challenges facing diasporas at the beginning of the twenty-first century, as should be clear by now, one should avoid generalizations and make very careful and clear distinctions between the various types of diasporas and diasporans. The most significant distinction that needs to be elaborated is between "transnational" and "transstate" diasporas.[11]

Let's begin by stating that there are of course certain similarities between these two categories of diasporas. Nevertheless, some basic characteristics, such as the identity, connections, organization, and behavior and the survival and demise of the diasporic identity of the members of each of these two types are different. Hence, the challenges that each of the two diasporic types confront are also different.

The following are only relatively brief distinctive characterizations of these two categories. Essentially, the first category—the transnational one—consists of large groups, some of which, but certainly not all members of these entities, regard themselves as forming coherent diasporas. Yet all persons who regard themselves or are regarded by others as forming such a diaspora are not of the same ethnonational origin. Rather, they have in common some other characteristics that in their own perception and in the eyes of outsiders—such as the general publics in their hostlands and worldwide, politicians, and analysts—determine their belonging to such entities, entities that usually are ill defined. Thus, they may have in common religious beliefs and affiliation to a church or sect, or the same regional geographical background, or the same language, or even shared ideological beliefs. Hence, respectively, groups such as the "Muslims," "Buddhists," and "Catholics"; the "Africans," "Latinos," and "Arabs"; the "Francophone" diaspora and the "Chinese-speaking" diaspora; probably also the "Green" and, in the past, the "Communist" diasporas should be included in this category. It should be noted here that these groups are included in this category mainly on the basis of the subjective views of their members and some outside observers.

The second category, that of the transstate diasporas, includes, for example, the Irish, Armenian, Greek, and Jewish diasporas.[12] The most significant feature that determines the similarity between these transstate entities is that their core members, as well as some peripheral members of each diaspora, are of the same ethnonational origin. These members are persons that very clearly belong, according to their ethnonational background and own awareness and self-definition, as well as according to the perception of relevant external observers, to a certain diasporic entity, and their identification with it is either not questionable or not objectionable. It should be emphasized that this applies not only to first-generation diaspora members, but also to later generations of historical, modern, and incipient diasporas, whether these are state-linked or stateless.

---

11. William Miles and Gabriel Sheffer, "Francophone and Zionism: A Comparative Study of Transnationalism and Transstatism," *Diaspora* 7, no. 2 (1998): 119–48.

12. For a profile of these diasporas, see Sheffer, *Diaspora Politics*, chapter 2.

To a great extent, as a result of the growing realization that perceptually and, probably also actually, these two types of diasporas exist and therefore that distinctions should be made between them, there have emerged also two main theoretical/explanatory approaches to the entire diasporic phenomenon. Actually, the adherents to the transnational approach, which has been the more popular approach, regard and portray all present-day dispersed persons permanently residing out of their countries of origin as transnational entities.[13] They strongly argue that, like other existing nations and ethnic groups, such diasporas are, to use Benedict Anderson's famous term, "imagined communities."[14] They also argue that diasporism is essentially a modern phenomenon. This approach is very influenced by postmodern epistemological trends, as well as by various actual aspects of globalization, such as ease of migration, modern communication, individualization, and spreading hybrid cultures.

The main specific arguments of the transnational approach are well known, and therefore the following is not an exhaustive list of their definitions and characterizations. Essentially, the adherents to this approach argue that membership in these entities is based on the utterly subjective feelings and decisions of individuals, who, especially when they do not have noticeable physical markers, can relatively easily change their affiliations and loyalties, up to the extreme stage of full assimilation into their hostland societies; that the main glue tying together these persons, and hence also their entities, is cultural; that these entities are constantly changing; that their boundaries are very far from being clearly drawn, fixed, and stable; that most of these entities and their members who permanently reside in certain hostlands experience continuous processes of cultural hybridization that cause substantive heterogeneity in the entity at large and also in smaller subgroups residing in the same country, region, or city; that consequently they tend either to assimilate or to integrate fully into their host societies; that their memories of their historical and more recent ancestors or of their "original homelands" are not very significant for their existence; and that the possibility of their return to their homelands is almost inconceivable.

Adherents to this transnationalist approach also argue that the current processes of globalization constantly influence and cause major changes in the identity and identification of such persons, which are either "positive" or "negative" as perceived from the specific viewpoints of the diasporas' various leaders. Thus, on the one hand, globalization processes diminish the numbers of these diasporas' members and make their cultural

---

13. See for, example, Khachig Tölölyan, "The Nation-State and Its Others: In Lieu of a Preface," *Diaspora* 1, no. 1 (1991): 3–7, and idem, "Rethinking Diaspora(s): Stateless Power in the Transnational Moment," *Diaspora* 5, no. 1 (1996): 3–36; William Safran, "Diasporas in Modern Societies: Myths of Homeland and Return." *Diaspora* 1, no. 1 (1991): 83–99; Steven Vertovec, "Three Meanings of Diasporas," *Diaspora* 6, no. 3 (1997): 277–97; Kim Butler, "Defining Diaspora, Refining a Discourse," *Diaspora* 10, no. 2 (2001): 189–219; Brubaker, "The 'Diaspora' Diaspora"; and Dominique Schnapper, "De l'état-nation au mond transnational: Du sense et de l'útilite du concept de diaspora," in *Les diasporas: 2000 ans d'histoire*, ed. Lisa Anteby-Yemini, William Berthomière, and Gabriel Sheffer (Rennes: Press Universitaires de Rennes, 2005).

14. Benedict Anderson, *Imagined Communities: Reflections on the Origins and Spread of Nationalism* (London: Verso, 1991), and Benedict Anderson, "Exodus," *Critical Inquiry* 20, no. 2 (1994): 314–27.

and social boundaries even less defined and more porous, but on the other hand, due to current means of communication, such processes increase the number of such diasporas' members and enhance their solidarity and connections to their "communities," or rather entities. As mentioned above, one of the main diasporic entities that is supposed to fit this characterization is the "Muslim diaspora." But there are widespread doubts about the inclusion in this category of, for example, the "Arab" and "Latino" diasporas.[15]

Generally, it seems in fact that there is a certain decline in the acceptance and application of the transnational approach to the diasporic phenomenon.[16] The other approach—the transstate approach—argues that a distinction should be made between the two types of diasporas and that as far as their age, collective identity, organization, and behavior are concerned, diasporas constitute a perennial phenomenon.[17] This means that, although over the centuries certain historical diasporas that still exist today, such as the Chinese, Indian, Jewish, and Armenian, have indeed changed quite considerably, these are ancient entities that have overcome many actual as well as more abstract acute threats to their identities and existence. In fact, they have survived planned and actual attempts to annihilate them totally or to assimilate them. It also means that their members are capable of existing as distinct groups in today's globalized, postmodern world in which there have emerged some expectations that ethnic minorities and diasporas will totally disappear, either through assimilation or by a return to their homelands. This portrayal applies to modern and incipient stateless and state-linked diasporas, such as Basque, Palestinian, Polish, and even to some reawakening Scandinavian diasporas in the United States.

Furthermore, according to this second approach, the cores of such diasporas are more united, and they demonstrate greater cohesion and solidarity than the transnational diasporas. This is the case because of a number of factors. The identity of their members is more firmly established because it is a complex and changing integrative combination of primordial, psychological, and instrumental factors.[18] Also, there is no tremendous gap between their identity and identification. These days, such diasporans are not so shy or reluctant to identify themselves publicly as belonging to these entities, and it is becoming even fashionable to do so and to behave like a diasporan. In addition, in comparison with the purported transnational diasporas, transstate diasporas are better organized, their connections to their real or perceived original homelands are constant and intensive, and their involvement in their homelands' cultural, social, political, and economic affairs and in the affairs of various hostlands where their brethren reside is significant. On various occasions, they are involved in conflicts in or pertaining to their homelands and to other states that host their brethren, and some members of such diasporas consider a return

---

15. Sivan, *Clash Inside Islam.*

16. See, for example, Braziel and Mannur, eds., *Theorizing Diaspora.*

17. Smith, *The Ethnic Origins of Nations.*

18. John Kelass, *The Politics of Nationalism and Ethnicity* (New York: St. Martin's Press, 1991); Sheffer, *Diaspora Politics.*

or actually return to their homelands. This is the case, for example, with the Irish, Jews, Turks, and even Japanese.[19]

Based on these arguments, it seems that the current processes of globalization and liberalization would cause neither total assimilation, full integration, and hybridization nor an eventual total disappearance of the cores of these entities. By the same token, though these diasporas' geographical and demographical boundaries are constantly changing and though these boundaries are porous, they are still quite clearly drawn and can be maintained and sustained. In fact, there are signs that the current trends of globalization, liberalization, and multiculturalism, and consequently their effects, strengthen many diasporas. These trends provide them with additional cultural, ideational, economic, and social resources and means that ensure their sustained existence.

After the downfall of the Soviet Union and its empire and because of the latest wave of the establishment or reemergence of sovereign states, the number of stateless diasporas has declined—thus, for example, the Armenians, Poles, and Croats have gained their full independence and sovereignty, and consequently their diasporas' status has changed. All these and others are modern diasporas that have reformulated their collective goals and strategies, which are now geared to support their brethren in their real or imagined homelands states. Hence, now, most of the existing diasporas are state-linked, rather than stateless. However, there are still ethnonational diasporic entities fighting for their independence in their real or imagined homelands. When considering this factor, the cases of the Palestinian, Tamil, Basque, and Kosovar diasporas and segments of the Turkish-Kurdish diaspora immediately come to mind. Individual members and various groups within the remaining stateless diasporas are deeply involved in the struggles of their brethren in their homelands to gain their independence and extend to them various types of support.

Yet all diasporic entities, whose number and size, as has been mentioned before, are increasing, and who on the whole are not facing tremendous pressures from host countries' governments to assimilate, or to integrate fully, or to refrain from organizing and acting either as autonomous or separatist collectives nevertheless face major challenges. These will be conceptualized and presented below.

The Challenges Facing Diasporas

The following are not all, but only the most critical cultural-ideational, organizational, and behavioral challenges facing the two types of diaspora, the transnational and transstate. And again, as can be seen below, while the challenges facing the two types of diaspora are not totally diametrically opposite, they are substantially different.

These critical challenges are, first, the need of diasporas' core and peripheral members to clarify their individual and collective identity and identification. Probably these

---

19. Sheffer, *Diaspora Politics*.

issues—identity and identification—constitute the hardest challenge facing all incipient transnational as well as state-linked and stateless transstate diasporas. However, in view of various current cultural, social, political, and economic environmental temptations, which will be specified below, members of historical and modern transstate state-linked and transstate stateless diasporas also must work hard at maintaining the nonessentialist primordial elements of their identity.

The second major challenge, which is closely interlinked to the first, is connected to the need to define the actual and virtual boundaries of these entities, which now are very blurred and porous.

The third significant issue facing these entities concerns the need to define and recognize the actual or virtual location of each of the diasporas' centers. Closely interconnected is the need to clarify the relations between the diasporas' actual or perceived centers and their dispersed members and organizations.

The fourth major dilemma that generates significant challenges is that of loyalty to either the imagined center or actual homeland or to the host countries.

The fifth challenge is that of the development and use of strategic and tactical policies and activities, including the use of violence and terrorism and connections to criminal groups, tactics and policies that are intended to ensure the accomplishment of the maximal interests of the various categories and subcategories of diasporas and diasporans.

The First Challenge: Identity and Identification

The first basic and most significant challenge facing *all* diasporas as collectivities and *all* their members as individuals concerns identity and identification. It would seem that in an article in this volume, there is no major need to reemphasize that, as is the situation with all national majorities and minorities, identity and identification are the most critical factors determining and ensuring the sustainable existence of all diasporic entities. Although these two interconnected factors are essential in any discussion of the future of such entities, with some exceptions,[20] their academic discussion has been relegated to a secondary place in recent studies and publications in the field of diaspora studies.

As far as their identity is concerned, diasporic entities can exist when two significant preconditions are met. The first precondition is met when, in addition and to an extent "on top" of the existence of individual and familial emotions and cognitions concerning their "belonging," individual diasporans and small familial groups have a very clear cognitive sense of belonging to a wider group that cultivates solidarity and fosters commit-

---

20. The exceptions include Philip Gleason, "Identifying Identity: A Semantic History," *Journal of American History* 69, no. 4 (1983): 910–31; Stuart Hall, "Cultural Identity and Diaspora," in *Identity: Community, Culture, Difference*, ed. Jonathan Rutherford (London: Lawrence and Wishart, 1990); Egon Mayer and Barry Kosmin, *American Jewish Identity Survey 2001. AJIS Report: Exploration in the Demography and Outlook of a People* (New York: New York Center for Jewish Studies, the City University of New York, 2002); Braziel and Mannur, eds., *Theorizing Diaspora*; Waltraud Kokot, Khachig Tölölyan, and Caroli Alfonso, eds., *Religion, Identity, and Diaspora Transnationalism* (New York: Routledge, 2003); and Vijay Agnew, ed., *Diaspora, Memory and Identity: A Search for Home* (Toronto: University of Toronto Press, 2006).

ment to the entire ethnonational entity. The second precondition is met when there is an inherent readiness of individual diasporans, their families, and larger diasporic groups to identify themselves publicly as members of these entities.

As noted above, contrary to some observations of insiders and external observers, such recognition, feelings, and commitments are not confined to core members. Actually, some peripheral members of these entities—that is, those persons who have greatly integrated into their hostland society, politics, and economics—share and maintain their diasporic ethnonational identity. However, especially because of the still widespread opposition to diasporas and their concomitant rejection, which are engendered by hostile surrounding cultural, social, political, and economic environments in their hostlands, peripheral diasporans refrain from public identification with the entire entity. Despite their vacillations and hesitations (not so much concerning their identity, but more frequently concerning their identification), very often these persons are generally written off from the attention, memory, and formal and informal membership in these entities. For example, these days, this trend is notable in the study of the "classical" Jewish diaspora, especially in the United States. Though in different ways, when analyzing this entity and attributing to it figures and numbers, most writers make the distinction between core and periphery, or core and enlarged Jewish population.[21]

However, the greatest difficulty in this respect, and the one that causes the most significant challenges facing diasporic entities, is experienced especially by members of the imagined transnational diasporas. Again, according to the vast literature on transnationalism, the main reason for this difficulty is that the identity of their members is not inherently entrenched and based on primordial factors. Rather, according to various writers, their identity is freely or autonomously imagined, subjectively constructed, and individually espoused by actual or virtual members of these entities. Hence, this interpretation rightly implies that the original ethnonational or religious identities of such diasporans can easily be neglected, totally altered, or hybridized.[22] Such a capability to alter fundamentally one's basic ideological and religious beliefs can lead such persons to total assimilation or to full integration into host societies and thus to considerable demographic losses, especially for transnational diasporas.

Usually—and this observation is not confined to diasporans belonging to transnational diasporas, but applies to other diasporans, as well—both cognitive and emotional confusion and uncertainty about the fundamental identity of disaporans also prompt severe emotional and cognitive doubts about the need and benefits that they can gain from identification as members of diasporic entities. In turn, such positions and decisions

---

21. Uzi Rebhun, "Centers and Peripheries of Jewish Identity in the US: A Structural Analysis of Attitudes and Behaviors," in *Les diasporas: 2000 ans d'histoire*, ed. Lisa Anteby-Yemini, William Berthomière, and Gabriel Sheffer (Rennes: Press Universitaires de Rennes, 2005).

22. On hybridization, see, for example, Pnina Werbner, "The Materiality of Late Modern Diasporas," in *Les diasporas: 2000 ans d'histoire.*, ed. Lisa Anteby-Yemin, William Berthomière, and Gabriel Sheffer (Rennes: Press Universutaires de Rennes, 2005).

will lead to new difficulties facing such individuals and to major challenges to the leaders of such collectivities who are interested in maintaining "their" entities.

Therefore, if leaders and core members of such transnational entities—for example, the leaders and core members of what is now referred to as the Muslim and the Latino diasporas—indeed determinedly intend to organize, prevail, and then maintain some sort of cohesion, commitment to the diaspora and to its causes, and an ability to act politically and economically as an effective group, the basic challenges facing them are whether and to what extent to define more clearly their identity. It seems that recently, such leaders have relied on a combination of religious ideas plus economic and social promises to encourage and strengthen the commitment of vacillating and indecisive persons to remain members or at the least to maintain close connections with the diaspora.

In most cases, the maintenance and encouragement of such truly united and organized transnational diasporas will require on the part of actual and potential members of such entities an ideational, emotional, and practical substantial detachment from the ethnonational elements of their emotions and beliefs. Basically, this means that such individuals and groups must decide whether they give up their primordial ethnonational identities and instead join these less-defined transnational entities and later remain or become active members in these entities, thus helping shape a larger, persistent core that is coherent and capable of demonstrating solidarity and initiating and implementing actions. The diametrically opposite option is that they can try to assimilate or to integrate fully into their hostland societies. Given favorable conditions in their host countries, the latter decisions may lead to a situation that would prevent the establishment of truly united and coherent transnational diasporas.

It can be very easily understood that such decisions concerning their identities will have a tremendous impact on individuals' public identifications. If these persons decide that membership in and support of the emergence of more coherent transnational diasporas are preferable, members of existing transstate diasporas originating in separate Muslim or Latino homelands will have to identify themselves clearly, publicly or secretly, as such. Moreover, in many instances, they will have to denounce the primacy of their actual belonging to a transstate ethnonational diaspora.

This does not exclude the possibility that some diasporans would try to identify as members of both the transnational and transstate diasporas. As the cases that will be discussed below indeed show, actually, in most cases, such persons do not discard their original ethnonational identities. At most, these persons "add" such transnational identities to their original ethnonational identities, and they either suffer or enjoy a dual identity—the identity of their ethnonational and of their transnational entity.

The examples of individuals and groups that may face or are already facing this dilemma include Pakistanis in Britain and elsewhere, North Africans, such as the Moroccans and Algerians in France, and, of course, Africans in Europe and the United States. Because of the significance of this challenge, the illustrations below will occupy a significant portion of what remains to be discussed.

Let's begin with a brief discussion of the Pakistani diaspora, especially in Britain, as an example of this significant issue of identity and identification. Many Pakistanis have left their country in pursuit of higher education or better employment opportunities. At present, there are about four million Pakistanis abroad. This diaspora is steadily increasing in number. Many persons in the Pakistani diaspora have maintained close relations with their homeland and consequently have had a great social and economic impact on Pakistan in the past. According to most assessments, this will not decrease with time. The relatively economically secure large Pakistani diaspora, especially in Britain, has played an important role in continuous attempts at directing Pakistan toward democratization and greater economic prosperity. This could have been achieved only through a shared vision about their country's future. The organization of the Pakistani diaspora has been done through the establishment of religious centers located in many mosques, but also through the formation of civil-society and politically oriented organizations (as in other diasporas, it is difficult to asses the numbers of members and activists in these organizations). Yet older and younger Pakistani diasporans, as well as newcomer and veteran immigrants, especially in Britain, face difficult questions concerning their identity. Since it would be difficult for most Pakistanis to assimilate fully into the British society, like most other diasporans, they have to decide whether to integrate fully or partially into British society. At the same time, they have to make up their minds about their relations with other growing Muslim entities in Britain and Europe, especially to what extend they should identify with the "Muslim diaspora" and actively support its legal and illegal activities. As noted before, this creates a need to decide about preferences concerning their emotional and cognitive ties with their ethnic origins and the religious demands and calls for identification and support of the general Muslim cause.[23]

Very similar dilemmas are facing the North Africans in various European hostlands and especially the relatively large Moroccan entity in France.[24] In this respect, one should differentiate between the Berbers and the rest of Moroccans. It seems that some of the latter are more inclined to identify themselves with the general Muslim cause. Because of the Moroccans' proximity to their homeland and the relatively easy communication with it, they have stronger links with Morocco, and thus they are both capable of maintaining and willing to maintain their ethnonational identity and to identify as such. In any case, one of the indicators for the critical decision of these diasporans in regard to this issue is their cooperation and support for organizations such as al-Qaeda.

For many generations, the identity issue and challenge have been facing African Americans who are not descendants of recent immigrants or who are immigrants

---

23. Pnina Werbner, *Imagined Diaspora among Manchester Muslims* (Santa Fe, NM: James Currey, 2002), and Pnina Werbner, "The Predicament of Diaspora and Millennial Islam: Reflections in the Aftermath of September 11," available on-line at www.ssrc.org (last accessed on October 16, 2007); Yvonne Haddad and John Esposito, eds. *Muslims on the Americanization Path* (New York: Oxford University Press, 2000).

24. Stefano Allieve and Sorgen Nielsen, eds., *Muslim Networks and Transnational Communities in and across Europe* (Leiden: Brill, 2003).

themselves. Most members of the latter groups remember and maintain their original identities, retain contacts with their homelands, and support them. Their main dilemma is to what extend to integrate into American society. On the other hand, the former have to decide whether they are a diaspora at all and from which country they draw their identity. There is no question that the majority of African Americans do not regard themselves as members of a diaspora, and despite their troubled history, their identity is basically American.[25]

In view of the more firmly established base of identity and identification in core members of transstate diasporas, questions related to the need for protecting and promoting identity and identification are not as severe in these cases as they are in the cases of transnational entities. However, in view of current cultural and social temptations for assimilation and full integration in the more liberal democratic hostlands, members of transstate diasporas must also invest emotional and concrete resources in maintaining the given primordial elements of their identity. In other words, if they are inclined to maintain their memberships in their ethnonational diasporas and willing to augment their activities, they must try to prevent processes of sweeping hybridization of their individual and collective identities that may lead to its blurring and, later, when circumstances in their hostlands would permit, also to full assimilation. In turn, this may result in the total eradication of their identities and thus to the end of their membership in organized entities.

Examples of transstate diasporas facing such a practical challenge include the American and British Jewish diaspora and the case of Swedish Americans. Let's begin with a brief discussion of the Jewish diaspora. Subjectively and probably also objectively, the future of this "classical diaspora"—world Jewry—is uncertain. On the one hand, there are leaders, activists, and researchers who demonstrate a certain degree of optimism, but on the other, there are those who show great concern about it and especially about the future of European Jews.[26] In view of this mood and these assessments, the recent general and specific discussions within American Jewry and the various surveys and studies of the situation there indeed focus on the question of the "continuity" of the American Jewish entity. (The same applies to other Jewish diasporic entities, such as that in Britain, that will be discussed below.)

---

25. Paul Gilroy, *The Black Atlantic: Modernity and Double Consciousness* (Cambridge, MA: Harvard University Press, 1993); Paul Gilroy, "Diaspora and the Detours of Identity," in *Identity and Difference*, ed. Kathryn Woodward (Thousand Oaks, CA: Sage, 1997); and Paul Gilroy, "It Ain't Where You're From, It's Where You're At: The Dialectics Of Diasporic Identification," *Third Text* 13 (1991): 3–13; Charles Green, *Globalization and Survival in the Black Diaspora: The New Urban Challenge* (Albany: State University of New York Press 1997); Ronald Segal, "Globalisation and the Black Diaspora," Transnational Communities Working Paper WPTC-98-15 (Oxford: ESRC Transnational Communities Programme, 1998); Michael Hanchard, "Afro-Modernity: Temporality, Politics and the African Diaspora," *Public Culture* 11, no, 1 (1999): 245–68; and Michael Hanchard, "Identity, Meaning and the African American" *Social Text* 24 (1990): 31–42.

26. Bernard Wasserstein, *Vanishing Diaspora: The Jews in Europe Since 1945* (Cambridge, MA.: Harvard University Press, 1997).

Actually, these discussions and studies deal with the ongoing processes of assimilation and full integration of Jews in their hostlands and therefore with the decreasing numbers of identified and active members in that disapora. Among other things, these ponderings refer not only to actual operational aspects of the issue, but also to more general issues such as the fundamental question of "who is a Jew?" It is obvious that such issues and questions pertain to the basic question of identity discussed here. Recent studies of this matter clearly show not only that Jews assimilate and totally desert Jewry and its various communities, but also that a fundamental debate is going on among many Jews concerning the nature of Judaism. In the United States, this discussion deals with the centrality and role of the religious element versus the ethnic and national components of the Jewish identity. The surveys indicate that fewer Jews define their identity as purely religious, and more Jews define their identity in national or ethnic terms.[27] This trend indicates that more Jews "liberate" themselves from the bonds of religion and its leaders and revive the ethnic elements of their existence. Similar processes occur in British Jewry. The number of identified Jews is decreasing in that host country, as well, and the discussions about the future of this veteran entity, which is closely connected to issues of identity and identification, is continuing, but in a less passionate manner.[28]

As is well known, since the nineteenth century, about eight million Swedes emigrated to the United States. The more or less generally accepted public perception of these persons has been that eventually, they either assimilated into the American society or totally integrated into it. However, this has not been the actual situation of Swedish Americans—certain segments of this group have settled in certain urban concentrations that have helped them maintain their ethnonational identity, and they even have organized certain diasporic associations. More recently, there has been a clear reawakening of various segments of this Swedish diaspora, as well as, for example, of members of the American Polish, Norwegian, and other diasporas. This reawakening is expressed not only in emotive and ideational aspects, but also in the economic, trade, and tourist spheres.[29]

The Second Challenge: Actual and Virtual Boundaries

The second major challenge facing existing diasporas is closely interlinked to the challenge concerning their identities and identification patterns. This challenge pertains to

---

27. Mayer and Kosmin, *American Jewish Identity Survey 2001*; Daniel Boyarin and Jonathan Boyarin, "Diaspora: Generation and the Ground of Jewish Diaspora," in *Theorizing Diaspora: A Reader*, ed. Jana Evans Braziel and Annita Mannur (Oxford: Blackwell, 2003); Chaim Waxman, "Identity of Jewish Boomers," in *Contemporary Jewries: Convergence and Divergence*, ed. Ben Rafael Eliezer, Yosef Gorny, and Yaacov Ro'I (Leiden: Brill, 2003).

28. Marlena Schmool, "British Jewry: Prospects and Problems," in *Jewish Centers and Peripheries*, ed. Ilan Troen (London: Transaction Books, 1999).

29. See, for example, Steven Schnell, "Creating Normatives of Place and Identity in 'Little Sweden' USA," *Geographical Review* 93 (2003): 1–29, and Allyson McGill and Sandra Stotsky, *The Swedish Americans (The Immigrant Experience)* (New York: Chelsea House, 1997).

the definition, protection, maintenance, and expansion of the virtual and actual bound-aries of these entities. This has been recognized by various writers as one of the most critical aspects of diasporism.[30]

While the identities of core members of transstate diasporas are more firmly estab-lished and solid, and consequently, while the boundaries of their collective entities are more clearly defined, the challenge facing transnational diasporic entities in this respect is different from the challenge facing transstate diasporas and a challenge with which it is more difficult to cope. Thus, if there really exists a wish to form, consolidate, and later maintain a transnational organized collective, such diasporans must define and draw more clearly the boundaries of their entity, which today are almost nonexistent—for example, there are no defined boundaries of the global African and Muslim diasporas whatsoever.

If the leaders and activists of these potential or existing diasporas wish them to have a chance actually to be formed and to exist for longer periods, their leaders and activists should do their utmost to delineate the boundaries of these "communities," either after or simultaneously with the definition of their identities. From their own point of view, there are a number of "positive" and "negative" reasons for this. Two of these "negative" reasons are, first, because the total lack of well-defined boundaries makes it very difficult for leaders and activists to recognize, reach out to, and mobilize members, to organize, and to locate needed political, diplomatic, and economic resources and recruit activists. Second, the definition and drawing of more or less clear boundaries (of course not in physical terms) facilitate the diaspora's efforts to resist attempts by hostland govern-ments, societies, and competing ethnic and religious groups to penetrate these diasporic entities and cause their weakening, shrinking, and even demise in order to punish them for patterns of belonging and actions that they perform or that they avoid, patterns of behavior and actions that infuriate their hosts.

The difficulties that are involved in such attempts to create meaningful boundaries are demonstrated, for example, by the efforts of moderate Muslim leaders who oppose radical Islam and the claims of its proponents and activists that global Islam is by far more important than the existence of various separate ethnonational diasporas. These moderate leaders prefer to maintain their own entities and advance their own ethnona-tional homelands' interests, and they oppose attempts to expand the virtual boundaries of transnational Islam and the obligations to it, wishing to prevent the departure of certain transstate diasporans, such as the Lebanese, Palestinians, and Syrians in Latin America, from their diasporic entities. They also are eager to prevent the neglect of homelands

---

30. Fredrik Barth, "Introduction," in *Ethnic Groups and Boundaries: The Social Organization of Cultural Difference*, ed. Fre-drik Barth (London: George Allen and Unwin, 1969); John Armstrong, "Mobilized and Proletarian Diasporas," *American Political Science Review* 70, no. 2 (1976): 393–408; Gabriel Sheffer, "A New Field of Study: Modern Diasporas in Interna-tional Politics," in *Modern Diasporas in International Politics*, ed. Gabriel Sheffer (London: Croom Helm, 1986), and Sheffer, *Diaspora Politics*; Safran, "Diasporas in Modern Societies"; David Laitin, "Identity in Formation: The Russian-Speaking Nationality in the Post-Soviet Diaspora," *Archives Européennes de Sociologie* 36, no. 2 (1995): 281–316; Tölölyan, "Rethinking Diaspora(s)"; and Cohen, *Global Diasporas*.

and diasporic interests and eventually "defection" to the more radical elements of the transnational Muslim diaspora.

We are talking here about Muslim communities founded by immigrants from Syria, Lebanon, and Palestine who arrived in Latin America at the end of the nineteenth century and the first half of the twentieth and permanently settled in various countries there. It should be noted that these entities are predominantly Sunni in origin. Because of their economic success, they ran the risk of being assimilated or fully integrated into their host countries' societies. That is why the aim of the first organizations founded by these immigrants in the 1920s was to bring the communities together and organize them around ethnonational linguistic and religious traditions. Thus, their communities acquired an ethnic character. The communities were started as closed groups and were not open to diffusion outside of the original group. This ethnic character began to lose strength at the end of the 1990s, when Islam entered the international scene in a dramatic fashion and individuals began to show interest in joining the new frameworks. Leaders of radical and extremist groups such as al-Qaeda and Hezbollah try to draw and determine much broader boundaries for the transnational diaspora, according to their beliefs and views, by including all separate transstate diasporic entities in the general radical Muslim framework.[31]

On the other hand, if the leaders and activists of core transstate diasporas wish that these entities will continue to exist, they must work hard not so much at drawing the lines of their entity's borders, but at protecting the existing boundaries of their entities and at preventing their further blurring and porosity. They thus may avoid the possible consequent defection of core and peripheral members to either transnational diasporas or to hostland societies, a situation that may lead to a major decrease in their size and resources.

At the beginning of the twenty-first century, preserving existing diasporas is a major challenge, since the current boundaries of these entities have become less defined and more porous than they used to be in the mid-twentieth century. The main reasons for these developments are members' assimilation and more often their greater integration into host societies, especially in democratic states. Yet because of the more firmly established nature of their members' multifaceted identities, if the leaders and activists of transstate diasporas invest extensive organizational efforts and substantial financial and educational resources, they are capable of maintaining their diasporas' boundaries and thus of preventing assimilation and full integration of large numbers of their members.

Examples of diasporas that have succeeded in maintaining their boundaries include the Basque and Turkish diasporas in the United States. For centuries, Basques have emigrated from Spain for economic reasons, and later, Basques emigrated to escape

---

31. Chris Zamblis, "Radical Islam in Latin America," *Terrorism Monitor* 3, no. 23 (2005); The Pew Forum on Religion and Public Life, *Islam and the Global War on Terrorism in Latin America*, event transcript. April 6, 2006. Riva Kastoryano, "Muslim Diaspora(s) in Western Europe," *South Atlantic Quarterly* 98, nos. 1–2 (1999): 191–202.

crushing poverty, civil war, and political oppression by the Franco regime. However, unlike other European immigrants to the United States, even after five or six generations of residence abroad, a surprising number of Basques have maintained their ethnic identity. The Basques in the United States have demonstrated remarkable allegiance to their ethnic identity and culture. They have maintained the elements of their traditional culture, the institutions that have encouraged identity maintenance, and connections with their brethren in Spain. Partly as a result of the well-organized connections between the Basque authorities and Basque communities in the United States, it seems that now there is a further determination to maintain the Basque community there.[32]

It should be added here that some dormant diasporas whose members are either fully integrated into their host societies or have been inactive for many decades or even generations are now awakening and reviving their organizations and their core members' joint activities. By doing so, they redraw the formerly indistinct virtual boundaries of their entities in their hostlands. As has been noted above, relevant examples of such processes affecting groups that were almost fully assimilated or totally integrated into their hostland society are some of the Scandinavian communities in the United States and Polish and Irish Americans.

The Third Challenge: Location and Relations with the Homeland or Center of the Diaspora

The third basic, very significant issue facing all diasporic entities concerns the definition and formal or informal recognition of the actual or virtual location of a diaspora's center. A very closely related issue is the nature of the relations between a diaspora's members, leaders, and organizations and its actual or perceived center.

An intrinsic ambiguity concerning or lack of actual or even perceived homelands or centers principally affects the transnational entities. The exception is probably found in the relations of various Christian churches with their putative centers. Thus, for example, while Catholics worldwide regard the Vatican not as their homeland, but as their cultural and to a certain extent also their political and economic center, and while the dispersed Greek Orthodox regard Athens as their center, there is certainly no agreement among Muslims or Africans about the center of their global entity.

The existence of a recognized center, the need to act on its behalf or to oppose its regime—in short, the wish and need to maintain continuous connections with it— dictates the need to organize. Organization is a sine qua non for the persistent existence of diasporas.[33]

Thus, if there is a recognized center, individual diasporans of all kinds can and do maintain contacts with it, and conversely, when there is no agreement about the loca-

---

32. Gloria Totoricagüena, *Identity, Culture, and Politics in the Basque Diaspora* (Reno: University of Nevada Press, 2004), and Gloria Totoricagüena, *Basque Diaspora: Migration and Transnational Identity* (Reno: Center for Basque Studies, 2005).

33. Sheffer, *Diaspora Politics*.

tion and legitimacy of a center, these groups experience severe organizational deficits that could have been prevented if such centers were recognized and contacts with them maintained. Because of this lack of established centers and the consequent diasporic organizational deficits, it is clear that in fact, these diasporas are merely virtual entities with a limited possibility to act and affect the international and national systems, except for their occasional substantial effect on regional and internal affairs in certain hostlands, such as the situation of the Sunni al-Qaeda, which is far from being recognized by the entire Muslim diaspora worldwide. The same applies to the terrorist activities of the Shiite Hezbollah, which is purportedly representing Iran, a state that is aspiring to become the center of the Shiite Muslim global group. It is highly doubtful whether and to what extent these two groups can systematically and continuously affect current affairs, especially in their host countries.

Because in most transnational diasporas there is no agreement about the location of a center, the challenge concerning the recognition of and relations with such a center is basically conceptual and abstract. For transstate diasporas, however, this challenge is neither hypothetical nor theoretical. Determining the location of the ethnonational center is a challenge facing members of these entities on almost a daily basis. This is so even though most core members of both state-linked and stateless transstate diasporas know exactly the *territorial* location of their imagined or real homelands. But for that reason, they must repeatedly decide on the nature of their relations with it and negotiate over who determines all cultural and practical decisions concerning the actions of both the diaspora and the ethnonational center—the center, or the diaspora.

There are only few cases of stateless ethnonational diasporans, including a minority among African Americans, who regard the whole continent as their homeland or some Romas who regard Northern India as their homeland. In other words, for these diasporans, the existence and location of their actual countries of origin is not clear. Otherwise, most of all other stateless diasporans—such as the Palestinians, Sri Lankan Tamils, Basques, Turkish Kurds,[34] Sikhs,[35] and, for the time being, the Albanian Kosovars—have a very clear idea where their center or homeland is. Usually they may have some doubts or specific wishes concerning the boundaries of these territories, but the location of the homeland is clear. In fact, large segments of these and other stateless entities invest substantial emotions and actual political, diplomatic, and economic resources in the usually protracted struggles for gaining independence and sovereignty in these countries of origin. As in the cases of the Palestinians and Kurds, not all diasporans may agree about the tactical moves intended to achieve that independence and sovereignty. On certain occasions, there may even emerge substantial disagreements between the diasporans and their brethren in their perceived homeland concerning these issues. Thus, for example, there have been difficult debates between Albanian Kosovars in the United States and

---

34. Eva Østergaard-Nielsen, *Transnational Politics: Turks and Kurds in Germany* (London: Routledge, 2003).

35. Darshan Singh Tatla, *The Sikh Diaspora: The Search for Statehood* (London: UCL Press, 1999).

their brethren in Kosovo about various conceptual and actual issues in regard to the separation from Serbia—as in other cases, the American Albanians have been more radical in this respect. The same situation characterized certain groups of Jews before the establishment of the sovereign state of Israel. In the Jewish diaspora, there were members who supported the right to launch a war against the Arabs and Palestinians in order to occupy the entire land of Israel.

After their brethren obtain independence in their homelands, stateless diasporas become state-linked diasporas. Later, up to a certain point and without asking too many critical questions about the policies and behavior of the new rulers in their homelands, members of such new state-linked diasporas tend to support the new systems in their homelands. Usually, during that initial period after independence, they continue to invest politically, diplomatically, and economically in enhancing their homeland's security and development. This was the case with the Armenian, Jewish, and Polish diasporas, as well as with various other diasporas. Later, former activists in such diasporas have tended to view more critically the situation in the homeland. In cases where the new rulers in the homeland pursue policies and behave in a fashion that does not fit the views of the diaspora, which in many cases are influenced by liberal and moderate norms of behavior prevailing in their hostlands, they might alter all or part of their previous relations with the homeland.

In any event, locating and recognizing the center of the entire ethnonational entity is a two-sided process. On one side, recognized homelands have tried and now more intensively continue to try to influence the situation and activities of "their" diasporas.[36] In this respect, there is a relatively new pattern: For many reasons—including obtaining remittances, donations, investments, political and diplomatic support, and so on—more homelands are showing a much-enhanced interest in their diasporas. Accordingly, many countries of origin have established special ministries or agencies to deal with "their" diasporas. For example, this is the case in Greece, France, Italy, and even Japan. Generally speaking, the overall purpose of these homeland governments is to enhance their relationships with and, in fact, their control over their diasporas, or at least to gain substantive influence concerning their positions and inclinations vis-à-vis their homeland and, possibly even more importantly, concerning the diaspora's activities on the hostland, regional, and international levels.

Thus, more homeland embassies and organizations are involved in the affairs of the diasporas, and more frequently, such governments attempt to "guide" the diasporas in what they should do in the social, political, and economic spheres in their hostlands. Moreover, homeland governments are now ready to invest more in cultural, educational, and socialization processes in their diasporas. Even the Israeli government, which was always eager to get from the Jewish diaspora maximum economic donations and investments, has changed its basic policy in this respect and recently began to invest in what is

---

36. Walker Connor, "The Impact of Homelands upon Diasporas," in *Modern Diasporas in International Politics*, ed. Gabriel Sheffer (London: Croom Helm, 1986).

called "Zionist-Jewish Education."[37] More homelands also encourage their diasporas to organize—this is the case, for example, with the Greek, Japanese, Turkish, and even Italian governments' positions and actual policies.[38] Such homeland governments wish that, in the final analysis, they and to an extent also their diasporas will stand a chance to gain from such close mutual relationships and homeland involvement in diaspora affairs.

Frequently, however, these connections with homelands and their interventions in the affairs of the diasporas are not welcomed by diasporas. Most organized transstate state-linked diasporas and their core members prefer to maintain their collective and individual autonomy in determining their strategies and actions in their hostlands and in fact also vis-à-vis their homelands. Consequently, more diasporans realize that in view of the new possibilities open to them in many hostlands and their better chances to survive as autonomous collectives for longer periods, they should either reform existing organizations or form new and more efficient ones that can either resist the interventions of the homeland or pursue their autonomous policies. The Indian diaspora has pursued just such a two-sided strategy in its relations with the Indian government.[39]

The Fourth Basic Challenge: Loyalty

The fourth interlinked basic challenge facing *all* diasporas is that of loyalty.[40] This challenge is connected to all three challenges already mentioned and particularly to the third—the issue of the location of the centers of ethnonational-religious entities. Members of all diasporas must decide whether—and probably more importantly, the extent to which—they owe loyalty either to the ethnonational-religious center or homeland or to their hostland. This is far from a new issue. It has accompanied and confronted diasporas from ancient times until now. However, this need to choose has become a major issue after 9/11 and in view of the very recent violent events in Madrid, London, Paris, and other cities, mainly in Europe.

Though, as noted above, the need to define to whom they owe their primary loyalty faces all diasporas, this is a major issue especially for the transnational group of diasporas. The main reason is, again, that diasporans belonging to these diasporas have no clearly defined centers. Thus, for example, Muslims and Arabs who regard themselves as belonging to such worldwide diasporas face the issue continuously and acutely. This is not only because of their own individual and collective priorities concerning to which social and political formation they belong and owe their loyalty, but because of a number of other reasons. It is due to the image that they project to all external actors, the

---

37. Gabriel Sheffer, *Who Governs the Jewish Nation?: Israeli-Jewish Diaspora Relations* [in Hebrew] (Tel Aviv: Hakibutz Hameuhad, 2006).

38. About the Italian case, see, for example, Donna Gabaccia, *Italy's Many Diasporas* (London: UCL Press, 2000).

39. Mark-Anthony Falzon, "Bombay, Our Cultural Heart: Rethinking the Relation between Homeland and Diaspora," *Ethnic and Racial Studies* 26, no. 4 (2003): 662–83.

40. Yossi Shain, *The Frontier of Loyalty: Political Exiles in the Age of the Nation-State* (Middletown, CT: Wesleyan University Press, 1989); Sheffer, *Diaspora Politics*.

emotional and rational reactions that they provoke from these actors, and the actions taken these days by hostland societies and governments to counter real or imagined threats. Hostland societies and governments are now very determinedly inclined to do all that they can to prevent the use of force and terrorism, tactics that are wrongly attributed especially to members of such emerging transnational diasporas.[41]

Such intense reactions to these diasporas, which are accompanied by racist and violent responses by host societies and governments, cause ideational and practical splits within these diasporic entities. Thus, on the one side, the moderates insist on loyalty to local societies and states. They are advocating restrained actions in accordance with the prevailing legal norms and requirements in their hostlands. On the other side, the radicals, who insist on loyalty to the causes of their emerging diasporas, frequently tend to use tough tactics, including terrorism vis-à-vis their hostlands.

Though less critically, transstate diasporas that usually accept the rules of the game in their hostlands and that opt for either full loyalty to their hostlands or at least adopt a vague posture in this respect also face this challenge and must make some critical decisions concerning its various aspects. The issue is grave in cases where and when there are conflicts or clashes between their hostlands and homeland. This is the case, for example, with the Cuban diaspora in the United States. In this case, however, many Cuban Americans oppose the Castro regime and government and cooperate with the United States. Generally, the decisions that these diasporas must make pertain to their remittances, other unilateral transfers of money, economic investments, political involvement, lobbying, and criminal cooperation with various elements in their homelands.

Most of the stateless diasporas find themselves in a delicate and problematic situation concerning the loyalty issue. They must decide to what extent they would support the struggle of their brethren for independence and sovereignty in their homelands. If there is no inconsistency between their own inclinations and strategies and the position of their hostland's authorities, their ability to make autonomous decisions concerning their assistance to their kin in the homeland is ensured. Things are by far more complicated in cases in which a hostland adopts a policy that contradicts the inclination of core leaders and members of a stateless diaspora. This issue confronts, for example, Muslim Palestinians who are either citizens of or permanently reside in the United States and Great Britain. They must decide whether to refrain from helping the more radical Palestinian organizations, such as Hamas, or to show loyalty to those two hostlands, which oppose that movement and try to disarm it and turn it into a purely social-political organization. The same applies to Turkish Kurds living in Germany and to Tamils in the United States.

The Fifth Challenge: Strategic and Tactical Policies and Activities

A whole range of strategies is available to diasporas, from active political, social, economic, and practical support of violence and terrorism in hostlands, homelands, and third and

---

41. Gabriel Sheffer, "Diaspora and Terrorism," in *The Roots of Terrorism*, ed. Louise Richardson (New York: Routledge, 2006).

fourth countries to legal attempts to promote their interests publicly and openly. Generally speaking and as already noted, most state-linked diasporas pursue quite moderate and balanced communitarian policies.[42] More often than not, these entities prefer to act in accordance with the laws and the rules of the prevailing social and political games in their hostlands and in the international system.

On the other hand, the more radical activist members of transnational and stateless diasporas tend to adopt more radical policies, including violent and terrorist tactics, as well as cooperation with criminal groups, which is a rapidly expanding problem facing all the actors involved. In fact, most, if not all diasporas are involved in various criminal spheres.[43] In view of the tough reactions of hostland governments in countries such as the United States, Britain, Spain, and Germany, diasporas have been forced to make difficult decisions in this respect. In fact, it seems that as time has passed since the 9/11 events, in view of the tough reactions of these and other hostlands, the extremist activists in these diasporas have moderated their positions, strategies, and actions. It is clear that despite the recurrent terrorist attacks launched by members of such diasporas, on the whole, Western democracies are not seriously threatened by such radical postures and actions on the part of these diasporas. This fact must lead these diasporas to rethink their positions concerning the methods to achieve their goals. However, the abandonment of the more radical postures and actions may alienate and further radicalize certain segments and individuals in these diasporas.

Concluding Comments

The diasporic phenomenon is alive and growing at the beginning of the twenty-first century. Though there might be cases of the assimilation and full integration of diasporans into hostland societies, nevertheless, the cores of these diasporas and significant parts of the peripheries will continue to exist and will be influential on many levels. There is a wide agreement that the phenomenon is complex. Therefore, when discussing the main issues, dilemmas, and challenges facing diasporas, one should avoid generalizations and make very careful and clear distinctions between the various types of diasporas and diasporans. The main distinction suggested here is between transnational and transstate diasporas. Generally speaking, it seems that transnational diasporas face more substantial dilemmas and challenges in comparison to the various subcategories of the transstate diasporas.

Despite the differences between the two types of diasporas and in addition to their specific problems and challenges analyzed above, diasporas in both categories and subcategories share a number of additional concerns that have not been elaborated in this article but that should be very briefly mentioned here. Among other issues, these are the

---

42. Sheffer, *Diaspora Politics.*

43. Sheffer, "Diaspora and Terrorism"; U.S. State Department Counterterrorism Office, *Patterns of Global Terrorism, 1995–2003*, available on-line at http://www.state.gov/s/ct/rls/crt/ (last accessed on October 16, 2007). Center for Defense Information, available on-line at www.cdi.org (last accessed on October 16, 2007).

need to establish and maintain cultural, religious, educational, and health systems; organizing social and legal support systems; and defining their relations with other diasporas and minorities in their hostlands. Each of these tasks involves very difficult decisions that affect the resources at the disposal of these entities.

In this context, however, one important thing should be very strongly stated: Diasporas are not only perpetrators of difficulties, unrest, conflicts, disloyalty, terrorism, and crimes. Rather, diasporas immensely contribute—in the form of literature, poetry, movies, plays, TV programs—to the cultures and the economies of their host countries. Therefore, they deserve a lot of understanding and patience from host societies and governments.

Finally, while there is a multitude of studies concerning specific diasporas, and the numbers of these studies is increasing and their quality is improving, there is still a noticeable lacuna in the study of certain aspects of the entire phenomenon, including the challenges that has been discussed here. Thus, the number of comparative and theoretical studies in this field is still limited. Hence, there is a need to develop such studies further and to create theoretical islands that eventually will serve as bases for a more comprehensive theoretical exploration of diasporism, a phenomenon that is not going to disappear, but rather to grow.

Bibliography

Agnew, Vijay, ed. *Diaspora, Memory and Identity: A Search for Home*. Toronto: University of Toronto Press, 2006.

Allieve, Stefano and Sorgen Nielsen, eds. *Muslim Networks and Transnational Communities in and across Europe*. Leiden: Brill, 2003.

Anderson, Benedict. *Imagined Communities: Reflections on the Origins and Spread of Nationalism*. London: Verso, 1991.

———. "Exodus." *Critical Inquiry* 20, no. 2 (1994): 314–27.

Anthias, Floya. "Evaluating 'Diaspora': Beyond Ethnicity." *Sociology* 32, no. 3 (1998): 557–80.

Armstrong, John. "Mobilized and Proletarian Diasporas." *American Political Science Review* 70, no. 2 (1976): 393–408.

Barth, Fredrik. "Introduction." In *Ethnic Groups and Boundaries: The Social Organization of Cultural Difference*. Edited by Fredrik Barth. London: George Allen and Unwin, 1969.

Boyarin, Daniel, and Jonathan Boyarin. "Diaspora: Generation and the Ground of Jewish Diaspora." In *Theorizing Diaspora: A Reader*. Edited by Jana Evans Braziel and Annita Mannur. Oxford: Blackwell, 2003.

Braziel, Jana Evans, and Anita Mannur, eds. *Theorizing Diaspora: A Reader*. Oxford: Blackwell, 2003.

Brubaker, Rogers. *Accidental Diasporas and External "Homelands" in Central and Eastern Europe: Past and Present.* Political Science Series no. 71. Vienna: Institute for Advanced Studies, 2000.

——. "The 'Diaspora' Diaspora." *Ethnic and Racial Studies* 28, no. 1 (2005): 1–19.

Butler, Kim. "Defining Diaspora, Refining a Discourse." *Diaspora* 10, no. 2 (2001): 189–219.

Center of Defense Information, www.cdi.org.

Clifford, James. "Diasporas." *Cultural Anthropology* 9, no. 3 (1994): 302–38.

Cohen, Robin. *Global Diasporas: An Introduction.* Seattle: University of Washington Press, 1997.

Connor, Walker. "The Impact of Homelands upon Diasporas." In *Modern Diasporas in International Politics.* Edited by Gabriel Sheffer. London: Croom Helm, 1986.

Falzon, Mark-Anthony. "Bombay, Our Cultural Heart: Rethinking the Relation between Homeland and Diaspora." *Ethnic and Racial Studies* 26, no. 4 (2003): 662–83.

Gabaccia, Donna. *Italy's Many Diasporas.* London: UCL Press, 2000.

García, John. *Latino Politics in America: Community, Culture, and Interests.* Lanham, MD: Rowman and Littlefield, 2003.

Gilroy, Paul. *The Black Atlantic: Modernity and Double Consciousness,* Cambridge, MA: Harvard University Press, 1993.

——. "Diaspora and the Detours of Identity." In *Identity and Difference.* Edited by Kathryn Woodward. Thousand Oaks, CA: Sage, 1997.

——. "It Ain't Where You're From, It's Where You're At: The Dialectics Of Diasporic Identification." *Third Text* 13 (1991): 3–13.

Gleason, Philip. "Identifying Identity: A Semantic History." *Journal of American History* 69, no. 4 (1983): 910–31.

Glick-Schiller, Nina, Linda Basch, and Christina Blanc-Szanton. "From Immigrant to Transmigrant: Theorizing Transnational Migration." *Anthropological Quarterly* 68 (1995): 48–63.

——. "Towards a Transnational Perspective on Migration." *Annals of the New York Academy of Science* 645 (1992): 1–24.

Green, Charles. *Globalization and Survival in the Black Diaspora: The New Urban Challenge.* Albany: State University of New York Press 1997.

Gunderson, Cory Gideon. *Swedish Americans.* Philadelphia: Chelsea House, 2003.

Haddad, Yvonne, and John Esposito, eds. *Muslims on the Americanization Path.* New York: Oxford University Press, 2000.

Hall, Stuart. "Cultural Identity and Diaspora." In *Identity: Community, Culture, Difference.* Edited by Jonathan Rutherford. London: Lawrence and Wishart, 1990.

Hanchard, Michael. "Afro-Modernity: Temporality, Politics and the African Diaspora." *Public Culture* 11, no, 1 (1999): 245–68.

——. "Identity, Meaning and the African American" *Social Text* 24 (1990): 31–42.

Kastoryano, Riva. "Muslim Diaspora(s) in Western Europe." *South Atlantic Quarterly* 98, nos. 1–2 (1999): 191–202.

Kelass, John. *The Politics of Nationalism and Ethnicity.* New York: St. Martin's Press, 1991.

King, Charles, and Neil Melvin. *Nations Abroad: Diaspora Politics and International Relations in the Former Soviet Union.* Boulder, CO: Westview Press, 1998.

Kokot, Waltraud, Khachig Tölölyan, and Caroli Alfonso, eds. *Religion, Identity, and Diaspora Transnationalism.* New York: Routledge, 2003.

Kolstoe, Paul. *Russians in the Former Soviet Republics.* London: Hurst, 1995.

Koser, Khalid, ed. *New African Diasporas.* London: Routledge, 2003.

Laitin, David. "Identity in Formation: The Russian-Speaking Nationality in the Post-Soviet Diaspora." *Archives Européennes de Sociologie* 36, no. 2 (1995): 281–316.

Lie, John. "From International Migration to Transnational Diaspora." *Contemporary Sociology* 24, no. 4 (1995): 303–6.

Mandelbaum, Michael. *The New European Diasporas: National Minorities and Conflict in Eastern Europe.* New York: Council on Foreign Relations Press, 2000.

Mayer, Egon, and Barry Kosmin. *American Jewish Identity Survey 2001. AJIS Report: Exploration in the Demography and Outlook of a People.* New York: New York Center for Jewish Studies, the City University of New York, 2002.

Miles, William, and Gabriel Sheffer. "Francophone and Zionism: A Comparative Study of Transnationalism and Transstatism." *Diaspora* 7, no. 2 (1998): 119–48.

Morwaska, Ewa. "Immigrants, Transnationalism, and Ethnicization: A Comparison of This Great Wave and the Last." In *E Pluribus Unum? Contemporary and Historical Perspectives on Immigrant Political Incorporation.* Edited by Gary Gerstle and John Mollenkopf. New York: Russell Sage Foundation, 2001.

Münz, Rainer, and Rainer Ohlinger, eds. *Diasporas and Ethnic Migrants: Germany, Israel, and Post-Soviet Successor States.* Portland, OR: Frank Cass, 2003.

Østergaard-Nielsen, Eva. *Transnational Politics: Turks and Kurds in Germany.* London: Routledge, 2003.

The Pew Forum on Religion and Public Life. *Islam and the Global War on Terrorism in Latin America.* Event transcript. April 6, 2006.

Rebhun, Uzi. "Centers and Peripheries of Jewish Identity in the US: A Structural Analysis of Attitudes and Behaviors." In *Les diasporas: 2000 ans d'histoire.* Edited by Lisa Anteby-Yemini, William Berthomière, and Gabriel Sheffer. Rennes: Presses Universitaires de Rennes, 2005.

Safran, William. "Diasporas in Modern Societies: Myths of Homeland and Return." *Diaspora* 1, no. 1 (1991): 83–99.

Saint-Blancat, Chantal. "Islam in Diaspora: Between Reterritorialization and Extraterritoriality." *International Journal of Urban and Regional Research* 26, no. 1 (2002): 138–51.

Schmool, Marlena. "British Jewry: Prospects and Problems." In *Jewish Centers and Peripheries*. Edited by Ilan Troen. London: Transaction, 1999.

Schnapper, Dominique. "De l'état-nation au mond transnational: Du sense et de l'útilite du concept de diaspora." In *Les diasporas: 2000 ans d'histoire*. Edited by Lisa Anteby-Yemini, William Berthomière, and Gabriel Sheffer. Rennes: Presses Universitaires de Rennes, 2005.

Schnell, Steven. "Creating Normatives of Place and Identity in 'Little Sweden' USA." *Geographical* Review 93 (2003): 1–29.

Segal, Ronald. "Globalisation and the Black Diaspora." Transnational Communities Working Paper WPTC-98-15. Oxford: ESRC Transnational Communities Programme, 1998.

Shain, Yossi. *The Frontier of Loyalty: Political Exiles in the Age of the Nation-State.* Middletown, CT: Wesleyan University Press, 1989.

Sheffer, Gabriel. "Defining Ethno-National Diasporas." *Migration* 33/34/35 (2002): 69–92.

——. *Diaspora Politics: At Home Abroad.* Cambridge: Cambridge University Press, 2006.

——. "Diaspora and Terrorism." In *The Roots of Terrorism.* Edited by Louise Richardson. New York: Routledge, 2006.

——. "A New Field of Study: Modern Diasporas in International Politics." In *Modern Diasporas in International Politics.* Edited by Gabriel Sheffer. London: Croom Helm, 1986.

——. *Who Governs the Jewish Nation?: Israeli-Jewish Diaspora Relations.* [In Hebrew.] Tel Aviv: Hakibutz Hameuhad, 2006.

Sivan, Emanuel. *Clash Inside Islam.* [In Hebrew.] Tel Aviv: Am Oved, 2005.

Smith, Anthony. *The Ethnic Origins of Nations.* Oxford: Basil Blackwell, 1986.

Smith, Robert. "Diasporic Memberships in Historical Perspective: Comparative Insights from the Mexican, Italian, and Polish Cases." *International Migration Review* 37, no. 3 (2003): 724–59.

Tambiah, Stanley J. "Transitional Movements, Diaspora, and Multiple Modernities." *Daedalus* 129, no. 1 (2000): 163–94.

Tatla, Darshan Singh. *The Sikh Diaspora: The Search for Statehood.* London: UCL Press, 1999.

Tölölyan, Khachig. "The Nation-State and Its Others: In Lieu of a Preface." *Diaspora* 1, no. 1 (1991): 3–7.

———. "Rethinking Diaspora(s): Stateless Power in the Transnational Moment." *Diaspora* 5, no. 1 (1996): 3–36.

Totoricagüena, Gloria. *Identity, Culture, and Politics in the Basque Diaspora*. Reno: University of Nevada Press, 2004.

———. *Basque Diaspora: Migration and Transnational Identity*. Reno: Center for Basque Studies, 2005.

United Nations High Commissionner for Refugees (UNHCR). Fifty-sixth General Assembly, Third Committee, November 19, 2001.

U.S. State Department Counterterrorism Office. *Patterns of Global Terrorism, 1995–2003*. Available on-line at http://www.state.gov/s/ct/rls/crt/.

Vertovec, Steven. "Three Meanings of Diasporas." *Diaspora* 6, no. 3 (1997): 277–97.

———. *Trends and Impacts of Migrant Transnationalism*. COMPAS Working Paper WP-04-03. Oxford: Centre on Migration, Policy and Society of the University of Oxford, 2004.

———, and Robin Cohen, eds. *Migrations, Diasporas, and Transnationalism*. The International Library of Studies on Migration. Cheltenham, UK: Edward Elgar, 1999.

Wahlbeck, Östen. *Kurdish Diasporas: A Comparative Study of Kurdish Refugee Communities*. Houndmills, Basingstoke, Hamphshire, UK: Macmillan, 1999.

Waldinger, Roger, and David Fitzgerald. "Transnationalism in Question." *American Journal of Sociology* 109, no. 5 (2004): 1177–95.

Wasserstein, Bernard. *Vanishing Diaspora: The Jews in Europe Since 1945*. Cambridge, MA.: Harvard University Press, 1997.

Waxman, Chaim. "Identity of Jewish Boomers." In *Contemporary Jewries: Convergence and Divergence*. Edited by Ben Rafael Eliezer, Yosef Gorny, and Yaacov Ro'I. Leiden: Brill, 2003.

Werbner, Pnina. *Imagined Diaspora among Manchester Muslims*. Santa Fe, NM: James Currey, 2002.

———. "The Materiality of Late Modern Diasporas." In *Les diasporas: 2000 ans d'histoire*. Edited by Lisa Anteby-Yemin, William Berthomière, and Gabriel Sheffer. Rennes: Press Universutaires de Rennes, 2005.

———. "The Predicament of Diaspora and Millennial Islam: Reflections in the Aftermath of September 11." Available on-line at www.ssrc.org.

Zamblis, Chris. "Radical Islam in Latin America." *Terrorism Monitor* 3, no. 23 (2005).

Stateless Power and the Political Agency of Diasporas: An Armenian Case Study

By Khachig Tölölyan

Two of the terms in my title—"diaspora" and "power"—require a definition and discussion that is more than a fussy excursus into terminological distinction. Distinctions must be made because "diaspora" is a term that still means several things, and this leads to misunderstanding within the young field of diaspora studies, and "power," though always a fact of life, is actually now used to mean fairly different things in the literature of the social sciences.

The contemporary discourse of diaspora studies all too often lumps together two terms, "dispersion" and "diaspora." For example, a book on human evolution that discusses the early migration out of Africa of *Homo sapiens* and related species titles itself *The Great Human Diasporas: The History of Dispersion and Evolution.*[1] Properly used by contemporary scholarly discourse, "dispersion" is a far more general term than "diaspora," Dispersion is a set of which diaspora is a subset. But in this title, the authors make the terms virtually synonymous; one substitutes for the other. The semantic field designated by these terms in fact encompasses many kinds of scattering—for example, both the dispersion of seeds away from the parent body of a plant and, metaphorically, the movement of people away from their homeland. The dispersion of people is by definition connected to mobility, sometimes alternating with sedentariness.[2] Such forms of dispersion can range

---

1. Luigi Luca Cavalli-Sforza and Francesco Cavalli-Sforza, *The Great Human Diasporas: The History of Dispersion and Evolution* (Reading, MA: Addison-Wesley, 1993).

2. For an extended discussion of these terms, their use, misuse, and the effects of doing so, see my "Restoring the Logic of the Sedentary to Diaspora Studies," in *Les diasporas: 2000 ans d'histoire*, ed. Lisa Anteby-Yemeni, William Berthomière, and Gabriel Sheffer (Rennes: Presses Universitaires de Rennes, 2005) and my "From Diaspora Studies to Dispersion Studies: Changing Definitions, Altering Methods, Moving Targets," *Comparative Studies of South Asia, Africa and the Middle East* 27, no. 3 (Winter 2007): 647–55. Special issue edited by Ato Quayson.

from sojourns and homecomings to permanent emigration and colonial settlement. The category of the dispersed can also include exiles; expatriates; migrant laborers; great merchants and minor traders constantly on the move, buying and selling; refugees and asylum seekers; seasonal agricultural workers; transnational domestic and service-sector workers; in the past, slaves, bond servants shipped to colonies, and deported populations; trafficked sex workers; and many others, such as Chinese and Korean children, almost always girls, adopted into families in countries ranging from Sweden and Spain to Canada and the United States. Only one subset of the set designated by "dispersion" is the social formation and concept that we call a "diaspora."

"Diaspora"

Though it is etymologically closely connected to "dispersion," the term "diaspora" is a historically distinct word from Attic Greek, first applied on or around 275 B.C.E to the Jewish dispersion,[3] which by then was three centuries old and had become a well-organized social formation linked to Jerusalem while thriving in Hellenic Alexandria, in Egypt. Eventually, the term came to mean the *coerced* scattering of indigenous populations away from their home territory, fatherland, or homeland, followed by the survival of the fragments, their transformation into an enduring set of linked communities, and the willed, organized maintenance of an old, inherited collective identity, as well as the construction of new identities.

Until the 1960s, scholars applied "diaspora" to only three groups: the earliest, the Jewish, then also to Armenians (starting in the eleventh century C.E.), and then to Greeks (around 1650 C.E.). Starting in the 1960s, for reasons I have explored elsewhere,[4] the term gained wider currency, in part as a response to increasing transnationalism and globalization. The discourse and rhetoric of diaspora have been adopted by scholars in many disciplines; today, four decades later, it is applied to at least three dozen dispersions and transnational communities. The strict sense of the term thus has diminished and has become more accommodating. However, even after this enlargement and loosening of the meaning of the term, not all mobile transnational dispersions can also be called "diasporas." To call such dispersions "diasporas" is to put, if not the cart before the horse, then the subset before the set.[5]

---

3. "Diaspora" is most commonly named *galut* in Hebrew. Although *golah/galut* are the Hebrew terms best known to modern scholars, the Hebrew Bible does not consistently use that single word to describe the Jewish condition. Variations of the noun *fotz* and the verb *hefitz* (the scattering, the dispersion) are commonly used, for example in Genesis 11:4, the Tower of Babel episode.

4. Khachig Tölölyan, "Rethinking Diaspora(s): Stateless Power in the Transnational Moment," *Diaspora: A Journal of Transnational Studies* 5, no. 1 (1996): 3–36; idem, The Nation-State and Its Others: In Lieu of a Preface," *Diaspora: A Journal of Transnational Studies* 1, no. 1 (1991): 3–7. Reprinted in *Becoming National: A Reader*, ed. Geoff Eley and Ronald Suny (New York: Oxford University Press, 1996.

5. The duality appears in a different form in John Armstrong, "Mobilized and Proletarian Diasporas," *American Political Science Review* 70, no. 2 (1976): 393–408, where he juxtaposes what he names "mobilized" and "proletarian" diasporas. The former are my primary concern here; the latter are not synonymous with, but overlap with what I here call "dispersion."

Scholars who have studied the topic for some time know that during the first twenty-one centuries of its existence, "diaspora" denoted the melancholy situation of a dispersed, dislocated, uprooted minority that lived in an enclave hierarchically encapsulated within the larger host society or state, an enclave with more or less porous communal boundaries. Even on the occasions when it prospered economically, it lived precariously and lacked security, let alone power. Within many states, members of diasporas were regarded as second-class citizens of their host societies, and they were viewed both by others and by themselves as marginalized remnants of a nation that was, a nation to be, or a nation elsewhere, linked by nostalgia to an old homeland or, in the absence of a homeland, to some territory or region, sustained by shared language, memory, religion, rituals and institutionalized practices, struggling to maintain and to reproduce their social formation and collective identity under the threat of anything from massacre to assimilation.

"Power"

This is not a situation in which the term "power" naturally comes to mind. And yet, by and in the 1960s, much had changed, both in the conceptualization and in the geopolitical situation of diasporas,[6] and it became possible to acknowledge that diasporas could exercise some forms of power. I first used the term "stateless power" in 1990 to describe this emergent attribute of diasporas. It appeared in one of the pamphlets that described the forthcoming *Diaspora: A Journal of Transnational Studies* (which I edit, and whose first issue appeared in May 1991). Subsequently, I used the phrase in the title of an article published in 1996.[7] In 1992, Jonathan and Daniel Boyarin titled their book about Jewish diaspora culture *The Powers of Diaspora*. Their use of the term and my own overlapped, but also differed. By "power," they mean something similar to the currently popular "soft power," the ability of one culture to be a prolific cultural producer of representations of itself while also influencing others through them.[8] My own use of the term includes the soft power that the Boyarins examine and more: by "stateless power," I also refer to the ability of diaspora elites to obtain voluntary contributions—a sort of self-taxation—from their own community; to their capacity to use these funds to perform social and cultural services that states would not or could not perform; to their effective nurturing of organizations and institutions within the community; and to their ability to extend the diasporan community's reach, through financial contributions, political lobbying, and media

---

At any rate, while Armstrong's first term is still used, the second adjective has not to my knowledge been used since its first publication—it simply refers to a dispersion before it has been organized as a diaspora.

6. For a historical survey of the origin of the term "diaspora" and the changes in its use and meaning, see my "Rethinking Diaspora(s)," as well as Khachig Tölölyan, "The Nation-State and Its Others: In Lieu of a Preface," *Diaspora: A Journal of Transnational Studies* 1, no. 1 (1991): 3–7. Reprinted in *Becoming National: A Reader*, ed. Geoff Eley and Ronald Suny (New York: Oxford University Press, 1996)

7. Tölölyan, "Rethinking Diaspora(s)."

8. Jonathan Boyarin and Daniel Boyarin, *Powers of Diaspora: Two Essays on the Relevance of Jewish Culture* (Minneapolis: University of Minnesota Press, 1992).

representations, to influence policies and legislation, indeed, to participate energetically in the public sphere, where so many discourses and practices of political power are first formulated. Furthermore, I include in "stateless power" the admittedly unusual circumstances in which some diasporas have elected representatives to parliament, participated in terrorism, and even maintained armed militias.[9]

The terms and discourses that scholars use often commit them to underlying assumptions from which we might, in fact, wish to distance ourselves. The terms "power" and "politics" elicit such a tacit commitment from the scholar of diasporas. To see why, we need first to acknowledge that within the discourse of political science and of worldly political practice, "power" is to "politics" as "market" is to "economics." In both cases, the first term is indispensable to the practice of the second, yet it can be elusive and polymorphous. There are many kinds of power and markets in different times and places, but it would be very difficult indeed to consider politics and economics without alluding to them, changeable and slippery as they are.

In the case of the modern politics of nation-states as practiced since the eighteenth century, "power" has meant "state power," and it has presupposed, in turn, the gathering and focusing of several kinds of resources. The first of these resources has been a delimited *territory*, which is metaphorically considered the body that houses the nation and its spirit. Such a territory is not just land—not real estate that can be traded, like some Louisiana or Alaska territory—but a sacred whole that must remain indivisible, sovereign, not open to forced entry, the body-homeland of national soul and essence. The people that dwells on this territory, however diverse it may be, is conceived as situated in a narrative trajectory that will eventually eliminate problematic differences, so that all inhabitants will form members of one society and the people a nation, sharing rights, duties, a single standard language, and a unitary culture. Such a population is converted by the Foucauldian "bio-power" of censuses, categorized and disciplined, encouraged to proliferate, to be economically productive, and to provide citizen-soldiers as necessary. Territory, population, a unified national society—these produce economic, military, and cultural power that can sustain the security and sovereignty of the nation and the state and that can be projected externally when necessary. This is the first meaning of "power" in the discourse of political science, where "politics" is the process by which elites attain the levers of this power and exercise it to achieve their own interests and, in good times, those of the mass of citizens.

On the face of it, this prevailing notion of power and politics cannot be applicable to diasporas. They very rarely dominate a territory.[10] Their culture rarely remains pure and

---

9. Tölöyan, "Rethinking Diaspora(s)," 32–33 n. 21.

10. There are at least two striking exceptions: Cilicia, a territory in what is now southern Turkey, was once inhabited by Greeks and Syriac-speaking peoples, yet came to be dominated by immigrant Armenians and was the site of a principate, later a kingdom, ruled entirely by Armenians between 1071 and 1375 C.E. Singapore was a thinly populated, marshy island, which is now a multiethnic state dominated by diasporic Chinese. Of course, if we agree to consider colonizing settler populations as diasporas, then "diasporic power" radically expands its range and meaning. Robin Cohen and Leonard

homogeneous. Over time, diasporas acquire the characteristics of the different societies of settlement and thus become "impure," heterogeneous, diverse—most diasporans are bicultural, and most long-lived diasporas develop hybrid cultures and subjects. Language is often the first casualty of migration and resettlement. As to the economic element of power, though some diasporas develop wealthy merchant or financial elites, they cannot claim powers of taxation—one of the two foundations of state power. The other element, the Weberian monopoly on violence, also remains exclusively the state's prerogative.

How, then, is it possible to argue that, on occasion, mobilized diasporas—unlike other transnational dispersions—develop stateless power? Because power is more complex than state power crudely conceived (formidable and decisive as state power can be in wars, genocides, expropriations and nationalizations of the property of diasporas, etc.). The complexity of alternative forms of power has been theorized by a variety of thinkers since Macchiavelli, but particularly in the twentieth century by Georg Simmel, Michel Foucault, Anthony Giddens, and Steven Lukes. The elements of their thought that are relevant to my argument—concerning the ability of diasporas to possess and wield stateless power—all have to do with reconceptualizing power not merely as a rich treasury, a large GDP (gross domestic product), and a powerful army, the chief agents of *realpolitik*, but as a set of relations that can constrain or enable. We are of course familiar with such: A court may have the power to order a prisoner's execution, but legal arguments may dissuade the state from carrying out the sentence, from exercising its power of life and death. Territory, treasury, and armies are not the determining factors here. Once power is understood as an endlessly ongoing interaction/relation among many actors, an interaction in which the flow itself alters the space of action and where personal wealth or wealth voluntarily concentrated into communal hands, along with skills, ideas, will, and determination also play a role, it becomes clear that well-organized, self-consciously theorizing, and dedicated diasporas can exercise some forms of power. Such power can be deployed to secure the interests of a particular diaspora community in the competition of interests between minorities and elites that characterize the United States and Canada, above all, but also, increasingly, other diversified societies and nation-states, as well. It may also be used to lobby for the interests of another, kin community of the diaspora embedded in another society. Finally, specific diasporic communities or an entire transnational diaspora may seek to act in ways that benefit a homeland.

In what follows, in order to explore how diasporic agency—or stateless power—can become relevant to both the home state in which the diaspora is situated and to the homeland, I will focus on certain actions of the Armenian diaspora during a conflict into which the emerging (1988–91) and then newly independent post-Soviet Republic

---

Tennenhouse have argued that there may be good reasons for doing so. See Robin Cohen, *Global Diasporas* (Seattle: University of Washington Press, 1997), and Leonard Tennenhouse, *The Importance of Feeling English: American Literature and the British Diaspora, 1750–1850* (Princeton, NJ: Princeton University Press, 2007).

of Armenia was drawn (1991–94).[11] Some years ago, Gurharpal Singh, a scholar of the Sikh diaspora, wondered whether a diaspora autonomously initiates political moves that affect the homeland and the conflicts in which it becomes involved, or whether its agency is reactive and leads it only to respond and contribute to initiatives emerging from the homeland. In a memorable phrase, he asked: "is the [Sikh] diaspora the leading actor, or is it a weathervane responding to developments in Punjab and India?"[12] There is no general, theoretical answer to this question, but I believe that my Armenian example will demonstrate that diasporas may both act and react.

How Diasporas Deploy Power to Assist Their Homelands

In the period of post-Soviet globalization, scholars of international relations and of the emerging discipline of diaspora studies have focused on the ways in which contemporary diasporas become active agents in international politics.[13] Whether the investigation is framed in the discourse of international relations or with the concepts of diaspora studies, scholars usually focus on a small number of political activities that result from the solidarity that mobilized, transnational ethnic groups—"diasporas"—feel toward homelands caught up in conflict.

The most visible of these activities is the lobbying through which diasporas address the governments of the countries of which they are citizens with the intention of inducing them to conduct policies favorable to their kin states or ancestral homelands. (Such activity may leave diasporas vulnerable to charges of multiple and divided loyalties.) The second activity consists of diasporic attempts to influence the media and public debate of the countries they inhabit with the intention of having their homelands (and the causes or conflicts they are engaged in) represented in a favorable light. The third, most heterogeneous activity includes, for example, appeals to supranational organizations such as the United Nations or engagement with and investment in transnational nongovernmental organizations (NGOs) in order to further the security, health, environmental, or

---

11. The tradition in diaspora studies is to refer to the "hostland" and the "homeland," but I find that usage untenable. It is wrong to refer to the United States as the "host" of Jews and Armenians whose ancestors arrived, say, in 1887, 120 years ago, and who are fourth-generation Americans. The so-called "hostland" is their home. What I am calling the "homeland" was once the home of their ancestors, toward which diasporans retain loyalties and attachments. In the past five years, I have increasingly heard young diasporans utter some variation of a remark that I first heard twice within a month of each other in 2002, once at an Armenian American gathering in Watertown, MA, and again at an international conference in Poitiers, France. "My home is the USA; the homeland of my ancestors (Armenia, Israel) is the other country that I care about a lot."

12. Gurharpal Singh, "A Victim Diaspora? The Case of the Sikhs," *Diaspora: A Journal of Transnational Studies* 8, no. 3 (1999): 293–308.

13. Gabriel Sheffer and the contributors to the volume he edited, *Modern Diasporas in International Politics* (1986; New York: St. Martin's Press, 2002), did pioneering work. He and Yossi Shain have been the most systematic students of the connections between diasporas and international affairs. In *Identity and Global Politics: Theoretical and Empirical Elaborations* (New York: Palgrave Macmillan, 2004), Patricia F. Goff and Kevin C. Dunn provide an overview of the ways in which the attempt to exercise diasporic political power is often motivated by "identitarian" concerns. Identitarian concerns and political actions reciprocally shape each other.

developmental aims of homelands. Fourth, at least some diasporas seek to influence the behavior of the governments of their original homelands or kin states, especially during the transitional phase that marks the passage to sovereignty, for example, in Armenia after the collapse of the Soviet Union. Some diasporas working from within Western democracies do so with the intention of furthering democracy. Often, the definition and consequences of the form of democracy promoted by the diaspora are shaped by the interests and pressures of the host state. Finally, some diasporas have agendas—usually grouped under the label of nationalism—that seem problematic to many Western scholars and governments. Their diasporic attempts to influence homeland governments or to contribute to and intervene in the economic, social, and cultural life of the homeland may have as their goal the strengthening of a particular form of national identity in both the homeland and the diaspora.

Our understanding of the workings of the power and agency of diasporas can be extended by looking into the specific case of the struggle between Armenia and the neighboring state of Azerbaijan over Karabagh.[14] Karabagh was a part of historic Armenia that was ruled for centuries by Turks, Persians, and Russians. The vast majority of the population was Armenian, but Joseph Stalin, pursuing a policy of creating multiethnic Soviet Socialist Republics that were internally divided, placed the region inside Azerbaijan (which also ruled a region, Nakhichevan, entirely cut off from Azerbaijan, as Karabagh was from Armenia). In 1988, the Armenians of Karabagh, following Soviet law, sought to benefit from Mikhail Gorbachev's declared policies of *perestroika* and *glasnost*, voted to secede from the Azerbaijani Soviet Socialist Republic, and requested permission to join the Armenian Soviet Socialist Republic (SSR). This was denied by Moscow and was followed by repression and massacres exercised by the Azerbaijani majority against Armenians living in and near the country's capital. The hostilities between the Armenians and Azerbaijan, which began in February 1988 as a local political struggle, soon was militarized, escalating from clashes and massacres into a war, then was slowed down by a cease-fire in 1994 and remains unresolved, even as the attempts to broker a peace have become fully internationalized and involve Russia, Turkey, the European Union, and the United States, as well as the Armenian diaspora.[15]

---

14. The long prehistory of this conflict is adequately covered in Levon Chorbajian, Patrick Donabedian, and Claude Mutafian, *The Caucasian Knot: The History and Geopolitics of Nagorno-Karabagh* (London: Zed, 1994), and Thomas de Waal, *Black Garden: Armenia and Azerbaijan through Peace and War* (New York: New York University Press, 2003). It should be noted that the region named "Karabagh" in this paper is called "Artsakh" in Armenian and "NKR," the Nagorny-Karabagh Republic (that is, the Mountainous-Karabagh Republic) by Russians. They are identical.

15. By now, there is a considerable literature in Armenian on this war, scattered in the diaspora's numerous newspapers. In English, there are useful articles by Edward Walker, "No Peace, No War in the Caucasus: Secessionist Conflicts in Chechnya, Abkhazia and Nagorno-Karabakh," Occasional Papers of the Strengthening Democratic Institutions Project (Cambridge, MA: Harvard Center for Science and International Affairs, 1998), and Charles King, "The Benefits of Ethnic War: Understanding Eurasia's Unrecognized States," *World Politics* 53 (2001): 524–552, and helpful books by de Waal, *Black Garden*, and Dov Lynch, *Engaging Eurasia's Separatist States: Unresolved Conflicts and De Facto States* (Washington, DC: United States Institute of Peace Press, 2004). However, even Lynch's excellent analysis lacks a thorough understanding of the Armenian diaspora's role.

Diasporic Political Action in the West

There is a degree of scholarly consensus that the early years of the transition of Armenia from Soviet rule were the ones during which diaspora communities were most able to influence events. The spheres of the diaspora's action include the military, the political, the economic, the humanitarian-philanthropic, and the discursive and cultural sphere of debates over national identity. All of these, in turn, influenced the less easily defined psychosocial realm of collective morale and will in the homeland's combat zones.

As the conflict began, the intrastate Karabagh diaspora[16] was the first to act. Estimates of the number of its members range from one hundred and fifty thousand to three hundred thousand; in 1988 there were sizeable groups in Baku, Azerbaijan, as well as in Armenia, Georgia, and Russia proper. Karabagh Armenians speak a dialect that is nearly unintelligible to speakers of the two major standard Armenian dialects. They tend to be fluent in Russian and to identify themselves in the intrastate diaspora as being specifically from Karabagh. This diaspora became active immediately after February 20, 1988, when the representatives of the Armenian majority of what was then, officially, the Nagorny-Karabagh Autonomous Region (with a 78.5 percent Armenian population of roughly one hundred and forty-five thousand and a 21.0 percent population of roughly forty thousand Azeris) resolved to petition that the USSR's Supreme Soviet approve the administrative transfer of the region from the Azerbaijani SSR to the Armenian SSR. The speed with which the Karabagh diaspora began to agitate for support of the resolution suggests the strength of the links maintained with the homeland leadership. Off-the-record conversations confirm the likelihood of prior coordination. Between 1988 and the collapse of the USSR at the end of 1991, several members of the Karabagh diaspora, above all Igor Mouratian, played a significant role in generating political support in Armenia and among Russophone Armenians in Russia.[17]

What is less frequently mentioned in the English-language literature and not at all understood by diaspora specialists is the crucial *military* role played by the intrastate Armenian diaspora of the USSR, especially by the descendants of emigrants from Karabagh. The Armenian leadership of Karabagh proper was unprepared for the armed response by the Azerbaijani police and the militia of the Ministry of the Interior, let alone the full-scale war that developed as the USSR began to collapse. This lack of preparation was due to the fact that at the outset, the Armenian leadership viewed itself as initiating a political and administrative transfer, not a futile armed rebellion against the Soviet state. Given the lack of preparedness, intrastate diasporic assistance was indis-

---

16. "Intrastate" diasporas are those that exist within the borders of a multinational, often "imperial" state that rules the homeland. In the USSR, there were around 1.5 million Armenians who lived outside the Armenian SSR but within the USSR's borders as an intrastate diaspora.

17. Abel Aghanbekian, head of an important economics institute and adviser to Gorbachev, is of Karabagh origin. Russian in outlook and speech, he is said to have cautiously supported the transfer of Karabagh to Armenian sovereignty. If so, he illustrates the way in which almost fully assimilated ethnics can, in moments of crisis, develop diasporic attitudes and rally to the homeland.

pensable. Early in the conflict, the diasporic communities in the Crimea, Moscow, and later the Armenian community of Abkhazia, eighty to one hundred thousand strong, sent crucial assistance in the form of weapons and money to purchase weapons on the black market.[18] But what enabled first the ragtag Karabagh forces and then Armenia's own militia to become a disciplined army that was more rapidly professionalized than Azerbaijan's better-financed and better-armed forces were the intradiasporic Karabagh and Russian Armenian officers, along with local NCOs and ordinary soldiers who had gained experience while fighting in Afghanistan. The appendix to this article offers data on such high-ranking officers, but four others who played a pivotal role early on must be discussed here. Then-Colonel and now Major General Arkady Ter-Tatevosian, born in the Karabagh diaspora of Georgia, was probably the first high-ranking officer to take retirement from the Soviet Army (in 1990) and move to Karabagh, where he eventually became chief of staff of the defense forces. Colonel General Gurgen Dalibaltayan, also born in Georgia, retired in 1991 from his post as deputy commander for combat training of the North Caucasus Military District, then moved to Armenia, where he became chief of staff of the Armenian Army and later its inspector general. Colonel General Norad Ter-Grigoriants, born in the Russian Armenian diaspora, formerly deputy chief of staff of Soviet ground forces, moved to Armenia in 1992 and served as a staff officer. Finally, Colonel General Mikayel Haroutunian, born in Azerbaijan, formerly chief lecturer on reconnaissance in the Academy of the Soviet General Staff, moved to Armenia in 1992 and became chief of staff of Armenia's armed forces. The expertise of these officers contributed to the ability of the Karabagh forces to recover from initial setbacks in 1988–92 and to win in 1993 and 1994.

In addition, a handful of ordinary combatants and several officers came to fight in Karabagh from Lebanon, France, and the United States (see the Appendix). Of these, Monte Melkonian—a Californian who had earlier joined an Armenian terrorist movement—was a charismatic leader who fascinated diaspora Armenians by the depth of his commitment and his eloquence about it. From Lebanon, a handful of fighters trained during the long Lebanese civil war of 1975–90 also went to Karabagh. What made them significant is that several, including Lieutenant Colonel Jirair Sefilian, had been cadres of the diaspora-based Dashnak political party, which has always prided itself on its heroes and martyrs. Two who were killed in Karabagh continue to be remembered by the Lebanese Armenian diaspora community as embodiments of the spirit of sacrifice that is a key element of diasporic discourse in general and Dashnak Party culture in particular. Commemoration rituals have an essential role in the consolidation of the Armenian diaspora everywhere.

---

18. A small, but symbolically important shipment of weapons—250 Kalashnikovs—was sent from Lebanon in 1991, according to two scholars familiar with local fighters in Karabagh. A resourceful and prosperous Armenian from Greece is also generally acknowledged to have been responsible for crucial early shipments of weapons, for which he was decorated by the de facto state of Karabagh. The identities of diaspora Armenians involved in these acts are known, but not published for security reasons.

As the struggle continued, diasporic politics emerged as an important factor. There have been two kinds of diasporic activity, one having to do with lobbying the government of the United States and other governments, the second with attempts by three diasporic political organizations to become registered, election-contesting parties in Armenia. In the former sphere, the strongest contribution has been that of the U.S. Armenian community, which, in the decade from 1972 to 1982, had already organized to lobby for its interests in Washington, DC and in particular to press the U.S. government to acknowledge the Turkish genocide of the Armenians during World War I. After 1988, although genocide-related lobbying continued, lobbying on behalf of the diplomatic and economic interests of Armenia and Karabagh became primary. Two lobbies have operated quite effectively.[19] One, the Armenian National Committee, represents the Dashnak Party's viewpoint. The other, the Armenian Assembly of America, was always well-funded by a small group of wealthy contributors, but is now broadening its initially narrower popular base. It was the primary architect of Section 907 of the Freedom Support Act, signed into law on October 24, 1992, as Public Law 102-551.

The strictly material effect of Section 907 was not great, because Azerbaijan is a major source of oil. The law placed restrictions on some kinds and amounts of aid that the United States could extend to Azerbaijan, while significant nonmilitary assistance ($80 to $105 million per year) went unimpeded to Armenia, where it made a real contribution to the Armenian economy. At the same time, fiscally trivial, but symbolically and politically significant U.S. funds also went to Karabagh. After years of Azerbaijani and Turkish lobbying and White House pressure, in October 2001, in the aftermath of 9/11, Congress loosened and modified, but did not entirely rescind the restrictions. The president can now waive, at his discretion, the restrictions for a one-year period on the grounds that aid to Azerbaijan would serve overriding national security interests. Each year since January 25, 2002, the White House has waived the section.

Section 907 has come to stand for all the efforts of the U.S. Armenian diaspora to secure political and diplomatic support for Karabagh's right to self-determination. A remarkably large proportion of the experts I consulted before writing this article, both in Armenia and in the diaspora, identify it as a major factor in the conflict, shaping the homeland's diplomacy and morale to some degree. It has come to stand for (and sometimes even has led to a lack of recognition of) other important actions by the U.S. diaspora, such as its success in speeding recognition of the Republic of Armenia and especially in establishing a fully functioning embassy in Washington, DC, at a time when the republic lacked the funds to purchase an appropriate building. Even the stubbornly continuing, if ultimately unsuccessful attempts of the U.S. lobbies (as well as French and

---

19. One index of this effectiveness is the size of the Armenian Caucus in the House of Representatives. As of November 1, 2007, 159 members of congress, or 36.6 per cent of the total, belonged to it. See http://www.anca.org/legislative_center/armenian_caucus.php (last accessed November 30, 2007), Armenians make up 0.3 percent of the total U.S. population. At one point in October 2007, some 220 congressmen indicated a willingness to vote for an Armenian-backed genocide resolution opposed by the White House.

Canadian Armenian lobbies) to obtain recognition for the genocide committed by Ottoman Turkey trouble Azerbaijan, not only because of its close identification with Turkey, but also because the persistence and near success of the enterprise are taken as evidence of Armenian diasporic power.[20]

In related efforts, the U.S. diaspora combined political work and financial assistance to enable the emergent de facto state of Karabagh to maintain offices and representatives in Washington, Moscow, and Paris. No other Eurasian separatist state—Abkhazia, South Ossetia, Transdnistria, let alone Chechnya—enjoys the level of quasi-official representation in several capitals that Karabagh has enjoyed since the collapse of the USSR, thanks primarily to the efforts of the Armenian diaspora. During this time, members of Congress belonging to the Armenian Caucus have repeatedly spoken out in favor of Karabagh's self-determination on the floor of the House. United Kingdom notables such as Lady Caroline Cox have frequently visited the area on humanitarian missions while calling attention to the unresolved conflict and what a just resolution of it might be. Even after the waiver of Section 907, the Armenian diaspora continues to send delegations to Karabagh that are sometimes accompanied by members of the U.S. Congress and by French officials, without asking for Azerbaijan's permission. This has an effect in Azerbaijan, which protests each visit to the region, over which it retains de jure sovereignty. Together, these events serve as a reminder that if the "front" in the conflict is the cease-fire line, the "home front" of Karabagh encompasses both Armenia and significant portions of the Armenian diaspora.

Overall, these efforts have kept Azerbaijan, Turkey, and their allies in Washington aware that the U.S. Armenian diaspora, in particular, has been, is, and will remain a factor in the debate about what U.S. actions in the Transcaucasus would best serve America's interest. One of the scholars interviewed anonymously for this article recalled a closed seminar in the United Kingdom in 1997 during which UK officials criticized the senior participating U.S. diplomat for failing to overturn Section 907. Exasperated, the official replied: "If you had to deal with a million Armenian citizens every day, you'd behave differently, too." Although the true figure is closer to eight hundred thousand, the remark encapsulates a reality. The U.S. Armenian diaspora is an actor in the political arena where the interests of the United States in the Karabagh conflict are formulated. This participation may be more important than the exact tally of votes won and lost in individual cases. It matters to the mobilization of the diaspora in the United States and elsewhere (especially in France and, now, increasingly, at the headquarters of the European Union in Brussels). It almost certainly matters to the calculations of Azerbaijan and Turkey. And it has certainly strengthened, albeit to an incalculable degree, the political will of Armenia and Karabagh, to which we must now turn.

---

20. Armenian diasporic groups have achieved partial successes in "genocide recognition" in Uruguay, Argentina, the Parliament of the European Union, France, Canada, and Germany.

Diasporic Influence on the Republic of Armenia

The diaspora's political actions have not been limited to lobbying outside the homeland. They have extended to Armenia proper. In February 1988, the Karabagh movement began. In December 1988, a catastrophic earthquake rocked northern Armenia. Both were badly handled by Gorbachev's government. From then until December 1991, the diaspora sent medical and humanitarian assistance at the same time that its organizations interceded politically, both abroad and in the homeland. (The latter was regarded by many locals as interference.) Diaspora groups (especially from France) exerted effective pressure on Gorbachev, through the European media and the EU Parliament, to free the arrested members of the Karabagh committee, whose leadership, headed by Levon Ter-Petrosyan, later became the first government of Armenia. Several diaspora organizations that rarely cooperate nevertheless signed a joint statement calling on homeland Armenians who were advocating independence to move cautiously, arguing that the Soviet Army was the guarantor that Turkey and Azerbaijan together would not launch an attack, even a second genocide. The appeal was not heeded, and it became a paradigm for many in Armenia for what they came to view as the negative nature of some of the diaspora's political actions. By contrast, in the diaspora, ignorance of local dynamics combined with insistent advice resulted in indignation when diasporic views were not welcomed. The path of homeland-diaspora interaction has been rocky.

Soon after 1988, the major diasporic organizations felt the need to be active in Armenia through their own official representatives. Faced with the likelihood that the diaspora's political dynamic would itself undergo massive upheaval in response to the homeland's move toward independence, they wished to have a role in the process, and so they invested funds and sent personnel to Armenia in order to secure a foothold on the ground where questions of Armenian identity as well as transnational politics would henceforth be contested.[21] The Ramgavar Party (the Armenian Democratic Liberals) failed to establish a strong position, but a newspaper it launched, *Azg* (Nation), is now one of the most trusted and influential in Armenia. The diasporic Dashnak Party contested the first presidential election, in which it won an embarrassing 4.5 percent of the vote, but it persisted, was prosecuted by the government for reasons and in circumstances that remain obscure, and has since recovered. It participates in parliamentary elections (in the most recent of which it won 13 percent of the vote), is currently a junior partner of President Kocharian's government, in which it holds some ministerial posts,

---

21. Diasporic intellectuals, artists, scholars, and political leaders all realize that henceforth, new diasporic Armenian identities and commitments will be shaped to some extent in Armenia and Karabagh, as well as through the transnational migration and cultural circuits that are rapidly altering Armenia's own identity. The uneven, but reciprocal penetration of the homeland by the diaspora and of the diaspora by the homeland continues. Many citizens of the Republic of Armenia emigrate, and Armenia establishes embassies in countries with large diaspora populations. Meanwhile, diasporic organizations increase their presence in the homeland, with cadres, media, money, ideologies. In "American Jews and the Construction of Israel's Jewish Identity," *Diaspora: A Journal of Transnational Studies* 9, no. 2 (2000): 163–202, Yossi Shain closely examines analogous Jewish diasporic penetration of Israeli society.

and functions as an extraordinary transnational organization, both global and local, with offices in communities ranging from Los Angeles, Washington, DC, and New York to Paris, Moscow, Yerevan, Beirut, Teheran, and beyond.

Meanwhile, as in other formerly Communist countries, ranging from Estonia to Croatia, talented and ambitious diaspora individuals went to work in Armenia. Both the first foreign minister of Armenia, Raffi Hovannisian, and the long-serving current foreign minister, Vartan Oskanian, are diaspora Armenians, as is Jivan Tabibian, Armenia's ambassador to Austria, and as was Sebouh Tashjian, another minister. Hovannisian, who remains active in Armenia, resigned from President Ter Petrosyan's government over a dispute concerning the extent to which the question of genocide could be tacitly put aside in order to make negotiations with Turkey more productive. His brief tenure established one of the paradigmatic problems that haunt Armenia's relations with the diaspora, where so many are descendants of genocide survivors. Whereas in Armenia, the danger to Karabagh is primarily and correctly understood as the danger of ethnic cleansing (Azerbaijan wants the land of Karabagh without Armenians), in the diaspora, the ethnic cleansing is viewed through the exterminatory lens of genocide itself, to which the appropriate response is "Never again." This attitude underpins many diasporic Armenians' commitment to Karabagh.

The diasporic Hovannisian's career can be usefully contrasted with that of another diasporan, Jirair Gerard Libaridian, a Lebanese-born U.S. citizen who became, with Levon Ter-Petrosyan, the architect of Armenia's foreign policy and its most important negotiator on Karabagh during the first five years of Armenia's independence. The aim and achievement of this foreign policy was to maintain balance, to secure U.S. aid (an average of close to $100 million a year) with the help of the U.S. Armenian lobby while also securing Russian assistance to arm both Karabagh's and Armenia's military, to establish full diplomatic relations with Turkey (an effort rebuffed by Ankara), and to find a formula that would let Azerbaijan retain de jure sovereignty over the region while also accommodating the near independence of the de facto state that has emerged. This effort came close to success, but ultimately failed because of multiple forms of intransigence in Turkey and Azerbaijan and among many Armenians. An important faction in Armenia, backed by the Dashnak Party and much of the diaspora's public opinion, believed and continues to believe that time is on Karabagh's side, that Russia's restored power and its willingness to help Armenia, along with hoped-for resettlement in Karabagh and prosperity in Armenia, will eventually create irreversible geographical, economic, demographic, and political facts on the ground.

Azerbaijan's leadership has been at least equally misled by a notion that time is on its side. Several factors have contributed to this conclusion. Baku has come to believe that oil wealth, plus the Western arms (especially air power) that wealth will buy, will eventually result in military superiority. Its optimism about the future also results from a belief that assistance from Turkey and the United States will continue, even as Russian influence in the region weakens. Finally, this optimism about the future counts on the abiding primacy of the principle of territorial integrity. President Levon Ter-Petrosyan predicted in 1994, in an interview with me, that each side's belief that "time is on our side" would lead to what he called, in Armenian, "Kipratsoom"—"Cyprusization." It appears that he was right. A faction of the diaspora, most vigorously but not exclusively represented by the Dashnak Party, has had a significant, though not determining role in the process of promoting that view and freezing the situation.

The differences between the positions taken by Ter-Petrosyan and Libaridian and those held by both the Dashnak Party and many others in the diaspora have been constitutive, determining the approaches of many diasporic groups to conflict resolution. For the first camp, of which Libaridian has been the most eloquent theorist, distinctions between the proper roles of the government of Armenia and of the diaspora are and must remain clearly demarcated. This camp views Armenia's government as primarily the government of the citizens of Armenia, responsible for them and obligated to prioritize their interests and issues. By contrast, many in the diaspora look for leaders in Armenia who will commit themselves not just to local citizens, but also to the interests of "the Armenian people/nation," terms that encompass ethnic Armenians living in Armenia, Karabagh, *and* the diaspora. They imply that they have the best insight into the pannational (*hamazgayin*) interests at stake in the Karabagh conflict. This position is partly shared by those in Armenia's government and elites who either sincerely agree with it or, more commonly, profess agreement because they believe that to declare solidarity with the view strengthens their position as they pursue more local interests. Still others, both in the homeland and in the diaspora, oppose the position taken by Ter-Petrosyan and Libaridian because they think, rightly, that the way it was articulated unnecessarily alienated the diaspora. Individuals holding one or more of these positions currently influence current President Kocharian's policy, paying lip service to the notion that, though the combatants in the conflict are locals, the cause is pannational.

In the early 1990s in Karabagh, the diasporic Dashnak Party assisted and influenced several of the early dissidents, fighters, and administrative leaders of the emerging regime. Once again, this was a case not of a diaspora organization shaping local realities, but rather of meshing with and so to some extent directing an already existing movement. Here, as in Armenia, it is essential to underscore that the positions of the diaspora and/or of the Dashnak Party have not been decisive on their own. Rather, dominant diasporic factions have formed alliances with some major factions in Armenia, who fought and won the battles. Rhetoric and convenience shape that alliance as much as, or more than, fully shared views. Part of the ongoing political, ideological, and cultural contestation has to do with whether those views will converge and become a new, hegemonic, transnational Armenian view of the political interests at stake in the Karabagh conflict.

No overview of the diaspora's influence on the Karabagh conflict as it involved Armenia can neglect the economic dimension. First, the two Armenian lobbies in Washington have been crucial in securing well over $1 billion in U.S. aid for Armenia since 1991. A small part of that would have gone to Armenia without such lobbying, but not most of it. That averages about $86.5 million a year for a government whose budget sank to less than $200 million in U.S. dollars at its nadir in 1994 and whose gross domestic product was $1.2 billion. By 2005, the budget had grown to $900 million and the GDP to $4.86 billion, but dependence on diasporic sources remains strong. As of September 2007, remittances to Armenia from Armenians working abroad remain the largest source of foreign currency and are estimated at $1.2 billion for the first nine months of the year,[22] more than one-fifth of the GDP.[23] Tourism (318,000 in 2005, mostly by Armenians, either post-1988 emigrants returning for a visit or members of the older diaspora) contributed an estimated $250 million to the GDP. Philanthropic diaspora organizations such as the Hayastan Fund, the AGBU (the Armenian General Benevolent Union), the United Armenian Fund, and the Armenian Relief Society have also contributed millions, though here the figures are less reliable because much of the assistance came in the form of donated goods, from ageing kidney dialysis machines, to computers, to clothes and medications. These have approached the $1 billion range.

In these various ways, both the older Armenian diaspora and the newer one that has emerged as a result of labor migration from post-Soviet Armenia since 1991 contribute significantly to Armenia's economy. These sums are of material significance. They raise morale and the will to resist an unfavorable settlement of the Karabagh issue. And that difference in morale has been a major factor throughout the conflict. Not surprisingly, Azerbaijan's leadership has taken steps to promote the organization of its own dispersed emigrant populations into a diaspora.[24]

What does this record of diasporic influence on Armenia and Karabagh enable us to say about the future? First, that, though the diaspora does not speak with one voice, some solidarities emerge around certain positions: I know of no group that envisages a simple return of Karabagh to Azerbaijani control—a control that is universally regarded as guaranteeing bureaucratic persecution that would coerce Armenians to emigrate from the territory until they were ethnically cleansed. This consensus forms the core ground for cooperation both between diasporic factions and between the diaspora and Armenia. In addition, homeland and diaspora Armenians agree that the security of Armenia and Karabagh must be guaranteed by creating a situation in which violence and economic blockade will no longer continue to coerce Armenians into leaving their ancestral lands.

Beyond such a consensus, diasporic views diverge. Most groups agree on the importance of "well-crafted third party mediation" between Armenia and its enemies.[25] The

---

22. Armenpress news release, October 11, 2007, "Money Remittances to Armenia in Nine Months Reach $1.2 Billion." Posted on-line on the Groong Armenian News Network, October 12, 2007, http://groong.usc.edu (last accessed November 20, 2007).

23. In "Migrant Money Flow," in the *New York Times* of November 18, 2007, Jason DeParle writes that the share of Armenians' GDP that stems from remittances is 19 percent, very close to the one-fifth estimated above. "Week in Review section," 3.

24. See http://www.regnum.ru/english/607105.htmli (last accessed November 20, 2007).

25. Lynch, *Engaging Eurasia's Separatist States*, ix.

diasporic Armenian Assembly organization and the shapers of Armenian foreign policy have both felt that involving the Organization for Security and Co-operation in Europe, especially Russia, the United States, and France, is likely to guarantee a more just mediation, even if it might take longer to achieve unanimity. Interestingly, much of the leadership of the diaspora as well as of the homeland is wary of advocating mediation by one country, even if that were Russia, currently Armenia's ally. In this, the Armenian parties to the Karabagh conflict differ significantly from Western theorists of conflict resolution. Although agreeing that conflicts may be resolved more rapidly when the number of influential secondary parties to the conflict is kept small, they believe that a just and lasting peace requires multinational participation, endorsement, and guarantees.

On other issues, such as the form and direction of state building in Armenia and Karabagh during and after the conflict, there is more disagreement: Presidencies on the Yeltsin-Putin model, which weaken the parliament in which the Dashnaks have power, are, unsurprisingly, opposed by the Dashnaks. More and more diasporic intellectuals are voicing their unease about corruption (which is easy to condemn in general terms) and governmental abuse of concentrated power, both because these are immoral in themselves and because they lead to the disillusionment of the general population, who may come to neglect the distinction between fighting for Karabagh and fighting for corrupt elites that rule in Armenia. A similar disenchantment of ordinary Azeris with their own oil-rich elites also exists; curiously, this may contribute to the freezing of the conflict, because neither side is eager to test the true resolve of immiserated and disenchanted populations during active and prolonged combat. In earlier years, the crisis of war and economic blockade silenced criticism because there was a country to be saved. Now that there is a state to build and a society to be reconstituted, the diversity of opinion is becoming more vocal. It is helpful to recall that diasporas often sustain their homelands while opposing particular governmental measures. Such opposition is now emerging in the Armenian diaspora.

Three final generalizations can be ventured. First, the diaspora feels itself to be important to Armenia and Karabagh and to the ability of both to resist a resolution of the conflict that is unjust to Armenians. Armenia's leadership tries to downplay that (sense of) importance while maximizing the forms of support it can extract by accommodating it to some degree. President Kocharian's current regime, more than former President Ter-Petrosyan's, understands that to maximize the diaspora's contributions requires not puncturing its sense of importance, even when it would be possible and justifiable on some specific occasions to do so. Vartan Oskanian, the foreign minister, himself of diaspora origin, has proved adept in this matter. Second, any diasporic group's attempt to influence either Armenia or Karabagh is maximized when it can ally itself with a local group strong enough to establish a movement, but not strong enough to win by itself. Smaller diaspora groups that lack resources to bring to the homeland table in order to make a consequential difference cannot find partners and are sidelined—that is what happened to the Hnchags, an old and once prestigious diasporic political organization (founded 1887), which has been unable to insert itself into the power structure in Armenia. Third, the major diasporic lobbies and organizations (including new ones emerging in Moscow) will have a role to play in reminding the likely international mediators that "settlement is possible only if it is premised on some form of acceptance of the current existence of the de facto states."[26]

At the moment, as diaspora money and other forms of assistance continue to flow to Armenia, there is no agreement either in the diaspora or in the homeland about how the settlement of the Karabagh conflict is to be accomplished, because each action that reinforces the de facto state can have a backlash. For example, some in Armenia and many in the diaspora opt for increasing the settlement of Armenians, not only in Karabagh, but also in the areas of historical Karabagh that are now occupied by Armenians, but were not within the borders of the pre-1988 region. As the Israeli example shows, the settlement of occupied territories is a double-edged sword. On the one hand, it alters the facts on the ground and forces those in Azerbaijan and the West who continue to wish to deny Karabagh its proper place at the negotiating table, and who wish to minimize Armenia's power, to take both into account. But to construct such facts on the ground is also to give a hostages to the future. It becomes ever more traumatic to dislodge settlers, who themselves resist, as does a diaspora that fears that the settlements, roads, canals, and power lines it has funded will be torn up by bulldozers or turned over to the other side. The key problem, for the diaspora, for Armenia, and for Azerbaijan is to see that time is not predictably on anyone's side.

While that problem remains unsolved, the diaspora and its allied faction—and it is only a faction—in Armenia's government have succeeded in changing the law of citizenship in Armenia. The constitution forbade dual citizenship; now, provisions are about to be put into place that make it possible for many Armenians to hold dual citizenship.[27] Once again, the effect of this change is not clear. Many diaspora Armenians who are eager to hold some form of citizenship have no desire to settle in Armenia or to serve in its army, but hold the symbolic recognition by the state of their commitment to the homeland to be indispensable. The diaspora has demonstrated the surprising efficacy, but also the clear limits of its stateless power to the Armenian state, as well as to Western states. We are now at a moment in which each agent is recalculating what it can demand of the other and deliver to the other. It is a testimonial to the importance of the Armenian diaspora—and, by extension, other mobilized diasporas—that their stateless power participates in such circulations of power.

---

26. Ibid., 9.

27. Anna Ohanyan, "The Developmental Value of Dual citizenship for Armenia," *Diaspora: A Journal of Transnational Studies* 13, nos. 2–3 (2004) offers a history of the debate and struggle concerning various forms of such citizenship both in Armenia (where many oppose it) and in the diaspora (where most favor it) and argues that the new law will help Armenia develop much more rapidly if and only if the government alters institutions and behaviors in Armenia.

Appendix: High-Ranking Diasporic Officers Who Joined the Armed Forces of Armenia or Karabagh.

Major General Enriko Apriyamov. Born in Georgia. He commanded a Soviet missile artillery division. Moved to Armenia in 1992, where he serves as deputy chief of staff of the armed forces.

Lieutenant General Hrachya Andreasian. Born in Russia, former chief representative of the Warsaw Pact headquarters to the Czechoslovak armed forces. Retired in 1990, moved to Armenia in 1992, served as chief of staff of the armed forces. Died in 1999.

Major General Vagharshak Haroutyunian. Born in Georgia, served as a naval captain, second rank, in the Soviet Pacific Fleet. Moved to Armenia in 1991. Served as Armenia's representative to Russia, and as defense minister. Discharged, lives in Yerevan.

Lieutenant General Khristofor Ivanian. Born in Georgia. A veteran of World War II, he served as director of a Soviet artillery and missile school and retired in 1979 to live in Leningrad. Moved to Karabagh in 1992, where he served as chief of staff of the defense forces. Died in 1999.

Officers from the Non-USSR Diaspora

Colonel Hovsep Hovsepian. Born in France. Moved to Armenia in 1991. Commanded a regiment. Retired, lives in Yerevan.

Monte Melkonian. Born in the United States. Moved to Karabagh in 1991, Commanded the Third Defense Region (Pashtpanakan Shrjan) of Martuni. Killed in action, June 1993.

Lieutenant Colonel Jirair Sefilian. Born in Lebanon. Commanded the Dashnak Party's irregular units in Karabagh, then the Seventh Defense Region, which includes the occupied Azerbaijani territory of Kelbajar. Retired, withdrew from the Dashnak Party and is now under arrest for political reasons.

Bibliography

Armstrong, John. "Mobilized and Proletarian Diasporas." *American Political Science Review* 70, no. 2 (1976): 393–408.

Boyarin, Jonathan, and Daniel Boyarin. *Powers of Diaspora: Two Essays on the Relevance of Jewish Culture.* Minneapolis: University of Minnesota Press, 1992.

Cavalli-Sforza, Luigi Luca, and Francesco Cavalli-Sforza. *The Great Human Diasporas: The History of Dispersion and Evolution.* Reading, MA: Addison-Wesley, 1993.

Chorbajian, Levon, Patrick Donabedian, and Claude Mutafian, *The Caucasian Knot: The History and Geopolitics of Nagorno-Karabagh.* London: Zed, 1994.

Cohen, Robin. *Global Diasporas.* Seattle: University of Washington Press, 1997.

De Waal, Thomas. *Black Garden: Armenia and Azerbaijan through Peace and War.* New York: New York University Press, 2003.

Goff, Patricia F., and Kevin C. Dunn, *Identity and Global Politics: Theoretical and Empirical Elaborations.* New York: Palgrave Macmillan, 2004.

King, Charles. "The Benefits of Ethnic War: Understanding Eurasia's Unrecognized States." *World Politics* 53 (2001): 524–52.

Lynch, Dov. *Engaging Eurasia's Separatist States: Unresolved Conflicts and De Facto States.* Washington, DC: United States Institute of Peace Press, 2004.

Ohanyan, Anna. "The Developmental Value of Dual citizenship for Armenia" *Diaspora: A Journal of Transnational Studies* 13, nos. 2–3 (2004).

Shain, Yossi. "American Jews and the Construction of Israel's Jewish Identity." *Diaspora: A Journal of Transnational Studies* 9, no. 2 (2000): 163–202.

——. *Marketing the American Creed Abroad: Diasporas in the U.S. and Their Homelands.* Cambridge: Cambridge University Press, 1998.

Sheffer, Gabriel. *Diaspora Politics at Home and Abroad.* Cambridge: Cambridge University Press, 2003.

——, ed. *Modern Diasporas in International Politics.* 1986; New York: St. Martin's Press, 2002.

Singh, Gurharpal. "A Victim Diaspora? The Case of the Sikhs." *Diaspora: A Journal of Transnational Studies* 8, no. 3 (1999): 293–308.

Tennenhouse, Leonard. *The Importance of Feeling English: American Literature and the British Diaspora, 1750–1850.* Princeton, NJ: Princeton University Press, 2007.

Tölölyan, Khachig. "Elites and Institutions in the Armenian Transnation." *Diaspora: A Journal of Transnational Studies* 9, no. 1 (Spring 2000): 107–36.

——. "From Diaspora Studies to Dispersion Studies: Changing Definitions, Altering Methods, Moving Targets." *Comparative Studies of South Asia, Africa and the Middle East* 27, no. 3 (Winter 2007): 647–55. Special issue edited by Ato Quayson.

——. "The Nation-State and Its Others: In Lieu of a Preface." *Diaspora: A Journal of Transnational Studies* 1, no. 1 (1991): 3–7. Reprinted in *Becoming National: A Reader.* Edited by Geoff Eley and Ronald Suny. New York: Oxford University Press, 1996.

——. "Restoring the Logic of the Sedentary to Diaspora Studies." In *Les diasporas: 2000 ans d'histoire.* Edited by Lisa Anteby-Yemeni, William Berthomière, and Gabriel Sheffer. Rennes: Presses Universitaires de Rennes, 2005.

——. "Rethinking Diaspora(s): Stateless Power in the Transnational Moment." *Diaspora: A Journal of Transnational Studies* 5, no. 1 (1996): 3–36.

Walker, Edward. "No Peace, No War in the Caucasus: Secessionist Conflicts in Chech-
    nya, Abkhazia and Nagorno-Karabakh." Occasional Papers of the Strengthening
    Democratic Institutions Project. Cambridge, MA: Harvard Center for Science and
    International Affairs, 1998.

NOTE:

This article draws on interviews with a number of officials, scholars, and analysts who supplied information that greatly enhanced my analysis. Many have been or still are involved in diasporic politics and have asked not to be identified by name except in this fashion. They are, alphabetically: Khatchik Der Ghougassian, Richard Giragosian, Arman Grigorian, Richard Hovannisian, Hovsep Khourshoutian, Jirair Gerard Libaridian, Robert Owen Krikorian, Van Krikorian, Gaidz Minassian, Razmik Panossian, Simon Payaslian, Hovan Simonian, Emil Sanamian, Ara Sanjian, Hratch Tchilingirian, and Ross Vartian.

The Political Agency of Ethnic Diasporas: Paradiplomacy and the Construction of Political Communities in the World System

By Gloria Totoricagüena

Diplomacy has never been exclusively a state function, but rather has been and is an organic system of multilevel governmental and nongovernmental interactions. The latest reconfigurations of these political institutions and of the overall international scene have facilitated diaspora politics, but diaspora politics are not a new phenomenon. Traditional foreign affairs may have focused on the definition, the defense, and the promotion of the state. However, today's political issues lie less and less in the realm of the state-controlled questions of territorial borders, military powers, or border-controlled trade and more in the areas of identity politics and cultural, social, linguistic, political, and economic rights. Nonstate actors have exerted a growing and cumulative agency in these areas, and diaspora politics increasingly are about identity politics and ethnic recognition. Because diplomacy today is unambiguously multilayered, we also recognize that diaspora activities often exemplify the localization of international relations via examples of amateur citizen diplomacy.

There has been a development in the machinery and scale of diplomacy from mostly professionally trained experts representing the state to regularly include representatives of special-interest entities such as public-interest nongovernmental organizations (NGOs), commerce and business, and ethnic diasporas. However, I will argue that these developments in the character of the machinery of diplomacy do not demonstrate a causal decline of the state or of its role. Such actors pose no ultimate threat to the state system. They have always been involved in diplomacy at some level of influence and in the end have supported the existing international framework. Neither are nonstate actors totally autonomous or extraneous to the state, and states still remain the main target for nonstate actors' agency and activities. We know that central governments, noncentral governments (or mesogovernments), such as the semiautonomous governments of the Spanish Basque Country, and nongovernmental organizations intersect and interact in various ways.[1] The statecentric and the multicentric systems of foreign policy actually develop alongside each other, not in competition with or exclusively of each other, and diasporas often attempt to influence these spheres of decision making simultaneously, hoping for success in one or the other, or both. These changes thus simply add actors to the lists of existing global players in the making of foreign policy, in which the magnitude of transgovernmental and transnational relations has increased. Countless individuals have become involved in transnational activism. In this volume, Robin Cohen discusses "forms of power found in collective shifts of attitudes and social behavior," and one of these may be diaspora involvement in foreign affairs. With the number of migrants worldwide having reached nearly two hundred million, we are witnessing the expansion of the available domains for political decision making, and the opportunities for their entrance have also increased in number, as well as arguably in substance and influence.

The dynamics of the effects and opportunities of globalization influence the restructuring of the relationships between public and private actors in foreign affairs, and many functions that previously were central to the state now have been devolved to or have been assumed by other noncentral government actors. However, globalization does not affect each community in the same way at the same time; there are multiple stages of development, and development is not necessarily linear. Cross-border migration has increased, and so has the ease of communication and travel, thereby encouraging ongoing links between the original homeland and the current land of residence. Widespread migration and easy communication, in turn, have encouraged the construction of new identities and creolization as groups living outside their homelands initiate new solidarities and social networks that incorporate their homelands and their new places of residence.

Diaspora community activities and diaspora institutions often serve as links between homeland and host country and between the homeland and the international stage, providing an effective external dimension for the homeland's foreign affairs.[2] The Basques, for example, have established diaspora communities in over twenty countries, and this multilocality of presence around the globe is an asset in terms of agency and mobilization for their attempts to influence policy at various political points. Multilocality increases possibilities for access to many different policy-makers at various levels of importance. For example, Basque diaspora activists facilitate relations between Basque territorial governments and the governments of their own host countries, as well as between cultural

---

1. The activities of noncentral governments are actually parallel structures that attempt to accomplish independently what they cannot achieve within the existing hierarchical framework of statecraft.

2. For an excellent overview of ethnic group involvement in United States foreign affairs and questions about their successes and failures, see Thomas Ambrosio, ed., *Ethnic Identity Groups and U.S. Foreign Policy* (Westport, CT: Praeger Publishers, 2002), chapter 1.

institutions, universities, public and private institutions, and so on through political, economic, cultural, academic, artistic, and sports exchanges.

The evolution of international law has encouraged diversification and a shift to polycentric conceptions of legal sovereignty, affecting attitudes toward noncentral governments. Structural conditions of state constitutions and regional autonomy, together with international opportunities also provide new avenues for nonstate action in global affairs.[3] Thus, diplomacy today is much more than the conduct of relations between states and other entities with political standing. It is merely one dimension of global interactions. Nonstate actors can use suprastate entities and transnational networks to promote their national identity beyond the state border and into the international arena. Wolfram F. Hanrieder first discussed these changes in diplomacy as involving access, rather than acquisition, presence, rather than rule, and penetration, rather than possession.[4] The main focus is no longer only on getting the political and economic attention of other states, but also on getting attention in the market and in the worldwide media.

We know that the nonstate actor has always been present in what is known as the Westphalian system of international relations, in which the state is considered the sole source of political legitimacy in domestic affairs and is the most important actor in international relations. Religious orders—for example the Jesuits, founded by Basques—served as prototypes of globalization and transnationalism. Workers' movements, banking, international crime, and nationalist movements all have been and are powerful influences on the system of international relations, and there is continuity in the existence and significance of nonstate actors in the last five hundred years of diplomacy. The International Red Cross and Amnesty International are two contemporary representative examples of influential nonstate actors with tremendous legitimacy. Thus, perhaps we may find that the state has actually served as an obstacle to "world order" and that an alternative—and more democratic—diplomacy including nonstate actors and nongovernmental actors might be welcomed.

Global governance structures and suprastate structures such as the European Union continue to use the nation-state as the main vehicle for decision making and for the execution of policy, yet concurrently, there are additional spheres of authority alongside it that form a part of today's dynamic and more fluid diplomacy. The state's "suturing" functions tie together actors and agencies from multiple levels in order to solve issues. They distribute power up, over, or down to the appropriate level, yet persevere in gener-

---

3. See Michael Keating, *The New Regionalism in Western Europe* (Cheltenham, UK: Edward Elgar, 1998); Gurutz Jáuregui, *La Comunidad Autónoma del País Vasco y las relaciones internacionales* (Oñati: Instituto Vasco de Administración Pública, 1989); and Angela Bourne, ed., *The EU and Territorial Politics within Member States: Conflict or Cooperation?* (Leiden, Netherlands: Brill, 2004).

4. Wolfram F. Hanrieder, "Dissolving International Politics: Reflections on the Nation-State," in *American Political Science Review* 72. no. 4 (1978): 1276–87.

ally dominating the overall manipulation of policy.[5] Yet globalization has highlighted the deficiencies of state governments, showing that most have ignored questions of identity and migration and issues of interest to migrants. The postmodern state's inadequacies, including minimized bureaucracy and operational responsibilities in domestic and global citizen welfare, have complicated its ability to maintain knowledge assets such as specialists for information gathering or to generate innovative ideas and address new issues of globalization in diplomacy. These functions are increasingly transferred to NGOs and the private sector or not addressed at all.

Euskal Herria: The Basque Homeland and the Basque Diaspora

Diaspora players, unlike the institutions of states, are nimble and ready to act, often without caring about ramifications, because they are not specifically accountable to anyone for anything. They use technology and communications to their advantage, and often there is little in the way of bureaucratic or hierarchical baggage, norms, or rules to move. Today's diplomacy in general is not linear, but has many points of entry and manipulation, and diasporas are able to benefit from this decentralization in world affairs and often gain agency before the states themselves do. Contemporary global affairs are marked by a proliferation of power centers and opportunity structures for nonstate actors that significantly affect policy-making and governance. My question here is whether or not the Basques and the Basque diaspora are taking full advantage of the new opportunities.[6]

The Basque homeland antedates the rise of nation-states and historically has stood athwart them. Today, Basque foreign policy emanates from a historic space defined by shared cultural, economic, and linguistic ties, which is currently delineated in three administrative, political, economic areas. The Basque Autonomous Community of Euskadi includes the historic territories of Araba (Alava), Bizkaia (Vizcaya), and Gipuzkoa (Guipuzcoa), which fall inside the state boundaries of Spain. The Foral Community of Navarre, or Nafarroa in Basque, is its own separate autonomous community, also within the Spanish state. The northern area of the Basque Country is known as Iparralde and includes the three provinces of Lapurdi (Labourd), Zuberoa (Soule), and Behe Nafarroa (Lower Navarre), which are in today's southwestern France. In 2008, there are also nearly two hundred Basque diaspora organizations in twenty-one different countries that are involved in varying degrees in the maintenance of Basque identity.

---

5. Paul Hirst and Grahame Thompson, *Globalization in Question: The International Economy and the Possibilities of Governance* (Cambridge: Polity Press, 1999), 184. This is one of the reasons that the Basque government focuses on Europe and "defending itself" from Spanish state policies that advantage non-Basque autonomous communities of Spain.

6. At the Fourth World Congress of Basque Collectivities, held from July 8 to 13, 2007, in Bilbao, I gave the inaugural address to the delegates, Basque government officials, and invited guests and referred to what I see as a lack of strategy and also a lack of preparation for doing so. The speech can be found at http://www.euskosare.org/euskal_mundua/egmb_2007/gloria_totoricaguena_inaugural_keynote_address_2007?set_language=en&cl=en (last accessed August 27, 2007).

There are contested visions of collective identity, and even within the homeland, as within the diasporic Basque cultural organizations, there are disagreements about what it means to "be Basque." The latest significant study of Basque identity and culture was conducted and published by Eusko Ikaskuntza, the Basque Studies Society, headquartered in Donostia–San Sebastián, Gipuzkoa. Results of interviews and questionnaires of a representative sample of residents in all seven homeland territories demonstrated that there was not one single defining factor of "Basqueness" on which even 50 percent of the respondents could agree, although many respondents embraced more than one characteristic as being decisive (thus the percentages add up to more than 100 percent). Forty-two percent defined as Basques those people who wish to be Basque. Forty-one percent categorized Basques as those persons who live and work in the Basque Country. Thirty-nine percent defined as Basques those people who are born in the Basque Country. Though the Basque language has often been used as an ethnic marker, only seventeen percent choose being a Basque speaker as a necessary condition for being defined as a Basque.[7]

The dominant definition in the diaspora communities generally follows a conservative, traditional delineation focusing on ancestry, is quite nostalgic and folkloric, and is centered in cultural traditions and not necessarily in a political or religious identity. A majority of the Basque cultural centers in the diaspora maintains a homeland culture of the 1920s to 1960s—the period of the last great immigrations into their communities.[8]

The goals of the Basque government's ruling coalition, led by the Basque Nationalist Party, include an external projection of the Basque Country in its post-Franco ultramodern presence. However, although the Basque diaspora is heterogeneous and not necessarily centered on the homeland, the real interests of the diaspora elite are homeland tradition and history. Of the approximately 200 Basque diaspora cultural organizations around the world, there are currently 173 that are officially registered with and recognized by the government of the Basque Autonomous Community of Euskadi. This official registration allows specific benefits and rights for the individual member of an organization and other rights for the organization itself in regard to access to homeland cultural patrimony.[9] These rights include activities that will strengthen Basque commu-

---

7. Erramun Baxok, et al., *Identidad y cultural vascas a comienzos del siglo XXI* (Donostia–San Sebastián: Eusko Ikaskuntza, 2006), 52–57. Data from this study show that in the political administrative unit of Euskadi (Araba, Bizkaia, and Gipuzkoa), a majority of residents define themselves as Basques, and they respond that people who wish to be Basque and who live and work in the Basque Country ought to be considered as Basques. However, in Nafarroa (Navarre), there is a separate and specific Navarrese identity and respondents defined themselves as Navarrese, equally Navarrese and Spanish, or Basque Navarrese. In Iparralde, the majority of respondents defined themselves as French. Ibid., 54.

8. Gloria Totoricagüena, *Basque Diaspora: Migration and Transnational Identity* (Reno: Center for Basque Studies, 2005). See especially chapter 19, 449–66.

9. See Gloria Totoricagüena, *Identity, Culture, and Politics in the Basque Diaspora* (Reno: Nevada Press, 2004), 155–91, especially 162. Privileges include among other things: access to information of a public nature with a social, cultural, or economic content; the right to participation in different forms of expression of Basque homeland social, cultural, and economic life that contribute to the diaspora's external diaspora; treatment identical with that of homeland associations; the right to ask the Basque Autonomous Community to participate in activities organized by a diaspora Basque center

nities and centers, preserve and reinforce links between Basque communities, project a knowledge of today's Basque Country, give financial help and protection to Basques living outside the Basque Autonomous Community, and facilitate channels of communication among Basques.[10]

After General Francisco Franco's death in 1975 and during the subsequent transition to democracy after nearly forty years of dictatorship, since 1985, there has been a continued and unprecedented proliferation in the number of new Basque diaspora centers. Although this worldwide Basque diaspora is currently generally latent, without leadership or unified political or cultural direction, and not mobilized toward any collaborative political or cultural strategy, increasingly, there is an emerging cadre of transnational activists. A few are academic specialists, others are young professionals and recent emigrants out of the Basque Country, and others are Basques and friends of Basques who are interested in the conflict and peace process for the Basque territories. Their uncoordinated and in some cases even unintentional promotion of a deterritorialized Basque identity and interconnected diasporic population could eventually mobilize segments of groups to mutual collaborative action.[11] However, the configuration of the relations between the homeland government and the diaspora are murky. The mechanics of these relations are not yet established or formalized beyond the arena of cultural issues, and there remains a vacuum in the planning for both content and process for diaspora mobilization. The Basque diaspora communities do not necessarily share a common language for communications, either, but in general, e-mail and other virtual exchanges are conducted in Spanish.

Other areas of Basque Autonomous Community foreign policy have been measurably successful, including the 1986 opening of the Basque Delegation of Euskadi in Brussels, responsible for Euskadi's relations with the European Union (EU), and the subsequent opening and development of delegations in Madrid, Mexico, Chile, Argentina, and Venezuela in the late 1990s and early 2000s and in the United States (New York City) in 2007. Plans for additional delegations include Paris (2008), London (2009), and Berlin (2010),[12] and further discussions have also included mentions of Italy and possibly Finland in Europe, and then Canada. In 2005, the Basque government executive-branch cabinet approved a ten-year strategy road map for its foreign affairs, extending to

---

in order to promote Basque culture; participation of the diaspora Basque center in programs, missions, and delegations organized by Basque homeland institutions in the center's territorial area; the right to request and receive advice on social, economic, or labor matters in the Basque Country; the right to a supply of material designed to facilitate the transmission of knowledge of Basque history, culture, language, and social reality; collaboration in media activities centered in the Autonomous Community, such as EITB (Basque Radio and Television, and the *Euskal Etxeak* journal; the right to be heard via the Basque government's diaspora advisory council and to attend the World Congresses of Basque Communities; and the organization of courses to learn the Basque language.

10. See Ley 8/1994, Public Law 8 of 1994, passed by the Parliament of the Basque Autonomous Community.

11. Totoricagüena, *Basque Diaspora*, 518.

12. Interviews and discussions with Iñaki Aguirre, Basque government secretary of foreign affairs. Bilbao, July 8, 2007.

multilateral interregional cooperation in Europe, global networks with other noncentral governments, and intensified relations with United Nations UNICEF and UNESCO programs. There was a mention of the historical importance of the Basque diaspora collectivities abroad, but no clarification of political content or processes for relations between the government and the existing diaspora organizations. Existing relations are quite positive and efficient between individual Basque diaspora organizations and the office of the Directorate for Relations with Basque Collectivities (a section of the Secretariate of Foreign Action in the Office of the Presidency) and are very close between the two federations of Basque centers in Argentina and the United States with the homeland directorate.[13]

While the Basque diaspora is mainly in the Americas, this 2005 strategic plan saw Europe as the "nucleus" for international affairs, because at least half of the legislation in effect in Euskadi today is conditioned by EU decisions.[14] By working with other noncentral government actors in the EU, the Basque government may be able to design and implement policies and relations that actually make them less dependent on Spain and that will allow them to use their own "identity economy," that is, their own national cultural and political characteristics, in order to respond efficiently to international competition.[15] The delegations in Latin America have as an objective to "serve as the organ of communication on behalf of the Basque Government and to lend assistance to the resident Basques,"[16] and though there was recognition of the need for a unified communications policy that would promote a more positive image of the Basque Country, there was no mention of engaging the existing Basque diaspora communities to this end or of operationalizing the positive status of the existing Basques for the homeland's advantage.

This changed with the Konpondu (to solve) initiative by the Basque president, Juan José Ibarretxe, which is an attempt to involve the Basque diaspora and the opinions of its members in the conflict management process of the homeland. The Web page of Konpondu informs its readers:

> As other international experiences have shown, the road to political normality in the
> Basque Country needs to be reinforced through the opinions and contributions of Basques

---

13. Alexander Ugalde Zubiri has published several books, chapters, and journal articles regarding the history of the Basque government's chronology of foreign relations with its diaspora, as well as its influence in the building of European community politics. The latest is *Memoria de la dirección de relaciones con las colectividades vascas en el exterior del Gobierno Vasco (1980–2005)*, published in Spanish by the Basque government as a volume in the Urazandi Series (Vitoria-Gasteiz: Servicio Central de Publicaciones del Gobierno Vasco, 2007).

14. *Euskadi: Estrategia de acción exterior de la Comunidad Autónoma Vasca* (Vitoria-Gasteiz: Servicio Central de Publicaciones del Gobierno Vasco, 2005), 41.

15. Guy Lachapelle, "Identity, Integration and the Rise of Identity Economy: The Quebec Case in Comparison with Scotland, Wales and Catalonia." in *Globalization, Governance and Identity: The Emergence of New Partnerships*, ed. Guy Lachapelle and John Trent (Montréal: Presses de l'Université de Montréal, 2000), 212n.

16. Interview with Iñaki Aguirre, secretary of foreign action for the government of the Basque Autonomous Community. July 9, 2007. Bilbao, Bizkaia. Spain.

abroad. This initiative backed by the Lehendakari Juan José Ibarretxe invites you to take part directly receiving information, sending your message to Basque political parties, or contacting Basque Centres to discuss the possibility of arranging forums of discussion on this issue (https://www.konpondu.net/?page_id=16).

During Ibarretxe's travels in Latin America during 2006, he also included repeated mention of diaspora involvement in creating a new image of the Basque Country in their own home-country media.

State and Nonstate Actors: Structures and Agency in Diplomacy

Diplomacy is one area in which, in recent decades, diasporas have become increasingly active. The historical operational principles of diplomacy are in transition, and states are confronted with challenges to their singular authority to control diplomacy. In world diplomacy, global affairs have been localized and local affairs globalized. States' central governments are "adapting the management of their external policies" to specialist groups with expertise in specific areas.[17] The complexities of the issues and the uncertainties of alliances in international affairs result in the stimulus and emergence of epistemic communities—networks of knowledge-based experts. Indian Americans, for example, are preparing themselves with the Indian-American Leadership Initiative Public Action Committee (IALIPAC), seeking to train young activists in political advocacy with hopes to have a dozen Indian Americans in elected office by the end of the decade. In 1983, Greece founded the Secretariat General of the Hellenic Diaspora, which coordinates action among the Greek diaspora communities. In 1996, they established the World Council of Hellenes Abroad, which actively lobbies and promotes the transnational identity of Greeks abroad, "hoping to maximize support for Greek foreign policy in countries with large diasporic constituencies."[18] Jews, Armenians, Chinese, Cubans, Haitians, Koreans, and many others have also established their own lobbying groups. Basques also could aim to create epistemic communities with recognized competence and expertise in Basque Country issues that could gain legitimacy and authority in the political arena, but Basques thus far have only sporadically attempted orchestrated joint action and, not having met with significant success, Basque diaspora policy formation remains decentralized and intermittent.

In numerous other cases, amateur diplomats have successfully gained credibility and agency. For example, NGOs are necessary for implementing much of the foreign humanitarian assistance of state governments, businesses are essential in shaping trade policy, and diasporas are involved in attempting to influence the foreign policy of hostlands toward their homelands, especially in the arena of human and civil rights. State-

---

17. Brian Hocking, "Privatizing Diplomacy," *International Studies Perspectives* 5 (2004): 148.

18. Victor Roudometof and Anna Karpathakis, "Greek Americans and Transnationalism: Religion, Class and Community," in *Communities across Borders: New Immigrants and Transnational Cultures* (London: Routledge, 2002), 54.

centered diplomatic systems of state representation are giving way to multivariate entities such as the Basque delegations named above. Spain is having to adjust to its own internal political changes and—having tried to control and determine the international activities of each of its autonomous communities—has found it impossible to quell or to limit their diplomatic activities, especially those of Galicia, Catalonia, and the Basque Autonomous Community. Madrid itself deals regularly with noncentral government entities from around the world, yet it has attempted to forbid its own autonomous communities from establishing their respective international trade, political, educational, and cultural markets. Currently, though the Spanish Constitution and the Basque Autonomous Community Statutes of Autonomy confound the issue of autonomous community powers in international arenas, the Spanish Constitutional Tribunal decision 165 of May 26, 1994, ruled in favor of the Basque Autonomous Community and clarified its legitimacy to act in certain foreign affairs. It ruled that because the autonomous communities have assumed the public functions of their societies, in order to do so effectively, not only do they need to have the power to act outside of their own boundaries, but they must also have the authority to act outside of the state of Spain.[19] Despite their not having a clear picture of the diplomatic impact, Spain's central government actors have repeatedly favored state-to-state relations at the expense of the conceivable growth in foreign affairs of its autonomous community governments.[20]

Gabriel Sheffer argues that the lack of data demonstrating the influence of diasporas on hostland and homeland politics is not accidental: "In most cases the problem stems from deliberate policies of homelands and host governments intended to suppress or falsify information about modern diasporism, that is, to conceal its actual impressive magnitude, rapid growth, and emerging significance."[21] However, diaspora networks are creating another mode of foreign assistance and investment. Economic stimulus results from self-organizing diaspora networks generated by civil society and the private sector, albeit legitimized and sustained by governments and multilateral institutions. For example, the report of the World Bank's Global Economic Prospects (GEP) for 2006 illustrates that remittances recorded worldwide in 2005 are estimated to exceed $232 billion. Of this amount, developing countries are expected to receive $167 billion, which is more than twice their level of development aid from all sources combined. The figures for South Asia are quite compelling, with the region expected to receive an estimated $32 billion in remittances, a 67 percent increase since 2001. The figure for worker remittances to India, $21.7 billion, is followed by China at $21.3 billion and Mexico at $19 billion, all flowing into the hands of homeland relatives and businesses from abroad.[22]

19. *Euskadi: Estrategia de acción exterior de la Comunidad Autónoma Vasca*, 13.

20. See Carlos Closa and Paul M. Heywood. *Spain and the European Union* (Basingstoke, UK: Palgrave MacMillan).

21. Gabriel Sheffer, *Diaspora Politics: At Home Abroad.* (Cambridge, MA: Cambridge University Press, 2003, 99).

22. World Bank, *Global Economic Prospects 2006: Economic Implications of Remittances and Migration*, 2005. Available on-line at http://www-wds.worldbank.org/external/default/WDSContentServer/IW3P/IB/2005/11/14/000112742_200511141749 28/Rendered/PDF/343200GEP02006.pdf (last accessed on December 10, 2007).

Workers' remittances are critical to the economies of these and a number of other states. They represent the single most valuable source of new capital for Latin America and the Caribbean and are higher to that region than foreign direct investment, portfolio investment, foreign aid, or government and private borrowing. The Chinese, Lebanese, and Indian trading networks exemplify economic activity with significant political and social implications. In the Basque case, historically, remittances to the homeland were often decisive to economic development from the 1600s to the early 1900s and then were mostly symbolic from the 1960s forward. Improved economic conditions in the Basque territories and the declining economies of Latin America (home to the majority of the Basque communities abroad) have resulted in an actual reversal of fortune, and now Basque homeland communities often sponsor aid to diaspora Basque centers, as was the case for Basques in Argentina receiving humanitarian aid at the end of the 1990s and early 2000s. The town of Oñati, Gipuzkoa, continues sending household goods and used clothing to the Basque organization of José C. Paz in Argentina, which are then distributed to local families in need. Homeland Basques have received their Uruguayan, Venezuelan, and Argentine Basque "cousins" in their homes and have tried to help them find employment in order to stay in the Basque Country. The migration is now "return migration" of latter-generation Basques born in the Americas looking to the homeland for economic, academic, and personal opportunities.

Today, there are official Basque government trade delegations in Mexico City, Caracas, Santiago, Buenos Aires, Chicago, and Shanghai, funded and partly administered by Basque government officials and employees, with amateur Basque diplomats encouraging and assisting with arrangements for international trade offices in their hostlands. With the exception of the one in China, these trade offices were negotiated and opened with the facilitation of diaspora Basques instrumentalizing their identities, but not usually their financial capital, in order to gain access for their homeland government.[23] This reconfiguration of agency and access empowers diaspora communities and non-state interests and contributes legitimacy to the Basque homeland-diaspora diplomatic infrastructure.

When discussing structures and agency, we cannot omit a mention of the influence of the Internet in facilitating diaspora political entrepreneurship. States have been involved in protection and management of scarce resources, but the cybereconomy is one of shared resources, shared information, shared software, and the spread of knowledge resources, music, video, markets, information, and data. This helps nonstate entities enter into new transactions and, in this case, what is involved in the transaction is the ethnic identity itself. Experts discuss information as an environment, not as a product,

---

23. Basque government trade missions are not one and the same as the Basque government delegations mentioned earlier. The trade missions were initiated first in these countries, and then in 2005 and 2006, those of Mexico, Chile, Argentina, and Belgium were designated as official delegations. In the United States, the trade mission office will remain in Chicago and the delegation offices will be opened in Manhattan, according to the United States delegate of the Basque government, Aitor Sotes. Interview with the author, July 13, 2007.

and identity as a good or service that states do not control. Though I am not convinced there is a causal relationship between access to the opportunity to participate and subsequent actual activism in the Basque diaspora, when analyzing digital activism on the part of diasporas, we have to recognize that cybertechnologies do broaden the opportunity structure for diaspora engagement. Alejandro Portes, Luis Guarnizo, and Patricia Landolt write:

> If technological innovations represent a necessary condition for the rise of grass-roots transnationalism, it follows that the greater access of an immigrant group to space- and time-compressing technology, the greater the frequency and scope of this sort of activity. Immigrant communities with greater average economic resources and human capital (education and social skills) should register higher levels of transnationalism because of their superior access to the infrastructure that makes these activities possible.[24]

Technology does empower networks and social movements, and the collective actions of diasporas do influence the existing state-centered system of foreign policy creation and implementation.

Time-space compression, intensified communications using the Internet, access to watching and creating media, and access to homeland information, newspapers, people, and Web sites, all facilitate the manifestation of multiple identities and identification with multiple localities. Diasporas have adopted transstate institutional mechanisms to effect intrastate changes. New technologies of representation are available, and the relative isolation of expatriates in their new locations has been effectively offset by the presence of a large, virtual, instant community that may be geographically disconnected but is electronically—and sometimes epistemologically and ideologically—connected. Internet communities such as EuskoSare, or the Basque Network, designed and operated by Eusko Ikaskuntza, the Basque Studies Society, has numerous on-line groups that communicate in combinations of Spanish, Basque, English, and French regarding myriad Basque issues. Euskal Irrati Telebista, Basque Radio and Television, is seen and heard around the planet on the Internet and on satellite television. This "despatialization" of social realities results in a scenario in which physical geography and interests no longer need coincide in order to produce activism.[25]

Christopher Hill argues that states and transnational actors in the globalized environment have to be prepared for "constant change, mixed actorness and lack of structure."[26] State relationships have been structure-driven, but transnational relations are actor-driven.

---

24. Alejandro Portes, Luis Guarnizo, and Patricia Landolt, "The Study of Transnational Communities: Pitfalls and Promise of an Emergent Field," *Ethnic and Racial Studies* 22, no. 2 (1999): 222.

25. For discussions of "spatial and visual neighborhoods," see Arjun Appadurai, *Modernity at Large: Cultural Dimensions of Globalization*, Public Worlds, vol. 1 (Minneapolis: University of Minnesota Press. 1995), 213. For other discussions of space-compressing effects on identity see Zygmunt Bauman, *Globalization: The Human Consequences* (Cambridge: Polity Press, 1998), 77–102.

26. Christopher Hill, *The Changing Politics of Foreign Policy* (New York: Palgrave Macmillan, 2003), 193.

Each policy area may necessitate a mix of players and frameworks for diasporas to target, and effective policy influence will occur through numerous levels of contacts, as well as through bilateral and multilateral relations. The following diagrams are based on those of Joseph Nye.[27] However, I have added "IGO," intergovernmental organizations, to the statecentric world politics diagram, and "NGO," nongovernmental organizations, to the diagram of transnational interactions and interstate politics.

STATE-TO-STATE RELATIONS AND TRANSNATIONAL RELATIONS

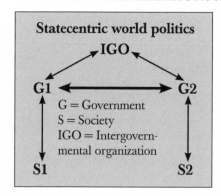

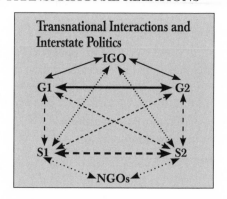

Traditional statecentric model   Transnational network model

In traditional statecentric thinking about world politics, any actors of a particular state's society (S1) would have to work through its central government (G1) in order to relate to another government (G2) or its society (S2), or to an intergovernmental organization (IGO) such as the United Nations. Regardless of the content of the issue or policy, the process is through the state government apparatus. The transnational paradigm of interactions reveals a much more accurate picture of contemporary politics, where any segment of any society of any state can directly contact any other segment of any another state, its central government, an IGO, or an NGO. Here, regardless of the content, the process is transnational and focused on noncentral governments. An Armenian diaspora community in Canada indeed has uncomplicated access to the decision makers of the Canadian government, but also to those of the United States government and to the Armenian government, as well as to the European Union and the United Nations. Basque communities have in fact employed these various types of processes of transnational interactions for centuries: from intra-Basque-diaspora "multinational" trading companies established during the times of Spanish colonization of the Americas,[28] to Basque center communications, to diasporic political and financial support for the

27. Joseph S. Nye, Jr., *Power in the Global Information Age: From Realism to Globalization* (London: Routledge, 2004), 3.

28. See William A. Douglass and Jon Bilbao, *Amerikanuak: Basques in the New World* (1975; Reno: University of Nevada Press, 2005), especially chapter 2, 61–115.

Basque government-in-exile (1937–77),[29] to Basques lobbying the United Nations and Amnesty International.

Be that as it may, the Basque Country governments and diaspora communities (and other stateless homeland governments and their diasporas) may not be utilizing the full spectrum of today's available resources for foreign affairs. It may also be that there exists a disconnect between the diaspora's and the Basque government's strategies and definitions of *content* and *process* for effective foreign affairs. The Basque government's message of a progressive and ultramodern Basque Country is sometimes not recognized, and in extreme cases is even rejected, by those diasporans who want the content to focus on traditional cultural definitions of identity, that is, on the Basque Country's unique language, historical traditions, history, music and dance, and so on. Diasporas could map their foreign-affairs strategies through other transnational networks and benefit from the many avenues available for international relations. Why not focus energy on a path that has less resistance? Why not band with other noncentral government entities, NGOs, diasporas, and economic actors? Why not develop their virtual diasporas and use the Internet to develop strategic alliances with other grassroots activists?

These questions highlight the differences between the traditional hierarchical model and the network model. The network model for political agency is interdependent, more fluid, and the process changes according to content, but historically, the state and the hierarchical model have been totalitarian, with the state as the only representation of the people's and the society's will. Diaspora transstate organizations, networks, and agency have the ability to exemplify a future model of self-empowerment for social movements on the international stage that circumvents the international state structure. As illustrated below, diaspora communities have the opportunity to interact with numerous administrative levels for cultural, economic, political, educational, and other interests.

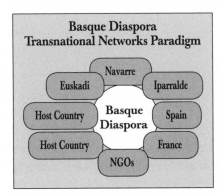

29. See Koldo San Sebastián, *The Basque Archives: Vascos en Estados Unidos (1939–1943)* (Donostia–San Sebastián: Editorial Txertoa, 1991); Xabier Irujo Ametzaga *La hora vasca del Uruguay: Génesis y desarrollo del nacionalismo vasco en Uruguay (1825–1960)* (Montevideo: Sociedad de Confraternidad Vasca Euskal Erria, 2006); and Alexander Ugalde Zubiri, "La actuación internacional del gobierno vasco en el exilio (1939–1960): Un caso singular de acción exterior," Programa de Becas Postdoctorales de Perfeccionamiento de Personal Investigador del Gobierno Vasco (Leioa: Universidad del País Vasco, 1995–97).

For the Basques seeking to influence the global stage and to return to the positive image they had in their communities before the inception of the violent activities undertaken by Euskadi 'ta Askatasuna (ETA: Basque Homeland and Liberty) during the last decades, there are many junctures for action. However, the political landscape is also complex and requires in-depth knowledge of the issues, the actors, and their relationships to one another, as well as an understanding of the politics of the new paradigm itself.

Strategies for Diasporas

What is the foreign-policy goal or mission of the Basque diaspora, what are its targets, and what are the strategies to be implemented? Who is framing the image and message for Basque issues on the international stage? The diaspora? The Basque government itself? The Spanish central government? Nongovernmental Basque organizations? What if there is no coordination whatsoever in formulating and/or in answering these questions? Current Basque government activities include what Ivo D. Duchacek names "paradiplomacy," consisting of noncentral governments' political relations with trade, industrial, and cultural centers in other states, including relations with foreign state governments.[30] He categorizes global "protodiplomacy" as activities of noncentral governments that project a separatist or independentist message onto programs and projects with entities in other countries: "In such a context, the regional/provincial authority uses its trade/cultural missions abroad as protoembassies or protoconsulates of a potentially sovereign state. Such missions may be sometimes viewed and treated by the recipient foreign government in a similar fashion."[31] Iñaki Aguirre Zabala preferred to call the international involvement of noncentral governments (NCGs) "postdiplomatic," because it is a process that moves beyond the state, that is, "beyond diplomacy."[32]

In the Basque diaspora, there is no recognized strategy or coordination of policy formulation for attempting to promote Basque issues onto the international stage. The established Basque Delegations of Euskadi have focused almost entirely on economic and commercial trade issues and, more recently, in 2006 and 2007 began discussing political activity. There have been occasional private attempts by several individuals in different countries to build coalitions across the global diaspora, but nothing permanent has resulted. In 2006, Juan José Ibarretxe, president of the Basque Autonomous Community, designed an innovative initiative to include certain elite of the Basque diaspora in organizing and participating in think-tank discussion forums called the Grupo Pensamiento. Currently, there is one section dedicated to leading intellectuals, academics,

---

30. See Ivo D. Duchacek, *The Territorial Dimension of Politics: Within, Among and Across Nations* (Boulder, CO: Westview Press, 1986), 246–47.

31. Ibid., 248.

32. Gloria Totoricagüena, "Diasporas as Non-Central Government Actors in Foreign Policy: The Trajectory of Basque Paradiplomacy," *Nationalism and Ethnic Politics* 11 (2005): 266. See also Iñaki Aguirre, "Making Sense of Paradiplomacy? An Intertextual Inquiry about a Concept in Search of a Definition," in *Paradiplomacy in Action: The Foreign Relations of Subnational Governments*, ed. Francisco Aldecoa and Michael Keating (London: Frank Cass, 1999), 205.

and opinion leaders in the Basque diaspora and friends of Basques living outside of the Basque territories, whose charge it is to promote a more accurate and updated image of Basques in their own spheres of influence, as well as to provide the Basque president with their analyses in regard to the place of Basque society in the globalized world. The Basque government officials might be hesitant of opening a Pandora's box. However, by not leading, they are following and are reacting to Basque amateur diplomats mostly in the United States, Mexico, Venezuela, Uruguay, and Argentina. If deemed desirable, and with a little planning, it could be possible to build a coherent international relations strategy that would include the homeland and the diaspora, both promoting attention to various policy issues that affect Basque society.

The key to mobilizing might be based in the essentialist element of identity. William Bloom's "identification theory" tells us that given equal environmental circumstances, people actively seek their group identity and that there is a tendency for people to act collectively to protect and enhance this shared identity.[33] If we look for relationships between this "national identity dynamic"[34] and the political environment, we will see that diasporas introduce additional identity variables into the making of foreign policy that have the ability to sway outcomes. Bloom shows us that the general public is more likely to mobilize when it perceives that the national identity is threatened or when there is an opportunity for enhancing the national identity, and this dynamic is prevalent both in homeland politics and in diaspora politics. Some of the most highly mobilized diaspora communities are groups whose identities are linked to stateless and marginalized peoples in danger of losing their cultures. If one's identity group is already secure back home, then the need to develop political activities abroad is less compelling, and diasporans may enthusiastically come together to celebrate their common culture, but not involve themselves in politics.

Following Bloom's theory of the national identity dynamic, we can argue that public opinion in the Basque diaspora will likely mobilize when diasporans perceive either that Basque national identity is threatened or that there is an opportunity for enhancing their Basque identity. A handful of Basques in the homeland and in the diaspora have indeed attempted to activate this national identity dynamic, although there have been no resolute attempts to centralize or to coordinate these efforts or to prepare special amateur diplomats and spokespersons for the epistemic communities discussed above. Basque nationalist advocates around the globe have desired a Basque nation-building project for the diaspora, but these requests to the homeland actors have been ineffectively communicated, have fallen on deaf ears, have been ignored, or have been given very low priority. When individual Basques have attempted this strategy, they have found it is nearly impossible to implement, because the diaspora is not monolithic, but decentralized and

---

33. William Bloom, *Personal Identity, National Identity and International Relations* (New York: Cambridge University Press, 1990), 23.

34. Ibid., 79.

heterogeneous, and perhaps because the Basque national identity dynamic is shared with the creolized identities of the diaspora host country.

In the homeland, the ruling Basque Nationalist Party could use the argument of enhancing all Basques' identities around the world to strengthen their own homeland national identity dynamic (and to win votes), but they are not following this strategy, either. There is no effective effort to demonstrate to homeland Basques how positively the Basque government's educational and cultural programs are affecting Basques abroad. In this millennium, there are Basque trade delegations in seven countries, but until 2006 there were no determined (funded) push for academic chairs in universities, no significant targeted publishing or media agenda, and a lack of—or silence about—an overall strategy for relations with the diaspora. In 2007, the platform of the ruling Basque Nationalist Party included sections referring to the importance of the diaspora communities and individuals, and the president regularly refers to the role that the diaspora could play in the homeland peace process and in the separate discussion of the political future of the Basque territories.

The art of diaspora politics is to tap a psychological motivation to help get people mobilized and then to use this momentum to one's advantage by making calculations as to how to affect the political environment.[35] It is important to understand that the national identity dynamic can be exploited as a foreign-policy resource if governments evoke it with homeland and diaspora populations for the pursuit of strategic goals. Regarding the Basque scenario, the Basque government could benefit from activating the dynamic for use in foreign policy as a tool for homeland and diaspora Basque nation building. Although Basque Country political parties may not be able to rely on any specific Basque national identity dynamic in the homeland because of the extreme pluralism of Basque society, this dynamic may indeed exist in the Basque centers of the diaspora. Currently, homeland politicians cannot rely on the dynamic for delivering votes in homeland campaigns, and they do not instrumentalize it at all; therefore the diaspora is still without leadership or political mobilization unless from local initiatives.

Diaspora Basques have not applied confrontational strategies such as aggressive demonstrations, hunger strikes, or physical violence against persons or property in order to gain agency. Instead they have employed institutional and elite contacts who move within established channels and have targeted powerful individuals in the European Union and United Nations, as well as national congressional deputies in Argentina, U.S. senators and representatives, provincial and substate governors, and writers, artists, and business leaders to ask for influence in promoting Basque Country economic, cultural, and political issues. Basques have also discerned that when the diaspora's agenda conflicts with their hostland's politics, they may have to change strategies and target a different audience, as they have had to do recently. The post–September 11 Bush-Aznar alliance and the newfound friendship between the United States and Spain necessitated that Basques in New York organize activities aimed at the United Nations, instead of at

---

35. Ibid., 82.

the U.S. Congress, and that Basques in California would go directly to Amnesty International for assistance instead of their own California Assembly. Kurds, Tibetans, and Palestinians generally also have had to target other nonstate actors as sources for attention. Therefore, transstate advocacy networks of NGOs that function at both the state and international levels can be extremely useful, because these organizations facilitate contact with various levels of policy-makers that are otherwise inaccessible for nonstate entities.[36] It is a strategy on which Basques have not capitalized to its fullest potential.

Homeland governments do have an interest in maintaining a relationship with their diaspora communities in order to use them in the future for their own goals. The economic policies of the Basque government have included benefiting from the status of certain diaspora Basques in order to establish their own economic institutes and, more recently, to constitute the legal Basque delegations. The Basque diaspora communities have repeatedly expended their cultural and identity capital in their host countries in order to promote a positive awareness of homeland Basque society to counteract the negative news of political violence. The focus on raising the national identity dynamic is mutually beneficial for homeland and diaspora populations when the social recognition and status for a group are positive.

In regard to strategies for selecting appropriate issues for international agency, it is likely wiser for diasporas to focus on advocating for issues of human and civil rights in their homelands and not for issues of territorial nationalism, partisan politics, or complex homeland historical questions. The greater the acceptance of a group's issues and their institutionalization in the international arena, the more legitimate and accepted are the activities of the diaspora actors. The higher the degree of international institutionalization of a concept, such as civil rights, the more admissible the transnational activities of the diaspora group, which increases access to local, national, and international politics and the ability to then influence policy-making.[37]

36. Eva Østergaard-Nielsen, "Diasporas in World Politics," in *Non-State Actors in World Politics*, ed. Daphné Josselin and William Wallace (New York: Palgrave, 2001), 225.

37. Thomas Risse-Kappen, ed., *Bringing Transnational Relations Back In: Non-State Actors, Domestic Structures, and International Institutions* (Cambridge: Cambridge University Press, 1995).

Basque diaspora activists interested in spotlighting Basque issues might well point to Spanish judges' restrictions on freedom of press and the closing of the Basque-language newspapers *Egin*, in 1998 and *Egunkaria*, in 2003; the prohibition of Basque political parties such as Herri Batasuna;[38] or the restrictions on freedom of political speech and assembly in the Basque territories. If the issues raised are conventionally recognized and regulated by international norms of cooperation, the likelihood of the diaspora group successfully gaining access to opinion leaders and influencing policy-making circles is higher. For example, the Global Organization of People of Indian Origin was founded at the First Global Convention of People of Indian Origin in New York in 1989, and its initial thrust was fighting human-rights violations of people of Indian origin. Diasporas can use these human-rights and civil-rights questions as the issues for their entry into the foreign-affairs scene. They can call for implementation of universal norms of human rights in the homeland territories and for international protection for endangered languages and cultures.

However, Basque elites in the diaspora are miscalculating and focusing on the wrong issues—trying to explain or rationalize the history of political violence or advocating the right to self-determination, which are extremely complex polemics with centuries of detailed histories that most citizens and politicians will not take the time to study. They often are also using the traditional process of attempting to influence the international stage by going through their own states' central governments. Basques could be focusing on the international institutionalized issues mentioned above in order to gain attention and access, and later, with epistemic communities of experts, move on to more specific debates with specialists, using the transnational model of process. There is a history of this being successful for the Basques.

In the mid-twentieth century, the Basque government-in-exile created delegations that had political and public relations missions. The Basque government-in-exile fled the Spanish Civil War (1936–39) and established delegations and offices in Paris and London and in smaller European capitals, in New York, and throughout Latin America, with influential offices in Mexico City, Caracas, Bogotá, Panama City, Santo Domingo, Havana, Buenos Aires, and Montevideo. Between the 1930s and the 1970s, these delegations were effective at mobilizing the Basque diaspora communities, and the delegation in New York successfully lobbied until 1955 to keep Franco's Spain out of the United Nations.[39] The ministers and leaders of the Basque government-in-exile persuasively activated the national identity dynamic of their constituencies and simultaneously launched an international lobbying effort focused on the human-rights and civil-rights abuses of

---

38. The name of the political party has changed each time it was declared illegal by the Spanish courts: Herri Batasuna (Popular Unity) 1978, became Euskal Herritarrok (Those of the Basque Country), which then became Batasuna (Unity). This party has generally received between 10 and 20 percent of the popular vote, even when illegal.

39. See Alexander Ugalde Zubiri, "La actuación internacional del primer Gobierno Vasco durante la Guerra Civil (1936–1939)," *Sancho el Sabio, Revista de Cultura e Investigación Vasca*, no. 6 (1996): 187–210, and San Sebastián. *The Basque Archives*.

the Franco regime (1939–75). They fashioned epistemic communities of specialists who met regularly with Catholic Church officials, United Nations representatives, academics, intellectuals, and the media—using transnational networks, rather than focusing only on state central-government actors to advance the Basque cause of a republican and autonomous government. After the end of the Franco dictatorship and the ongoing transition to democracy in Spain, the elected governments of the Basque Autonomous Community have taken a different approach to the Basque diaspora and have cultivated almost exclusively short-term cultural projects and programs.

When determining a diaspora's strategy, one must also consider at which entry points the group would have the highest likelihood of success. Local politics? State or international institutions? NGOs? Academic institutions? The United Nations? What are the characteristic forms of Basque diaspora activity that are intended to help shape public policy? Should they attempt to influence mass mobilization, or should they target elite involvement? Are there any intellectual efforts on behalf of the Basques to reshape the language of the debate about the Basque Country in academia or in the media? How do Basques effectively mobilize and generate local, domestic, and international constituencies? What resources are employed, and are they self-sustaining? What and who are the typical targets? Is there any attempt to shape an international consensus among Basque diaspora populations? The Basque diasporic communities have not yet "arrived," in that their political participation has not yet shifted from symbolic to tactical-strategic goals. They have not yet created social and/or political fields for interaction and agency or even begun the debate regarding on which issues and images to focus.

The Basque government has been especially concerned with the image of the Basque Country around the world, and its international relations often focus on portraying a postmodern, service-industry society. This introduces additional dissonance, because they are attempting to "reeducate" their diaspora, where identity is firmly based on the past and on traditional agrofishery lifestyles, not necessarily the present or the future. Government officials have aimed their pesetas and euros at Basque cultural centers, which were originally immigrant receiving centers and which promote cultural identity, and not usually political education or militancy. Homeland attitudes of diaspora Basques as "decaffeinated" or "vascos light" demonstrate the pejorative attitudes toward the lack of authenticity or lack of legitimacy of the diaspora Basques. Homeland Basques are also likely to see the dual orientation of diaspora Basques (Canadian Basques, Belgian Basques, Basque Americans, etc.) as a factor that diminishes the Basque identity. They often understand identity as a zero-sum game, where for every ounce of Americanness, one must lose ounces of Basqueness, and transnational and creolized identities are suspect. Conversely, the postmodern edition of Basque ethnic identity that Basque homeland institutions often attempt to export is received abroad with some skepticism. However, in the last two decades, Basque homeland political policy toward the diaspora has indeed developed: from symbolic words, to cultural programs, to economic trade missions, and then to official delegations. It is possible that perhaps the next stage is political mobilization. Strategy for activism could include:

- Creating social fields for interaction among Basque diaspora opinion leaders
- Using time-space compression to advantage
- Identifying specific issues to address publicly
- Determining opportunity structure entry points
- Establishing Basque diaspora epistemic communities
- Instrumentalizing the "national identity dynamic"
- Preparing intellectuals and training amateur diplomats
- Targeting elite contacts in policy-making circles
- Working within the transnational network paradigm

To conclude our discussion of strategies regarding relationships between homeland and diaspora communities, we can ask several questions: What are homeland governments doing today to generate constituencies, to campaign to elites and decision makers, to shape and reshape the language of debate and the global image of their homeland society? How is the Internet being used to do the same to a global audience? In what arenas are they "advertising" or participating on an international level? Academic conferences? International media? Educational, business, cultural, or political exchanges? Who are they inviting to the homeland? With which other diasporas and NGOs are they aligning to gain attention and to use the power of numbers?

Institutional and Social Mechanisms that Structure Diaspora Activism

Diasporas are able to trigger a national identity dynamic among their own ethnic community members by gaining the attention of other transnational actors and by establishing their own international images. They can serve as interest groups, providing information and working in domestic and international politics, and can assist homeland governments and institutions, or they can attempt to discredit them, as in the case of the Cuban diaspora in the United States, discrediting its homeland leadership.

Homeland governments usually think of diasporas as a foreign-policy asset, and not a liability, though they can be. Recent studies by World Bank scholars identify diasporas as critical to the funding and support of insurgent groups engaged in civil wars. Yossi Shain and Aharon Barth quote a World Bank investigation that concluded: "By far the strongest effect of war on the risk of subsequent war works through diasporas. After five years of post-conflict peace, the risk of renewed conflict is around six times higher in the societies with the largest diasporas in America than those without American diasporas. Presumably this effect works through the financial contributions of diasporas to rebel organizations."[40] The Tamil diaspora provides critical funding to the Liberation Tigers of Tamil Eelam, for example, and the links between diaspora fundraising and conflict have been noted repeatedly in research and in the general media with regard to the Kurdish Workers Party, the Provisional Irish Republican Army, and Croatian political and military movements.[41]

When homeland conflict is the axis of diaspora identity, diaspora social organizations tend to mobilize to provide support for actors engaged in the struggles back home. These organizations abroad thereby often become factors that complicate the processes of conflict management or resolution and may make homeland hostilities more protracted. They tend to be less willing to compromise and therefore reinforce and exacerbate those dimensions that prevent constructive conflict management in their homelands. A number of scholars have recognized the key role of an "opposition" in the construction of diaspora group social identities, and, in addition, the trauma associated with emigration and dispersal often lead to a desire for the imagined homeland to be protected or granted independence and/or for the ethnic identity to be maintained and guarded.

Beyond the provision of financial resources, diasporas can play important roles in setting the terms of debate around issues of conflict and identity. The concept of homeland is inherent in the diaspora identity and therefore serves as a focal point of diaspora political action and debate. As the intrinsic value of territory diminishes, with day-to-day activities focusing on the new place of residence, the homeland's *symbolic* importance may actually increase and intensify. For the immigrant, geographical detachment converts the territorial concept of homeland from the physical to the virtual and imagined realm and from one that has relatively known boundaries to one that is unbounded and abstract. As Shain and Barth note, for many homeland citizens, territory serves multiple functions: It provides sustenance, living space, and security, as well as a geographical focus for national identity. If giving up a certain territory, even one of significant symbolic value, would increase security and improve overall living conditions, a homeland citizen *might* find the tradeoff worthwhile and give up a fight for sovereignty or independence. In his essay in this volume, William Safran emphasizes that, by contrast, for the diaspora, while the security of the homeland is of course important, as well, the territory's specific identity function is often paramount.

The devotion to the cause by the diaspora may make it more difficult for political actors back home to accept compromise solutions that may be condemned as appeasement or treason among the émigrés. On some occasions, a move by a leader in a conflict to seek a negotiated outcome will be undermined by diaspora leaders committed

40. Paul Collier and Anke Hoeffler, *Greed and Grievance in Civil War*, Policy Research Working Paper 2355 (Washington, DC: World Bank, Development Research Group, 2000), quoted in Yossi Shain and Aharon Barth, "Diasporas and International Relations Theory," *International Organizations* 57 no. 3. (Summer 2003): 449.

41. A brief, but especially informative article with excellent quantitative data regarding diaspora involvement in homeland voting, nationalist movements, and civil wars is *The Economist*, "A World of Exiles" 366, issue 8305 (January 4, 2003), 41.

to hard-line positions. In Armenia, for example, the first post-Soviet president, Levon Ter-Petrossian, sought to constitute Armenia's foreign policy out of state interests and to make conciliatory gestures toward Turkey. The Armenian diasporas in the United States and France, however, regarded this as capitulation on their core issue of recognition of the Armenian genocide at the hands of Turks. Ter-Petrossian eventually fell to Robert Kocharian, who followed the diaspora's traditional anti-Turkish attitudes.

Diaspora communalist and corporatist strategies use voluntary and loose frameworks for preserving ethnic identity away from the homeland, defending the group whenever necessary and organizing activities for the members.[42] Communalists aim to prevent full assimilation into the new host country's society and its values and strive for integration with and organization around the homeland and its own diaspora, not necessarily adopting host country ideas. Communalists maintain transstate networks in order to keep the global diaspora interconnected. Corporatist strategies differ slightly and often have a formal status to represent the group to the hostland or to the homeland government. In the Basque case, the North American Basque Organizations (NABO), a federation of thirty-five Basque organizations in the United States, has gained a formal representative political status, with communications and grant money moving between the Basque Autonomous Government and NABO. Argentine, Uruguayan, and Venezuelan Basques also have politically recognized federations, and in the many other countries, each separate Basque center has been officially recognized and certified by the Basque government and each represents its affiliated members to the Basque government. The institutional mechanisms structuring cultural activities in the Basque diaspora are firmly put in place by the diaspora Basque centers, the Basque government, or both.

Conclusions

Basques living abroad do not lobby for themselves or their individual circumstances in their host countries, but have instead demonstrated interest in promoting recognition and understanding of Basque homeland reality in the global landscape. Their sense of self-help seems to be projected out to the homeland, primarily, and by improving the circumstances and image of the homeland, they believe they help all Basques around the globe. Over the centuries, they have served as sources of foreign investment, as diplomatic links, and as amateur ambassadors. Today, distance-shrinking technologies facilitate diaspora activism and effectiveness through easy and cheap communications and information sharing. These globalization processes have intensified in depth, breadth, and in the speed of global interactions and interrelations. However, the process itself is not new. In addition, although the number and the depth of issues and types of networks in the global arena have increased and additional actors have been added to the scene, states, though not univocal, are still dominant in world affairs. The state is in

---

42. Sheffer, *Diaspora Politics*, 164.

transformation, but not in decline. Yet noncentral governments may be bypassing central state government structures with transsovereign relations with other actors, such as the Basque government has by establishing its own trade missions and now delegations in several countries.

Different international issue areas have different systems of actors, and in identity politics, diaspora communities are increasing their influence and agency. Interdependence among the leaders of the Basque communities is low. They do not know each other, in most cases, nor do they have any agreed-upon agenda. Although there is a Basque diaspora World Congress organized by the Basque government every four years, the structure is highly controlled, with meetings, speeches, and presentations, and usually delegates do not have much free time for open debate, which is another lost opportunity for dynamic discussion and idea sharing.[43]

What points of entry for political, economic, social, and cultural influence are available to diasporas? Which is more likely to directly effect a successful outcome as a result of diaspora intervention: the number of people involved and supporting the issue, or the status and influence of the specific people who participate in the network? Should Basque homeland institutions be focusing on the Basque diaspora cultural centers and an overall grand, general network to promote Basque society, or would it be more effective to pinpoint specific experts in various policy areas and entry points and to train and equip specialized amateur diplomats, emphasizing quality or quantity, or either, depending on the issue?

"Success" for the Basque diaspora could be measured simply in terms of having gained access to the media and/or opinion leaders or policy-makers. Simply having opened a channel of information and dialogue can be a significant triumph. "Success" also differs widely according to the opportunity structures available. Often, the political playing fields vary and may not allow for single-issue attention. For example, in some environments, the institution of the political party is strong, and diasporas must work through the parties for representation and exposure, while in others spheres, interest groups have agency, and diasporas can form their own representational bodies. However it is accomplished, lobbying and access to decision makers is essential to the transnational paradigm of paradiplomacy.

The Basque diaspora remains a potential mobilizing force, and it seems that community leaders are indeed using their resources in innovative ways, yet they still lack any strategy or centralized plan. Basques have no detectable politically progressive or

---

43. The Fourth World Congress of Basque Collectivities was held from July 8 to July 13, 2007, in Bilbao and was attended by over one hundred and fifty delegates representing Basque diaspora organizations from eighteen countries. The congress is held every four years. This congress witnessed the return of many delegates who have represented their countries at each congress, while others were attending for the first time. Interviews with first-time delegates revealed that once again, there was a sense of disappointment at the lack of time given for discussion and debate, and too much time was taken for presentations that resulted only in the passive participation of listening by the delegates. Several mentioned that the information in the presentations could simply be sent by e-mail prior to the congress and that the gathering should be spent in discussing those presentations, ideas, and possible projects and programs.

even well-defined diaspora agenda. Basque government officials have not tried to identify instrumentally the strengths and weaknesses of their diaspora, nor have they investigated methods of possible collaborations with the communities for everyone's advantage. Certain elite diaspora players have acquired agency as brokers and facilitators in hostland political circles and have established individual authority and legitimacy with hostland institutions and the media. Although the political resources of the Basque diaspora rest firmly on their established social status in each host country, in general, they have not fully capitalized on this intangible networking resource.

The Basque Country and its institutions want to raise their profile and status in European and world affairs, and yet they are not capitalizing on the availability of their own diaspora transnational networks. If the Basque government has believed that it has had the sole authority and exclusive capacity as the gatekeeper and encyclopedia of Basque identity and that it alone has had the power to define the identity of the homeland and to transmit that image to the rest of the world, it has been mistaken. President Ibarretxe's opening speech to the Fourth World Congress of Basque Collectivities on July 8, 2007 demonstrated that this is no longer the case—or the attitude of leading Basque politicians. However, the Basque government's lack of political activity with Basques abroad is being perceived by some leaders in the Basque diaspora as a lack of confidence and even a lack of interest. It is also being perceived by bolder critics as incompetence. The diaspora communities each have actors that are ready to take on the role of the paradiplomat, whether or not the homeland institutions assist them. Homeland leaders can either take advantage of these diaspora activists and prepare them to promote Basque culture and identity policies or spend their energy reacting to the results of the diaspora individuals' actions. Diaspora and nonstate government actors also need to readjust their statecentric conceptions of the system of international relations and capitalize on transnational relations in order to gain access to decision makers.

State-society relations are changing, and the state as the spokesperson, protector, and controller of its people, territory, and economy is no longer accepted carte blanche. States have been quite ineffective at diplomacy and at negotiating and creating lasting solutions for the planet. Diplomacy has to evolve with human knowledge, but it seems we are often using the same old methods of destruction to solve new problems related to identity. Diplomacy, which is generally defined as the activities of professional representatives of the state, must be expanded to the reality of multilevel and multifaceted interrelationships, including diaspora politics. The Westphalian system has demonstrated the inability of the state system to promote a peaceful globe, and the state system has been unsuccessful at protecting cultures, identities, and the environment. Perhaps the involvement of nonstate actors and the democratization of diplomacy can more effectively and efficiently improve the conditions of human existence.

Bibliography

Aguirre Zabala, Iñaki. "Making Sense of Paradiplomacy? An Intertextual Inquiry about a Concept in Search of a Definition." In *Paradiplomacy in Action: The Foreign Relations of Subnational Governments*. Edited by Francisco Aldecoa and Michael Keating. London: Frank Cass, 1999.

Ambrosio, Thomas, ed. *Ethnic Identity Groups and U.S. Foreign Policy*. Westport, CT: Praeger Publishers, 2002.

Appadurai, Arjun. *Modernity at Large: Cultural Dimensions of Globalization*. Public Worlds, vol. 1. Minneapolis: University of Minnesota Press. 1995.

Arts, Bas, Math Noortmann, and Bob Reinalda, ed. *Non-State Actors in International Relations*. Non-State Actors in International Law, Politics and Governance Series. Aldershot, UK: Ashgate Publishing, 2001.

Bauman, Zygmunt. *Globalization: The Human Consequences*. Cambridge: Polity Press. 1998.

Baxok, Erramun, Pantxoa Etxegoin, Terexa Lekunberri, Iñaki Martinez de Luna, Larraitz Mendizabal, Igor Ahedo, Xabier Itzaina, and Roldan Jimeno. *Identidad y cultura vascas a comienzos del siglo XXI*. Donostia–San Sebastián: Eusko Ikaskuntza, 2006.

Bloom, William. *Personal Identity, National Identity and International Relations*. New York: Cambridge University Press, 1990.

Bourne, Angela, ed. *The EU and Territorial Politics within Member States: Conflict or Cooperation?* Leiden: Brill, 2004.

Closa, Carlos, and Paul M. Heywood. *Spain and the European Union*. Basingstoke, UK: Palgrave MacMillan.

Douglass, William A. "Creating the New Basque Diaspora." In *Basque Politics and Nationalism on the Eve of the Millennium*. Edited by William A. Douglass, Carmelo Urza, Linda White, and Joseba Zulaika. Basque Studies Program Occasional Papers Series no. 6. Reno: Basque Studies Program, 1999.

——, and Jon Bilbao, *Amerikanuak: Basques in the New World*. 1975; Reno: University of Nevada Press, 2005.

Duchacek, Ivo D. *The Territorial Dimension of Politics: Within, Among and Across Nations*. Boulder, CO: Westview Press, 1986.

——, Daniel Latouche, and Garth Stevenson, eds. *Perforated Sovereignties and International Relations: Trans-sovereign Contacts of Subnational Governments*. New York: Greenwood Press, 1998.

The Economist, "A World of Exiles" 366, issue 8305 (January 4, 2003).

Government of the Basque Autonomous Community. *Euskadi: Estrategia de acción exterior de la Comunidad Autónoma Vasca*. Vitoria-Gasteiz: Servicio Central de Publicaciones del Gobierno Vasco, 2005.

Haas, Peter M. "Introduction: Epistemic Communities and International Policy Coordination." *International Organization* 46, no. 1 (Winter 1992): 1–35.

Hanrieder, Wolfram F. "Dissolving International Politics: Reflections on the Nation-State." *American Political Science Review* 72, no. 4 (1978): 1276–87.

Held, David, Anthony McGrew, David Goldblatt, and Jonathon Perraton. *Global Transformations: Politics, Economics and Culture.* Stanford, CA: Stanford University Press, 1999.

Hill, Christopher. *The Changing Politics of Foreign Policy.* New York: Palgrave Macmillan, 2003.

Hirst, Paul, and Grahame Thompson. *Globalization in Question: The International Economy and the Possibilities of Governance.* Cambridge: Polity Press, 1999.

Hocking, Brian. "Catalytic Diplomacy: Beyond 'Newness' and 'Decline.'" In *Innovation in Diplomatic Practice.* Edited by J. Melissen. London: Macmillan, 1999.

———. "Privatizing Diplomacy." *International Studies Perspectives* 5 (2004): 147–52.

Irujo Ametzaga, Xabier. *La hora vasca del Uruguay: Génesis y desarrollo del nacionalismo vasco en Uruguay (1825–1960).* Montevideo: Sociedad de Confraternidad Vasca Euskal Erria, 2006.

Jáuregui, Gurutz. *La Comunidad Autónoma del País Vasco y las relaciones internacionales.* Oñati: Instituto Vasco de Administración Pública, 1989.

Josselin, Daphné, and William Wallace, eds. *Non-State Actors in World Politics.* New York: Palgrave, 2001.

Keating, Michael. *The New Regionalism in Western Europe.* Cheltenham, UK: Edward Elgar, 1998.

Keck, Margaret E., and Kathryn Sikkink, eds. *Activists Beyond Borders: Advocacy Networks in International Politics.* Ithaca, NY: Cornell University Press, 1998.

Kennedy, Paul, and Victor Roudometof, eds. *Communities across Borders: New Immigrants and Transnational Cultures.* London: Routledge, 2002.

Keohane, Robert O. "Transgovernmental Relations and International Organizations." In *Power in the Global Information Age.* Edited by Joseph S. Nye, Jr. London: Routledge, 2004.

Koslowshi, Rey, ed. *International Migration and the Globalization of Domestic Politics.* New York: Routledge, 2005.

Kuznetsov, Yevgeny, ed. *Diaspora Networks and the International Migration of Skills.* Washington, DC: The World Bank, 2006.

Lachapelle, Guy. "Identity, Integration and the Rise of Identity Economy: The Quebec Case in Comparison with Scotland, Wales and Catalonia." In *Globalization, Governance and Identity: The Emergence of New Partnerships.* Edited by Guy Lachapelle and John Trent. Montréal: Presses de l'Université de Montréal, 2000.

McGrath, Conor. *Lobbying in Washington, London, and Brussels: The Persuasive Communication of Political Issues.* Studies in Political Science 26. Lewiston, NY: Edwin Mellen Press, 2005.

Molina, Ignacio, and Fernando Rodrigo. "Spain." In *Foreign Ministries in the European Union: Integrating Diplomats.* Edited by Brian Hocking and David Spence. New York: Palgrave Macmillan, 2002.

Nye, Joseph S., Jr. *Power in the Global Information Age: From Realism to Globalization.* London: Routledge, 2004.

Olzak, Susan. *The Global Dynamics of Racial and Ethnic Mobilization.* Stanford, CA: Stanford University Press, 2006.

Østergaard-Nielsen, Eva. "Diasporas in World Politics." In *Non-State Actors in World Politics.* Edited by Daphné Josselin and William Wallace. New York: Palgrave. 2001.

Panossian, Razmik. *The Armenians: From Kings and Priests to Merchants and Commissars.* London: Hurst and Company, 2006.

Portes, Alejandro, Luis Guarnizo, and Patricia Landolt. "The Study of Transnational Communities: Pitfalls and Promise of an Emergent Field." *Ethnic and Racial Studies* 22, no. 2 (1999): 217–37.

Risse, Thomas. "Transnational Actors and World Politics." In *Handbook of International Relations.* Edited by Walter Carlsnaes, Thomas Risse, and Beth A. Simmons. London: Sage Publications, 2002.

Risse-Kappen, Thomas, ed. *Bringing Transnational Relations Back In: Non-State Actors, Domestic Structures and International Institutions.* Cambridge: Cambridge University Press, 1995.

Roudometof, Victor, and Anna Karpathakis. "Greek Americans and Transnationalism: Religion, Class and Community." In *Communities across Borders: New Immigrants and Transnational Cultures.* Edited by Paul Kennedy and Victor Roudometof. London: Routledge, 2002.

San Sebastián, Koldo. *The Basque Archives: Vascos en Estados Unidos (1939–1943).* Donostia–San Sebastián: Editorial Txertoa. 1991.

Shain, Yossi, and Aharon Barth. "Diasporas and International Relations Theory." *International Organizations* 57, no. 3 (Summer 2003): 449–79.

——, with Tamara Cofman Wittes. "Peace as a Three-Level Game: The Role of Diasporas in Conflict Resolution." In *Ethnic Identity Groups and U.S. Foreign Policy.* Edited by Thomas Ambrosio. Westport, CT: Praeger, 2002.

Sheffer, Gabriel. *Diaspora Politics: At Home Abroad.* Cambridge, MA: Cambridge University Press, 2003.

Smith, Tony. *Foreign Attachments: The Power of Ethnic Groups in the Making of American Foreign Policy.* Cambridge, MA: Harvard University Press, 2000.

Tarrow, Sydney. *The New Transnational Activism.* New York: Cambridge University Press, 2005.

Totoricagüena, Gloria. *Basque Diaspora: Migration and Transnational Identity.* Reno: Center for Basque Studies, 2005.

——. "Diasporas as Non-Central Government Actors in Foreign Policy: The Trajectory of Basque Paradiplomacy." *Nationalism and Ethnic Politics* 11 (2005): 265–87.

——. Identity, Culture, and Politics in the Basque Diaspora. Reno: University of Nevada Press, 2004.

——. "Shrinking World, Expanding Diaspora: Globalization and Basque Diaspora Identity." In *The Basque Diaspora/La Diaspora Vasca.* Edited by William A. Douglass, Carmelo Urza, Linda White, and Joseba Zulaika. Basque Studies Program Occasional Papers Series no. 7. Reno: Basque Studies Program, 1999.

Ugalde Zubiri, Alexander. "La actuación internacional del gobierno vasco en el exilio (1939–1960): Un caso singular de acción exterior." Programa de Becas Postdoctorales de Perefeccionamiento de Personal Investigador del Gobierno Vasco. Leioa: Universidad del País Vasco, 1995–97.

——. "La actuación internacional del primer Gobierno Vasco durante la Guerra Civil (1936–1939)." *Sancho el Sabio: Revista de Cultura e Investigación Vasca,* no. 6 (1996): 187–210.

——. *Memoria de la dirección de relaciones con las colectividades vascas en el exterior del Gobierno Vasco (1980–2005).* Urazandi series. Vitoria-Gasteiz: Servicio Central de Publicaciones del Gobierno Vasco, 2007.

Wolfish, Daniel, and Gordon Smith. "Governance and Policy in a Multicentric World." *Canadian Public Policy—Analyse de Politiques* 26, special no. 2 (2000): S51–S72.

Zachary, G. Pascal. *The Global Me: New Cosmopolitans and the Competitive Edge—Picking Globalism's Winners and Losers.* New York: Public Affairs, 2000.

Index

List of Contributors

Kim D. Butler is a historian specializing in the African diaspora with a particular focus on Brazil. She holds masters degrees in history from Howard University and Johns Hopkins University and received her Ph.D. in history from Johns Hopkins University in 1995. She is an associate professor of history in the Department of Africana Studies at Rutgers University, with a joint appointment in the Department of History. From 2003 to 2006, she served as chairperson of the Department of Africana Studies.

Her first book, *Freedoms Given, Freedoms Won: Afro-Brazilians in Post-Abolition São Paulo and Salvador* (1998), was awarded the Wesley-Logan Prize in African Diaspora History from the American Historical Association and the Letitia Woods Brown Prize from the Association of Black Women Historians. Her current work focuses on African and comparative diaspora theory and the application of that theory to new approaches to African diaspora history. She also is engaged in continuing work on abolition-era Brazil.

Nergis Canefe (Ph.D., York, 1998, D.Jur. candidate, Osgoode Hall Law School) is associate professor of political science at York University, in Canada, and a member of the resident faculty at the Centre for Refugee Studies. She also taught at the London School of Economics and Bilgi and Bogazici Universities in Turkey. Her areas of interest are minority rights, diaspora politics, the transnational politics of religion, critical citizenship studies, and crimes against humanity. Her publications have appeared in journals including *Citizenship Studies, Nations and Nationalism, Balkanologie, Turkish Studies,* and *Rethinking History.* She has published a coedited volume, *Turkey and the European Integration: Accession Prospects and Issues* (Routledge, 2004) and has authored a volume in Turkish titled *Citizenship, Memory, and Belonging: Limits of Turkish Nationalism* (Bilgi University, 2006). She is currently coediting a volume with William Safran titled *The Jewish Diaspora as a Paradigm: Politics, Religion, and Belonging* (Edwin Mellen, forthcoming) and a second publication in Turkish titled *Local Entries in the Transnational Discourse of Cultural Studies: The Topic of Turkishness* (Bilgi University Press, forthcoming).

Robin Cohen is ESRC Professorial Research Fellow and a professor of sociology at the University of Warwick. He has held full-time appointments at the Universities of Ibadan, Birmingham, Cape Town, and the West Indies and sessional appointments at Stanford, Toronto, and U.C. Berkeley. His books include *Endgame in South Africa?* (1986), *The New*

Helots: Migrants in the International Division of Labour (1987, 1993, 2003), *Contested Domains: Debates in International Labour Studies* (1991), *Frontiers of Identity* (1994), *Global Diasporas: An Introduction* (1997, 1999, 2001, 2004), *Global Sociology* (coauthor, 2000, 2001, rev. 2007), and *Migration and Its Enemies* (2006). He has written, edited, or coedited twenty further volumes. His major works have been translated into Danish, French, German, Greek, Italian, Japanese, Mandarin, Portuguese, and Spanish. He has recently commenced a three-year research program on creolization, some results of which will shortly be posted at http://www2.warwick.ac.uk/fac/soc/sociology/research/cscs/.

William Douglass was born in Reno, Nevada, and attended the University of Nevada, Reno, majoring in Spanish literature. He received his Ph.D. in anthropology from the University of Chicago in 1967 and returned to UNR to establish the Basque Studies Program. He served as director of the program for thirty-three years, until his retirement in 1999. He also edited the Basque Book Series of the University of Nevada Press (about fifty titles in print).

He has authored over twenty books and over one hundred articles. His works on Basque migration, funerary rituals, rural exodus, family patterns, ethnonationalism, and border studies have all been groundbreaking in the various fields of Basque studies. Most people in the scholarly community consider him the dean of Basque studies. He has also written books on Italy, Australia, and Nevada gaming and mining.

Douglass is the recipient of many awards and honors. In 1984, he was given an honorary doctorate by the University of the Basque Country. In 1989, he was inducted to the Basque Hall of Fame by the Basque Studies Society of America. In 1998, he was named one of twenty corresponding members of Euskaltzaindia (the Basque Language Academy) and was also honored at Renoko Aste Nagusia (Reno's Basque Cultural Week). In 1999, Douglass was named the Outstanding Researcher of the Year at the University of Nevada, Reno, as well as given the Distinguished Faculty Award and named Basque Scholar Professor Emeritus. In October of 1999, he was given the Lagun Onari Award for distinguished service to the Basque people by Eusko Jaurlaritza, the Basque government.

Michel S. Laguerre is director of the Berkeley Center for Globalization and Information Technology and a professor at the University of California at Berkeley. He is the author of several books, including *American Odyssey: Haitians in New York City* (Cornell University Press, 1984), *The Military and Society in Haiti* (University of Tennessee Press, 1993) *Diasporic Citizenship* (Macmillan Press, 1998), *The Global Ethnopolis: Chinatown, Japantown, and Manilatown in American Society* (Macmillan Press, 2000), *Urban Multiculturalism and Globalization in New York City* (Palgrave Macmillan Press, 2003), *The Digital City: The American Metropolis and Information Technology* (Palgrave Macmillan Press, 2005), *Diaspora, Politics and Globalization* (Palgrave Macmillan Press, 2006) and *Global Neighborhoods: Jewish Quarters* *in Paris, Berlin and London* (State University of New York Press, 2008). His new volume, *Jerusalem, Rome, and Mecca: Network Governance of Global Religions*, is forthcoming.

William Safran (Ph.D., Columbia University) is professor emeritus of political science at the University of Colorado, Boulder. He has written numerous articles and reviews in professional journals and contributed chapters to more than forty edited books on French, European, and comparative politics and the politics of ethnonationalism, citizenship, language, religion, and diaspora. His most recent books include *Identity and Territorial Autonomy in Plural Societies* (Frank Cass, 2000), coedited with Ramón Máiz; *The French Polity* (6th ed., Longman, 2003); *The Secular and the Sacred: Nation, Religion, and Politics* (Frank Cass, 2003); *Language, Ethnic Identity, and the State* (Routledge, 2005), coedited with Jean A. Laponce; and *Politics in Europe* (4th ed., CQ Press, 2006), coauthor. He has lectured widely and taught at City University of New York, Hebrew University in Jerusalem, and the Universities of Grenoble, Bordeaux, and Santiago de Compostela. He is the editor in chief of *Nationalism and Ethnic Politics*.

Gabriel (Gabi) Sheffer is a professor of political science at the Hebrew University of Jerusalem and a senior fellow at the Jerusalem Van Leer Institute. He has served as director of the Jerusalem Group of National Planning at the Jerusalem Van Leer Institute and as director of the Leonard Davis Institute for International Relations of the Hebrew University. He has been the editor of several academic journals and is a member of several editorial boards. His research focuses on security policy-making networks in democratic states; ethnic politics, with a special emphasis on the politics of ethnonational diasporas; Israeli politics; and the Israeli-Arab conflict. He has been a visiting professor at Oxford University; U.C. Berkeley; the University of Wisconsin, Madison; Cornell University; the University of Maryland; Duke University; the University of South Wales, Sydney, Australia; the Woodrow Wilson Center, Washington, DC; and others. He has published numerous books and articles on all his research subjects, including *Moshe Sharett: Biography of a Political Moderate* (Oxford University Press, 1996), *Diaspora Politics: At Home Abroad*, (Cambridge: Cambridge University Press, 2006), *Middle Eastern Minorities and Diasporas* (Sussex Academic Press, 2002), and *Les diasporas: 2000 ans d'histoire* (Rennes Universitaires Press, 2005), and he has served as editor of three special issues of *Israel Studies*.

Khachig Tölölyan is a professor of literature, literary and cultural theory, and diaspora studies at the College of Letters, Wesleyan University, in Middletown, Connecticut, where he has also served as director of the Center for the Humanities. In 1979, he was one of the two founding editors of *Pynchon Notes*, a journal devoted to the study of the fiction of Thomas Pynchon. In 1991, he was the founding editor of *Diaspora: A Journal of Transnational Studies*, published by Oxford University Press from 1991 to 1996 and by the University of Toronto Press after that. The journal deals with old and new diasporas and other dispersions, as well as issues of nationalism, transnationalism, globalization, migration, ethnicity, exile, minorities, and postcolonialism.

He is the author of a book in his native language, Armenian, titled *Spyurki Mech* (In the Diaspora) (Paris: Haratch Press, 1980) and of some thirty-five articles on literary and political topics concerning diasporas, which have been published in *Diaspora, The Journal of Strategic Studies, Terrorism and Political Conflict, Conflict Quarterly, Nationalism and Ethnic Politics,* and *The Journal of Political Science.* He has lectured at conferences at the National Strategy Information Center of Washington, DC, the Conflict Studies Center at the Fletcher School of Law and Diplomacy at Tufts, as well as at the professional conventions of the American Political Science Association, the International Political Science Association, the American Anthropological Association, and at the Harry Franck Guggenheim Foundation. He has addressed scholars and members of the State and Defense Departments and analysts from the intelligence community on the topic of the cultural, political, and economic implications of increased diasporization. Currently, he is writing articles under the working title *Stateless Power: Diasporas in the Transnational Moment,* which he hopes to collect into a book.

Gloria Totoricagüena (Ph.D., London School of Economics, 2000) is a political scientist specializing in comparative diaspora studies and particularly in the Basque diaspora. She has conducted fieldwork with Basques from twenty different countries and currently collaborates in research projects with the Eusko Ikaskuntza–Society of Basque Studies in Donostia–San Sebastián, the University of Deusto, and with the University of the Basque Country. She also serves as a consultant for diaspora-related themes to the government of the Basque Autonomous Community and to various ethnic communities around the world. Totoricagüena is the former director of the Center for Basque Studies at the University of Nevada, Reno, and served as chair for this conference.

She has authored four books and numerous articles in the fields of Basque, diaspora, and migration studies and has taught as a visiting professor at Stanford University. Totoricagüena was selected by the president of the Basque government to represent diaspora Basques at the World Congresses of Basque Collectivities in 1995, 1999, 2003, and 2007 and was twice chosen as keynote speaker (2003 and 2007).

Totoricagüena has received much recognition and many awards for her research and teaching excellence, including selection as the finalist for the Idaho Librarians Best Book Award (for *Boise Basques: Dreamers and Doers,* 2004) and for the UNR Mousel-Feltner Award for Research and Creative Excellence, the University of Nevada Junior Faculty Research Award, and the Worldly Basque Award from Basque Country public and private institutions. Teaching awards include the Tufts University Inspirational Teacher Award, the University of Idaho Teaching Excellence Award, the Target Teachers Excellence Award, the State of Idaho Governor's Initiative Teaching Excellence Award, the Idaho Humanities Council Teacher Research Fellowship, and inclusion in *Who's Who among America's Teachers* in 1994, 2000, 2002, and 2004.

Current research interests include quantitative and qualitative analyses of the Basque diaspora political experience; relationships between globalization and transnational identity in diaspora populations; comparing the Basque diaspora infrastructure and organizational and political development to those of other ethnic diasporas; diaspora politics, foreign policies, and the paradiplomacy of homeland governments toward their diaspora communities; oral histories and associationism of Basque emigrants in various countries around the world; and ethnonationalism and ethnic identity in the Basque diaspora.